LYRIC LOGIC

Lyric Logic

HOW MODERN AMERICAN POETRY REASONS

Johanna Winant

Columbia University Press
New York

Columbia University Press
Publishers Since 1893
New York   Chichester, West Sussex
cup.columbia.edu
Copyright © 2026 Columbia University Press
All rights reserved

Library of Congress Cataloging-in-Publication Data

Names: Winant, Johanna author
Title: Lyric logic : how modern American poetry reasons / Johanna Winant.
Description: New York : Columbia University Press, 2026. |
Includes bibliographical references and index.
Identifiers: LCCN 2025029229 (print) | LCCN 2025029230 (ebook) |
ISBN 9780231217460 hardback | ISBN 9780231217477 trade paperback |
ISBN 9780231561747 EPUB | ISBN 9780231565295 PDF
Subjects: LCSH: American poetry—Philosophy | Reason in literature |
LCGFT: Literary criticism
Classification: LCC PS303 .W48 2026 (print) | LCC PS303 (EPUB)
LC record available at https://lccn.loc.gov/2025029229
LC ebook record available at https://lccn.loc.gov/2025029230

Cover design: Chang Jae Lee
Cover image: Artwork presented by Public Art Fund for Carmen Winant: *My Mother and Eye*, an exhibition on 300 JCDecaux bus shelters and newsstands across New York City, Chicago, and Boston, February 5–April 6, 2025.

GPSR Authorized Representative: Easy Access System Europe, Mustamäe tee 50, 10621 Tallinn, Estonia, gpsr.requests@easproject.com

For my parents, Deborah Rogow and Howard Winant

CONTENTS

Introduction: Philosophical Poetry   1

Chapter One
Walt Whitman's Enumerations   30

Chapter Two
Emily Dickinson's Analogies   50

Chapter Three
Contingency and Gertrude Stein   78

Chapter Four
Consistency and Marianne Moore   109

Chapter Five
Coherence and Elizabeth Bishop   139

Conclusion: The Sonnet's Logic and
Gwendolyn Brooks   169

ACKNOWLEDGMENTS 187

NOTES 191

BIBLIOGRAPHY 235

INDEX 253

LYRIC LOGIC

INTRODUCTION
Philosophical Poetry

THIS BOOK

Poetry may reflect philosophy, allude to philosophy, discuss philosophy, and share knowledge and wisdom; all this is what's usually meant when a poem is described as *philosophical*. But poems also *do* philosophy—that is the fundamental claim of this book. More specifically, I'll argue that poems do philosophy by modeling logical reasoning, usually regarded as the least poetic sort of philosophy. And further, in modeling logical reasoning, poetry demonstrates the power of a kind of logic—inductive logic—that many philosophers regard as weak and problematic.

Inductive logic reasons by connecting particulars; many poems do as well, and this is most true of lyric poetry. When lyric poems leap between details, they are reasoning: demonstrating induction's sense-making powers as well as their own. I'll argue that not only is inductive reasoning visible in many lyric poems, it's an aspect of what we mean by *lyric* in the first place. Lyric is *lyric* in part because of its *logic*. And while inductive logic is present in poems across literary historical periods, it becomes foregrounded in modern American poetry, as ways of making sense of the world shifted rapidly and literary aesthetics did too. This book tells a story about that concurrence, but not the usual one about modern poetry reflecting history or illustrating philosophy, and, moreover, I'll argue that these poems have been misread as aesthetically experimental. Literary experimentation is the means and not the ends of poetry's project of modeling how we must and do reason in a new and surprising world.

Yes, it's true, both *poems* and *logical reasoning* are fairly abstruse categories—perhaps even more so *modern American poetry* and *inductive logic*—and, because this book argues that they overlap, it might seem like I'm threatening to multiply the perplexing by the recondite. So let me put it another way: *this book shows that two different stories—one in literary studies and one in philosophy—are sometimes the same story.* In literary studies, our basic account of American modernism is that it's an aesthetic movement arising from a historical process: the rapid, disorienting, exhilarating changes of incipient modernity in the United States from, roughly, the Civil War through the Cold War prompted a surge in literary experimentation. And in philosophy, the basic description of inductive logic is that it is a method of reasoning from the specific to the general, and its conclusions may be probable, but since induction (unlike deduction) does not invoke a general law or theory, they are not necessarily true.

These literary and philosophic stories may not sound similar, but they share a plot: both are about encounters with the new and unexpected, and about the resulting techniques by which the new and unexpected are made sense of and assimilated or just lived with and borne. In literary studies, modernism has been described as *making it new* since its own beginnings; modern literature reckons with modernity's transformations, and also offers aesthetic novelty to its readers.[1] Aesthetic novelty, and the challenge it presents to readers, is one account of modernism's famous difficulty.[2] In philosophy, induction was first clearly defined by David Hume, who pointed out that just because the sun has always risen in the past does not mean it will necessarily rise tomorrow. Inductive logic is often described as unreliable because a new event or phenomenon could falsify whatever generalization previously held. As Hume writes, "*That the sun will not rise tomorrow* is no less intelligible a proposition, and implies no more contradiction than the affirmation, *that it will rise.*"[3] Novelty is a challenge, whether aesthetic or epistemological. Modernism and inductive reasoning both perform and theorize this difficulty. Understanding inductive logic's concern with newness, and that novelty is part of the process of making sense of the world, helps to clarify that modernism's similar concern and commitment—visible in its poetics—also has to do with reasoning and also has philosophical weight.[4]

INTRODUCTION

Both logic and poetry reason formally. Indeed, *poetry and logic share a set of forms*. I am not using *form* at all loosely here; I don't mean "structures," "types," or "variations." Philosophy and literature are the two disciplines that have established sets of patterns made out of words. Even "philosophy" and "literature" are perhaps too broad; better to say *logic* and *lyric poetry*. In both logic and in the lyric, forms involve what is said and how, and they tell us what and how we may infer, which is to say what truth is and how we know it.

Deductive logical forms, which go back to the Classical world, are easy for an undergraduate studying philosophy to list—the basic forms of valid argument are hypothetical syllogism, disjunctive syllogism, modus ponens, and modus tollens—and in all of these, if the premises are true then the conclusion must also be true.[5] These forms are termed *valid* because they offer epistemic security; the inference they support is described as *impeccable*. There are not many such forms because there are limited ways to be sure a conclusion is true. Not all logic, though, is impeccable; there are also inductive logical forms. Inductive logical argument does not guarantee that a conclusion is true if the premises are true—the conclusion is *probably* true, but not definitely—so induction's forms are not valid. There's an indefinite number of ways to be less than perfect; no one can list all of them. Enumeration and analogy are among the most fundamental; both work from particular examples toward a broader generalization that would allow prediction.

Now, in poetry: some poetry could be described as aspiring toward the tight validity of deductive logical forms. For example, some religious poems present themselves not as making proofs but by being a proof for something that doesn't demand further proof, or in Ana Schwartz's words about the religious poems of Anne Bradstreet, they "show her interest in strong theory, deductive abstractions that could be used to organize a wide range of phenomena."[6] But most poems are not that deductive, especially not lyric poems. In this book, I'll discuss poems that are invested in reasoning, but reject the impeccable as impractical, if not impossible. These poems use the forms of inductive reasoning.

In addition to modeling inductive reasoning, the poems in this book defend it. I identify induction in modern American poetry, but I also find in modern American poetry strong versions of induction and claims for it. Inductive reasoning is viewed by philosophy as flawed, unreliable, unjustifiable, and weak, but these poems display its powers. Here is where the two stories diverge: the poetry I discuss is doing philosophy precisely because it's going beyond what philosophy has already done by reconceptualizing one of modern philosophy's central problems.

I could describe these poems as borrowing philosophical forms, but I am making a different argument. Philosophy has a robust vocabulary to describe reasoning—that's what logic is, and I am using those terms—but that doesn't mean that reasoning—or logic—are proprietary to philosophy. Children reason even before they can speak and can do logic shortly thereafter. In this book, I discuss reasoning in poems, but that's just the location; more importantly, the poems here reason *through* poetry; they reason by means of poetry's resources; they reason with poetics. This book only appears to be interdisciplinary: poetics preexists the disciplines and logic transcends them. I am not writing a book of compare/contrast between lyric poetry and formal logic, but instead making visible the intellectual ambition of poems as they try to make sense of the world.

HOW POEMS REASON: EZRA POUND

Logic generally formalizes reasoning in and through language, telling us "what follows from what."[7] Inductive reasoning tells us what *might* follow, what *usually* does, and what *always has before*—and also that it might not, that the unexpected might occur instead.

How do we read a poem paying attention to its reasoning? How do poems reason, and how do they teach us about how reasoning works? What does inductive reasoning look like in poems? Often, inductive reasoning is understood to be synonymous with *generalizing*. That's not wrong, but generalizing is a vaguer term, implying a sort of survey as if scanning from above. Inductive reasoning, though, is best figured not in space but in time: *this, then this, then this*.

Ezra Pound's "In a Station of the Metro" is two lines long, with one image on each line; we can describe its moves as: *this*—the title—*then this*—the first line—*then this*—the second.

> The apparition of these faces in the crowd;
> Petals on a wet, black bough.[8]

Even after reading this poem countless times, if I go slowly enough, I can still feel the unexpectedness of the second line, especially what Hugh

INTRODUCTION

Kenner calls "the pivotal word."[9] *Petals?* Weren't we just in a busy subway station? How can we make sense of this new line, this new image, following the first? It's not hard to answer: there's a comparison being made between the faces, ephemeral and pale in the underground gloom, and petals; as Kenner observes, "it is a simile with 'like' suppressed."[10]

When we interpret poetry that offers us two or more details (perhaps luminous ones), and when we ask about the connection between particulars, including particular images, we are reasoning inductively. Induction describes having a working theory; each new detail might overturn the generalization-in-process, or affirm it, or complicate it.[11] *This*, then *this*, then *this*, then—maybe—*that*. The working theory usually has to do with causality: this apple drops to the ground because of the same force that, yesterday, made an orange fall, and tomorrow if I drop a pear, it will also fall; or an inference is made about why *this* phenomenon occurs, and then *this* one. One particular after another, all from the same cause: this is also what it's like to read a poem, image by image, line by line. We work off an expectation of how things have been, and we—not always but often—are confronted by an unexpected detail. Afterward, we might reread a poem and see it as a whole. But we don't experience it as a whole, or at least not without neglecting that breath-catching leap across the line break from "crowd" to "Petals." Poems require readers to reason inductively. The fact that New Criticism works inductively is well-established, even if it's not often labeled as such.[12]

But my argument in this book is not that we read poetry inductively, but that poems themselves model inductive reasoning. I rotate the subjects and objects of the close reading to argue that *some poems close read the world*. At the beginning of this section, I asked about inductive reasoning, not in us, but in poems. By describing these poems as modeling induction, I'm arguing that they're reasoning and thereby showing what reasoning is and how it can be done. When poems say *this, then this, then this*, they develop causal inferences. These poems aren't a transcription of thinking, but the organization and display of that transcription into forms that secure (or leave insecure) inferences: logic. When we read a poem like this, we retrace the steps of its logic.

The speaker of "In a Station of the Metro" is reasoning about the people he sees by means of the comparison to flower petals stuck on a branch, making inferences based on particulars without recourse to laws or theories.

This poem could be described in terms of its literary form—a couplet or, if you include the title, a sort of haiku—or in its logical form—an analogy. (I write more about how poetry uses analogy as a logical form in chapter 2, focusing on the work of Emily Dickinson.) "In a Station of the Metro" has been described as philosophical in its concern with the afterlife, aesthetics, and modernity. But we can also read it as philosophical in the more fundamental way of demonstrating a method of reasoning, and, implicitly, making a claim for it. Because the speaker is not reasoning deductively, his inferences—our lives, like other natural phenomena, are brief, fragile, and luminous, even or especially in the modern era—are not impeccable, and they may turn out to be false. But the poem, in modeling this reasoning, stands behind an insecure inference as, nonetheless, a working theory about how the world works. And it can be powerful, offering some predictions about how we catch the light as we move through time and space (perhaps faintly, but soon not at all).[13]

When Pound is read as a philosophical poet, it usually has to do with his invocation of large-scale theories about art and value.[14] While I offered a reading of "In a Station of the Metro" as invoking mortality—a subject about which poems often offer wisdom—its choice of topic is not the grounds on which I'm describing Pound's short poem as philosophical. I'm describing "In a Station of the Metro" as philosophical because of its logic, the language and form that its reasoning takes.

In this book on modern American philosophical poetry, I discuss some of the poets you might expect—Pound, Eliot, and Stevens—but I don't devote chapters to them. (Pound and Stevens feature briefly in this introduction with readings like the one above that run a bit aslant to established accounts of modernist philosophical poetry.) These three have been, each in their turn, championed as the defining king of modernism, the one who linked up modern poetry's aesthetics with large-scale philosophical theories of art and value.[15] The assumption that lies under describing Pound, Eliot, and Stevens as philosophical is that offering a large, abstract theory or set of theories is the central work of philosophical poetry.[16] But large, abstract theories are not, in and of themselves, philosophical, nor are they the only way to write philosophical poetry. The poems in this book avoid large, abstract theories, and they reject the deductive reasoning such theories afford. They are philosophical in how they reason, not what they reason about.

INTRODUCTION

LYRIC

There is a fair amount of overall agreement about what we mean by *lyric*; the most prominent three accounts are that the lyric is closest of all poetry to music, that the lyric is the voice of a single person heard or overheard in emotional or meditative speech, and that the lyric is made lyric by its readers. Susan Stewart notes the first two of these as "The most obvious facts of lyric practice—lyric as first-person expression and lyric as the most musical of literary forms."[17] But there is also ambiguity about the lyric and even pointed conflict. Daniel Albright begins *Lyricality in English Literature* with "the tormenting question, 'What is a lyric?' Every hypothesis I tried, of course, was vitiated by some opposing hypothesis; the lyric seemed definable only as a tissue of paradoxes."[18] Stephanie Burt maps some consensus, some confusion, and some direct disagreement in "What Is This Thing Called Lyric?," her review essay of Virginia Jackson and Yopie Prins's *The Lyric Theory Reader*.[19] Burt takes issue with aspects of Jackson's fundamental claim that the lyric is a "modern invention,"[20] writing, "Lyric poetry was not just the same in 1850 or 1400 as in 1950, but neither was an apple."[21]

Because descriptions of the lyric overlap and diverge, split and recombine, when we talk about the lyric, we are describing a category governed more by family resemblance than by criteria.[22] And yet, here I'll offer the observation that a common thread through many of these interwoven accounts is the lyric's relationship to novelty: the lyric's ability to leap, to turn, to surprise, to depend on the unexpected.[23] And this recognition—that often when we describe a poem as a *lyric*, we are noting that, at least on some level of its aesthetics, it is new or surprising—is useful. Here, it helps me tell the story I offer in this book about how what we've understood as modern poetry's aesthetic experimentation is part of a broader intellectual history from the mid-nineteenth to the mid-twentieth century and centered in the United States. More broadly, I hope it suggests routes to examine why, at different moments in history, other experimental aesthetic movements also coincided with epistemological upheaval. And also, sliced at another angle via poetics instead of modernism, this account of the lyric is connected to particular places and time—what's new and surprising depends on historical and cultural context—but also supports a more general theorization of lyric. Indeed, this is one of the powers displayed by inductive reasoning, and by inductive reasoning as it occurs in lyric poems. But it also offers us a way to avoid thinking of the lyric as either historically contingent or an eternal truth.

So, for example, if we read the lyric as close to song, some scholars argue that the lyric becomes surprising because of its proximity to music, and others despite it—but in either case, surprise remains a constitutive feature of the lyric. Mark Booth, for example, differentiates between lyric poetry and song lyrics with the case study of Feste's song in *Twelfth Night*, much of which he describes as "highly conventional,"[24] and therefore argues that the lyric, unlike song, embraces the unexpected.[25] Albright also agrees on the proximity of lyric to music: "lyric poetry is fundamentally an attempt to approximate the condition of music within the slightly alien and prosaic domain of words."[26] And Albright also uses Shakespeare's songs as an example, but for him, they show that the lyric makes us "avid for novelty."[27] That is, these scholars agree on the lyric's musicality, and though they use the same example, they disagree on whether those songs are examples of the lyric—but they still agree that the lyric is characterized by surprise.

When the lyric is read less as an instantiation of song and more as the representation of first-person utterance, definitions further proliferate: the lyric speaker can speak rhetorically, emotionally, meditatively, or intellectually, about personal subjects, with ethical or interpersonal or social goals, as part of ordinary human experience in time or as a rupture with it, and the voice may be close and available to us as readers, or distant, even absent. What many of these accounts share is that the lyric speaker is motivated into speech to do necessary work, but that the success of the poem in doing that work—which might be as small as provoking a smile, as great as reordering the world, or as immeasurable as provoking a smile that reorders the world—requires them to work slantwise, from a surprising angle.[28]

For example, one of the most granular thinkers about poetry, Helen Vendler, demonstrates repeatedly not just how lyric poems choose unexpected details—images, words, even punctuation—but how reading the lyric requires marking these turns; examples of her noting her surprise, or even instances of the exact phrase "to our surprise," pepper every one of her many books. (My favorite is when she discusses "The Wild Swans at Coole," nearly sighing, "It is a ravishing surprise . . . that the punctuation following 'sky' is *not* a period but a semicolon."[29]) And one of the most abstract thinkers about poetry, Allen Grossman, begins the essay

INTRODUCTION

"Hard Problems in Poetry, Especially Valuing" with this statement about how successful lyric poetry is premised on the unexpected, the new: "Poetry is the means of last recourse, the artistic form of communicative action. The use of poetry in which I wish to interest you is its intention to interrupt the continuity of cultural understandings. That's what I think poetic 'originality' means. That's what poetic novelty, the new thing, is."[30] Grossman—whose academic career was dedicated to theorizing the lyric—defines the lyric in *Summa Lyrica* in a way that might appear to be straightforward: "Lyric is the mode of visibility of the speaking person."[31] But making another person visible is no easy task; Grossman takes John Stuart Mill's well-worn definition of the lyric poem, via Northrop Frye, as utterance that is overheard and transforms the reader from illicit eavesdropper to someone who must reckon with the Cartesian problem of other minds: "The lyric speaker is overheard in the same way in which the mind of another person is known, that is to say, *per impossibile*."[32] But also: "Wherever the philosopher says *per impossibile* the poet shows the way."[33] How does the poet show the way, how does the poet solve a very hard, or even an impossible problem? With novelty: "poetic novelty, the new thing."

So—although Vendler makes few if any general statements about the lyric, and Grossman, it often feels, does mostly that—both understand the lyric as representing a single perspective that's not omniscient, and so is capable of and even obligated to registering and representing the surprise of human experience.[34] Surprise, the unexpected, novelty: this might be a very common feature on which to hang a family resemblance of the lyric, but it is there.

However again: asking what the lyric is, or even what the lyric does, could be the wrong questions. Jonathan Culler asks instead something more like how the lyric works; he describes four "parameters"—voice, event, ritual, and hyperbole—but writes that "they do not constitute a set of necessary features or invariants or a definition of the lyric, but they have, I believe, the virtue of being more central to the functioning and the power of lyrics than elements likely to be cited in any attempt at definition."[35] And according to Virginia Jackson, rather than looking for definitions of the lyric in the poems, we should look at how we've come to read them.[36] Lyric theory in the twenty-first century has been shaped by the debate between Culler and Jackson—a debate that is overt enough to be featured in their respective books—but although they disagree on how to define the lyric, that disagreement occurs against their shared and unquestioned background agreement that we do conceptualize the lyric as a genre.

Their question, then, can be described as not about what the lyric is, does, or works, but about how we recognize it. There's an element of pragmatism here; Culler writes, "a compelling argument for lyric as a genre is that we have no better alternatives."[37] And genres, as sets of expectations, offer a way to handle what Albright called the "tormenting question 'What is a lyric?'" by asking instead about the way we use that term and the work it does for us. Emphasizing the lyric as a genre with established expectations—whether they stem from the long tradition of poetics or from modern reading practices—shifts focus from an individual lyric's surprises and novelties to the overall lyric genre's conventions and traditions. That said, the past can still have unexpected presence; as Culler writes, "A genre is not just a historical evolution but a historically evolving set of possibilities with potential to surprise."[38] We can be surprised, and even surprise ourselves, with how we have categorized and continue to categorize poems.[39]

Why is novelty a throughline in discussions of the lyric? It's one way, I'll venture, that people writing about the lyric have gestured toward what I'm identifying as its logic. This book intends to follow through and make good on this widespread intuition that the lyric is connected to newness or surprise, particularly in modernity. Earlier, I quoted the definition of logic that tells us "what follows from what," a statement that deduction's conclusions have logical necessity; I noted that, in contrast, induction's conclusions are always contingent and so can surprise.[40] And I described lyric poetry as "what follows what" too—*this, then this, then this*—though here *following* is not a statement of entailment but of observable fact—one detail succeeds another—and so any necessity is harder to anticipate if it exists at all.

Logic and lyric poetry are both concerned with coherence: when that sequence becomes connection, how parts make wholes that are greater than the sum of those parts. And both logic and the lyric are concerned with coherence in its conceptual sense as well: sense-making. Deductive logic coheres—it hangs together and is lucid—when there are no surprises in what follows what. But the lyric coheres—in both meanings—when there are surprises. Lyric's necessity requires that each new detail *feel new*. The problem of induction names novelty as a problem, but as I've traced here, scholars of poetics understand novelty as central to the lyric. But even more,

INTRODUCTION

I'm arguing that novelty—surprise, the new, the unexpected—is how the lyric *addresses* problems, including philosophical problems. Philosophers see the world's novelty as a problem with no solution. Poetry reverses the direction of problem and solution; poetry sees novelty as, if not a solution, at least an adequate or even the best possible response to a thorny philosophical problem.[41]

Along with Grossman, Stanley Cavell also argues that literature can respond to philosophical problems; indeed, both Grossman and Cavell argue that literature succeeds better than philosophy in recognizing how to frame an adequate response to skepticism. Both focus on the problem of other minds, that skepticism which Grossman calls *impossibile*, and which Cavell describes as having truth that results in tragedy.[42] The problem of other minds is one of the two great problems of skepticism that catalyzed modern philosophy. The other is the problem of induction. Like the problem of other minds, the problem of induction is impossible and true. It is unsolvable. But the poems in this book use the resources of lyric poetry to find a place to stand—which is to say to leap unexpectedly, to turn to the new—relative to it. The world surprises, and the lyric does too.

HOW POEMS REASON: WALLACE STEVENS

By paying attention to how poems reason, I am shifting the grounds on which a poem can be described as philosophical from content to form. I'm arguing that lyric poetry is characterized by its engagement with a philosophical problem—novelty—and it represents that problem formally. By formally, I don't mean only in such formal characteristics as meter, rhyme, or stanzaic structure, but rather, in the shape of its reasoning, in the way the poem moves and makes connections. My claim is that reasoning in and through poetic form counts as logic. I'll have more to say about form in chapter 1, but I'll show what I mean here with Wallace Stevens's aubade, "Nomad Exquisite."

More than any other, Stevens has been described as the poet whose work reflects philosophy. But, like other modernists, that characterization often rests on the poems that display the influence of the philosophers these poets knew or read: those poems are usually read as philosophical because of what is in them.[43] Like Pound's "Metro" poem, Stevens's poems may also be philosophical, but not by echoing philosophical topics, but in how these poems model reasoning and make formal logic their own as they reckon with the new. While Pound and Stevens are often contrasted with one another, there's kinship in how they build their short poems. The logic of "Nomad Exquisite," for example, works along the same lines as the logic of "In a Station of the Metro," and it then takes an additional step. A comparison is made between phenomena, then also with the speaker: *this, then this, then this, and so, in me, this.* In Pound's poem, the faces and the petals are alike in their lightness against a dark background, and also, connected as a tenor to those vehicles, in their mortal ephemerality.

In addition to offering a generalization based on likeness, these poems also show reasoning in time, step by step, and also both show reasoning about time. (This is not itself surprising: novelty can only emerge relative to temporality.) The duration of "In a Station of the Metro" is very brief but it's not a single instant; the faces were not there, then they are, then there's a leap to another image, the petals. "Nomad Exquisite" takes place over the course of a sunrise, observing the dawn's flaming colors and ending with the inspiration—the internal sunrise of "Forms, flames, and the flakes of flames"—that presumably led to the writing of the poem we're reading. The sunrise is, of course, also Hume's example of an event that because it seems to be the most unexceptional, literally everyday occurrence is all the more devastating when one realizes its contingency, the possibility of something unexpected happening. Stevens's poem presents the kind of reasoning the lyric can do best because as it moves from detail to detail—*this, then this, then this*—it shows how each new detail changes a working theory that ends up cohering, even if in a surprising way. It connects a series of new dots about a new morning and perhaps a new world.

> As the immense dew of Florida
> Brings forth
> The big-finned palm
> And green vine angering for life,
>
> As the immense dew of Florida
> Brings forth hymn and hymn
> From the beholder,

Beholding all these green sides
And gold sides of green sides,

And blessed mornings,
Meet for the eye of the young alligator,
And lightning colors
So, in me, come flinging
Forms, flames, and the flakes of flames.[44]

The first two stanzas of "Nomad Exquisite"—like "In a Station of the Metro"—affirm an unexpected likeness between a person and a plant. In Pound's poem, both are ephemerally luminous; in Stevens's, both produce extravagantly when unstintingly nourished. "Nomad Exquisite" then adds two additional images and so additional terms and comparisons: the young alligator, who watches the dawn, and the speaker, who experiences cognitive or creative illumination. As Charles Altieri writes of "Nomad Exquisite," "The basic force here is the grammatical power of 'as' and 'so' to set in motion a chain of equivalents that draw worlds together without relying on the abstracting power of ideas."[45] Like "In a Station of the Metro," the poem is not only asking readers to reason; it is itself modeling such reasoning that grows out of and depends on surprising connections between particulars that then settle into sense.

If my argument is counterintuitive, it might be on these grounds: poems, especially poems about inspiration, such as "Nomad Exquisite," have long been described as representing *unreason*. This description is at least as old as Plato's "Ion," in which the titular rhapsode accepts a description of poetry as divinely inspired, a definition designed specifically to exclude *technē*, knowledge or skill. One of my aims in this book, then, is to show that what may look inspired, what may be about inspiration, can still be recognized as technical, knowledgeable, and reasonable. But this is not a book that consists of pointing out examples of inductive reasoning in poetry. I'm *not* simply arguing that poems use a particular kind of logic. Instead, I am arguing *on behalf of* the inductive reasoning in poems.[46] I'm arguing that reasoning in poems should count as logic, or rather, even further, reasoning in poems should count as what philosophers call *metalogic*. The poems in this book are using logic to make arguments, and also the arguments they are making are about how logic works and what it can do.

If we recognize that such poems as "In a Station of the Metro" and "Nomad Exquisite" are modeling inductive logic, then we see their formal organization in new ways. But the philosophical account of logic should also shift after this recognition. The enabling assumption of modern literary studies is that poems *work*, and that by closely analyzing their careful design, we can see how. But much of modern philosophy begins by assuming that inductive reasoning does not work, or not reliably enough, so any success is accidental. In describing poems as modeling inductive reasoning, I'm arguing that in poetry we see what induction looks like if we begin by granting that it can and does work. Inductive logic may not be valid or guarantee truth, but it still might succeed in the absence of or in the gaps between laws or theories. Induction can work as well as lyric poems do.

WHO

Who uses poetry to model inductive reasoning? To answer the question, I'll start by turning it inside out to answer another: while writing this book about inductive reasoning and modern poetry, I've been asked frequently about whether poems can model *deduction* as well. The answer is *yes*, and self-consciously, and also that literary scholars already talk about the two common ways in which deduction is used in and by poems.

The first way that poems use deduction is: some poems present themselves as an example or set of examples of a covering law that already exists, complete and powerful. This poetry is not necessarily itself an argument or even evidence—it has very little to prove and even less to discover. Rather, it is itself only comprehensible in reference to another, bigger idea. This is a large category of poetry, including much religious poetry (such as Bradstreet's), but also poetry that forthrightly reflects and uncritically endorses other kinds of abstract beliefs, ideologies, or intellectual commitments, such as Ezra Pound's *The Cantos*. Readers of *The Cantos* have to educate themselves on Remy de Gourmont, C. H. Douglas and Silvio Gesell, and Leo Frobenius extracurricularly, because—despite Gertrude Stein's description of Pound as a "village explainer"—*The Cantos* does not explain theories.[47] Pound refers to the work of various theorists and those theories clarify the particulars of his poetry.[48]

INTRODUCTION

The second common way that poems use deduction is: some poems incline toward the forms of (or forms resembling the forms of) deductive logic. In her notes to an edition of John Donne's poetry, Janel Mueller points out his use of the dilemma and disjunctive syllogism, identifying a number of Donne's poems as imitating deduction's logical forms.[49] And Paul Fussell has written about Andrew Marvell's use of syllogism as a poetic form as well:

> ["To His Coy Mistress"] is argued like a classical syllogism: (1) if we had world enough and time, your coyness would be tolerable; (2) we do not have sufficient world or time; (3) therefore, we must love at a faster rate than gentility or modesty permit. Although he has written his poem in a continuous sequence of iambic tetrameter couplets, Marvell has separated the three elements of his argument into three indented verse-paragraphs, and, more important, he has proportioned each according to the logical weight of the part of the argument it embodies: the first (the major premise) contains twenty lines, the second (the minor premise) twelve, and the third (the conclusion) fourteen.[50]

As Fussell's reading shows, we can talk about a poem's form using the vocabulary of logical form.

Scholars also describe poetry along these lines without using any philosophical terms at all. For example, see how Gordon Teskey compares John Milton's long poetry to Edmund Spenser's:

> The Spenser of *The Faerie Queene* is a poet so very different from the Milton of *Paradise Lost*.... Spenser is ideologically incoherent and subversive, whereas Milton is not; Spenser is uncertain, tentative, and exploratory, whereas Milton never is; Spenser is distractible, whereas Milton is not; Spenser surprises himself by thinking new things, which Milton never does; above all, Spenser's poem moves forward in pulsatile moments, whereas Milton's poems are architectonic structures. Milton's poems take time to read, of course, but they stand out of time, rigidly sublime and immobile, like mountains without weather. This is never so with *The Faerie Queene*. There is plenty of weather in it.[51]

Coherent, never "thinking new things," standing as "architectonic structure ... out of time, rigidly sublime and immobile, like mountains without weather"—this is a description of something like deductive reasoning. On the other hand, inductive reasoning is "exploratory," "mov[es] forward," dealing in "surprise" and in "thinking new things." Even the striking and strange description of Spenser's poetry as being full of "weather" chimes; weather forecasting is an example of inductive reasoning, as we know how past weather events have happened, and we have developed working theories, and new weather usually conforms to predictions, but *only usually*.

During the century or so discussed by this book—from the Civil War to the Cold War—several generations of philosophers considered, formalized, and argued about logic, and much of this conversation was about the status of inductive reasoning. Although those philosophic conversations began in different places—Vienna; London; Cambridge, Massachusetts—they converged in the United States by the beginning of the Second World War.

This book follows the generations of poets who were the contemporaries of those philosophers from the mid-nineteenth century through the late twentieth century, and it shows how American poets took up the logical forms of induction. This book is the story of how both modern logic and the modern lyric were developed at the same time in many of the same places for some of the same reasons. It positions modern American poetry as part of this intellectual history.

The first generation of poets I discuss—Walt Whitman and Emily Dickinson—created what we now call the modern American lyric at the same time as their contemporaries in philosophy developed modern logic. Induction becomes important, even central, in the philosophic conversations about logic emerging in the second half of the nineteenth century, from pragmatism to Bertrand Russell and Gottlob Frege. Induction also, I argue, is important, even central to the lyric at this time as well. But despite inductive reasoning's crucial place in each, the development of logic and the development of lyric ran in parallel with few intersections in the second half of the nineteenth century.

In the early twentieth century, these conversations cross-pollinated in the prestigious colleges and universities of the East Coast of the United States. By the First World War, pragmatism was well-established and Russell and Frege's logic had been formalized in university textbooks. By the Second World War, America had also become the adoptive home of philosophy of science, as the philosophers of the Vienna Circle and other German-speaking associated philosophers fled the Nazis. While these traditions in philosophy are profoundly at odds, they are also concerned with many of the same questions, and these philosophers read each other's work, and in some cases worked alongside each other at American colleges and universities.

When the young poets who would become modernists went to college, when they studied philosophy and learned directly about the problem of induction, the encounter between poetry and philosophy gained power and self-consciousness. In this book, modernism is primarily represented by Gertrude Stein and Marianne Moore, and then in the mid-century by Elizabeth Bishop. These poets were not just thinking alongside philosophers about the same problem; they were using philosophy and doing philosophy and they knew it. Both modern logic and some modern poetry can be understood as methods for working out, in lines of words, how to handle a particular unsolvable difficulty: the difficulty of not knowing what happens next. And so although the poets I discuss in this book have been categorized as aesthetically experimental, I argue that description doesn't fit the fact that they are using established forms. It's just that those forms are logical.

TWO DISCIPLINES, TWO RESPONSES TO UNDERDETERMINATION

Not knowing what's going to happen next, novelty, all that is solid melting into air—these are descriptions of a future that diverges from the past and is therefore underdetermined. Twentieth-century philosophy and twentieth-century literary studies have conceptualized underdetermination in opposite ways: in philosophy, induction is one of the central problems of modern philosophy, while in literary studies, indeterminacy and contingency are aesthetic virtues.

A few centuries after it was first described by Hume, the problem of induction resurfaced in a significant cross section of the philosophic movements and schools at the end of the nineteenth century and through much of the twentieth.[52] Alfred North Whitehead describes induction as "an unsolved problem which has been bequeathed to us by the seventeenth century"; he's writing in *Science and the Modern World*, published in 1925. Whitehead sums up what's at stake: "The theory of Induction is the despair of philosophy—and yet all our activities are based upon it."[53] Whitehead's erstwhile collaborator Russell exemplifies that despair: he wrestled with inductive reasoning in his work on epistemology as early as 1907, writing, "We tend to believe the premises because we can see that their consequences are true, instead of believing the consequences because we know the premises to be true. But the inferring of premises from consequences is the essence of induction."[54] In 1946's *A History of Western Philosophy*, he offers the memorable assertion that if Hume cannot be answered, "there is no intellectual difference between sanity and insanity."[55]

Even with those stakes, it was not inevitable that induction was going to be one of the major philosophical problems of the twentieth century. Whitehead's and Russell's contemporaries, the pragmatists, also recognized inductive reasoning as a pressing subject—but they didn't despair. C. S. Peirce writes about how induction supports inference in the eleven Lowell lectures in 1866.[56] Peirce's work is the likely referent of William James's statement in 1907's *Pragmatism* that "One of the most successfully cultivated branches of philosophy of our time is what is called inductive logic."[57] James describes induction as how "mathematical, logical and natural uniformities, the first *laws*, were discovered," and states calmly, "most, perhaps all, of our laws are only approximations."[58] That the laws developed by induction may not be reliable clarifies the pragmatists' position that "truth in our ideas means their power to 'work.'"[59] Therefore induction—even as new and unexpected events occur—is not logic failing, but logic working. There's no problem here: James writes, responding to Hume's point that we can't be sure the sun will rise tomorrow because it has always risen, "Day follows day, and its contents are simply added . . . truth is satisfied by the plain additive formula."[60]

Other philosophers find other paths between (sometimes beyond) these poles of despair and serenity about the underdetermined future. Ludwig Wittgenstein supposedly said that reading Hume was a torture since he knew far too much about Hume's subjects,[61] and in 1921's *Tractatus Logico-Philosophicus*, Wittgenstein echoes Hume on induction's unreliable inferences, writing, "We *cannot* infer the events of the future from those of the present."[62] By the end of Wittgenstein's life, in *On Certainty*, he describes the problem of induction as nonsensical. In §287, he writes, "The squirrel does not infer by induction that it is going to need stores next winter as well. And no more do we need a law of induction to justify our actions or our predictions."[63] Wittgenstein's later writings frustrated the logical empiricists, whose tradition evolved into what we now call philosophy of science; it is they who write about induction the most and the most critically. Rudolf Carnap devoted decades to evaluating the reliability of inductive reasoning to try to solve Hume's dilemma.[64] Carl G. Hempel developed a theory of scientific explanation: explanations must be deductive-nomological; induction, necessarily, cannot meet these criteria.[65] But he also held open the possibility for what he called "inductive-statistical explanation," whose purpose would be to offer reliable predictions, though what information would be relevant and adequate for such inductive explanations was never settled, and it was immediately contested.[66] Hempel's paradox of the ravens is his well-known account of the unreliability of inductive reasoning; it shows how difficult it is to confirm inductive reasoning since the claim "all ravens are black" is confirmed by both examples of black ravens *and* by examples of nonblack nonravens.[67] Karl Popper took a harder line, arguing that Hume is correct and that induction *never* supports scientific inference. Induction, he writes, "is a myth . . . neither a psychological fact, nor a fact of ordinary life, nor one of scientific procedure."[68] Particulars may not lead to scientific theories, according to Popper, only falsify them.

The next generation of philosophers of science outflanked the logical empiricists on induction. Thomas Kuhn undermined the premises of the problem of induction with his argument about successive scientific paradigms; there can't be a problem of induction if there's no such thing as "true" science.[69] W. V. O. Quine, claiming Hume for naturalism, takes the problem of induction seriously and writes an almost Joycean pun: "the Humean predicament is the human predicament."[70] Nelson Goodman combines philosophy of language, logical empiricism, pragmatism, and Quinean naturalism—all of which were previously in tension with one another—and becomes one of the foremost thinkers about the problem of induction in the second half of the twentieth century. And at the same time, the study of probability made such enormous advances that induction is now sometimes considered a subcategory of probability rather than the reverse. The philosopher of science Ian Hacking writes, "probability is . . . *the* philosophical success story of the first half of the twentieth century."[71]

And also at this same time, during the first half of the twentieth century, literary studies takes shape as a discipline by taking up inductive reasoning as well. As Russell was laying the foundation of analytic philosophy, and James was outlining pragmatism, and Wittgenstein was writing the

Tractatus, and the Vienna Circle began meeting, and probability was emerging as a field of its own, New Criticism rooted literary analysis in its own version of inductive reasoning: close reading.[72] When reading a text closely, if there are any rules to be had at all, the rule is to build up our account of a poem as a whole from minute attention to its particulars. But in literary studies, underdetermination is reliably identified as an aesthetic virtue, not a problem.

The modern world's "variety and complexity" meant that modern poetry, as Eliot writes, "must be *difficult*."[73] This kind of claim is common throughout the twentieth century; George Steiner's classic essay outlines four different types of difficulty and the last, and arguably hardest, is ontological difficulty, caused by obscurity in the world.[74] And as literary studies became an academic discipline, the difficulty of literary texts was valued; as Leonard Diepeveen writes, "difficulty, then, was the early twentieth century's central tool for arguing about what literature is."[75] John Guillory argues, "the linguistic difficulty of literature ... revalued literature as the cultural capital of the university."[76] But no matter how unsolvable modern literature's difficulty might be, that difficulty is a credit to literary texts and to the discipline of literary studies. New Critical literary scholars resolve the difficulty, so that difficulty is rarely described as a problem, much less a philosophical one.[77]

Literary studies' embrace of underdetermination as aesthetic merit becomes even clearer by the late twentieth century. But the cause and effect switch: rather than the underdetermined modern world making modern poetry difficult, now literary critics tend to argue that modern poems create underdetermination as an aesthetic effect; scholars aren't meant to resolve it, and so difficulty drops away. Marjorie Perloff, in 1981's *The Poetics of Indeterminacy*, describes indeterminacy in twentieth-century poetics as an aesthetic effect of "irreducible ambiguity" causing a kind of readerly "undecidability."[78] More recently, indeterminacy has been subsumed under another kind of underdetermination: contingency, a term brought to literary studies by Richard Rorty and Barbara Herrnstein Smith, both of whom argued in the 1980s that value and values are contingent.[79] David Wellbery's 1992 essay, "Contingency," also helped bring Niklas Luhmann's thinking about contingency—"also being possible otherwise"—to English-language scholars of literary studies.[80] Wellbery argues that while sometimes the contingent is a subject of literary texts, *all* literary texts can be described as contingent as a literary text always could have been otherwise; it's "a divine toss of the dice."[81] By the twenty-first century, literary scholars generally use "contingency" to mean both narrative uncertainty for a character or plot and interpretive uncertainty for the reader. Christina Lupton, introducing a special issue on literature and contingency in *Textual Practice* in 2018, describes contingency both as "a theme" and "a way of reading."[82] The former is similar to Wellbery's claim, and the latter is not unlike Perloff's "indeterminacy," and indeed, it has replaced it. As Gillian White writes in that same issue, contingency is "a word and a concept that in the late twentieth century had become central to critical accounts of what differentiates modernity from postmodernity, and the supposed 'mainstream' of poetry from the 'avant-garde' of contemporary US poetry and poetics."[83] She notes that Charles Altieri, Michael Palmer, and even Perloff all use "contingent" by the end of the twentieth century to describe avant-garde poetry they admire.[84] Even when the word contingency itself isn't used to describe avant-garde poetry, its traces are apparent; for example, in Sianne Ngai's "The Cuteness of the Avant-Garde," she writes that avant-garde poetry represents a "fantasy about the very capacity to fantasize or imagine an *otherwise*."[85] These days, it is rare for literary scholars, critics, or poets from the avant-garde tradition to describe underdetermination as an experience of difficulty.[86] Finding a poem "difficult" is a sign that you are not approaching it the right way, or even that you may not be the right reader.[87] For example, Charles Bernstein's tone, in "The Difficult Poem" from *Attack of the Difficult Poems*, is tongue-in-cheek as he describes his essay as a guide to "coping."[88] The avant-garde and the mainstream are united not in *what* poetic difficulty is but *where* it is: it's an experience of the reader's. If a poem is difficult, that's a reader's problem, and they probably shouldn't be having it. The reader may experience indeterminacy and contingency, but that open-endedness is not difficult, nor a problem.

I shift the location of underdetermination in order to describe aesthetic difficulty as philosophical difficulty, and one worthy of having: the difficulty of this poetry doesn't describe the reader's struggle of making sense of the poem, but the difficulty of the sense-making that the poem is doing. I argue that by the same process that we use to reason about poems—the logic of induction—they reason about the underdetermined world. *Poems do philosophy*. Poems show how reasoning works. This is what I mean when

I say these poems are *miscategorized as aesthetically experimental*: they are using forms from philosophic logic. Because poetry and logic share a set of forms—the forms of inductive reasoning—poems can be difficult in the same way that a philosophical problem is difficult.[89]

HOW POEMS REASON: GWENDOLYN BROOKS

Gwendolyn Brooks's poem "kitchenette building" does not obviously appear to show the difficulty of reasoning logically about an underdetermined world. To the extent to which the poem depicts reasoning, it could initially be seen as the reverse: the world depicted in this poem appears to be *unrelentingly determined* by the laws of racist and misogynistic capitalist America. By recognizing what Brooks's poem knows about deduction and induction, however, we can see that this poem uses poetic form as logical form.[90] Or more specifically, Brooks's use of a truncated sonnet suggests an analogous limitation of deductive logic: that if you make sense of something by referring to a set of established laws, then you may not be able to make sense of new things. And that failure to accommodate novelty reveals that the determinations of those laws may nor may not have the force of necessity.

The poem's plural speaker begins by announcing that their lives are shaped by "the involuntary plan."

> We are things of dry hours and the involuntary plan,
> Grayed in, and gray. "Dream" makes a giddy sound, not strong
> Like "rent," "feeding a wife," "satisfying a man."[91]

"The involuntary plan" requires the speakers to act in ways that are practical, not "giddy," and most of all, financially obligatory. Their activities are necessitated by capitalism, and they are also only legible relative to capitalism; for example, "satisfying a man" is what women, financially dependent on their husbands' work outside the house, provide in exchange for him "feeding a wife." The activities become terms—they are in quotation marks in the poem—because they are terms in an equation of what may be exchanged for what.[92]

We might say that Brooks's speakers are reasoning deductively: based on capitalism's logic, they assert that their activities are worthwhile because they have an exchange value, and that the speakers themselves are commodified "things," interchangeable and also able to be exchanged. All of this only makes sense in reference to capitalism in America. In some ways, "kitchenette building" appears, in its first few lines, to be akin to a religious poem; like Bradstreet's poetry, it seems to have an "interest in strong theory, deductive abstractions that could be used to organize a wide range of phenomena."[93] Bradstreet's speakers' reasoning only makes sense in reference to the laws of Christian doctrine, as, we could say, Brooks's speakers' reasoning only makes sense in reference to capitalism. And in these poems, doctrine—either religious or economic—makes sense of everything.

But then the deductive reasoning of these early lines of "kitchenette building" cracks open. In the middle of the poem, the speakers "wonder" if their lives could accommodate something new and surprising:

But could a dream send up through onion fumes
Its white and violet, fight with fried potatoes
And yesterday's garbage ripening in the hall,
Flutter, or sing an aria down these rooms

Even if we were willing to let it in,
Had time to warm it, keep it very clean,
Anticipate a message, let it begin?[94]

Merely asking if it's possible to dream conjures the dream briefly into being, or almost into being. The speakers clarify that the dream lies beyond the daily exchange of labor for survival; it is not a commodity to be consumed or that has been consumed; it is not today's "fried potatoes," nor "yesterday's garbage ripening in the hall."[95]

The speakers have been reasoning deductively about how their world appears to be determined, but here they show that there's a difference between having something be materially determined—as these speakers' lives are—and having something be purely logically determined. The speakers may initially conflate logical determination and material determination, but then the poem distinguishes them. If something is logically determined, there is no other option—there's nothing outside or beyond it—and here, the dream is not encompassed nor digestible by the deductive reasoning of the speakers. The dream is outside of capitalism; it cannot be made sense of for or by capitalism. And so we learn that the speakers' lives are not logically determined, because the poem moves beyond the material to show that deductive reasoning based on historically contingent conditions *is itself contingent*. Something new, something that it cannot accommodate, can overturn it. Material determination is powerful, but it's not *all* powerful. The speakers can imagine what would have been possible otherwise.

Because the dream cannot be made sense of in reference to capitalism, the speakers must reason about it by comparing it to experiences that lie beyond exchange value, such as holding a new baby or a spiritual transport. And so, like them, the dream would take "time to warm it, keep it very clean,/Anticipate a message, let it begin?'"[96] This sort of comparison of particulars is inductive reasoning; the speakers are reasoning without laws. We might say here that the speakers are considering, in Teskey's words, "surpris[ing] themselves by thinking new things." Then the speakers return to what Teskey calls "architectonic structures"; these structures are the literal structure of a kitchenette building, and also their (our) society's economic structures. Walt Hunter writes about how, for Brooks, "the house is inseparable from matters of racism, segregation, gendered labor, and class politics."[97] Farah Jasmine Griffin writes of these speakers, "The act of dreaming seems a waste of time in light of the realities confronting them, realities of providing shelter, food, and some degree of sensual pleasure; but they dream nonetheless."[98] For these speakers, though, considering a dream at any length ultimately isn't possible, because it doesn't pay off. It doesn't pay off because it's not explicable by the logic of exchange value, of *paying off*, in the same way that love isn't. The speakers return to the deductive logic they use to make sense of their lives and its laws about what value means, about what counts as "well" or what's worth "a minute."

> We wonder. But not well! not for a minute!
> Since Number Five is out of the bathroom now,
> We think of lukewarm water, hope to get in it.[99]

And yet, the poem knows what the speakers themselves don't quite know, or don't know *yet*, about the limitations of deductive logic. And we readers know that the poem knows it because of its form. The poem is nearly a sonnet—it's thirteen lines—but, like many of Brooks's sonnets and almost-sonnets, it doesn't fall clearly into an octave and sestet.[100] Instead, divided into four stanzas, the poem yawns open across the middle, as the possibility of a dream wafts and waltzes through the building's cramped rooms and also through the poem's tight stanzas. And then both structures reassert themselves at the end, returning to "the involuntary plan." The hours at the close of the day are only potentially less "dry" than they were at its start, as the speakers long to wash themselves in dirty bathwater. But it's not clear they manage to take baths at all; they only "think of lukewarm water, hope to get in it."[101] But they are thinking and also hoping.

The poem is nearly a sonnet, and also, the dream is almost called into being: these two very near misses, both close enough to feel as they brush by, are two ways in which the poem leaves a lacuna that shows what lies beyond its grasp. A sonnet, like the lives lived in the kitchenette building, can also be described as having "an involuntary plan," one that traditionally has served as an example of restriction in space ("narrow room") and time ("moment's monument"); the sonnet's structure might not be "architectonic" but it is lastingly, if somewhat flexibly, engineered. For Brooks, at least at times, the sonnet embodied the white tradition of poetry whose power she resolved to reject.[102]

But because "kitchenette building" is only thirteen lines, what I'd like to suggest is not that it's a sonnet that has a line missing, the way someone might have a sock missing, but that it's a sonnet that *is missing* a line, in the sense that someone can miss the point, can fail in an attempt to catch a ball. Brooks's point is *that the point might be missed*. The poem models deductive logic, and it models inductive logic, and it shows how deductive logic is more powerful, *but only as long as nothing new occurs*. The plan appears to be "involuntary" but, it turns out, there's something that escapes it, that *can* escape it, that will not be caught. Something—something new, *anything new*—lies beyond its grasp. Novelty—a new baby, a new message, a dream—cannot be made sense of by this framework. It cannot be seen or said or grasped fully or made to comply.

The speakers' dream never takes a firm shape; not even they can see it clearly; it never really exists at all—or it only exists enough to glimmer at the possible undermining or overthrowing of the laws that make sense of, and so govern, the speakers' lives. The speakers' dream cannot be seen clearly because it can't be made visible by exchange value, and so the speakers cannot realize or visualize it all the way. And so, too, the unshaped, only-glimmeringly-existing line that would make this poem a sonnet is also missed by it, and also threatens to undermine or overthrow it because of what we make legible, and how, in reference to which laws. And by not showing the dream or that line, "kitchenette building" shows us what those laws can't help us see or understand.[103]

In this poem, a dream is not just a dream—it's the recognition that not all determination has deductive necessity because deduction may not be able to make sense of novelty. Capitalism, racism, misogyny—these aren't timeless and inescapable truths. They aren't necessary, in both philosophical and colloquial meanings. This poem models deductive logic that fails to reason about novelty, and it shows us how inductive logic might tell us more about what we need to know to live in an unpredictable world, because the unpredictable world is the better one to live in. It shows us that it's possible—and that it's difficult.

CHAPTER SUMMARIES

The first half of *Lyric Logic* focuses on the parents of modern American poetry, Walt Whitman and Emily Dickinson, and on how their characteristic formal poetics—the list and the analogy—are also the two fundamental forms of inductive reasoning.

Walt Whitman's Enumerations

Walt Whitman's catalogues, his characteristic technique of generating long lists, have long been recognized as central to his poetics. The list, or enumeration, is also the most basic form of inductive reasoning. In this chapter, I argue that we should understand the Whitmanian catalogue not just as formal, as in a traditional feature of long poems, but as a poetic form that is also a logical form: enumerative induction. I introduce formal logical reasoning to readers who aren't trained in philosophy, and I show that by recognizing that Whitman reasons logically through his poetic form, not only is the common account of Whitman changed, but the concept of form must be revised in three crucial ways. First, form should not be defined in opposition to poetic content—this is a false definitional binary. Second, form and free verse are another false binary, as poems can be written in free verse and also have form, as Whitman's poetry is and does. Third, form is not just a rubric with which critics interpret poems, but the logic by which poems interpret the world.

INTRODUCTION

Emily Dickinson's Analogies

Just as Walt Whitman is known for his expansive catalogues, Emily Dickinson is famous for her condensed images. These images are usually described as metaphors or similes, but I argue they should be understood as analogies. Along with the list, analogy is the other fundamental form of inductive reasoning, and its logic is crucial to scientists, legal theorists, and the reasoning that ordinary people do in everyday life. This chapter shows how Dickinson's use of analogy is a form of logical reasoning. Dickinson, unlike Whitman, is already regarded as a difficult poet, but while I argue that Whitman's difficulty has been unrecognized, Dickinson's has been misrecognized. Both use logical forms as poetic forms and aesthetically model logical reasoning. Their aesthetic difficulty is actually philosophical.

If the first two chapters can be described as about induction's poetic *forms*, the next three move a generation or two later to discuss its *problems*. When reasoning inductively, when does one have enough particulars to generalize? And can one ever confidently offer a prediction on the basis of that generalization? The third and fourth chapters of *Lyric Logic* describe how the poetry of Gertrude Stein addresses the problem of generalization and the poetry of Marianne Moore addresses the problem of prediction through their formal poetics. Both poets studied philosophy at college with well-known pragmatists, and both depart from pragmatism in describing induction's problems as serious, but neither find those problems paralyzing. Rather, both defend induction, however unreliable, as the type of reasoning best suited for an unpredictable world. Its difficulty, which is also the difficulty of their poetry, is both real and necessary. The fifth chapter focuses on the poetry of Elizabeth Bishop, who takes as a poetic form the other type of nondeductive logical reasoning. Abduction, or what modern philosophers call "inference to the best explanation," makes a virtue out of induction's necessary contingency.

Contingency and Gertrude Stein

Stein's writing is notoriously difficult, and, like I suggest in my chapter on Dickinson, we've misunderstood that difficulty. It's not aesthetic difficulty but epistemological difficulty: the difficulty of knowing what the facts tell.

Stein presents this philosophical problem via her poetics by presenting readers with facts rather than laws or theories. In addition to exploring the limits of inductive reasoning—through the presentation of facts alone—Stein defends it, not despite its contingency but *because* of it. Stein argues that explanation based on deductive reasoning may appear dependable, but that is misleading; deductive laws and theories are contingent in their own way and may change with the addition of new facts. And while she's influenced by her professor William James's pragmatism, Stein finds contingency to be a real problem. She makes it clear that the contingency stemming from the problem of generalization isn't solvable or escapable, though it can be generative.

Consistency and Marianne Moore

This chapter discusses how Moore transforms induction's contingency—the problem of predicting based on inductive reasoning—into poetics. Moore is commonly thought of as describing, but she's describing *mechanisms*; Moore shows us that mechanisms are reliable until they are not. But Moore defends inductive reasoning by insisting that we have to accept unpredictability. She argues that while inductive reasoning may not be reliable, we can still wish and work for, if not entirely expect, certain future events. Her model is the pangolin's grace, and this grace also shapes her own formal poetics, which enact inconsistency and the difficulty of prediction.

Coherence and Elizabeth Bishop

The final chapter departs slightly: Elizabeth Bishop's poetry also makes use of a philosophical form of logical reasoning, but instead of induction she uses *abduction*. Abduction, also known as inference to the best explanation, shares with inductive reasoning a dependence on individual experience and perspective, and like induction it is not necessarily true, but it does not oppose deduction as much as invert it. Instead of understanding logical reasoning as beginning with laws and theories, as it does in deduction, or ending with them, as induction does, abduction uses laws and theories as hypotheses to guide inference. Bishop does not just describe what she sees, but uses abductive reasoning to infer about what she can't see, what remains out of sight, hidden within or behind or as the invisible causes of visible objects. Bishop's poems—in pointing, then tracing backward—model the logic that readers use on them.

INTRODUCTION

Conclusion: The Sonnet's Logic and Gwendolyn Brooks

This book ends with a conclusion about the sonnet, which, I argue, we already implicitly recognize as a form of logical reasoning. The book's chapters discuss forms of reasoning that philosophy has names for that poetics does not, though these forms are in practice shared. With the sonnet, poetics has a name for a form—a logical form and a poetic form—that philosophy doesn't. I make a claim for what poetics has long known about its own relation to reasoning and also its own resources. Both inductive reasoning and modern poetry work by connecting particulars, and the sonnet—specifically the volta—models this kind of conjunction. I look again to Gwendolyn Brooks, one of the greatest modern practitioners of the sonnet, to show how voltas are the central attribute of the sonnet because of their logical work. But also, more broadly, the volta shows the characteristic power of both logic and the modern lyric poem are the same.

Chapter One

WALT WHITMAN'S ENUMERATIONS

LISTS

Walt Whitman lists. His enumerative catalogues have long been recognized as a, or even the, characteristic aspect of his poetics. An early review of *Leaves of Grass* said Whitman should have been an auctioneer because he's "perpetually haunted by the delusion that he has a catalogue to make."[1] Ralph Waldo Emerson described Whitman's "Catalogue-style of poetry" as "easy and leads nowhere."[2] Whitman adopted the term himself, referring to his "catalogue business."[3]

We are still discussing Whitman's lists: Allen Ginsberg, in "A Supermarket in California," addresses Whitman: "I went into the neon fruit supermarket, dreaming of your enumerations!"[4] Harold Bloom theorizes tallying,[5] and Allen Grossman identifies the "manifest structure" of Whitman's lists, punning on the ship's manifest that tallies passengers and cargo.[6] More recently, scholars have situated Whitman's catalogues in their social and historical contexts to discuss their influences, including the nineteenth-century flipbook,[7] the slave auction,[8] and the urban experience of a flaneur.[9]

In this chapter, I will argue that we should understand Whitman's catalogues as a form. In many ways, we already do. It is uncontroversial to say that Whitman's poetics depends, formally, on listing. And what the flipbook, the slave auction, and the experience of a flaneur share *is* their form:

they list one item, then another, then another. The Whitmanian catalogue has been taken up as a form by a huge range of poets including, to name just a few in addition to Ginsberg, A. R. Ammons, Bernadette Mayer, Claudia Rankine, and Donika Kelly.[10]

More generally, lists themselves are at the very least *formal* in the sense that the epic (and mock-epic) catalogue can be recognized as a traditional element of many long poems, from the *Iliad*'s catalogue of ships, to Chaucer's lists in *The Parliament of Fowls*, to Alexander Pope's *The Rape of the Lock*. But although listing is formal, the list is not usually described as a form. Some literary scholars don't describe lists as forms because a form is understood to be, in Caroline Levine's words, "an ordering principle," and lists disrupt order.[11] For this reason, Eva von Contzen, introducing a special issue of *Style* on lists in literature, describes it as a "non-form" because it undermines narrative authority.[12] Other literary critics argue the opposite: lists *make* order, even if they disrupt narration. Paul Jaussen says so straightforwardly: "Literary criticism has primarily focused on the catalogue as a mechanism for order";[13] as one example, Paul Tankard describes lists as "managerial devices."[14] Some critics are stranded in the middle: Umberto Eco tries to split the difference by distinguishing between a list in a literary text, which is a "breakdown of form" and a "pragmatic list" like a grocery list, which "confers order (and hence a hint of form)."[15] But even for these critics who understand the list to be an ordering principle, it's described as *formal*—a structure, a technique—but not exactly a *form*. For example, Robert Belknap describes the list, in both life and literature, as "formally organized" and a "framework."[16] For Jaussen, the catalogue is a "formal . . . device";[17] he cites Caroline Levine and discusses the catalogue's affordances, as does von Contzen.[18] But they avoid describing the list as a form, presumably because of this unclarity or even uneasiness about whether lists make order or disrupt it, or because lists can both make and disrupt order.

I won't be arguing that lists are or aren't ordering structures; the lack of clarity about whether lists are forms already demonstrates that it's a mistake to conceptualize form as establishing order. Describing a form as an ordering principle depends on a definitional dichotomy between form and content, one in which form brings order to unruly content, that many scholars, including me, would not want to defend at length. Moreover, the lack of clarity about whether lists are formal aspects of texts or are themselves forms is, I think, a function of the same legitimate reluctance to endorse a dichotomy between form and content. One common route around this problem, one way that scholars avoid thinking of form as simply and broadly ordering content, is to focus instead on formal features of texts. Relegating forms to aspects of formality means releasing form from any ordering obligation or expectation. But this option surrenders as much as it preserves.

I will offer an account of form in this chapter that's akin to the account of form in philosophical logic. This is less a redefinition or even reconceptualization of form via interdisciplinary borrowing, and more an attempt to affirm our existing disciplinary practices in literary studies by regrounding them in a transdisciplinary or even predisciplinary idea of what form is and how it works.[19] And it allows us another route, one that doesn't run around a dichotomy between form and content, nor endorses form following content, nor even form as content, but identifies content as formal too. Alongside literary studies, philosophy is the other discipline that identifies forms made of delineated language.[20] A syllogism's form is three lines but also requires certain content in each of them; a sonnet's form is fourteen lines but also the volta must pivot relative to the poem's topic or subject or perspective and not just in its rhyme scheme.

In this light, I'll describe the list as a form, no matter how variable and baggy it is, whether it disrupts order or establishes it. Walt Whitman's listing—also variable and baggy, also disrupting order and establishing it—is not just formal, but a form. Whitman's form is one that philosophic logic has maintained a better name for, and conceptualization of, than literary studies: his catalogues are, formally, enumerative induction.[21] Recognizing them as such means that Whitman's characteristic poetic technique also counts as logical reasoning. And by recognizing Whitman's lists as a form in the logical sense, we can see how they are doing work not just of inventorying the world, but of reasoning philosophically about it in and by means of the strengths of lyric poetry.

LITERARY FORM

In this section, I offer a series of observations about what form means in literary studies. I show how this term has become increasingly vexed by interlocking problems rooted in how we discuss form in our scholarship, and also that it doesn't need to be. In the spirit of the rest of this chapter, my observations are enumerated.

First, there has been a much-remarked-on resurgence in the term's use in the twenty-first century.[22] Returning to form itself is a return to form. Looking at the last half century, we could say that literary studies has both never forgotten about form but also is always remembering about it: multiple waves of literary or scholarly movements in literary studies in the twentieth century were dubbed *new formalism*, as Susan Wolfson describes in her introduction to the 2006 essay collection *Reading for Form*, a book that itself is described as, once again, new formalist. Wolfson states that formalism had "gone underground" at the beginning of the twenty-first century, and that the essays show "if no consensus about what form signifies, then a conviction of why it still has to matter."[23] The next year, in a review essay for *PMLA* about the most recent wave of new formalism (including *Reading for Form*), Marjorie Levinson writes, "Because new formalism's argument is with prestige and praxis, not grounding principles, one finds in the literature ... no efforts to retheorize art, culture, knowledge, value, or even—and this *is* a surprise—form."[24] The still-newer new formalism of fewer than ten years later, ushered in by Levine's *Forms* in 2015, does claim to attempt retheorization; Levine writes, "This book makes a case for expanding our usual definition of form in literary studies to include patterns of sociopolitical experience."[25] In the past decade, scholarship that has retheorized form, discussed form, and retheorized our discussion of form has proliferated beyond the capacity or duty of this brief section to itemize. At this point, form is definitely not underground any longer in literary studies; form is invoked almost everywhere and there are manifold accounts of how it matters. Scholars influenced by Karl Marx and his heirs, particularly Fredric Jameson, write about form. Scholars of Victorian fiction write about form. Scholars of the Black experimental tradition write about form. Scholars write about form across media. Scholars reflecting on the discipline itself write about form. And all of these conversations are so extensive and have cross-pollinated so broadly and thoroughly that attempting to list or sort them into discrete categories is silly.

However—this is my second observation—scholars in literary studies agree that we do not agree on what is meant by the term *form*. These many different works of scholarship discussing form offer prismatic and even diverging accounts of it.[26] Indeed, the conversation about form has turned to its own failure to yield a rigorous and unified account of the term. Sandra Macpherson writes about realizing her own use of form as a key term in her recent book was typical in that it lacked "any rigorous discrimination between form, structure, and necessity," and notes that she didn't "know what distinguished form from genre."[27] Jonathan Kramnick and Anahid Nersessian argue that form has become fuzzy through the term's varied and widespread use, and they polemically suggest that this isn't a problem, writing, "there is no reason to maintain or to desire a consistent use of the term *form*."[28] Levinson, among others, disagrees with them, maintaining that "conceptual clarity" about form is indispensable.[29]

But—this is my third observation—in our classrooms, especially with our undergraduate students, we *do* act as if we know what form means, *which is to say that we know what it means*. Form was an uncontroversial term in literary analysis for a long time, and overall, at least in practice, it continues to be. When we teach form, we have this conceptual clarity: form names the premise—or even the promise—that a text is more than the sum of its parts, that a sonnet is more than a set of miscellaneous lines or even words, that a novel is more than a collection of assorted chapters or even sentences. Assuming that a text has form licenses much if not most of the literary interpretation that we do that links together the facets of texts, particularly close reading, our foundational disciplinary practice. We have naturalized this to the extent that we might not always even note that a text has form out loud, but what we teach our students is not just that it does but that it must—it must have been formed, it must have form, even it must have *a* form—in order for us to interpret it with our fundamental analytical techniques. We talk about not just how form and content tie together but how they extend each other, how they ramify. We think it is meaningful that a sestina follows or stretches the appropriate rules for its repeating end words, and that doing so is what makes the sestina cohere. Asserting that we should look at our ordinary use of form to know what it means is not the same as saying anything goes. I'm asserting the reverse: we have, in practice, a robust and even radical account of form that we rarely acknowledge.[30]

Fourth, *form* is not the same as *formal*. *Formal* is a term that lets us talk about a text's parts and techniques—a poem's meter, rhyme, stanzaic structure, or a novel's breakdown into chapters or its use of free indirect discourse—but by shifting its focus there, it does not deal as directly with the strange math by which the whole exceeds these parts. Labeling the formal aspects of a text is an aspect of literary interpretation, but it is not the license for literary interpretation. If there is confusion in the classroom, in our practice, about what form means, it is due to this distinction: sometimes scholars use *form* for something like *formal*, swapping our fundamental good-faith assumption of a text's coherence for the identification of aspects of its formal poetics or stylistics. In pedagogy, this can mean something like understanding form as the answer to a question on a quiz that ends interpretation rather than the premise that supports it and sets it in motion.[31] In scholarship, this can mean describing form as, or perhaps as a function of, meter, rhyme, or other formal aspects of a text—but this is still a reversal of the assumption that form exists and therefore, indeed as a direct result, formal aspects of a text do too.[32]

Fifth, the abundant disagreement about form at the professional level shares some qualities with the *lack* of disagreement about form at the pedagogical level. We teach undergraduates that identifying a poem's form is a means to an end—at best, attention to aesthetic techniques, at worst, the answer to the professor's question. And at the professional level too, form is theorized to serve as the means to a scholar's interpretive end; because scholars have varying goals, *form* has multiple meanings. What looks inevitable in the undergraduate classroom looks indeterminate in scholarship. In either case, though, form is an interpretive tool in our hands: a lens, a series of boxes for sorting, a set of rulers for measuring. Poets, though, see form differently; they suggest that form is not an exegetical tool that scholars use in order to do our work, but rather what poems use in order to do *their* work. Robert Hass, in *A Little Book on Form*, defines poetic form as "shapes of thought and feeling," as opposed to the "external shape" of New Critical well-wrought urns.[33] In *The Making of a Poem*, Eavan Boland and Mark Strand organize their selections according to recognized poetic forms—the sonnet, ballad, villanelle, sestina, couplet—but also the elegy, the ode, and the pastoral. Boland, Strand, and Hass matter-of-factly include content in their descriptions of form. *Shapes of thought and feeling is form. Remembering the dead is form.* These poets are not suggesting that form is content—as Cleanth Brooks states—but rather, *that content is formal*.[34] Poets may or may not have special authority when it comes to poetics, and it's true that these poets are writing for students, particularly in creative writing, more than for literary scholars. But currently, scholars generally either avoid form when talking about poetry, or offer theorizations of form that aren't particularly literary, or argue for deliberately thin accounts of form that are, so it's notable that poets themselves offer accounts of form that have none of these problems, and that poets do so by rejecting the binary that scholars understand as definitional. Recognizing that content is formal—that we can include content in our talk of form without setting them in opposition to each other—shows us how to recuperate the term and also why we should desire to.[35] And understanding that content can be formal also lets us talk about poems that have been written off, incorrectly, as formless: like Walt Whitman's.

WHITMAN'S FORM

The poetry of Walt Whitman appears so elastic that it might seem shapeless, with its long lines piling up into baggy stanzas—can we talk about its form? Whitman is the father—even the patron saint—of free verse, but that does not mean his poetry isn't formal, because it is: Whitman's poetry is written in free verse *and* it has form, indeed, if we think it hangs together, a form.

There's a long-standing identification of Whitman with free verse, and an identification of both Whitman and free verse with freedom, which usually is understood to mean freedom *from* form. Ezra Pound identifies Whitman as the "pig-headed" father of free verse who inaugurates modernism by giving the "first heave" "to break the pentameter."[36] The imagery here is of meter as restricting, and the comparison of poetic form to imprisonment was well-established by Pound's time; John Milton describes the "modern bondage of Riming,"[37] and William Wordsworth writes in "Nuns Fret Not at Their Convent's Narrow Room" that the sonnet allows solace from "the weight of too much liberty."[38] The comparison of form to a prison continues to the present day: Levine does not describe forms as prisons, but does describe prisons as forms.[39] Whitman's poetics are seen as having thrown off that restriction; Martha Nussbaum and Betsy Erkkila both write about Whitman's "freedom of form"[40] and his "revolution in literary form."[41]

While it is clearly true that Whitman does not write in rhyme, it is just as clearly true that his poetry follows formal traditions; for example, the first line of "Song of Myself"—"I celebrate myself and sing myself"—is iambic pentameter. The echoes of formal poetics in Whitman's poems suggest that the binary of poetic form and free verse is constructed incorrectly.[42] A poem is not *in* or *out* of form the way one is *in* or *out* of prison. Even the freest of free verse sometimes uses the most traditional of formal techniques. And, after all, descriptions of Whitman's "freedom of form" and "revolution of literary form" don't deny that he's still writing in form; they just suggest that his form is new. They do not name it, but the absence of a name doesn't mean there's nothing there to name. A poem may not fulfill the criteria of sonnet or elegy, but saying that a poem has form—even if it doesn't have a form named in the *Princeton Encyclopedia of Poetry and Poetics*—is asserting that it is a single artifact that is interpretable. A half-written poem may be formless; Elizabeth Bishop's drafts of "One Art" are not in the villanelle form and they may not have form at all.[43] If all poems have form, then each poem could have *a* form as well. We know the names of many poetic forms, and there are still other forms for which one could imagine future entries in reference books: maybe "poems that echo nursery rhymes," or (following Frank O'Hara) "lunch poems," or (following Terrence Hayes's homage to Gwendolyn Brooks) "golden shovels."

It's expedient for poets writing both in traditional poetic forms and in free verse to describe form as a prison in opposition to free verse. Wordsworth's speaker, in his sonnet-prison, is humble-bragging about his contentment with how "scanty" it is.[44] And poets writing in free verse are also happy to identify form with imprisonment because they can then cast themselves as bringing forth a more liberated and authentic aesthetic. Whitman himself explicitly connected his revolutionary poetics to revolutionary American democracy. In the Preface to the 1855 edition of *Leaves of Grass*, he writes that the qualities that make Americans—"their manners speech dress friendship . . . the terrible significance of their elections . . . these too are unrhymed poetry."[45] Whitman is responding to Alexis de Tocqueville, who wrote in *Democracy in America* about what would characterize "the poems of democracy" while asserting that "the Americans have no poets."[46] Whitman's description of his own free-verse poetics as implicitly democratic—and of himself as a homegrown American genius—has stuck. Patrick Redding summarizes the basic consensus: "Whitman is perhaps best known for associating democracy with the rejection of traditional poetic meter and rhyme."[47] But accepting this self-description at face value not only means buying Whitman's self-promotion, it also means reducing form to formal devices and to thinking of the whole of a poem as less than the sum of its parts.

Free verse is invested in form and not liberated from it. Whitman's poetry is formed and it has a form. The remainder of this chapter will discuss the form of Whitman's poetry; it's a form not usually thought of as a literary form but a logical one. And on a larger scale, if we decide ahead of time that modern poetry's explosion of poetic innovation is merely a reaction against Victorianism's imprisoning formality, then we'll never be able to see what forms can do.

LOGICAL FORM

As I wrote earlier, philosophy is the other discipline with shaped language; undergraduates in literary studies learn about such forms as the sonnet and villanelle, and undergraduates in philosophy learn about such forms of logical argument as the syllogism. A syllogism, for example, is comprised of two premises and a conclusion. Like other forms of valid arguments, it's deductive, and if its premises are true, then its conclusion must be as well. Here is how it's written:

All A are B.
All B are C.
Therefore all A are C.[48]

Or, the most famous syllogism, often attributed to Aristotle:

All men are mortal.
Socrates is a man.
Therefore Socrates is mortal.

In philosophy, it is not controversial to say that content is formal. Logical forms, like literary ones, organize both what the form says and how it says it. Aristotle describes the syllogism as having a major premise and a minor premise; the major premise contains the major term—here, "mortal"—which is the predicate of the conclusion, and the minor premise contains the minor term—"Socrates"—which is the subject of the conclusion.

For the categorical syllogism above, the major premise, the minor premise, and the conclusion must be affirmative and universal. The middle term—"man"—doesn't occur in the conclusion at all.

In poetry, we use symbolic letters to record a poem's rhyme scheme, so a rhyming quatrain might be written ABAB, or AABB, or more combinations. Logic uses symbolic letters to stand in for terms in reasoning, so the major term will be represented as A, the middle term as B, and the minor term as C. (Other letters—A, E, I, and O—indicate the moods of a syllogism's propositions.) Without collapsing these disciplinary distinctions, there's more than a superficial likeness between how we map out the work that these lines do in literary and logical texts. In the syllogism above, that minor term—"man"—works as a turn from the major and minor premises—is it a volta?—toward the conclusion. I could even describe the syllogism as a three-line stanza in which the A term, the major term—"mortal"—returns in the third. This three-line stanza could be related to terza rima, the form used by Dante and Percy Bysshe Shelley—ABA, BCB, CDC, etc. Like the famous syllogism above, both Dante and Shelley use the tercet to evoke mortality and unavoidable fate. And no wonder: in both the syllogism and terza rima, that apparent wandering away of the second line is actually the perfect set up for the third line's airtight snap.

Form is logical and each form offers a logic. What makes a sonnet a sonnet is not simply that it's fourteen lines, but that its logic is built on the relationship of the octave to the sestet, turning on the volta.[49] In Wordsworth's "Nuns Fret Not," the volta marks the shift from the octave's list of nuns, hermits, maids, weavers, and students, all content with their restricted lives, to the sestet's revelation that they were evidentiary preamble for the speaker's own assertion of contentment. My claim that form is inherently logical is a stronger statement than simply saying that form, whether literary or philosophical, involves content, though it builds on that point. Interpreting a text involves its literary form and its logical form. Or rather, literary forms and logical forms are not distinct: literary forms, like all forms, have a logic.

Understanding that form is logical also means recognizing that texts interpret the world. Texts offer arguments about how we should understand events and phenomena. Nersessian and Kramnick cite the twentieth-century philosopher of science Carl G. Hempel on explanation in their article to argue that identifying a text's form is part of literary-critical explanation. Drawing on Hempel's work on explanation, they ask: "What does form explain?"[50] But, as Marjorie Levinson notes in her response, they don't seem to understand the conversation about philosophical explanation.[51] Kramnick and Nersessian get Hempel backward: Hempel does not argue that form is explanatory; rather, he argues that *explanation itself is a form*. Hempel (along with Paul Oppenheim) wrote the deductive-nomological theory of scientific explanation, which says that an explanation of a given phenomenon must show that it is logically deducible from general laws.[52] Nersessian and Kramnick's question about how we use form in our interpretations of texts is second-order, but the first-order question remains: how literary texts, in having a form, are *already* logical. Form is not just the way that we scholars interpret and explain the text; a text's form embodies its logic, and shows how it interprets.

Hempel argues that explanation is a form with specific criteria, and so some statements are merely descriptive, not explanatory, by Hempelian standards. Hempel's theory that explanation must be deductive was first published in 1948, and it has been questioned for over half a century now precisely about the question of where to draw the line between the descriptive and the explanatory. Another twentieth-century philosopher of science, Wesley Salmon, phrases it this way: "If explanation does something over and above mere description, just what sort of thing is it? . . . What, over and above descriptive knowledge of the world, is required in order to achieve understanding? This seems to me to pose a serious philosophical problem."[53] Some of the sharpest attacks against Hempel's deductive-nomological model have been from philosophers who ask: How, if every explanation must deductively depend on an existing law, are new laws ever discovered?[54] Indeed, many new laws are discovered not through deduction but through empirical observation, that is, description.

Here we return again to the Whitmanian catalogue. A list is a form—but what kind of form? Most logical forms that philosophy undergraduates learn—modus ponens, modus tollens, and syllogism—belong to the category of "valid argument," which means that if the premises are true, then the conclusions will also necessarily be true. Because these logical forms are deductive, they are valid; because their premises are true, their conclusions will also be true. But there are logical forms in which validity and truth have a less stable relationship, and among these are the logical forms of induction. In inductive forms, the premises can be true but the conclusion can still be false. For example, all the men you've ever heard of met are mortal: your neighbor, Abraham Lincoln, even Prince. Therefore, your father is mortal as well. That is probably, but not necessarily, true. There is no general law being invoked from which the conclusion is being logically deduced. Rather, the reasoning depends on assembling together particular examples to suggest a generalization that can then be applied to another example. Hempel does not consider inductive reasoning to be explanatory because for as long as philosophers have discussed induction, inductive reasoning has been considered unreliable. David Hume most famously states the problem of induction's unreliability; he writes that it is impossible to justify the prediction that the sun will rise tomorrow just because it has always risen in the past.[55] The sun rises every day; one could list each dawn. That catalogue of particular descriptive examples might allow one to predict the next time the sun will rise, but it will never guarantee that it will. Without more advanced knowledge of astronomy, there is no general law from which to deduce.

Inductive reasoning can take the form of a list, and lists are the most basic form of induction. Slave auctions and the urban experience of a flaneur are, like sunrises, catalogues from which laws can be generalized such that the next particular can be—uncertainly—predicted. From a description of a slave auction, we can generalize about racism and who will go on the block next, and from the experience of a flaneur, demography, clothing styles, or pedestrian habits. Philosophers call this form *enumerative induction*.

Noting Whitman's "enumerations" is commonplace. And Whitman's lists may look unstructured, like they have broken free of form. But if we recognize that a discussion of form involves not just how something is said, but what is said, then we can see that lists are a form. They are a form at which literary studies gestures vaguely, but for which philosophy has a specific name and account. They may look simply descriptive, but that description has real, albeit uncertain, philosophical heft.

In the form of enumerative induction, each particular observation—the dawn, what the person passed on the street wore—can support a general law which would then allow the next particular in the series to be predicted. That prediction is never necessarily true the way that a prediction based on a deductive explanation would be.[56] But having an uncertain relationship to predictive truth does not mean that the list has no value at all. Whitman insists on its value.

"YOUR ENUMERATIONS!"

Section 15 of "Song of Myself" contains nearly seventy lines that list different people and their activities. To choose just a few: "The carpenter dresses his plank"; "The duck shooter walks by"; "The bride unrumples her white dress"; "The squatter strikes deep with his axe."[57] Each line contains a subject, verb, and object, usually in that order. This list is usually seen as thwarting close reading in two ways: it is both too long and also too straightforward.[58] One could try—noting two different uses of the word "dress," both quoted above—but it's unclear what that kind of granular analysis would render. Its clearest significance is that it is, formally, a list, and is described as a kind of representative census of the country and evidence for Whitman's democratic poetics.

The list as a logical form—enumerative inductive reasoning—means that these particulars support a general law, as all enumerative catalogues do. Here, the implicit generalization supported by this list is about what it means to be American. The particulars are people, and their inclusion in this list supports a generalization that American democracy is diverse and inclusive. Grossman's description of Whitman's "nonequivalent, but equipollent lines" comes from his argument along these lines that Whitman's catalogues are the technique with which he attempts a "poetics of union" akin to Abraham Lincoln's.[59] Grossman continues: "Whitman's originality consisted in the discovery of a regulative principle that permitted an art based in the representative function itself, and organized in its ideal-typical moments (for example, the world-inventories in #15 and #33 of 'Song of Myself') as a taxonomy of which the sorting index is mere being-at-all."[60] In that each person listed has the same amount of power, Whitman's is a democratic poetry. And Grossman is right that the list has criteria that determine what gets included. But "a sorting index" of "mere being-at-all" is a contradiction in terms—the list does not and cannot include everyone, and a sorting index that is all-inclusive is not a sorting index in the first place. Still, the Whitmanian catalogue does have a logic.

Here is the end of section 15 of "Song of Myself":

And these tend inward to me, and I tend outward to them,
And such as it is to be of these more or less I am,
And of these one and all I weave the song of myself.[61]

"These" are the descriptive particulars, the people, in this catalogue. In this first line, Whitman's speaker is set at the center of this crowd, like the middle of a bullseye, as all the other people "tend inward" toward him and he "tend[s] outward" toward them. Although he is placed last on the list, he is central to it.

In both the second and third lines, Whitman says that he is "of these" people that he has listed: "of these more or less I am/And of these one and all." But this assertion of being "of these" has a different meaning in each line. In the second line, Whitman describes his own position among the catalogued masses. He is one "of these" people at the center of this group. There are varying extents to which they tend inward and he tends outward, but still, "such as it is to be of these more or less I am." He belongs in this catalogue.

The third line uses "of these" to claim another, different relation between the speaker and the group. "Of these one and all I weave the song of myself," he says. The most basic interpretation of this statement is as an account of the poem's composition. "Song of Myself" includes descriptions of lots of different people; *of these* descriptions of different people the poem is made. But there's another way to read the claim. Rather than referring to the poem we hold in our hands, Whitman is also saying that he produces *himself* out of this list of descriptions of other particular people. He doesn't just belong with "these," he is made of them. There's that half-rhyme between "these" and "weave." The catalogue of people establishes the logic by which Walt Whitman is at all.

When Walt Whitman is one of this list, as he is in the second line quoted above, the general law supported by the particular examples is presumably one about what it means to be American. There are general laws that govern who is American and that determine a person's status (for example, being born in the United States) and Whitman also establishes his Americanness by deductive criteria; he is "born here of parents born here...." But in this catalogue, Whitman is working inductively, from the bottom up, using particular examples to distill laws about Americanness. He's not after a legal definition, but instead is trying to develop a law of Americanness that could only be discovered inductively through the accumulation of examples. If all of these people are American, then being American must not simply be a matter of race, class, or place of birth, but rather, being American can be described as—according to this list in which each person is attending to their characteristic activity—a pursuit of one's own happiness. Whitman is central to this catalogue because he is yet another example of the catalogue; he's American because he, like the carpenter, bride, and duck-shooter, is doing the thing that makes him who he is. Whitman's characteristic activity, though, is paying attention to the people around him and listing their activities in his poetic, free-verse form. Cataloguing is arguably the characteristic aspect of Whitman's poetics, and here he is included in a catalogue because by pursuing the activity characteristic to him, he is modeling the behavior that makes one American.

But what about when Walt Whitman is the particular produced by this list, as he is in the third line? When he is not just the best example in the catalogue, but produced by it? When he writes "of these one and all I weave the song of myself"? Enumerative induction allows singular predictive inference, which is to say that listing particulars allows one to develop or discover a general law that supports the prediction of the next particular on the list. He is the last person catalogued in section 15 of "Song of Myself," and he's suggesting that he is predicted by all the other people listed. What would it mean to take this seriously and to understand Whitman as claiming that he is predicted by the list that he has written?

Here the stakes of the list as a logical form sharpen: if a catalogue of people allows the enumerative inductive reasoning that predicts Walt Whitman as the next example of that catalogue, then he is like today's sunrise, uncertainly predicted by the ones that came before. There is no guarantee that prediction based on inductive reasoning will work. An explanation that depends on deduction is valuable precisely because its valid logical form means that its predictions are true. For example, we can know that the sun will rise tomorrow—at a specific time, no less—if we refer, deductively, to the laws of astronomy. But a prediction based on induction's logical forms, such as the enumerative list, will never be able to predict as reliably. And yet, Walt Whitman lists, and bases predictions on those lists, even, or especially, the prediction of himself.

VALIDITY

More than a century after Hume's death, prediction based on inductive reasoning reemerged as a particular problem for the modern era. As Lisi

Schoenbach writes, "One might even claim that the problem of relating present to future, whether by proleptically managing the subjectivities of a polity or simply by considering the ramifications of a life lived in time, was the central preoccupation of the modernist moments."[62] One can point to different reasons, ranging from the commonplaces of modernity's rapid changes foregrounding the difficulty of prediction—when "all that is solid melts into air," as Marx writes—to more specific cases of the emergence of the field of probability[63] and the business of insurance.[64] Schoenbach writes about how at the end of the nineteenth century and the beginning of the twentieth, "intertwined debates about history and causality ... including discussions of logic, induction, memory, risk, probability, certainty, and chance" connected thinkers in philosophy, mathematics, law, history, and politics, as well as writers.[65] By the mid-twentieth century, the problem of induction, and particularly prediction based on inductive reasoning, was a central issue in philosophy, with major figures such as Hempel, Salmon, Nelson Goodman, Hilary Putnam, and Rudolf Carnap engaged with the question of how we make possibly unreliable sense of an often unpredictable world.

On one end of this philosophical conversation, philosophers of science, led by Hempel, rejected inductive reasoning as the basis for prediction. On the other, pragmatists such as John Dewey and Richard Rorty, and philosophers of language such as Ludwig Wittgenstein, were attentive to what we actually do, ordinarily, pragmatically, on a daily basis. And regardless of whether inductive forms are reliable, it is undeniable that we depend on generalizing from particular instances and examples to predict, not only in empirical research or in legal theory's attention to case law, but also constantly, every day. Somewhere in the middle, between the philosophers of science and the philosophers of ordinary language and pragmatic daily life, is Goodman, who directly tackles the issue of prediction based on inductive reasoning. Goodman notes: "As principles of *deductive* inference, we have the familiar and highly developed laws of logic; but there are available no such precisely stated and well-recognized principles of inductive inference."[66] For Goodman, inductive validity depends on the language used in the prediction; the terms must be, as he writes, "entrenched," by which he means that they have been used to predict previously. Goodman uses his "new riddle of induction" as an illustration, distinguishing between predicting an emerald's color with the predicates "green" and "grue." I described Goodman as related to pragmatists and philosophers of language because he argues that inductive reasoning depends on our ordinary use of language.[67] "Grue" is not an entrenched predicate, and won't let a speaker make a valid prediction.

Is Whitman's prediction of himself as the last instance, produced by the others listed, in the catalogue in section 15 of "Song of Myself," a *valid* inductive prediction? Is "Walt Whitman," the "I" of "Song of Myself," an entrenched predicate, in Goodman's terms? Is he like "green," or is he like "grue"? Making "Walt Whitman" into a term that is entrenched in our ordinary language is arguably one of the goals of "Song of Myself"—the speaker introduces "Walt Whitman" by name at the beginning of section 24, or arguably even earlier, in the engraving at the beginning of *Leaves of Grass*—and the extent to which Whitman succeeds in naturalizing himself to readers is exactly the extent to which he can be validly predicted by a catalogue of other people. Different readers might disagree on his success, but the foregrounding of himself is an attempt at his own entrenchment.

If Whitman succeeds in making himself into a projectable predicate accepted by a future reader, if he succeeds at making an enumerative catalogue that predicts himself, then that means that his particular use of the list is valid *as a form*. Goodman is a philosopher, but his investigation into what principles make inductive inferences valid is a question about form. Philosophical forms, like literary forms, involve both how something is written, and what it says. Goodman is clarifying the form of inductive reasoning, because while deductive reasoning depends on the "familiar and highly developed laws of logic," the criteria for valid inductive reasoning remain vaguer. Whitman puts inductive reasoning to the test, and the test is whether future readers will accept it as a valid form.

HENCE...

If Whitman succeeds in making himself into a term accepted by that future reader, if his catalogue form meets Goodman's criteria, then he pushes further, doubling down on prediction based on inductive reasoning: he predicts that future reader—us—as well. The last lines of "Song of Myself" project an image of someone reading his poem long after Whitman's death; he addresses that reader in the second person and instructs her to find him "under your bootsoles." So certain is Whitman of this future reader that he ends the poem, "I stop somewhere waiting for you."[68] The poem cannot fully end without the projected reader meeting him on the last page.[69]

If a reader accepts the term "Walt Whitman" as an entrenched predicate that makes his inductive reasoning into a valid form, then is his attempt to predict a future reader also valid? Is the final "you" of "Song of Myself" a term like "green" or one like "grue?" When I discussed section 15 of "Song of Myself," I argued that the enumerative inductive reasoning of that catalogue determines that Americanness does not depend on a deductive law of race, class, parentage, or place of birth, but rather, on a quality in which one pursues his or her own happiness. If, then, the reader understands herself as pursuing her happiness by reading Whitman's poetry, as he understands his own pursuit of happiness by writing it, then the "future reader"—that "you"—can also be argued to be, or to have become through reading the poem, an entrenched predicate. Whitman is trying to make his own name and his first-person speaker into part of our language—if this works, then we accept that he is a projectable predicate—but he is also trying to make us, his readers, into a naturalized part of *his* language. If he succeeds in the first, his prediction of himself is valid. If he succeeds in the second goal, his prediction of us, his future readers, is also valid. His list will then include us, by predicting us as the next examples of a catalogue of Americans. We become so by reading his poem, and being enumerated by it.

Although Goodman asserts that the old problem of induction, as described by Hume, has been superseded by his own, he is not claiming that inductive reasoning is reliable. Instead, he is identifying another problem of induction that he considers to be prior to inductive reasoning's unreliable truth value; this more fundamental issue is that an inductive prediction can only be found to be true or false if it's validly formed in the first place.[70]

And yet, Whitman's listing succeeds: it is true. He is predicted by the catalogue of people in section 15, and he predicts a future reader. And his work does continue to be read, it has become entrenched in our language "ever so many generations hence." (Here I am writing about it.) But these predictions—both valid and true—should be read less as stress tests of inductive reasoning and more as claims about it: that it can, and does, work.

Whitman is, of course, rigging the game and stacking the deck. But my argument is less about inductive reasoning itself and more about poetry's use of it and claims about it.

Whitman affirms his commitment to inductive reasoning as a form. Why? What does induction offer Whitman? What is the value of the list and of inductive reasoning in general?

First: while inductive reasoning may not always afford reliable predictions, its unreliable predictions can still turn out to be true. That is to say, induction is more sharply problematic in theory, epistemologically—we can't know for sure that the sun will rise tomorrow simply because it always has—than it is on a daily basis, in practice, ordinarily, pragmatically. We live our lives predicting that the sun will rise, even if we know no astronomical laws that deductively guarantee it. Siobhan Phillips, in *The Poetics of the Everyday*, suggests that "a believer of Hume's era might well take such probability [as the sun not rising] as debilitating," but "a citizen of the disenchanted twentieth-century universe . . . could find the probability of sunrise to be a sufficient conviction as well as the single possible one."[71]

Second: inductive reasoning may be inherently unreliable, but deduction can also fail if, for example, its premises aren't true. And deduction can and does fail as premises are found false; Thomas Kuhn writes about when new scientific discoveries are made and scientists have to return to empirical data as they try to develop new explanations, because deductive laws are no longer reliable either.[72] In other words, even "a citizen of the disenchanted twentieth-century universe" who thinks that she bases her conviction that the sun will rise tomorrow on scientific laws can still end up facing the contingency of supposedly reliable science. And in such times of flux, inductive reasoning offers a way to stay closer to lived experience and may, in fact, end up being more true at some level than deductive laws. Induction may only support a reasonable guess, but reasonable guesses might be as good as any prediction can get, especially in times of great change.

Whitman lived in such a time; his present diverged violently from the past in ways that threatened how he made sense of his world. Most obviously, the Civil War presented this sort of rupture, but Whitman's response was not to turn against inductive reasoning. Rather, he doubled down. Ed Folsom and Kenneth M. Price argue that after 1860, Whitman's poetry was "radically altered . . . he would begin cataloguing mass death."[73] When Whitman faced a crisis of how to make sense of a changing world, he stayed committed to a method that rejects expertise as itself uncertain, instead holding "creeds and schools in abeyance." Listing the dead is, of course, one of the oldest purposes of Western poetry.[74] Enumerating them may comprise an argument about war, but that argument makes its sense through the use of the list as a logical form.

Finally, form is not just how critics explain poetry, but how poetry logically explains the world. Poetry can do this philosophical work, like philosophy, through form. And induction offers Whitman a form—the enumerative list, what we have come to call the Whitmanian catalogue—that is a logical form. Or rather, it is a logical form that can also be a poetic form, and it shows that poetic forms can have a logic, one that honors both the granular particularity of human experience and the grand uncertainty of our world.

Chapter Two

EMILY DICKINSON'S ANALOGIES

"THE JUGGLER'S HAT"

In 1862, Emily Dickinson included the following two-line poem in a letter to her close friend Samuel Bowles:

> The Juggler's *Hat* her Country is—
> The Mountain Gorse—the *Bee's*—[1]

Like so much of Dickinson's poetry, this poem is hard to interpret in some ways, mostly relative to questions about genre. Is the poem a draft or fragment or a finished, completed poem? How is it connected to three other brief poems included in the letter? (Are there *three* other poems or only *two*?) Is it part of the letter? Bowles was the editor-in-chief and owner of the *Springfield Republican*; this poem, with its reference to a country, may be an occasional poem or even an oblique message to a newspaperman presumably concerned with patriotism and politics? Is this even a lyric poem at all? Is it, in its extreme compression, a limit case or transitional example of the lyric? Or does that extreme compression in fact make it *exemplary* of the lyric? These are questions about the poem's genre, and the genre of Dickinson's poems has been the subject of much brilliant work in literary studies. As both an exemplar and limit case of lyric poetry, her poems have offered case studies for nearly every scholarly, theoretical, and critical frame in literary studies over the past century.

In other ways, the poem appears to be not all that hard to understand; its generic issues are complicated but its formal attributes can appear clear. It's a couplet, and the slant rhyme between "is" and "Bee's" both charms and grates the ear just as others of Dickinson's numerous slant rhymes do. And with its first line of iambic tetrameter and its second line of iambic trimeter, these two lines could be read as one half of a common measure quatrain, Dickinson's most frequently-used stanzaic form. In addition to being in the stanza form of common measure, the poem is also in the form of an analogy. The analogy here likens the relationship between a juggler and her hat to the relationship between a person and her country, as well as to the relationship between a bee and a mountain gorse flower.

This two-line poem is in the form of an analogy, and analogy is a form of logical reasoning. So while it's not controversial to describe the poem as an analogy, and while this kind of formal interpretation appears to be more straightforward than wading into the poem's thorny generic questions, its difficulty is of another kind. While formal aspects of the poem may not exemplify theoretical quandaries for scholars of literature, the poem's form—even the form of a poem this short and simple—demonstrates the philosophical difficulty involved in logical reasoning, and particularly the difficulty of reasoning inductively without referring to deduction's valid forms and sound covering laws.

Analogy is a form of logical reasoning, but unlike logical forms such as the syllogism, analogy is not deductive. There is no reference to an established law or theory, and that lack means there are no guarantees that inferences based on analogical reasoning will be accurate. As a result, analogies support arguments, but their relationship to the making of new knowledge is uncertain, even though analogical reasoning—and inductive reasoning more generally—is a crucial part of the sciences, the law, and the ways that we make sense of the world in our everyday lives. And yet, David Hume reminds us, describing the problem of induction, that we cannot know for certain that the sun will rise tomorrow just because it always has.

The *juggler* is to her *hat* as the *bee* is to the *mountain gorse* as a *person* (this term is missing in the poem but easy to plug in) is to her *country*. It falls neatly into the form of an analogy: *a* is to *b* as *c* is to *d* as *e* is to *f*. Through the analogy, this poem reasons about what it means to have a country. Dickinson uses the models of jugglers and their hats and bees and the mountain gorse flowers they frequent in order to argue that a country is not merely the place where one lives. The juggler is presumably itinerant, collecting money at the end of a show, and the bee flies around, visiting lots of mountain gorse flowers. But the juggler's hat and the flower are analogous: both collect resources that have been gathered by the means of their work. A country, then, is what rewards a person's skill and labor and so supports a person's life. It is not the same as the land itself, but rather, the poem suggests that a nation works along the lines of the political and economic philosophy of liberalism. The poem turns from the pastoral and premodern to a pressing question on the eve of the Civil War about what it means to have a country. The poem argues that a country is not a place and having a country emphatically does *not* mean inhabiting it physically. Rather, having a country means depending upon it economically. The juggler and the bee are both travelers who go from town to town, from flower to flower. A country can be the thing that travels with one, as the juggler's hat is. Or a country can be the thing that one works to find again and again, as the bee finds one mountain gorse, then another, then another, each, hopefully, with nourishment. A country is not where one lives, this poem argues, but rather, a country is *how* one lives.

In this chapter, I'll discuss Emily Dickinson's use of analogy as a version of this fraught form of logical reasoning, and I'll argue that Dickinson uses analogy as both a poetic form and logical form. What I mean by this is that reasoning may be a poetic form: not that reasoning may be poetic in its florid descriptions, but that the distinction between logical forms and poetic forms is false. There are conventional poetic forms that are logical, and reasoning is among the traditional formal resources of poetry. The difficulty of Dickinson's poetry stems from the difficulty of reasoning without being sure that her chosen form leads to truth or knowledge.[2]

ANALOGICAL REASONING

Analogy is a form of logical reasoning so fundamental that discussion of it crosses broad swaths of intellectual terrain. Often written $a:b::c:d$, or *a is to b as c is to d*, or sometimes in the lineation of a philosophic proof, analogy compares particulars, or rather, compares the parallel relations between particulars. Analogy is not deductive, in that it eschews reference to abstract laws and is not valid, much less sound.³ And yet, despite this unreliability, analogy is crucially important and widely used. It's a recognized part of human cognition—analogical reasoning is a subfield of cognitive science⁴—and its logic is understood to be central to legal, scientific, and philosophic reasoning. I won't discuss the cognitive science here, though it seems at least plausible, as Douglas Hofstadter and Emmanuel Sander write, that analogy is at the "core of cognition" because "without analogy there can be no concepts" and "without concepts there can be no thought."⁵ But my question is not exactly about Dickinson's *thought*, but rather, her *reasoning*: how she argues in a logical form that doubles as a poetic form. I'll briefly survey the formalization of analogy in different disciplines' modes of analysis and argument in order to clarify how Dickinson's poems share a form with logical reasoning.

In addition to cognitive science, analogy is particularly prominent in the law, the sciences, and philosophic ethics.⁶ Legal scholars write about the fundamental place of analogical reasoning. The principle of *stare decisis* is analogical—cases should be decided through comparison to a case that's a relevant precedent—and interpreting the law based on precedent is behind the entire tradition of common (or case) law. While some legal scholars worry about analogy's reliability because it is not necessarily valid or sound, the law's reliance on the logic of analogy is not disputed. Cass Sunstein begins an article on the subject by writing: "Reasoning by analogy is the most familiar form of legal reasoning."⁷ Lloyd L. Weinreb goes slightly further, writing "analogy is at the very center of legal reasoning."⁸

In the sciences, analogical reasoning underlies the use of models. Philosophers of science have long debated the importance of model-making in the sciences—models may help scientists discover or justify theories—for centuries. The eighteenth-century natural philosopher, chemist, and theologian Joseph Priestley writes of analogy that "all discoveries, which were not made by mere accident, have been made by the help of it."⁹ In the twentieth century, logical positivism attempted to unify philosophy and science under the umbrella of empiricism, and, as a result, described analogical model-making as unscientific and illogical, since scientific theorizing must be deductive only.¹⁰ Mid-twentieth-century philosopher of science Mary Hesse disagreed and defended analogical reasoning as "essential to the logic of scientific theories," and argued against her predecessors and peers, such as the logical empiricists Carl G. Hempel, Karl Popper, and "most contemporary philosophers of science ... [who] say that the use of models or analogues is not essential to scientific theorizing, and that theoretical explanation can be described in a purely formal deductive system."[11] In the social sciences, Mary S. Morgan, a historian of economics, also describes the importance of analogical models; she charts how over the nineteenth and twentieth centuries, economics became "heavily dependent on a set of reasoning tools that economists now call 'models': small mathematical, statistical, graphical, diagrammatic, and even physical objects that can be manipulated in various different ways."[12] Morgan cites cognitive scientists and also draws on Hesse and other philosophers of science as she writes about how models "[give] form to ideas."[13]

Beyond philosophy of science, philosophers in other fields—such as those in ethics, language, and mind—have written about thought experiments, many of which work analogically as an "imagined situation"[14] or "imaginary cases."[15] Many of these analogical thought experiments are in the field of ethics, such as Philippa Foot's trolley problem, Judith Jarvis Thomson's famous violinist, and many others. Like legal reasoning, these sorts of ethical thought experiments often involve an implicit or explicit argument that depends on analogical reasoning; Thomson's, for example, is an argument by analogy for abortion rights.[16] These sorts of thought experiments in ethics are also like thought experiments in the sciences in that they provide a "mental model" that's an "analog to a real-world phenomenon."[17] Like other versions of analogy, at least some thought experiments are "inductive argument forms."[18] And thought experiments are in no way limited to ethics; readers of such philosophers from Plato to Ludwig Wittgenstein will recognize that their writings also make use of thought experiments that use analogical reasoning (from the Ring of Gyges to the beetle in the box).[19]

And yet, despite its broad and fundamental importance as a mode of reasoning, because analogical reasoning is not deductive and so can never be sound, it's at best *likely* or *probably* true. There's always a risk that analogical reasoning could conflict with or even contradict deductive reasoning that's based on a covering law. In legal reasoning, common law and statutory law can differ or diverge, leading to inconsistent judgments. In the sciences, when analogical reasoning runs aslant of an established law, it could be the sign of the law being incorrect, and help to usher in what Thomas Kuhn has called "revolutionary science," when there's "a crisis induced by the failure of expectation and followed by revolution . . . thought experiment is one of the essential analytical tools which are deployed during a crisis and which then help to promote basic conceptual reform."[20] For example, in the second half of the nineteenth century, the analogy between how gas molecules bounce off of each other and how billiard balls do was a heuristic for scientists developing the kinetic theory of gases. But it's more likely *not* that the law is wrong, but that the analogy is. Gas molecules may behave like billiard balls, but they don't behave like bowling balls even if we analogize them to each other. In philosophy, whether ethics or another field, an analogy can be "double-edged" and "point to the opposite conclusion from the one which was proposed."[21]

How do we know if an analogical argument is true? There aren't any clear rules.[22] Hilary Putnam writes: "When Carnap and I worked together on inductive logic in 1953–54, the problem that he regarded as the *most* intractable in the whole area of inductive logic was the problem of 'giving proper weight to analogy.' No criterion is known for distinguishing 'good' from 'bad' analogies."[23] This chimes with David Hume's account of the problem of induction more generally: the difficulty in nondeductive reasoning isn't just epistemological—it's not only about how we make inferences—but also justificatory, in that we can't justify an inference based on inductive reasoning. Reasoning from analogy is "extremely tricky," and it's even been described as a fallacy, in that it's a mistake to suppose that it has "the certainty [of] deductive arguments."[24] Arguments using analogy are "legitimate *inductive* or probabilistic arguments," but they will never have the soundness of deductive arguments.[25] Hesse writes that analogy "depends on induction from known laws connecting the properties to each analogue; hence all such argument is inductive."[26] She's arguing for analogy's potential validity, so asks: "What is an analogy? [And] when is argument from analogy valid? . . . It is characteristic of modern, as opposed to classical and medieval logic, that the answer to the first question is taken to be either obvious or unanalyzable, while the second is taken to be a question involving induction, and therefore highly problematic."[27] In classical and medieval logic, the reverse is true: analogy required lengthy descriptions, but its logical power was taken for granted.

Why, then, use analogies, if they are unreliable in their argumentation and can't be justified? Sometimes, there aren't good alternatives; in many situations, there aren't any reliable deductive laws, and analogy is "often the most powerful and compelling type of argument we can use."[28] Kuhn writes about using thought experiments to remedy epistemological blind spots: "The outcome of thought experiments can be the same as that of scientific revolutions: they can enable the scientist to use as an integral part of his knowledge what that knowledge had previously made inaccessible to him. That is the sense in which they change his knowledge of the world. And it is because they can have that effect that they cluster so notably in the works of men like Aristotle, Galileo, Descartes, Einstein, and Bohr, the great weavers of new conceptual fabrics."[29] The word *fabric* shares a meaning with the etymological origins of *text*; Kuhn gestures toward the literariness of thought experiments when he asserts that simply by writing about the world, by describing the world differently, one can "change ... knowledge of the world."[30]

ANALOGY IN LITERARY STUDIES

Scholars in other disciplines often use literary texts as examples in their discussion of analogical reasoning, but the reverse tends not to be the case. For example, philosophers writing about thought experiments discuss whether literary fiction such as E. M. Forster's *Howards End* and Graham Greene's *The Third Man* count.[31] But in literary studies, analogy in a literary text is usually identified and discussed not as a form of logical reasoning at all, but as an example of imagery or figurative language; an analogical argument is usually described as a *metaphor*. There isn't necessarily a sharp distinction between analogy and metaphor—Aristotle writes about metaphors being based on the logic of analogy—but an analogy is *not* description. Analogy, unlike a metaphor, does not supplement our account of a tenor with new content about it. Rather, analogy is a form of reasoning, an argument. One could say that analogy is not figurative, as metaphor is, but *literal*; philosophers of language differ on whether a metaphor can be paraphrased, but there's no doubt that an analogy can be paraphrased.[32] Indeed, an analogy can be paraphrased so fully that there are several options for how to write its logical form.

Despite analogy not receiving a lot of attention in literary studies, there are several recent books that are exceptions; they suggest how analogy can be adapted into a literary technique. Devin Griffiths, in *The Age of Analogy*, theorizes "analogy as the primary formal constituent of *comparative historicism*,"[33] and argues that the nineteenth-century historical novel uses analogy as "a tool that brings the relation between previous ages and the present into focus."[34] Dahlia Porter, in *Science, Form, and the Problem of Induction in British Romanticism*, also writes about "the analogical project of conjectural history," locating it slightly earlier than Griffiths does, in the late eighteenth century, and in the poetry of Robert Southey.[35] For Southey, Porter argues, analogy is a technique of information management in that it provides a "procedure"[36] that handles the numerous "details that generate, fill in, and subsequently authorize the larger narrative framework that always, *invariably*, exceed its capacity for syncretism."[37] But although Griffiths and Porter both include the word "science" in their subtitles, neither directly connects analogy to theories of scientific model-making or debates in philosophy of science, much less thought experiments, legal theory, or other philosophical forms of logical reasoning. For both, analogy is historically focused and historically bound; a tool by which eighteenth- and nineteenth-century writers bring the present and past together, and one that originates in antiquarianism and draws on the work of Enlightenment and Romantic "philologists ... and anatomists ... as well as geologists, antiquarians, and biblical scholars"[38] and connects the contemporary genres read by those thinkers, including "travel narrative, natural history, ethnographic accounts, and literary works."[39]

Griffiths and Porter discuss analogical reasoning as a technique that isn't limited to literature, and here we share common ground. But this chapter offers a sharply different and in many ways more traditional philosophical account of analogy. Griffiths's interest is primarily in what he calls *"harmonic analogies,"* which are a process that "allow significant shared features to emerge," rather than analogies that "apply a previously understood pattern of relationships to a new context," as philosophers, legal theorists, scientists, and others usually understand analogy.[40] And Porter refers to induction, but she defines it as "compositional methods,"[41] not as a logical form of reasoning or argument. For both Griffiths and Porter, analogy is a way of generating and organizing content for a literary text. They both describe it as a form—in that, as Caroline Levine writes, form orders a text's content—but both of their accounts of the particular form of analogy, and logical form in general, are left vague.[42]

Daniel Tiffany, in *Toy Medium*, doesn't conceptualize analogy's relationship to literature within a historical period, but slices it transhistorically relative to a scientific problem of how to understand materiality. He argues for the relevance of literary studies in theorizing model-making about corporeality: "Most important, literary criticism has failed to address—though it is ideally suited to do so—the intrinsic role of pictures and elaborate analogies in shaping our knowledge of material substance, starting with the classical notion of the atom."[43] Tiffany shows that "scientific and philosophical theories of matter" have a "lyric dimension" in that both "science and poetry proceed, in part, by making pictures of what we cannot see (or what merely escapes our notice), by attributing corporeal qualities to inscrutable events."[44] My argument more closely resembles Tiffany's, in that I agree that literary criticism hasn't adequately discussed analogy, whether by reading it too shallowly as metaphoric description or too narrowly as a historical artifact. Tiffany's emphasis, though, is on corporeality, and he argues that scientific accounts of material substance are, though not recognized as such, lyric. My argument stresses the inverse: my focus is on form, and I argue that analogy in poetry is logical in its forms in addition to being literary.[45]

What's at stake here are analogy's powers. Just as philosophers of science, legal scholars, and others disagree about analogy's reliability, Porter, Griffiths, and Tiffany also differ in their sense of what analogy can tell us. In Porter's account, analogy fails; at best it offers "a far more pragmatic Romantic aesthetic than its Coleridgean counterpart, one that acknowledges the simultaneous necessity and impossibility of grasping the secret relations between things and forming them into a regular body of knowledge."[46] Griffiths takes an almost diametrically opposite position; he defends analogy as successful not in spite of its literariness but because of it: "the so-called literary features of analogy are precisely what afford its ability to capture natural patterns."[47] He writes of "the basic dilemma that constitutes the field of 'science and literature' insofar as it hopes to show the value of literary forms in producing scientific knowledge, and to prove that imaginative language generates real knowledge about the world."[48] He, perhaps unwittingly, is echoing Kuhn, who, five decades earlier, asked how rephrasing what we already know can tell us something new: "How, then, relying exclusively upon familiar data, can a thought experiment lead to new knowledge or to new understanding of nature?"[49]

Porter is right that analogy is a variety of inductive reasoning and inductive reasoning is always problematic. But Griffiths is right that induction—and analogy—often work *anyway*. And Tiffany's right that analogy might work better than any other alternative, and that in fact it's often already working, often unexamined. Analogy is powerful, analogy is persuasive, analogy can, simply by rearranging what we know into a new form and redescribing it, teach us something new about the world. And analogy might be wrong.

This is not just a critical issue in science, as Kuhn describes it, nor a basic dilemma in the relationship between science and literature, as Griffiths describes it, but a fundamental question about literature that has existed at least as long as Plato's dialogues: what is the relationship between literature and knowledge? How can *language* create *knowledge*? In Plato's *Ion*, Socrates makes Ion admit that poetry can't, that it does not contain knowledge. But can the relationship of poetry and knowledge be one of *form*, rather than content? Analogy is a logical form that is also a literary form. It's the foundation for a metaphor but also for an argument. Poetry—and bringing into alignment poetic form and logical form—can tell us more about analogy's powers. And doing so will also tell us about poetry's.

EMILY DICKINSON'S ANALOGIES

I've buried a lede, or rather, my lead. When I had just started graduate school, I happened across a slim book published nearly forty years earlier titled *Emily Dickinson's Poetry*. In it, Robert Weisbuch made an observation that sparked not just the origin of this chapter but of this whole book. Analogy, he writes, is for Dickinson the "poetic method which does not dress but illustrates, thus *is*, the pattern of her thought."[50] Weisbuch doesn't place analogy in the context of philosophical, legal, or scientific reasoning; he likens it to John Donne's metaphysical conceits, which is to say, to metaphor. What caught me is the assertion that in poetry what *illustrates* thinking *is* thinking. Or, framed differently, that *logic*, as we might use the term colloquially, can be *logic* in the philosophical sense.

But in the traditional language of literary studies, Dickinson's comparisons are categorized as *imagery*: metaphors, metonyms, and similes. Even Weisbuch distinguishes Dickinson's analogies from metaphors by degree, not kind. Suzanne Juhasz builds on Weisbuch's argument to describe Dickinson's analogies as materially enacting compulsive repetition, but she uses analogy and metaphor almost interchangeably.[51] In Sharon Cameron's

Lyric Time—which continues to stand as one of the best books about Dickinson's poetry—Cameron describes Dickinson's imagery as the mark of a lack of understanding and the gap between knowledge and language. She writes about how, in Dickinson's poems, "we fail at direct names because we fail at perfect comprehension, and that certain experiences evade mastery and hence definition—the best we can do is approximate or approach them; a simile is an acknowledgement of that failure and contains with it the pain of imperfect rendering."[52] Like simile, "metaphor and analogy are a last resort, they are also often all we have."[53] In this reading, Dickinson's analogies are not different from other comparisons, and all of them gesture toward what we do not know how to say, and their imagery illustrates this negative space. "Our minds produce images for which there are no verbal equivalents . . . unable to say what we mean, we also fail to know it."[54] Cameron's argument, along with Weisbuch's, is crucial to my understanding of Dickinson's poetry.

But while this may be true of Dickinson's imagery, analogies are not, or not merely, *imagery*. And while Dickinson's analogies may mark a failure of understanding, they also—if we understand analogies as logical forms of reasoning—make a step toward greater knowledge of the world. Cameron describes a lack or gap as an existential problem, as unapproachable for language, and so inaccessible or unresponsive to our thinking. But reasoning by analogy is not the sign of the impassable or impossible; analogy arises when a situation may not be covered by established laws, but it's still available to thought.

In other words, yes, an analogy might be a tool of last resort, but it's still a tool, and one that hasn't failed. Because analogy is not deductive, it is not as dependable as other forms of reasoning. But analogy *can* work, and sometimes it works very well, maybe even better than ostensibly more reliable tools. An analogy does not only mark a potential gap; it attempts to bridge it. And although it may be shaky, it sometimes does bridge it, and sometimes when nothing else would. Analogy need not be the sign of an existential problem and accompanying affective crisis; analogy can mark when reasoning is working exactly as it should.[55]

I'm distinguishing Dickinson's analogies, which reason and argue, from what several of Dickinson's best readers have described as an interest in defining words. Northrop Frye pointed this out when he wrote, "Many of her poems start out by making some kind of definition of an abstract noun."[56] Cameron writes about "Dickinson's poems of definition,"[57] and Jed Deppman positions Dickinson and her "definitional art"[58] of a "lyrical lexicon of some 250 poems" in conversation and competition with her Amherst neighbor Noah Webster's new dictionary.[59] "The Juggler's Hat" could be seen as a poem of definition because it could be read as defining what having a country means; according to the poem, it's not a political affiliation or personal identity, but the economic condition of being able to support oneself. *Citizenship* is not an experience where language fails, like *pain* is in Cameron's argument, but it's still a concept that the poem suggests may be better understood. And, more specifically, the concept can be better understood *through analogy*. Dictionary definitions don't reason or argue. Definitions may be one of the end results of analogical reasoning—a new definition of a word may be one of the implications of an analogical argument—but describing analogy *as definition* erases analogy's logical reasoning.

Some of these same poems that have been described as poems of definition have also been described as riddles, most prominently by Christopher Benfey, who has described the riddle as Dickinson's "favorite literary form."[60] This is less contradictory than it might first appear: riddles, such as those in the *Exeter Book*, work like inverse definitions in that they frequently describe a noun and ask the reader to name it. Benfey writes that the definitional poem is Dickinson's other favorite genre, and compares them: "Just as Dickinson's definitions often have built-in riddles, her riddles tend to have built-in definitions."[61] We can see this too with "The Juggler's Hat"—*What is it that's like a hat is to a juggler and a flower to a bee, but for a country?*—it asks us to solve the equation by filling in "citizen." But riddles, unlike definitions, don't offer new knowledge; they're solved by the knowledge we already have. So while describing some of Dickinson's poems as riddles reminds us of the process of logical reasoning she models, it's not the same point that I'm making by identifying them as analogies. Definitional poems contain new knowledge but not reasoning, and, inversely, riddles contain reasoning but not new knowledge.

"THERE IS NO FRIGATE LIKE A BOOK"

Analogies are a form of logical reasoning that attempts to produce new knowledge. In "The Juggler's Hat," Dickinson reasons logically about what it means to have a country, and argues using an analogy that countries are a necessary criterion for supporting oneself. Because the analogy likens countries to hats and flowers, it also argues that a country is transhistorical, and perhaps even natural. But "The Juggler's Hat" is only one example; Dickinson reasons logically with analogies throughout her poetry. Many, though not all, of what Cameron and Deppman and others call the definitional poems reason analogically. Many, though not all, of what Benfey calls the riddle poems also reason analogically.

I'll turn to a well-known poem of Dickinson's—"There is no Frigate like a Book"—which isn't thought to be particularly thorny. It could be read as a poem full of imagery, a poem of definition or a riddle, but it is best read, I'll argue, as an example of analogical reasoning.

> There is no Frigate like a Book
> To take us Lands away
> Nor any Coursers like a Page
> Of prancing Poetry—
> This Traverse may the poorest take
> Without oppress of Toll—
> How frugal is the Chariot
> That bears the Human Soul—[62]

This poem begins as an extended simile: a book is like a mode of transport. Only it's not quite: frigates and books aren't really comparable, asserts this poem in its first line, nor are horses and poems. Or, with more nuance: they may be *comparable*, but the experience of reading literature is so much better than other ways of traveling that the comparison is lopsided to the point of inaccuracy. They are not, I could say, *commensurate*; one cannot meaningfully be exchanged for the other (they are like monopoly money and dollar bills). The first two near-similes in the first half of the poem give way to a different metaphor in the fifth and sixth line, in which the point of the comparison again differentiates books and transport rather than simply likening them—reading is affordable, travel is not—but then the poem turns in its last couplet, the way a Shakespearean sonnet does. Here, there's a comparison that works by similarity, not difference. It might first appear that the last couplet continues the established comparison: a book is like a chariot in that reading feels like the soul is traveling, and a book is less expensive than a chariot, so books offer better ways to travel than actual modes of transportation. But there's also another possible comparison here, one that likens a chariot, carrying the soul, to the human body, the soul's usual mode of transport. Bodies are frugal in the noneconomic sense—meager, plain—especially compared to the magnificence of the soul.

If this poem were read as a poem of definition, it would be trying to bring the resources of language to describe the transporting experience of reading; what reading is like would be seen as unknown but available through elaboration and imagery. If it were read as a riddle, we might plug in "the experience of reading," believing that to be already known and adequately described by language. We would perhaps note the riddling on kinds of transportation; reading is a *transporting* experience.

These interpretations are still available if the poem is read as a series of analogies. But instead of the poem describing, it's reasoning: it's not describing the experience of reading, it's reasoning and, as a result, offering an *argument* about the distinction between body and soul. The analogies here argue that reading can feel like travel *because* of the soul's distinction, even detachability, from the body. Rather than letting the last several lines slide away, tangentially, from the main subject of the poem, I begin with the analogy at the end—both a *chariot* is to a *passenger* as a *book* is to a *reader* and also, completing the analogy in the other way, a *chariot* is to a *passenger* as a *body* is to a *soul*.

What this other option suggests as well is that a *book* is to a *reader* as a *body* is to a *soul*. Our bodies are one form of embodiment, and a book offers another form of embodiment in that it embodies the experience of reading. We could even say that the chariot is a model of what it means to be embodied; it lets us understand how embodiment works in the same way that billiard balls help us understand the workings of gas molecules. Now the negation of the comparison—the incommensurability—between *sailing* or *riding a powerful horse* and *reading* makes more sense. They are not quite exchangeable for each other, despite resembling each other, because one happens to the body and one happens to the soul. (Monopoly money and dollar bills also resemble each other but aren't commensurate.)

Another way of writing this is to say that *reading* is not a perfect metaphoric tenor for the vehicle of sailing or riding—the literal vehicles refuse to be metaphoric vehicles—because reading is not and cannot simply be likened to travel without flattening the poem into one about the joys of literature and disregarding the end and its concern with embodiment. The relation between reading and ways of physically traveling involves both similarity and difference, and while they can't be brought into a commensurate relation, they can be brought into an *analogical* one. Analogy allows—and operates by—recognizing both similarity and difference in its comparisons.

And analogy, because it is a logical form of reasoning, can argue. Read with attention to its analogical reasoning, this poem argues that reading is preferable to actual travel not because it is cheaper, but because the freedom it offers is the more extreme: it unencumbers one of a body. Based on that analogy between *body* and *soul* and *book* and *reader*, the poem argues that reading replaces the embodiment of being stuck in a human body with being embodied in a book. Both bodies and books are frugal, in both similar and different senses, and it turns out bodies and books are commensurate: one can be exchanged for the other.

ANALOGY'S POWERS

By attending to Dickinson's use of analogy in "There is no Frigate like a Book," I showed that the poem is reasoning logically. And, based on its analogy, the poem offers an argument not just about reading being pleasurable but about it being pleasurable precisely because it allows an escape from embodiment, or more specifically, the replacement of one's body with that of a book. "There is no Frigate like a Book" makes a claim about commensurability: frigates and books are comparable but not commensurate, but bodies and books are both comparable and commensurate.

But the implications of reading the analogies in Dickinson's poems as logical reasoning are larger than the expanded reading of what this one poem is doing, or even how a large number of Dickinson's poems use analogical reasoning. Analogy is a logical form, and recognizing that analogy is *formal* helps us develop a better account of Dickinson's poetic form and also of poetic form generally. When literary scholars talk about poetic form, it's often as another version of embodiment: the poem's soul is its content and its form is the structure housing the content, giving it shape. This is how most literary scholars from the New Critics to Caroline Levine have discussed form. In my previous chapter on Walt Whitman, I argue against this definitional binary because it leads to an impoverished account of form: one that is nearly universally applicable but means nothing beyond *organization*, and which betrays a kind of scholarly self-importance, in that we assume that form is *our* interpretive tool. Instead, I suggest a different version of form, one that's more akin to how form is understood in philosophical logic, in which form doesn't bring order to content, but rather, one where there is no conceptual opposition between form and content. Content itself can be formal. When poets use a logical form—such as analogy, or enumeration—as a literary form, they reveal that form isn't just an exegetical tool that scholars use in order to do our work, but rather an analytical tool that poems use in order to do *their* work. Readers interpret poems, but poems themselves also already interpret; poems reason and poems argue.[63]

Poems reason formally, through their form, and in "The Juggler's Hat," the logical form of analogy perfectly overlaps with the poetic form of the couplet. While it's more familiar for most readers of poetry to describe the poem formally as a couplet, it shouldn't feel too uncomfortable to recognize that it also has the form of an analogy. And by describing a poem as having a logical form, we can recognize that it makes an argument, and how it makes its argument, and what the strengths and weakness of its reasoning are. "There is no Frigate like a Book" also reasons analogically; while its eight lines may not map quite as tightly onto the *a is to b as c is to d* basic structure of analogy, it's not far from it. What happens if we also describe its form not just as two quatrains, but also as a set of linked analogies?

In the previous chapter, I argue that by recognizing the logical form of Whitman's poetry, we can see that his poems, though archetypically free verse, are not formless. No one describes Dickinson's poems as being formless. On the contrary, her poems are sometimes seen as burdened with too many formal characteristics; this overload of form is persuasively described as presenting problematic choices for readers to choose—or choose not to choose—as we interpret.[64] But first, we can recognize that Dickinson's logical form isn't mutually exclusive with what we might describe as her poetic form; we need not choose between asserting that she writes in analogies or quatrains. Second, we can also recognize that Dickinson's poems also offer interpretations. With a sharper sense of what form can be—so that we can include logical form—we can recognize a larger sense of what form can *do*, or rather: *what poems can do*. "There is no Frigate like a Book" may not be as neatly in the form of an analogy as "The Juggler's Hat" is, but it has the form of an analogy nonetheless. And it is by means of that form that it offers an argument about embodiment and commensurability. I could say that I interpreted both of these poems through their analogies and offered arguments, but really, their analogies are offering arguments already. That's what analogies do, and so what these poems do.

Using analogy as a form of logical reasoning offers benefits. One benefit, particularly important for Dickinson, is that analogical reasoning doesn't depend on expertise. It's inductive—it doesn't draw on abstract laws or theories—and so it makes interpretations and arguments from the ground up. Dickinson herself was well-educated for a woman of her time and was from a family that valued education. But in her poems, there's a pointed rejection of expertise.[65] For example, in the poem " 'Arcturus' is his other name—," the speaker expresses exasperation with an astronomer in the first stanza, a theologian in the second, and a scientist in the third.[66] In this poem and in two others ("A science—so the Savans say" and "If the foolish, call them 'flowers'—") the speaker refers to experts as "savans." "Savans," or savants, have genuine expertise that the speaker of these poems doesn't, either in the sciences or religion, but she does not value it. Indeed, in the very first lines of these poems, she insists on preferring colloquial names— "'Arcturus' is his other name—/I'd rather call him 'Star!'"—and describes the abstract scientific laws governing the classification of plants and animals as unhelpful and the words of the theologian as misplaced. Expertise, according to Dickinson, offers neither the divine knowledge of the "learned Angels," nor does it respect the other truth of one's direct experience.[67]

Dickinson is not suggesting that the experts of her time are wrong, exactly; she's not calling for a scientific revolution. But neither is she accepting their authority; although they are not wrong, neither she does acknowledge them as right. Or rather, there may be many versions of being right and the speaker of Dickinson's poems is concerned both with what is most correct and what is most useful. Both lead her to privileging empirical evidence and firsthand experience. Kuhn argues that in times of revolutionary science, abstract laws turn out to be untrue and so deductive reasoning fails; in this crisis, we have to return to inductive reasoning based on empirical evidence. Despite, or rather, maybe because, thought experiments are imaginary, they are part of that return to empiricism and induction. Cameron describes analogy, along with metaphor, as "a last resort, they are also often all we have."[68] Analogy is not *all* we have, but because analogy reasons using direct experience, precisely *because* it eschews the deduction of experts, Dickinson suggests that it's still the *best* we have.

There are links and echoes between my argument about analogical reasoning and feminist epistemology. Analogy reasons logically while rejecting the expertise of established male authorities in both the scientific and religious hierarchies, and Dickinson has been a central figure for feminist literary theory since Adrienne Rich's "Vesuvius at Home."[69] Further, there are potential alignments with queer epistemology; Dickinson's poetry has been discussed in that context by, for example, Eve Kosofsky Sedgwick.[70] Both feminist and queer epistemology draw on standpoint theory, and it could be argued that the speaker of Dickinson's poems, by virtue of her perspective as a woman and therefore a nonexpert offers an epistemological corrective. This strikes me, at least provisionally, as correct but not all that surprising. We could also say that she doesn't offer a new perspective or even a new epistemological method, but rather, an older one. She calls the bluff of expertise by returning to the fundamentals of knowledge, inductive reasoning based on empirical observation. And Dickinson doesn't offer something that hasn't been seen—the empirical observations are not new information—but rather, shows that rearranging and redescribing established knowledge can make new knowledge.

One more connection that I don't have the chance to explore at length here is how Dickinson's analogical reasoning chimes with the philosophical tradition of pragmatism.[71] Dickinson, like the monumental thinker of her time, Ralph Waldo Emerson, is sometimes described as a proto-pragmatist and sometimes as someone who wrestles with skepticism. These positions are usually held to be incompatible. For example, the dispute over Emerson involves eminent literary scholars as well as some of the greatest philosophers of the past century—for example, neo-pragmatist Richard Rorty claims Emerson for pragmatism, while Stanley Cavell, the ordinary language philosopher, describes Emerson as recognizing the truth of skepticism, and, in the face of it, seeking to redeem the meaningfulness of our words—and it hinges on how Emerson expresses his epistemology. Pragmatists and ordinary language philosophers share the conviction that philosophy belongs in the realm of everyday activities and language, neither are satisfied with philosophy of science's valuing of deductive knowledge only, arguing instead that large-scale theories are at best irrelevant and likely an impediment. But pragmatism and ordinary language philosophy differ sharply on knowledge and truth. In the pragmatic account, our inquiries lead to truth and knowledge about the world. For Cavell, though, if we demand that our language leads us to true knowledge about the world, we will fail, feel stricken, isolated, and experience skepticism.

Dickinson's analogical reasoning could be interpreted as a variety of pragmatism; its logic, shared and fundamental, reveals the closeness and continuity between everyday forms of sense-making and scientific and other intellectual inquiries. William James describes how pragmatic reasoning "clings to facts and concreteness, observes truth at its work in particular cases, and generalizes,"[72] and analogy too does this. But, for the pragmatist, according to James, truth is "what helps us get into a satisfactory relation with other parts of our experience . . . truth in our ideas means their power to 'work.'"[73] C. S. Peirce describes truth as what is "agreed to by all who investigate, is what we mean by the truth."[74] Is Dickinson comfortable with this "instrumental" view of truth, as John Dewey might have put it?[75] Or, asked differently, does her analogical reasoning always lead her to truth? No, Cameron is right: Dickinson's poetry—stricken, isolated—frequently demonstrates the failure of language to lead to truth or knowledge. For this reason, I'm also sympathetic to those readers who describe her as a skeptic. Dickinson knows that the knowledge she makes may turn out to be false, or not to be knowledge at all, but simply language encountering what can't be known.

ANALOGY'S FAILURES: "MY LIFE HAD STOOD—A LOADED GUN—" AND "I HEARD A FLY BUZZ—WHEN I DIED—"

Dickinson can be read equally as a skeptic and as a pragmatist because of her own recognition that analogical reasoning can be wrong. The unreliability of analogy—the contingency of any nondeductive reasoning—may not be a problem for pragmatists, but it is a problem for Dickinson. Sometimes analogies seem to work as a mode of reasoning for Dickinson and sometimes they do not. Sometimes an analogy remains incomplete, sometimes it's just incorrect, and sometimes it isn't available at all. Dickinson recognizes the risks of reasoning by analogy, and her poetry models its unreliability. In this section, I'll discuss two poems in which Dickinson shows us how analogical reasoning fails to lead to knowledge.

The poems discussed so far—"The Juggler's Hat" and "There is no Frigate like a Book"—are typical of Dickinson's poems in some ways, but they aren't among her greatest poems; they aren't as strange or difficult as the poems that are struggled with and revered. Of all of Dickinson's poems, the one that is most celebrated and agonized over is arguably "My Life had stood—a Loaded Gun—." My readings are all focused on the analogies in Dickinson's poems; here in this poem, too, there's an analogy at the heart of this poem between the speaker's life and a gun. But it's incomplete, and the interpretive work of reading this poem involves completing the analogy's terms so that the logical relationship of the gun to its owner is clarified relative to the speaker.

> My Life had stood—a Loaded Gun—
> In Corners—till a Day
> The Owner passed—identified—
> And carried Me away—
>
> And now We roam in Sovreign Woods—
> And now We hunt the Doe—
> And every time I speak for Him
> The Mountains straight reply—[76]

Who—or what—is the equivalent of a gun's owner in the speaker's life? The analogy continues and becomes more complicated throughout the poem, as the speaker describes "hunting the doe," then "smiling," and at night, "guarding" her master's head. The speaker tells us of their "Yellow Eye—/Or an emphatic Thumb—," and claims that they have "the power to kill,/Without—the power to die—."[77]

There are several options in how to read this nearly opaque poem. The first is that this poem is not analogical at all but metaphorical, and its language is figurative. And, as figurative language, it doesn't make an argument but rather decorates the poem. Theo Davis has written about Dickinson's "ornamental" poetry, which values attention to objects over thought about them.[78] But one need not even make an original argument and instead see this poem as doing the conventional work of poetry all the way back in the Classical Western tradition of writing in metaphors and imaginative figures of speech; most famously, Aristotle required that "above all the poet must be skilled in the use of metaphor."[79] In this reading, the speaker is like a gun in the way that Wordsworth's Lucy is like a violet in "She Dwelt Among th' Untrodden Ways"; they share one aspect of likeness that the poem elaborates, but there is no larger argument drawing on logical relation.

One could also argue that this poem is not metaphorical, nor analogical, but simply literal: the gun is speaking. This is also not inconceivable; there is a long list of it-narratives in literature, such as the novels, many from the eighteenth century, written from the perspectives of such objects as coins and pincushions. In this reading of Dickinson's poem, there is also no logical form, because it's a straightforward dramatic monologue.

But neither of these are the way the poem is most frequently read, in which there's an analogy set up between the gun and the speaker's life, and the task of the reader is to choose an analogical term that stands relative to the speaker as the owner does to the gun. The two conventional choices, as Cameron writes, are God or a lover.[80] Those aren't the only choices, though—there's Susan Stewart's essay on teaching this poem in which she offers the reading that the speaker is not literally the gun but also not human—rather, the speaker is a hunting dog, and the owner of the gun is also the master of the dog.[81] It's a brilliant, though kind of deflating, interpretation, almost making an it-narrative of the poem. And one could also follow Cameron in refusing to choose another term to complete the analogy, holding it open, deconstructing the association of identity and violence, and making something missing into a metaphysical drama.[82]

I'm not going to try to fill in the analogy and offer a different reading of this poem; rather, I'm pointing to the poem's form as an analogy, albeit a submerged and incomplete one. Because Dickinson doesn't complete the analogy—because the *b* term could be so many different things—she is not making an argument the way she does with "The Juggler's Hat" or "There is no Frigate like a Book." But this poem, because its form is analogical, still offers an opportunity to reason. It works in the same way that the beginning of a thought experiment does: "suppose that a person's life was likened to a gun . . ."[83] But then instead of making an argument based on that analogy, Dickinson leaves it incomplete, open, as if to invite readers to finish the analogy and therefore the argument. The reason that this poem has been catnip to scholars and critics who write about Dickinson is due to this form, its *logical* form. Because this poem is in the form of an analogy, and when that missing term is filled in like the blank spot in Mad Libs, it will generate an argument almost automatically. Or, to offer an analogy myself, the poem is an argumentative machine just waiting for a key to be inserted and turn it on; add the missing piece, and the poem roars to life. The poem's form *is* a loaded gun.

"My Life had stood—a Loaded Gun—" is famously difficult, but what critics and scholars seem to mean by that is that it's indeterminate, which I'm suggesting is because it's an incomplete analogy. It's underdetermined because of that missing term, but this isn't the actual source of its difficulty. I'm not arguing that this poem is easy to understand, but rather, that it has another kind of easiness: it's easy to make claims about. The poem may not make *sense*, but it's still *logical*. The speaker's situation may be strange, and her choice of words surprising, but its form—not its rhyme scheme but its logical form—is *not* hard to understand. The analogy fails to reason successfully because of its incompleteness, but this difficulty is, in many different ways, solvable.

Solving it—by completing the analogy and making the reasoning make sense—is what most readers of Dickinson do; we can describe this poem's analogy as a tool to outline a certain class or set of things that can complete it.[84] Other readers describe the poem's indeterminacy as the primary cause of Dickinson's difficulty. Indeterminacy is a kind of underdetermination, and it describes contingency in how we read a text; a text may be open to many different interpretations, any or all of which may be true. But there are other sorts of difficulty in Dickinson's poetry that are not easily solved, that remain difficult. I'm arguing that Dickinson's poems use analogical reasoning to model the difficulty of reasoning inductively, which is another kind of underdetermination. This kind of contingency is when a proposition may turn out to be true or may turn out to be false. And the associated difficulty is not one of too many options among which one can choose (or choose not to choose). Rather, the difficulty of contingency is that of the lack of choice because of a lack of power or knowledge. If indeterminacy is akin to being overwhelmed, contingency is experienced as scarcity or provisionality.

Theo Davis also describes Dickinson's poetry as interested in contingency, although one of Davis's lodestars in *Ornamental Aesthetics* is Martin Heidegger, and her discussion of Dickinson's poetry echoes him in describing how "Dickinson identifies ornamentation with contingent placing-upon."[85] For Davis, Dickinson's poetry "returns us to the uncertain, unfolding contingency of the immediate."[86] I don't share Davis's philosophical orientation, but I share with her the view that Dickinson's poetry must encounter the world's contingency because of its investment in truth. And we also agree that Dickinson's poetry doesn't seek to describe truth, but to use the particular resources of poetry to locate it. Davis writes, "Ornamentation can be found to have a *privileged* relationship to truth: it can point to what is unrepresentable, and indicate its presence and its value, without performing the transformative mediation of representation or the full merging of truth into the sensory and temporal."[87] When I say that Dickinson's poems use analogical reasoning to model contingency, I'm not suggesting that she represents truth through comparative imagery, but rather, uses the logic of analogical reasoning to discover truth, and to do so in the empirical "sensory and temporal" world, not maintaining the value of truth in another unmediated state. Precisely because the world is contingent, analogy is an appropriate form of reasoning. Dickinson shows how analogy's logic is, in addition to being indeterminate if left incomplete, also contingent, even if complete.

We see how analogical reasoning fails in "I heard a Fly buzz—when I died—."[88] The poem's difficulty is not due to the strangeness of the speaker recollecting her death, nor to the circularity of its narrative structure. It's due to the speaker's inability to reason logically because of the contingency of analogy.

At first, it appears that there are no analogies at all in this poem. After the first line's summary of events still to come in the poem, the second, third, and fourth lines are a long simile:

I heard a Fly buzz—when I died—
The Stillness in the Room
Was like the Stillness in the Air—
Between the Heaves of Storm—[89]

But this simile comparing the room's stillness to momentary stillness during a storm is closer to a figure of speech rather than a logical comparison;

the silence of the mourners shares a likeness with the silence between thunderclaps, but there isn't an argument based on this relation. The second stanza uses synecdoche; here the speaker uses eyes and breaths to represent the mourners gathered around:

> The Eyes around—had wrung them dry—
> And Breaths were gathering firm
> For that last Onset—when the King
> Be witnessed—in the Room—

But again, synecdoche, like simile, is a figure of speech, and there is no analogy behind the synecdochal reductions. One could link these two images and argue that both are comparing mourners to stormy weather, but it's not clear to me that the speaker is interested in making a claim based on that comparison; there may be an implication that death, like a thunderstorm, is unstoppable, and so both fearful and majestic, but that still seems descriptive rather than argumentative, since it's fact rather than analysis. And then the rest of the poem makes no comparisons at all.

But there *is* an implicit analogy here that supports an argument that may turn out to be true, though the speaker very much hopes it doesn't: that the "King" is analogous to the fly. The poem's third and fourth (and final) stanza are:

> I willed my Keepsakes—Signed away
> What portion of me be
> Assignable—and then it was
> There interposed a Fly—
>
> With Blue—uncertain—stumbling Buzz—
> Between the light—and me—
> And then the Windows failed—and then
> I could not see to see—

The "King" stands relative to the speaker's salvation as the fly does to the lack of salvation; the substitution of the "King" with the fly suggests an argument that the speaker is not saved. She cannot bring herself to accept it. If the fly arrived at the moment of her death when she expected the "King," did the fly come in his place, or block him from coming, or was the fly an incongruous incarnation of the divine? Or do the two have no relation at all? But the problem here is not indeterminacy—there are not too many right answers—but contingency. There *is* an answer, but we can't be entirely sure what it is. The argument that the speaker isn't saved because the fly arrived instead of the "King" remains speculative. To be sure, we'd need an update on the status of the speaker's soul beyond the poem's narrative loop.

Dickinson's poem models this particular moment of logical contingency, but, by extension, it also shows that all analogy is contingent. Even the description of the divine as the "King" who is expected to be "witnessed in the room" is a compressed analogy; the arrival of God is related to that of a sovereign whose presence underwrites the law, and so the possible desertion of the divine implies an ungoverned universe, but it also reveals that the description of the divine as a king might have been misguided in the first place. The analogy might have been simply wrong. The divine may not be part of a lawful system. The divine might not be all that powerful. The divine may not exist, despite any analogies arguing for the contrary.

And what if there's a blight of mountain gorse flowers? Or if the juggler goes hungry one season? What if one hates the next few books one tries to read or is too distracted, unhappy, happy, or whatever, to be carried away by reading? What if *it just doesn't work next time*? What if, to use Hume's example, the sun doesn't rise? This is a difficulty that won't go away.

POETIC REASONING

Reasoning by analogy will never overcome its fundamental unreliability; it will never be deductive. But sometimes it's all we have or the best we have. Dickinson thinks so—we can surmise that she's not simply or entirely a skeptic—because she keeps trying to use analogies to reason, even in the face of their contingency. Her analogies, like all analogies, may not produce knowledge, but also she cannot escape them or give them up.

How should one balance analogy's powers and its failures? How can pragmatism be brought into alignment with its absolute inverse, skepticism? I'll suggest an answer in a roundabout way, via an essay about quantitative literary studies that draws on statistics. Richard Jean So recently discussed the statistician George E. P. Box's aphorism, "All models are wrong, but some are useful"; he argues, via a discussion of Franco Moretti's *Distant*

Reading, that literary scholars, and particularly the practitioners and the readers of digital humanities scholarship, should let go of a long-held "suspicious and critical gaze toward modeling, which strikes them as offensively simpleminded and naïve."[90] According to So, Moretti produced "a statistical *description* of his corpus; what he has not done is produce a statistical *model* of this corpus," and this distinction is crucial if one is to understand the critiques of Moretti and the possibilities of quantitative literary studies.[91] "The purpose of my response," he writes, "is not to expose error and demand correction in his work; rather, it is to argue that error is a constitutive part of science and that quantitative literary criticism would benefit from viewing error as less something to be tolerated or avoided and more something to be integrated formally into our research."[92]

Like So, I'm noting the distinction between description and modeling, as an incorrect description doesn't have further epistemological stakes, and like So, I agree that the inevitable errors associated with modeling does not mean that models aren't still useful. All models are wrong, and models are still necessary. The worry that modeling always oversimplifies is another way of expressing the worry that analogical reasoning is contingent; both risk error as they seek to distill general laws from particular circumstances.

The difference between my argument and So's is not about the status of models, but rather, about literature. So is concerned with the analytical practices of literary scholars, particularly those in quantitative literary studies, while I'm concerned with poems. Which is to say, for So—as for most literary scholars—a discussion of how to analyze or interpret is a conversation about the practice of criticism and scholarship with other professional literary scholars and critics about our operations and activities. That literary texts are the *objects* of analysis and interpretation is so self-evident that writing it out feels banal. And yet, I'm arguing something quite different: that literary texts are also models—that *literary texts model*. They are the *subjects* of the action; they interpret and analyze the world. Literary texts of course offer an occasion for us to interpret and analyze them, but our actions and interests do not erase or override theirs.

So writes that for Box, the statistician, "models are recursive mechanisms for generative exploration"[93]; this neatly chimes with the literary scholar Marjorie Levinson's long-standing description of the lyric poem as "recursive" and her comparison of the lyric's recursive self-assembly to models of self-assembly drawn from the sciences.[94] In essays collected in *Thinking*

Through Poetry, Levinson traces and constellates the theoretical movements of the past few decades; she describes the "biggest recent innovation in humanities studies" as "reenchanting the object, transforming it from dead to vibrant matter."[95] Her conceptualization of recursion is one such version of this reenchantment, in that it recognizes form's *actions*: "What I have been describing, self-organization, could be termed a formalism in that, as I said at the start, its claims are operational, which means formal, albeit in a highly dynamic sense."[96] Levinson notes that both the sciences and the humanities encounter contingency—"in many cases or on many levels, both the objects and the explanatory models of the sciences are as fluid, as inter- or multideterminative, and as comfortable with contingencies as ours in the humanities"—but that error isn't harrowing, and unreliability is something with which we can be comfortable.[97] I read and reread Levinson's essays as I was writing this chapter, and—even more than the typical experience of seeing one's own thinking echoed in whatever one reads—found in her closing thoughts some of my own questions and ambitions. A footnote to her book's final pages felt almost like a personal note: "The status, uses, validity, and 'affordances' of models and/or metaphors in literary criticism badly needs theorizing, of a sort that would draw on current, recent, and classic work in history and philosophy of science."[98]

In this chapter, I've drawn on the current, recent, and classic work in the history of philosophy of science (as well as other sources), to argue about the status, uses, validity, and affordances of models. My focus hasn't been models in literary *criticism*, but models in *literature*, which is to say, those representations that have too frequently been read as metaphors, but should instead be understood as the actions of literary form. Another way to say this might be: my focus has been, like Levinson's, on what lyric poems can do. Though I recognize the validity of the broad-strokes argument about literary studies' return (again) to formalism with which Levinson closes her book, I have not thought of my own project as another version of reenchanting the dead matter of the text, in part because logical reasoning is resolutely unenchanting (I mean this as a compliment, and not even a backhanded one!), and in part because it has never made sense to me to think of poems as inert in the first place.

Poems reason logically through the resources of their form; logical reasoning is, like poetry, formal. Whitman's characteristic form—both logical and poetic—is the list, and Dickinson's characteristic form—both logical and poetic—is the analogy. Recognizing that logical forms and poetic forms can be one and the same has implications for our understanding of what poetry can do.

We analyze Dickinson's poems as critics and scholars, but that is second-order; more fundamentally, her poetry already reasons logically. The difficulty of Dickinson's poetry is connected to this often overlooked activity of logical reasoning, but it frequently has been misunderstood as obscurity or indeterminacy. Analogies are not an attempt to obfuscate or obscure; as one of the most widespread and fundamental forms of logical reasoning, they are the reverse. And while they might be left incomplete and as a result lead to indeterminacy, indeterminacy is not the most stubbornly difficult aspect of Dickinson's poetry. The difficulty of Dickinson's poetry is due to the difficult philosophical problem it models: the fact that even when complete, analogy is contingent. An analogy makes an argument, but its reasoning is inductive, and it will always be unreliable. Pragmatists (and Levinson) don't see this as a problem, and skeptics see nothing else. Dickinson, though, trusts to analogy, even when it's untrustworthy.

If we take seriously that poetic form can be logical form, and that it's how poems offer interpretations of the world, and that we see reasoning modeled in poems, then it's only one step further to make an evaluative claim and say that poetry is where we could or even *should* look to understand analogical reasoning. Dickinson's poems are among our very greatest. Why shouldn't we see her poems as, in their use of form, exemplifying the strengths of inductive reasoning, and also its weaknesses? Kuhn's question about thought experiments—"How, then, relying exclusively upon familiar data, can a thought experiment lead to new knowledge or to new understanding of nature?"—may be best answered not with reference to "the works of men like Aristotle, Galileo, Descartes, Einstein, and Bohr, the great weavers of new conceptual fabrics" but to *poets,* weavers of other texts.[99] It is in poetry—in poems such as Emily Dickinson's—that we see analogy at its strongest and most wild, at its most powerful and possibly its least reliable. One of poetry's particular powers, then, lies in rearranging and redescribing the familiar into new and yet everyday forms that help us reason about the world and so give us new knowledge about it. This is difficult, and it makes the poetry that tries to do it difficult as well; poetry as different as Whitman's and Dickinson's is difficult for the same reason: their opposite aesthetics are shaped by the same apposite philosophical concerns and ambitions.

Chapter Three

CONTINGENCY AND GERTRUDE STEIN

"FACTS TELL"

Gertrude Stein's first complete work is now known as *Q.E.D.* This semi-autobiographical novel, written in 1903 just before Stein moved to Paris, describes a gridlocked love triangle among three women, Adele, Helen, and Mabel, who meet each other on a ship crossing the Atlantic. As they part at the end of the novel, Helen scolds Adele, the stand-in for Stein, by saying, "Won't you ever learn that it is facts that tell."[1] Here, at the very beginning of Stein's writing career, we see her theorizing what will become her commitment to induction—"that it is facts that tell." Stein's commitment to reasoning without abstract laws or theories is unwavering, but she does not deny that inductive reasoning is problematic. Or, in Adele's words, following immediately on Helen's claim for induction—"But . . . there are many facts and it isn't easy to know just what they tell."[2]

Stein, in multiple texts over decades, insists that one can make sense of the world by accumulating particulars, even as she reckons with induction's contingency. Her central case study for defending inductive reasoning and the resulting contingency of its conclusions is *explanation*.[3] By experimenting with explanatory criteria—with what an explanation is and whether one can explain without reference to general laws—and by insisting that, yes, we can say why things happen using the particularity of our own experience,

Stein charts the limits of induction's powers. I will discuss three texts in three different literary genres from three different points in her career: fiction, *Q.E.D.*; poetry, "An Elucidation"; and a lecture, "Composition As Explanation." Each of these texts theorizes what explanation is, whether it is through the explanations that a lover may give to a beloved, or a teacher to a student, or a speaker to an audience. And in each text, Stein argues that explanation can work inductively, that one need not refer to laws or theories to understand why events or phenomena occur as they do.

The difficulty of making sense out of a large jumble of particulars, of never knowing if one's incipient theories are headed in the right direction, of feeling overwhelmed—of there being so many facts, of never being sure what they tell—this also sounds like what it's like to read Stein. This isn't a coincidence: I'll argue that Stein's theorization of explanation based on inductive reasoning happens within and through her poetics. Using the resources of literariness, such as the foregrounding of details and the embrace of the unexpected, Stein models the powers and pitfalls of making sense of experience using only our experience.

Another way of saying this is that explanation is formal and Stein's work also is formal. As I did in the first chapter, reading Walt Whitman's poetry as formal, I'll argue here that Stein's difficulty isn't due to formlessness, but to form. Logical reasoning has many forms: there are the well-known deductive forms in which true premises guarantee true conclusions, and there are also inductive forms, wilder, less certain in guaranteeing truth. Explanation is usually placed in the category of deduction, but Stein contests this placement and offers her own work as both argument and evidence. Her poetic form is a philosophical form disavowed by philosophy: explanation based on inductive reasoning.

EXPLANATION

What is an explanation? What distinguishes an explanation of an event or phenomenon from a description of it? Most simply, an explanation is the answer to a question that begins *why*. While discussion of the causes of events goes back to Plato and Aristotle, and causation is also an important topic for David Hume, they stop short of clarifying the criteria of explanation. Identifying one of Aristotle's causes might be descriptive instead of explanatory, such as the material cause of a statue being made of bronze.

Then, from the middle of the nineteenth century to the middle of the twentieth, while debating logic and reasoning, philosophers from a wide swath of fields and traditions directly took on the question of what counts as an explanation. That philosophers at this time would tackle this topic is not surprising; one way to describe the modern era is to say that old explanations were disappearing and new ones not only taking their seats but also rearranging the whole room. Friedrich Nietzsche, in *Beyond Good and Evil*, describes the modern era as "Nothing but new 'Whys,'" and that was in 1888, before the modern era was fully underway.[4] But this is part of the larger story told by this book: at the second half of the nineteenth century and the first half of the twentieth, induction reemerges as a philosophical problem. Explanation is the case study—and the battlefield—on which deduction's powers and pitfalls get worked out.

The philosopher who made explanation into a philosophical topic is the logical empiricist Carl G. Hempel, who, unlike pragmatists and ordinary language philosophers of his time, has absolute conviction in the scientific method. Hempel defines explanation as the answer to the question, "Why is it the case that p?"[5] To answer that question, Hempel, along with Paul Oppenheim, argues that an explanation must subsume the phenomenon under a covering law. Called the deductive-nomological (or D-N) model of explanation, this form requires that a phenomenon (*explanandum*) must be logically deducible from general laws and particular facts invoked (together called *explanans*), which must have empirical content and be true.[6] An explanation, according to Hempel, shows that a phenomenon is predictable because it is a logical consequence of the covering law.[7] What's most notable about Hempel's theorization of explanation is its emphasis on deduction. Requiring that an explanation refer to a covering law is a neat solution to the question of the criteria of an explanation, not least because if the deductive law is true (along with the particular facts), then the explanation will be true also. But also Hempel's D-N theory has been repeatedly criticized on its dependence on deduction and exclusion of inductive reasoning: this is its weakest point. As just one example, if an explanation must refer to existing laws and theories, how are new explanations based on empirical evidence ever developed? That is, what is the place of induction in explanation? This is the point that Mary Hesse takes up in her 1963 book *Models and Analogies in Science*, in which she argues that inductive reasoning through analogy is a crucial part of the discovery of new scientific explanations.[8] Bas C. van Fraassen makes a different point; he does not believe in the existence of induction, but also argues that deductive explanation is limited only to observable aspects of the world.[9] And more recently, the place of inductive reasoning in explanation is discussed relative to abduction by Peter Lipton in his 2004 book, *Inference to the Best Explanation*, in which he writes that scientists make predictions before they have established laws by using inductive reasoning (more specifically, abductive reasoning) to guide their explanations.[10] According to Lipton, when we develop an idea about how things work, we infer what would be the best explanation of the evidence we have. And, to be fair to Hempel, seventeen years after he first wrote about the D-N theory, he revisits the subject to elaborate further, expanding the category of "covering law" explanations beyond D-N to include both deductive and inductive statistical explanations. A covering law, then, can logically support, either deductively or inductively, why a phenomenon is likely or unlikely to happen, and not just why it did or did not.[11] But the expansion of covering-law theory to include inductive logic under the umbrella of statistical explanation raises more problems for Hempel. He spends one page on deductive-statistical explanation, and twenty on inductive-statistical explanation, finally allowing that while inductive-statistical does constitute explanation and does support prediction, it must meet more requirements, like being maximally specific (it must include all potentially relevant laws and facts),[12] and also has permanent problems, like ambiguity[13] and nonconjunctiveness (two inductive-statistical explanations will not work together to explain deductively).[14] Why does Hempel have such a difficult time finding a role for inductive reasoning in explanation? Because, above all, Hempel wants explanations to be reliably true, and induction is not reliable. He wants the form of explanation to be impeccable, valid and sound. But, as philosophers including Thomas Kuhn have pointed out: deduction is also, sometimes, not reliable.

This chapter argues that Stein participates in this intellectual history. While Stein's interest in explanation chimes with the intellectual history of the first half of the twentieth century, her claim that explanation can work inductively sharply diverges from Hempel's account. It is more extreme than Hesse's argument that analogical reasoning can be explanatory: Stein insists that description can explain. As Wesley Salmon writes several decades after the advent of Hempel's D-N model, "The current attitude leaves us with a deep and perplexing question, namely, if explanation does something over and above mere description, just what sort of thing is it? ... What, over and above descriptive knowledge of the world, is required in order to achieve understanding? This seems to me to pose a serious philosophical problem."[15] This is the problem Stein takes on.

Stein agrees with such philosophers as David Hume that inductive reasoning is unreliable. But returning to the quote from *Q.E.D.*—"there are many facts and it isn't easy to know just what they tell"—we can see that Stein understands this contingency differently than philosophers do. Stein describes the unreliability resulting from inductive reasoning as a kind of difficulty. This difficulty is twofold. First: inductive reasoning is harder than deduction; it's easier to apply an existing law or theory than build one's own way to understanding from the ground up. Second: it is also more reliable to apply an existing law or theory. The contingency that results from reasoning inductively—never being sure if what you've known in the past will help you understand what lies ahead in the future—is hard to live in. (Both kinds of difficulty are evoked in Adele's lament, as she doesn't understand Helen's behavior and is far, in every way, from stable ground.)

I'm focusing on this term, *difficulty*, because philosophers describe the problem of induction as impossibly insolvable. But there's real and important space to be found between *impossibility* and *difficulty*. Eschewing deduction isn't comfortable. Depending on one's own experiences and sense-making abilities isn't secure. But, Stein says, it may be done and should be done. Stein sees induction's contingency as inescapable, but she sees it as both a necessity and a virtue.

STEIN'S PHILOSOPHICAL CONTEXT

In *Q.E.D.*, Adele, the stand-in for Stein, spends the novel trying to figure out *why* things are as they are; she is seeking explanations. At the beginning, she is setting off to Europe, only slightly acquainted with two other women on the steamer, Helen and Mabel. Her first exchange with Helen, her future lover, ends: "Helen explained" that Adele's resistance to passion is "what makes it possible for a face as thoughtful and strongly built as yours to be almost annoyingly unlived and youthful and to be almost foolishly happy and content." Adele rises to her challenge about knowledge, daring her to explain: "I could undertake to be an efficient pupil if it were possible to find an efficient teacher."[16] Helen does teach Adele—they return repeatedly to the teacher-student joke—but although Adele has brief moments of insight, she never feels that she understands Helen. One evening as their transatlantic voyage is ending, Adele phrases her confusion in terms of having or not having an explanation. "Finally she began to explain to herself. 'No I don't understand it at all,' she said." This is the moment that Helen criticizes how Adele "explain[s] to herself," saying, "Won't you ever learn that it is facts that tell."[17]

Q.E.D. was written just after Stein left Radcliffe, and in *The Autobiography of Alice B. Toklas*, Stein writes, "the most important person in Gertrude Stein's Radcliffe life was William James."[18] Excellent critical work has been done on Stein's relationship with Jamesian pragmatism.[19] Adele, with her resistance to ideology, could be cast as a pragmatist, someone who, in the words of Louis Menand, held the "belief that ideas should never become ideologies."[20] Can James help us understand what it means to explain based on facts alone? It seems not; in *Pragmatism*, he rejects that idea that names for facts are then treated as explanatory:

> At a surgical operation I once heard a bystander ask a doctor why the patient breathed so deeply. "Because ether is a respiratory stimulant," the doctor answered. "Ah!" said the questioner, as if that were a good explanation. But this is like saying that cyanide of potassium kills because it is a "poison," or that it is so cold tonight because it is "winter," or that we have five fingers because we are "pentadactyls." These are but names for the facts, taken from the facts, and then treated as previous and explanatory.[21]

Possibly more useful would be to identify Adele as a radical empiricist, following the ideas laid out in James's posthumous book, *Essays in Radical Empiricism*. In trying to understand her relationship with Helen, Adele must, as James advocates, "lay explanatory stress upon the part, the element, the individual, and treat the whole as a collection and the universal as an abstraction," while depending entirely on what she has "directly experienced" rather than what has been reported to her.[22] Stein's radical empiricism is one of the primary subjects of Steven Meyer's book, *Irresistible Dictation*, which discusses "the correlations of writing and science" in Stein's work. Meyer argues that Stein, following James, practices "poetic science"[23] which rejects the "dominant vision of science, science understood as devoted exclusively to what James, in *The Principles of Psychology*, called 'knowledge-about' or descriptive knowledge."[24] Meyer describes Stein as a scientist—as indeed Stein often describes herself—but as Robert Chodat notes in discussing Meyer's account of Stein's work, "a lot rides on what we mean by 'science.'"[25] Chodat argues that literary texts "are hard to describe in scientific terms because they are both the product of an intentional action and essentially concerned with intentional action," and he points out that Meyer's " 'poetic science' is presented as a purely descriptive endeavor"—it makes use of "poetic description in order to extend the domain of science"—and so is unable to predict.[26] Science, Chodat reminds us, requires causal laws, not descriptions, to support prediction.[27] The only predictions that Stein's texts could offer, according to Chodat, are predictions about people; they may offer reasons but not causes. "Both reasons and causes are offered to explain the behavior of an entity, but unlike causal explanation, justification by reasons involves attributing the mental states of our folk psychology: beliefs, desires, wishes, hopes, hatreds, and so on. Both reasons and causes can be invoked when someone asks 'Why?' But a good account of, say, why a stalactite forms, or, to take a different example, why a sugar cube dissolves in water requires no reference to what the calcium carbonate deposit 'wants' or what the cube 'thinks.'"[28] Hence, "Reason-giving accounts resemble cause-giving accounts to the extent that they explain what Picasso did and anticipate what he will do next. But unlike scientific accounts, [they predict] 'roughly.'"[29] Ultimately, Chodat persuasively argues, "poetic science" is not science.[30] While I agree with Chodat's critique of Meyer, and agree that Stein is not best understood as a scientist, and agree that "poetic science" is not a coherent concept, there is still space here. I can grant—entirely grant—that Stein's poetry does not depend on causal laws, and still claim that it is interested in explanation. *That is, in fact, my argument: that Stein was interested in the extent to which facts can tell without laws.* Hempel argued that explanation consists of a causal law that is referred to deductively, but this theory of explanation has never completely resolved the possibility of inductive explanation. Stein can write about inductive explanation, that facts tell, without deductive reference to causal laws.

There is no question that Stein was, in her words about Adele's relationship to Helen, "an efficient pupil" of James. But when we look to James to understand Stein's work, we risk forgetting what it is to be a pupil. Adele shows us: she learns and accepts the argument of her teacher, Helen, that facts tell; then she develops an argument of her own, that it is difficult to know just what they tell. So, too, we can imagine that Stein learned James's arguments about how our individual empirical experiences allow us to make sense of the world, and we can imagine that she developed arguments of her own. Stein learned from James's thinking without being subsumed by it, developed her own ideas, and ultimately did philosophic work. One final reason why James cannot provide the only philosophic context to read Stein: James's philosophy consistently offers comfort and greater ease in the world, while Stein's literature generally offers discomfort and difficulty. Stein's difficulty is important, I argue (at greater length later), because she is demonstrating how difficult it is to explain, particularly without reference to theories or laws. James never describes explanation—or any part of his *"Weltanschauung"*—as particularly difficult to understand or undertake. James writes for the nonexpert (though well-educated) layman because expertise is not necessary, or even particularly helpful, for one to understand his thinking about how we make sense of our empirical experience. Stein may agree expertise is not helpful for someone seeking to discover explanations or even to define what we mean by "explanation," but *not* because it is easy to do so. Rather, explanation is a subject that is difficult enough that no expertise is particularly helpful.

The difficulty of the subject of explanation, though, illuminates Stein's oeuvre. Her work has often been sorted into two piles, her public writing and her experimental writing. Her public writing could be described under the title "facts tell," and we can see her charming, easy-to-understand work, such as *The Autobiography of Alice B. Toklas*, as straightforward presentations of facts. But the experimental writing, such as *Stanzas in Meditation*, can *also* be described as a presentation of facts. Seeing Stein as concerned with explanation based on inductive reasoning reduces the divide between her experimental and popular work. *The Autobiography of Alice B. Toklas* and *Stanzas in Meditation* were written in tandem, but readers of the former very rarely attempt the latter. And seeing Stein as a philosopher interested in inductive explanation provides a tool for close reading her oeuvre and talking about the way in which Stein makes sense. We do so by understanding how Stein thinks about sense-making—how she models reasoning.

THEREFORE CLEAR EXPLANATIONS ARE NOT CLEAR: STEIN'S PRINCIPLES OF EXPLANATION

Stein's interest in explanation can be seen as early as *Q.E.D.*, but it surfaces throughout her work, early and late, poetry and prose. An explanation is an answer to a why-question, and "Why" is one of Stein's favorite words, appearing in nearly every single one of her texts. Focusing just on her use of the word "explanation" and "explain," I find there are still far too many instances to list here, much less to discuss. To identify just a few: In *Tender Buttons* she writes, in "Rooms," "Explaining darkening and expecting relating is all of a piece."[31] In "Lifting Belly," her speaker returns repeatedly to the question of whether she has explained: "Did I explain it./Have I explained it to you./Have I explained it to you in season. Have I perplexed you. You have not perplexed me nor mixed me. You have addressed me as Caesar. This was the answer that I expected."[32] In "What Is English Literature," she offers an origin story of explanation in nineteenth-century England:

> And in order to understand, it must be understood that explaining was invented, naturally invented by those living a daily island life and owning everything else ... so there was invented explaining and that made the nineteenth century English literature what it is. And with explaining went sentimental feeling because it was of course it had to be explained all the owning had to be told about is being owned about its owning and anybody can see that if daily island life was to continue its daily existing there must be emotional sentimental feeling.[33]

In *Everybody's Autobiography*, she offers another theorization of explanation:

> I told him everything and he said that I talked so clearly why did I not write clearly. I do write clearly. That is not the answer that is a fact. I think I write so clearly that I worry about it. Not really, but a fact. However I began to explain to him then and at intervals all that winter I explained to him and then at last I wrote him letters about it explaining to him how explanations are clear but since no one to whom a thing is explained can connect the

explanations with what is really clear, therefore clear explanations are not clear.[34]

These examples show the consistency with which Stein is concerned with explanation throughout her oeuvre and they show Stein's understanding of explanation. We can see three preliminary principles.

First, Stein's explaining works inductively. Adele, in *Q.E.D.*, eschews laws and theories and agrees with Helen that facts tell, though she adds that it is difficult to know just what they tell. Adele is committed to facts and so is Stein. In these examples, when Stein mentions explanation, facts are invoked; laws and theories are not. We can look at the longer quotation from "Rooms," quoted more briefly above, and see that even when Stein seems to be generalizing, she is only pretending to refer to laws or theories, even parodying such references. "Explaining darkening and expecting relating is all of a piece. The stove is bigger. It was a shape that made no audience bigger if the opening is assumed why should there not be kneeling. Any force which is bestowed on a floor shows rubbing. This is so nice and sweet and yet there comes the change, there comes the time to press more air. This does not mean the same as disappearance."[35] "Any force which is bestowed on a floor shows rubbing" sounds like a law, but it is not, it is an imitation of a law that tells us only that the fact that this particular floor has marks on it where people have rubbed against it as they kindled the fire. It is a fact, and could only count as a generalization inductively, based on the speaker's experience with this floor—other floors where people have rubbed must also have marks showing—but calling the cause "force" is only renaming the blank space. It is akin to stating, as James writes, "it is so cold tonight because it is 'winter,' or that we have five fingers because we are 'pentadactyls.'"

Stein's second principle of explanation is that she understands what an explanation could provide: an explanation allows what she calls "expectation" but what we might call prediction. That is, even explanations based on inductive reasoning refer, obliquely, to the existence of causal laws. Hence, what Stein writes in *Tender Buttons*: "explaining ... and ... expecting ... is all of a piece." Because the explainer is able to predict, to expect, she has security, even power. We can see how providing an explanation secures a relationship in the erotic domestic scene in the poem "Lifting Belly." The speaker knows that, if the explanation succeeds, she will be addressed "as Caesar. This was the answer that I expected." Explanation allows prediction, including the prediction of power. If "Lifting Belly" shows the intimate version of explaining giving power over another, "What Is English Literature," is the political version, and shows how that power can be oppressive rather than erotic. In this lecture, Stein claims, "explaining was invented, naturally invented by those living a daily island life and owning everything else outside." The power of explanation, the expectations it supports and the way that such power of prediction gives one power meant that citizens of the imperial British Empire also "expected" to be "addressed... as Caesar." Explanation here is the reasoning behind oppression: "of course it had to be explained all the owning had to be told about."

The third principle about explanation that can be seen in these varied texts by Stein is that explanations rarely if ever work to convince anyone besides oneself. Stein's concerns about the listener's comprehension of an explanation in "Lifting Belly"—"Did I explain it./Have I explained it to you./Have I explained it to you in season"—are echoed throughout her oeuvre: her anxiety in "Lifting Belly": "I explain too much";[36] her insistence in *Geographical History of America*, "I wish to make this absolutely clear";[37] her repeated question in *Blood on the Dining-Room Floor*, "Lizzie do you understand."[38] In *Everybody's Autobiography*, she writes about her attempt to explain her work to Jo Alsop and admits that she is unable to explain it so that he can understand. It is worth noting here that we readers also generally *do not understand* Stein's explanations. As Stein writes in *The Making of Americans*, "I am full up now with knowing that mostly those to whom I am explaining are not completely hearing."[39]

STEIN'S DIFFICULTY

Many literary critical books on Stein's work have a section or chapter titled something like: "How to Read Gertrude Stein."[40] This is noteworthy; books on T. S. Eliot do not have similar chapters, nor do books on other American modernists such as William Carlos Williams, Marianne Moore, or even Ezra Pound. Many of Stein's critics offer contexts and methods to read her work, and her best critics do so brilliantly. Ulla Dydo looks to Stein's drafts in her *cahiers* and *carnets* in order to place her work in a biographical context. Marjorie Perloff argues that we should "see how carefully Gertrude

Stein has structured" her work, how "indeterminacy is created by repetition and variation, sameness and difference, a rhetorical pattern of great intricacy."[41] Perloff later offers the work of Ludwig Wittgenstein as another context for Stein's experimentation with semantics finding or losing meaning in use.[42] Lisi Schoenbach and Liesl Olson show us how to read Stein in the intellectual company of James; their excellent work is built upon that of Lisa Ruddick, who argues that Stein works through her psychological drama relative to James in her early work, and of Wendy Steiner, who argues that Stein develops a "theoretical framework" in response to James in her portraits.[43] Marianne DeKoven puts Stein in the context of Julia Kristeva's *écriture féminine* to make "her hitherto largely inaccessible and unread work accessible and readable."[44] Catharine R. Stimpson and Richard Poirier translate Stein's sexual codes; Stimpson writes, "Stein's coding of sexual activities ceases to be a suspect evasion and becomes, instead, a privileged, and a distinguished, 'anti-language';"[45] Poirier writes, "she can dissociate a word from its acquired significances, which is sometimes all she is credited with wanting to do, but she can then, at her convenience, revive and deploy that word with all of its conventional associations."[46] Poirier quotes Stimpson: Stein is "one of modernism's hardest writers."[47] Perloff, writing more recently about "the myth of Stein's 'unreadability,'" states, "It is easy to dismiss such commentary as no more than Philistine—the response to Stein of those who don't know any better." But, she continues, "Stein's admirers have often taken the same tack, except they turn 'unreadability' into a virtue."[48] Natalia Cecire argues that "Stein's unreadability discloses that the relationship between scale and style—between quantity and quality—is always a negotiation of value," and specifically the value of gendered labor; this, however, does not mean that Stein's work is less unreadable.[49]

There *is* something curious going on in Stein criticism. In these books, including Perloff's, that help us read Stein, there is simultaneously an acknowledgment of Stein's difficulty—critics don't feel the need to say how to read other writers who have been canonical for generations—and a denial that Stein's difficulty is all that difficult. Can we be more specific about what's so difficult about reading Stein? Why are we offered so many strategies? Why are all of the strategies helpful, but yet none of them seem to have taken the difficulty away? (As a contrasting case, think of *The Waste Land*. It has become increasingly less difficult as more criticism has been published on it, and is now regularly taught to college freshman.) At the end of the previous section, I wrote that Stein's readers, like Alsop, generally do not understand Stein's explanations; this is, of course, just a smaller version of the larger problem of Stein's difficulty, but it focuses, as Perloff does, on whether we can understand the referents of Stein's words rather than think of them as things.

The common critical account of why we do not understand Stein's explanations is that she is making sense but writing in coded language. If her explanations are inductive rather than deductive and deal only with her personal experience, then they are subjective and maybe even private. This reading assigns the difficulty of understanding Stein's explanations to her style. Deborah Mix writes that Stein offers "a variety of vocabularies."[50] This multiplicity of vocabularies is how many critics of Stein describe her difficulty. In this reading, her words will translate into meaning, though that meaning may be multiple. Ulla Dydo, Richard Poirer, and Catharine R. Stimpson all work to provide us with translations of Steinianisms; a "cow" is an orgasm,[51] for example, or a "cutlet" the vagina.[52]

Our sense that Stein's work is difficult because of its unavailable style is a complaint about subjectivity, but this account of Stein's subjectivity is framed incorrectly. If the problem is that her language has secret meanings— for example, that "may," even the month of May, was changed to "can" in *Stanzas in Meditation*, or a "cow" means an orgasm—then knowing these secret meanings would render Stein's texts available and therefore easier to read. But even when we know the secret meanings—when Dydo's research reveals the edits that turned "may" to "can"—Stein's work becomes more interesting, but not less difficult.

The other account of Stein's difficulty is that her language—not her words, but her grammar—is nonsensical, not multiple in meaning but risking being without meaning. These two accounts are sometimes collapsed, as, in both, Stein is performing, in Poirier's words, an "act of linguistic protest against traditional and agreed-upon systems of designation and against the structures of relative primacy and subordination that have been made to seem necessary, normal, and inevitable."[53] Those systems of designation and structures are often described as patriarchal. But in the first account, that act of linguistic protest could lead to feminist, even ecstatic language, while in this second account, the linguistic protest risks meaninglessness. Perloff flirts with a reading close to this in *Wittgenstein's Ladder* when she argues that Stein's work might appear to be nonsensical, such as the single-line sentence from *Tender Buttons*, "Roast potatoes for." While this line might appear to be, in Wittgenstein's words, "excluded from the language, withdrawn from circulation," Perloff argues that actually Stein is " 'draw[ing] a boundary,' not out of a refusal to 'make sense' or a predilection for pure nonsense, but because she wants to draw out specific semantic implications not normally present."[54] But while Wittgenstein argues that nonsense is "withdrawn from circulation," Perloff works very hard to drag Stein's language back into circulation; as a result, she ends up having to argue both that Stein's language is nonsense, that it is excluded from our language game like Wittgenstein's examples of nonsense, and that it is not, because of the literary critical work she can do to reveal its meaning.

But here I want to ask: *which* language game? Chodat argues, correctly, that it is nonsensical to misattribute agency and count reasons as causes for natural objects, such as saying that stalactite forms because of what "the calcium carbonate deposit 'wants.' "[55] But this is only a problem at all for deductive explanation. Stein is not playing by the rules of the language game of deduction; she's not appealing to laws and theories, and we already knew that. If one tries to explain inductively, then a stalactite forms because all previous ones have formed in just the same way—desires are just as irrelevant as laws. Recognizing that Stein is seeking to explain inductively does not erase the difficulty of her work, but it reframes that difficulty. "Roast potatoes for" is a statement of a fact—there are roast potatoes for someone or something. Who or what are they for? We can't know. Why are there roast potatoes? That's a request for an explanation, but there is no law or theory that would explain this fact. Perloff refers to the democratic simplicity of roast potatoes, but Chodat points out that such an association is arbitrary: "Why should the acoustics of 'Roast potatoes for' evoke *the simplicity of roast potatoes, which is everybody's food* rather than anything else— say, *the unhealthiness of a starch-heavy diet* or even *the Spanish control over Cuba in the seventeenth century*?"[56] All we can do is try to understand this fact, that there are roast potatoes presumably for a theoretical reason or lawlike cause—Picasso requested them, or potatoes are the only vegetable available in the wintertime—but without having that reason or cause, having only other facts. This is difficult—this is the difficulty of Stein—but it is not a difficulty that can be solved: it is the difficulty that results from the problem of induction.

Both accounts of Stein's difficulty come near to naming this difficulty as the problem of induction, but do not get it into focus. Stein's work is difficult for the same reason that explaining inductively is difficult—in Adele's words, it is difficult to know what the facts tell. Trying to explain using only inductive reasoning is more difficult than referring to a theory or law in order to explain. Stein is demonstrating explanation, theorizing explanation, and not simply explaining. The reason that this sort of explanation is difficult is that it is necessarily difficult—seemingly impossible—to overcome one's own subjectivity. How can Adele, or anyone, use her empirical experience to come to any objective conclusions?[57] The difficulty of knowing what the facts tell is the difficulty of induction. Stein's difficulty is more accurately described as the inherent difficulty of inductive reasoning. If one is not referring to a theory or law in order to understand why something has happened, if one is reasoning inductively from the facts, from the facts that only one person has subjectively experienced, then it is difficult to know what they tell because it is difficult ever to know if one has all, or enough, of the facts. Recognizing that Stein's difficulty is a philosophical difficulty allows us to recognize that understanding Stein's explanations is not a goal of reading her work; rather, our goal may be understanding her theorization of explanation.

THE PROBLEM OF HALVE

"An Elucidation" serves as a case study; it is a mature, experimental work that can be described as poetry. "An Elucidation" was written in 1923 and published in the first *transition* in 1927. In the first issue of *transition*, its pages were printed out of order, but receiving a corrected version did nothing to alleviate the confusion of its readers, who hadn't noticed it was out of order initially.[58] "An Elucidation" was brought to contemporary attention by Dydo, who included it in 1993's *A Stein Reader*. She introduces it by saying, "The title *An Elucidation* sounds philosophical and theoretical. We expect a credo, a statement of method, perhaps the key to meaning. Yet Stein refuses to explain writing and to distinguish theory and practice."[59] In Dydo's later *Gertrude Stein: The Language That Rises*, she writes again about her moments of confusion. "Here is a piece, 'An Elucidation,' which I read in the face of her refusal to explain and my trouble in comprehending."[60] Relying on Stein's biography and the *carnets* and *cahiers* in which she composed her drafts, Dydo finds French-English puns, as well as Toklas-Stein ones, and compares it to a classroom—"Instruction in Stein's school"—and also to the "moving waterways of the Rhone delta" as "the sections pull apart."[61]

As far as I'm aware, no other critic besides Dydo discusses "An Elucidation" at any length, although there are comments here and there about its "clearly perverse" title.[62] (Dydo, more charitably, calls it an "antititle.")[63] One thing that everyone agrees upon is that "An Elucidation" does not elucidate. I will suggest that it does, although not in the way we may have expected, and not with the goal of ending its readers' confusion. Rather, it elucidates why we readers are confused: as Stein wrote at the beginning of her career, it is difficult to know what the facts tell. The difficulty presented by "An Elucidation" will always be difficult, but that does not mean that we cannot see it clearly. We know so far that, in Stein's texts, we see a commitment to inductive explanation and the awareness that being able to explain gives one power over others. But we also see that explanation based on inductive reasoning, explanation that does not refer to objective laws or theories, is difficult for anyone else to understand. This is not due to cryptic style or vocabulary, but to the problem of inductive reasoning: how do you know if experience has provided enough information to support accurate explaining? "An Elucidation" sheds light exactly here.

"An Elucidation" begins:

Elucidation.
First as Explanation.
Elucidate the problem of halve.[64]

Explanation is an obvious subject of "An Elucidation," obvious even to the novice reader; the speaker uses varieties of the word "explanation" twenty-six times in a thirteen-page text and is constantly claiming to explain. Examples selected from only the first few pages include: "I have an explanation of this in this way"; "There is an excellent example and now I will explain away as if I have been sitting for my portrait every day./In this way I have made every one understand arithmetic"; "I will now explain dishes./I have explained that"; "To explain means to give a reason for in order. He adores her"; "I can explain visiting. I can explain how it happened accidentally that fortunately no explanation was necessary"; "I explain wording and painting and sealing and closing. I explain opening and reasoning and rolling, I was just rolling"; "Do you all understand why I explain"; "Did I say explanations mean across and across and carry. Carry me across."[65]

The speaker never makes "every one understand arithmetic." She never explains dishes. One can certainly think of a Stein-like speaker who could "explain visiting" or "explain wording and painting," but this speaker does not, she "was just rolling." Dydo writes that these lines "announce explanations but omit connectives and transitions."[66] That is, they present facts but not theories or laws. We see here a commitment to inductive reasoning, to telling facts. As in *Tender Buttons*, even when it seems like Stein is promising a deductive explanation—"a reason for in order"—she reneges, offering a fact instead—"He adores her." Dydo writes, it "sounds as if Stein was elucidating by examples, an easy principle to understand, but examples of what?"[67] "An Elucidation" elucidates, but it elucidates about explanation. In "An Elucidation," the speaker repeatedly claims to have explanations; Dydo asks what examples Stein is offering. I suggest that Stein is elucidating by examples of having explanations. Stein is not explaining. Rather, she is showing us something about explanation: an explanation is something one *has*. The speaker of "An Elucidation" has explanations, and having explanations gives the explainer power.

Dydo refers to "An Elucidation" as "Stein's school," writing "Elucidation belongs in the school room, between a teacher who proposes paradigms and models, asks questions, anticipates difficulties, and pupils who demonstrate understanding.... Instruction in Stein's school includes fun and games, hide-and-seek, peekaboo, 'Search for me,' 'Again search for me' ... This is the language that teaches."[68] We can remember that *Q.E.D.* repeatedly compared the relationship between Adele and her lover Helen to a student and teacher. Even in this early demand for further explanation—at the beginning of this novel at the beginning of Stein's career—we see that explanation is tied up with power. Helen has power over Adele as her teacher, as the person who has the explanations, as the person who (like in peekaboo) can see her without being seen in return. So too in "Stein's school," the speaker is a teacher who claims to have explanations, but who does not give us examples of the explanations she has, only examples of her having them.

And now we can see this principle in its negative form as well. Helen explains Adele and so has power over her, but Adele is never able to explain

Helen and never fully has her. Returning, then, to the beginning of "An Elucidation"—"Elucidation./First as Explanation./ Elucidate the problem of halve." "The problem of halve" is the problem of having, but having only half. My final point about Stein's conception of explanation is that she is aware that her explanations based on inductive reasoning are difficult for anyone else to understand. I argue that their difficulty is not due simply to their style or coded vocabulary—a superficial idea of subjectivity—but to the inherent, inextricable subjectivity of inductive reasoning. If one is reasoning inductively, trying to explain based on one's own experience rather than through reference to theories or laws, than one can never tell if one ever has enough facts. If any additional fact could change one's mind, then any explanation is only half-had. This is what happens to Adele who, without "a theory," must repeatedly revise her understanding of Helen with the addition of each new fact about her.

This is the problem of reading "An Elucidation"—"the problem of halve" that it promises to "elucidate" for us, and does—we do not know what makes this text complete. It could be rearranged. Our teacher, this speaker, may perhaps be withholding some of it from us. Dydo, one of Stein's very best readers, when she reads "An Elucidation," finds that she can only half-have it. This is the "problem of halve": facts tell, but it is difficult to know just what they tell, especially if one can never know if one has all the facts. "An Elucidation" shows us that every explanation based on inductive reasoning must be as contingent as human relationships, as contingent as Adele and Helen's, or any efficient teacher and efficient pupil, or a speaker and a reader of literature.

"THE THING SEEN BY EVERY ONE"

Explanations that are half-had may seem not to be predictive, or perhaps they seem to be predictive but are not. That is, a half-had explanation teeters on the edge of being able to predict. It is like the weather report—accurate until the winds shift, when everything must be adjusted for another prediction. The philosopher Donald Davidson writes in his 1963 essay "Actions, Reasons, and Causes," written in response to Hempel, that people's reasons for their actions count as those actions' causes. He writes, "We may call such explanations *rationalizations*. . . . In this paper I want to defend the ancient—and common-sense—position that rationalization is a species of causal explanation."[69] Davidson, that is, argues that reasons allow causal explanation for people's actions without reference to laws. Chodat, who cites this essay, points out that reasons do not count as causes to explain events and phenomena in the physical sciences (we do not ask what stalactites want). But what about the social sciences? Do groups of people operate more like individual people, with reasons supporting causal explanation? Or do groups of people operate more like events or phenomena in the physical sciences, like stalactites, and have explanations supported by causes?

Stein addresses this question in her 1926 lecture "Composition as Explanation." "Composition as Explanation," unlike "An Elucidation," is not obviously about explanation, despite its title. Aside from the title, Stein uses any variety of the word "explanation" only once, and it is when she performs starting over, making another attempt: "Beginning again and again and again explaining composition and time is a natural thing."[70] On the other hand, Stein uses the word "composition" repeatedly, using it to mean both the writer's product and also, and more importantly, the composition of the society of which the writer is part and which the writer influences. Stein writes, "composition is the thing seen by every one living in the living they are doing, they are the composing of the composition that at the time they are living is the composition of the time in which they are living."[71] The composition, "what is seen," is "the only thing that is different from one time to another."[72] And, further, "What is seen depends upon how everybody is doing everything. This makes the thing we are looking at very different and this makes what those who describe it make of it, it makes a composition, it confuses, it shows, it is, it looks, it likes as it is, and this makes what is seen as it is seen."[73] To paraphrase: the composition of the society is the crucial position from which the artist sees the world and so writes an artistic composition, which then influences the composition of society. Compositions of society change over time, influenced by artists, and so the art they make changes over time also.

Literary critics, following Stein's emphasis on the word "composition," write at length about what Stein means by "composition," but not what she means by explanation. Wendy Steiner, for example, writes, "'Composition' became both the vision of the time and its expression in writing.... The writer for Stein was one who was aware of the 'composition' of his time and thus could translate it into a written composition."[74] When critics mention explanation at all it is generally to stress its irrelevance in the lecture. Bruce

Bassoff writes, "The title of her essay" shows "causal explanation having been displaced by the reworking or permuting of elements common to a given situation."[75] Michael J. Hoffman and Bob Perelman both suggest that the essay offers explanations of sorts, as if the title of the lecture was "Composition as *an* Explanation." Hoffman writes, "This collective consciousness [of a culture] is what Stein means when she uses the term 'composition.' To understand its composition is to be able to explain a culture, and the artist's function is to express the composition of his time."[76] Perelman argues that the essay is an explanation about the "historical efficacy of art," since artists influence the composition of their cultures with their artistic compositions.[77] In order to see how "Composition as Explanation" is about explanation, first we have to understand what Stein means by explanation: how explanation is inductive, predictive, powerful, but very often difficult to understand because of the inherent contingency due to its subjectivity. And only then can we see how this lecture attempts to solve the problem of the contingency of inductive explanation.

My argument about explanation—how explaining through inductive reasoning means one can never know if one has all the facts—is not far from Jennifer Ashton's discussion of Stein's "problematic of 'wholeness.'"[78] As I've described the "problem of halve," it is the realization that, if one is trying to explain based on inductive reasoning, it is difficult to know if one has enough information. Ashton shows how Stein engages with the question of "what counts as a whole—whether it be a nation or a text (or a map or a masterpiece)" throughout her career, and finds that this problematic "entails both the ontological question of what makes it whole and the epistemological question of how we know it to be whole."[79] After the mid-1930s, Ashton reads a shift in Stein's representation of whole knowledge in which she becomes dissatisfied with inductive reasoning. Stein "dispenses with experience itself as the defining feature of knowledge" and "turns from a phenomenological model of wholes to a logical one, where the whole, instead of being attained through the cumulative experience of its parts, exists in an abstract form prior to and independent of any experience of its parts."[80] Ashton sees "Composition as Explanation," with its descriptions of "beginning again and again" and "present immediacy" and the famous "continuous present" as part of Stein's new theory of how artistic masterpieces are not accretive in nature, they do not begin and end, but rather, like knowledge, are whole before and apart from experience.[81]

Unlike Ashton, I do not see Stein abandoning inductive reasoning. In fact, Stein raises her bet. In "Composition as Explanation," we can see another model of how experience can lead to knowledge, and an attempt to deal with the "serious philosophical problem" of how much and what kind of information is necessary for a description to count as an explanation. Nine years after "An Elucidation," in "Composition as Explanation," Stein writes large the problem of explaining based on inductive reasoning and, by scaling it up, tries to resolve it. "An Elucidation" suggests that explanations based on inductive reasoning, based on the conviction that facts tell (even if it is difficult to know what they tell), are contingent. We never know if we have all of the facts, we can never know if we are too subjective, and so every explanation must be contingent, just as human relationships are. The "composition" in "Composition As Explanation" widens the scope of human relationships to include the entire society. The society's way of seeing constitutes what is seen. Earlier I wrote that if one tries to explain based on inductive reasoning, then one cannot tell if one ever has enough facts, and an explanation based on one's empirical experience can be dismissed as subjective. But the entire society's view, composed together, cannot be dismissed as simply subjective, although it is still inductive. Stein makes it clear that she does think of the composition, the culture's sense of itself, operating inductively because it is changed by each bit of new data, a new artist who influences how it sees, understands, explains. This model of whole knowledge (to use Ashton's term) is not based on accretive experience the way that it is in, say, *The Making of Americans*. Or rather, it is not based on one person's experience through many points in time, but many people's experience in one moment in time. Adele found it difficult to know what the facts tell because she didn't know if she ever had enough facts. In "Composition as Explanation," we are told that an entire society's experience is enough to vouchsafe explanation, to know what the facts tell, and without laws or theories, because there is no alternative. Adele says, "One must either accept some theory or else believe one's instinct or else follow the world's opinion. Now I have no theory and as much as I would like to, I can't really regard the world's opinion." This is an early clue that the world's opinion—composition—can stand in the place of a theory in order to support explanation. And though Adele rejects the world's opinion, in "Composition as Explanation," Stein suggests that Adele can't help but be part of the composition of her society: "No one is ahead of his time . . .

if they do not enter it they are not so to speak in it they are out of it and so they do enter it."[82] By refusing to refer to the world's opinion, she is still reasoning inductively, and, as a member of society, she is also part of shaping the world's opinion, her society's composition.

At the beginning of this section, I wrote that explanations that are inductive and therefore contingent are unreliably predictive. I compared them to weather reports, able to predict until very suddenly that prediction is wrong, and a new one is offered. This is exactly how Stein writes about art in this lecture, famously saying, "The creator of the new composition in the arts is an outlaw until he is a classic, there is hardly a moment in between.... For a very long time everybody refuses and then almost without a pause almost everybody accepts. In the history of the refused in the arts and literature the rapidity of the change is always startling."[83] This is also how Thomas Kuhn writes about scientific explanations in his famous book, *The Structure of Scientific Revolutions*. Every time there is a new discovery, the scientific community "altered its conception of entities with which it has long been familiar, and, in the process, shifted the network of theory through which it deals with the world."[84] This happens frequently, as oxygen is discovered, as DNA is discovered, as Matisse is accepted, as Warhol is. What the comparison to Kuhn suggests is *why* Stein commits to inductive reasoning as a basis for explanation: as contingent as inductive reasoning is, deductive laws and theories are contingent in their own way, as they very well may change with the addition of new information.

We will best be able to explain our world when we remember that facts tell, and we gather as many of them as we can with as wide a scope as possible. This is the inductive process at work, but its contingency no longer seems catastrophic. We have no alternative to being in our own time, even if we are aware that our laws and theories will very likely be revealed as temporary stops along a longer road of reasoning. We are only able to make sense of our world contingently; we learn from "Composition as Explanation" that trying to reason about it together makes it feel less contingent.

"A STANZA SHOULD BE THOUGHT"

There's no alternative to inductive reasoning, says Stein, and there are ways to mitigate its difficulty, to make its contingency feel less catastrophic—but that doesn't mean it's easy or free of trade-offs or costs. Contingency is still difficult affectively; it's bewildering and disempowering. It's also difficult epistemologically; it's puzzling and perplexing. This concern runs through her work: in "An Elucidation," Stein leans into the difficulty, experientially and intellectually, of explaining using only facts, and in "Composition As Explanation," she asserts that while it isn't easy to know just what the facts tell, this difficulty isn't catastrophic.

Similarly, in the second stanza of *Stanzas in Meditation*, Stein writes, "It is not only not an easy explanation."[85] A paraphrase of this line wobbles; the two negatives don't quite cancel each other out. If the line read "it is not not an easy explanation," Stein would be asserting that the explanation, in fact, *is* easy. But because the "only" modifies it, the line suggests that an explanation is difficult and also something more besides. Is that excess *beyond* difficult: even more difficult? Or is it described as *other* than difficult: obvious, comfortable, basic, uncomplicated? This statement—that explanation can be both extremely hard in some ways and also, from another angle, simple—dovetails with the rest of my argument in this chapter. Earlier I wrote about how the contingency resulting from inductive reasoning is difficult in two ways; it's epistemologically difficult to build new theories from scratch, and it's affectively difficult to never feel sure or secure. But I also argued that Stein insists that there is no alternative to inductive reasoning, even though this kind of explanation will never be objective nor sound. And there are upsides: inductive explanation, telling the facts, grows out of lived experience. This may be less epistemologically valid, or may not, but also may in the end offer more affective satisfactions. One may not be able to justify inductive reasoning except by more induction, but as Stein shows us, if induction counts at all, more induction might count more by including more people.

In this section, though, I'll do something beyond reading this line from *Stanzas in Meditation* as a claim about explanation. Instead, I'll use it as a springboard to explore the significant likeness between explanation based on inductive reasoning and lyric poetry. I'll argue that Stein's poetry works in the same way as her account of explanation, because what characterizes explanation based on inductive reasoning is the connection between disparate particulars—and that is also what characterizes the modern lyric poem. Both leap between luminous details; both consider what's a fragment and what's a whole. In other words, it is not a coincidence that Stein, in building her poems, is also showing how we build our understanding of the world. That this connection is not accidental, that this resemblance is the family resemblance of overlapping similarities because it stands on a deep history of relation—that the structures of reasoning and lyric are shared—is the central argument of this book. The stakes of this claim vis-à-vis poetry are that it is useful for readers of poems, especially in the modern era, to understand reasoning as a constitutive aspect of the lyric.

Or, as Stein writes in Part Five's stanza XXIX, "A stanza should be thought."[86] A stanza should be thought, and so far in this book, I have described how inductive reasoning inescapably conjures the difficulty of contingency. *Stanzas in Meditation*, as it happens, is shaped by contingency at multiple levels. Its textual history is a story of chance: as Stein began writing *Stanzas* in 1932, the long-lost manuscript of *Q.E.D.* resurfaced, upsetting Toklas with its depiction of Stein's early affair with May Bookstaver. As a result, all of the instances of the word "may" in the text were changed, at Toklas's insistence, to "can." It was not until 2012's *Stanzas in Meditation: The Corrected Edition*, edited by Susannah Hollister and Emily Setina, that the original words were restored.[87] "May," unlike "can," is itself a word that describes contingency, when a possibility is not dependent on your own power. Like Stein's earlier connection of explanation and authority, the alterations of *Stanzas in Meditation* also tell of facts of power and permission.

But there's more: even the qualified double negative of "It is not only not an easy explanation" suggests that events may unfold differently, that conditions may be reversed. Indeed, conditions are reversed and then reversed again over the course of reading this line. And this line has just one of many double negatives in this poem, especially doublings of "not"; no wonder the introduction by Joan Retallack in Hollister and Setina's edition is titled "On Not Not Reading Stanzas in Meditation."[88] There are also frequent "not only" constructions throughout the text. The line I've quoted from the second stanza is not the first example of this correlative conjunction; in the very first stanza, we find the lines "In which case in effect they could/Not only be very present perfectly/In each whichever they chose" and "Or in an especial case they will fulfill/Not only what they have at their instigation."[89] And, pulling these together, there are dozens of other lines in this poem where Stein combines double negatives and the qualification of "only"; picking just a few: "In any absent way we will not only not be there";[90] "Cherries not only not better not ripe/It was a mistake not to make not only a mistake with this";[91] "They could be not only not allowed but not clouded";[92]

"For me to me in not only not be/Not only not be how do you like not only not be/They will be satisfied to be satisfactory."[93] Literary scholars have described this phrasing as managing information relative to the reader—Chad Bennett likens it to "paraliptic" gossip—but what if it's not hiding knowledge but showing how it's made, how language is being crafted to tack close to thinking as thinking itself shifts over time?[94]

So then, what does it mean for a stanza to be thought? Or, to begin with, what does thinking look like in *Stanzas in Meditation*? We can already say that it looks like qualifications and possible reversals, in both the repetitions of "may"—even before they were replaced with "can"—and of "not not" and "not only" and "not only not." In these constructions and phrases, we see Stein slicing concepts thinly, seeking accuracy in the gradations of grammar, almost in real time, in a kind of continuous present of thinking as she weighs and half-rejects words, weighs probability and authority, and sketches out further suggestions. And we also see her leaving wiggle room for how conditions might change, registering "what would have been possible otherwise," in Niklas Luhmann's definition of contingency.[95] But thinking in *Stanzas in Meditation* also looks like the connections across and between stanzas, and also beyond stanzas, especially in the poem's echoing repetitions. Repetitions characterize Stein's poetics; remember her most famous line, "Rose is a rose is a rose is a rose," which first appeared in 1913's "Sacred Emily" but itself was repeated in other writings, including in *Stanzas in Meditation*. Dydo describes repetitions among a list of Stein's "language of poetry" that she relies on in multiple genres, essentially writing poetry "whether in poetry, plays, portraits, or novels."[96]

In addition to pointing out repetitions, we can also say what they're for—what repeating words does. For example in *Stanzas in Meditation*, the echoes of "may," the double negatives "not not" and the qualifications of "only"—among a long list of repeated words and phrases—link different moments together. These details make sense, or make more sense, in reference to other similar instances.[97] And together, they fit fragments together to make the whole text provisionally count as a whole. Earlier in this chapter, when I analyzed "An Elucidation," I described what Stein calls "the problem of halve"—having, but only having half, a similar problem to what Ashton calls Stein's "problematic of wholeness."[98] I described the difficulty of any explanation based on induction as one of parts and wholes, including those that one lover gives another, like Adele and Helen, or that a lyric speaker gives a reader. This is a problem of explanation: how many facts are enough to comprise an explanation, to tell? But it's also a problem of lyric: how many lines or images do you need to make a poem? How many of them repeat; at what point can one outline a set; when can one hazard predictions about what belongs and what doesn't? What makes a poem cohere? What makes a poem count as whole? As a poem at all?

Patterns of language that tie together the poem as a whole: this feels like a very familiar way to read poetry a century after New Criticism. Caroline Levine's first chapter of *Forms*, "Whole," traces how "a work of art" came to be identified with its wholeness, "its unifying power, its capacity to hold together disparate parts," as far back as Aristotle but most powerfully in the legacy of Cleanth Brooks and the New Critics.[99] Virginia Jackson has argued that it's the post–New Critical reader who assembles the parts of a lyric poem into that well-wrought urn; she describes the tradition of lyric reading which emerges through what she calls the process of lyricization: "The lyric takes form through the development of reading practices in the nineteenth and twentieth centuries that become the practice of literary criticism."[100] Biographically and historically, Stein was adjacent to the intellectual milieu that gave rise to New Criticism; *Stanzas in Meditation* was written nearly a decade after T. S. Eliot's *The Sacred Wood* but around a decade prior to the institutionalization of New Criticism in the pedagogy of university literary studies classrooms. Bennett writes about *Stanzas*, quoting Jackson, "The question of the lyric's workings and relevance was in the air as she composed her poem: the pedagogical practices that, Virginia Jackson writes, helped 'to forge a model of all poems as essentially lyric' and became 'the normative model for the production and reception of most poetry' were percolating on the college and university campuses Stein would soon visit on her American lecture tour."[101] Bennett's point is not that we read *Stanzas in Meditation* as lyric because of the influence of New Criticism on us, but rather, that Stein was also participating in the theorization of the lyric: "I understand Stein as entering into this unsettled conversation about the lyric through *Stanzas*, a poem we should encounter as not simply an object of lyric readings but as itself an actor in the collective invention of the modern lyric."[102]

I agree with Bennett that Stein is theorizing the lyric in *Stanzas in Meditation*, but not that Stein's account of the lyric chimes quite so neatly with established theorizations of lyric poetry. What I'm claiming here is threefold: first, that Stein is also thinking about how patterns make lyric poems into wholes; second, that *Stanzas in Meditation* shows that thinking and shows that it's on the page and not just in our heads; and third, that this thinking differs in important ways from how both New Critics and lyric theorists such as Jackson describe the workings of lyric poetry. Unlike the New Critics, Stein's stanzas conceptualize how patterns make wholes that can remain contingent. Poets such as Stein, writing at the same time as the New Critics, and at the same time as inductive reasoning reemerged as one of the foremost problems of modern philosophy, were also thinking about how a lyric poem works and what makes it cohere. For the New Critics, wholeness and contingency are mutually exclusive; a poem being whole means that it has been formed. For Stein, a lyric poem can be whole and still be contingent because form is a mode of thought. A poem's form, its whole, isn't the solidified resulting precipitate of thinking—it's not the ossified remnant, the glazed urn—it's thought in action. Reasoning is a gerund verb as well as a noun. *Stanzas in Meditation*, then, is also meditation—thinking—in stanzas. And it shows how thinking and stanzas, how logic and lyric, are alike or even akin to one another, how they share their forms.

Readers of *Stanzas in Meditation* tend to agree that it's among Stein's most lyric work, though "lyric" means different things. For example, Donald Sutherland, in his preface to the 1956 edition of *Stanzas in Meditation*, describes the poem as lyric in part because of its self-reflection on what counts as lyric; he interprets the poem's first line—"I caught a bird which made a ball"—as "meaning 'I captured a 'lyricity' that constituted a complete and self-contained entity.'"[103] For Sutherland, Stein's is a "lyricity of ideas" that are "not composed in their logical or persuasive connections."[104] More recently, Bennett traces the poem's "invocation of lyric tradition" from that first line of lyric bird and self-contained ball through the lyric's association with overhearing and its interest in the voicing of subjectivity.

So far my argument in this section has been organized somewhat syllogistically: a stanza should be thought, stanzaic form is an aspect of lyric poetry, and so lyric has to do with thinking. And reasoning, like poems, has to do with parts and wholes, the connections between parts, and the criteria for wholeness. But what's a stanza?

In *Stanzas in Meditation*, Stein is exploring the question of wholeness on the level of the work and also, fractally, on the level of individual stanzas. The stanzas are numbered, and Stein experimented with titling the book "81 Stanzas," "LXXXIII Stanzas," or "TWO HUNDRED STANZAS IN MEDITATION."[105] She wavered on whether to describe these poems as a sonnet sequence; Stein inscribed an exhibition copy of the 1932 Francis Picabia show, which included the earliest printed excerpt from *Stanzas in Meditation*, to Carl Van Vechten with "To Carl Sonnets in Meditation for Carl."[106] Stein's stanzas are sometimes close to sonnet-length, and use rhyme throughout but inconsistently; it can make sense to think of them relative to the sonnet and the sonnet sequence. Indeed, some stanzas are almost sonnets: Part Two's stanza XIV is thirteen lines and includes numerous rhymes, and Part Three's stanza VIII is fourteen lines and has only six end words. And even when they are not sonnet-length, their rhymes, which are another kind of repetition and qualification, a "not only not" in sound, can help to tie them together; most stanzas repeat sounds as rhymes or half-rhymes or even as end words somewhere. But variation in the stanzas is great. In length, most do not approximate the sonnet all that closely. Sometimes Stein's stanzas are just one line; here are just some examples: Part Two's stanza XV, "It is very much like it"; Part Three's stanza XIX, "Not only this one now"; three in a row in Part Four from stanza V, "I think very well of my way," stanza VI, "May be I do but I doubt it," through stanza VII, "May be may be men"; Part Five's stanza XI, "I feel that this stanza has been well-known"; and stanza XXXVII, "That feels fortunately alike."[107] On the other end, some of Stein's stanzas are very long, stretching for over one hundred lines. And while some stanzas contain many rhymes, some contain none.

Stein makes several suggestions about what a stanza is in *Stanzas*. Part Five's stanza IX is just two lines: "A stanza nine is a stanza mine/My stanza is three of nine."[108] But this brief couplet asserts qualities of a stanza. First, this stanza makes it clear, aside from the numbered title, that it is one of a series; a stanza can be a whole but unlike a sonnet which can be in a sequence or stand alone, a stanza can't be singular. A stanza is both a whole and also always already a part. *Stanzas in Meditation* shows what it looks like to have a whole—the poem—made of parts, each of which is a whole made of parts, and each of which, at every level, could have been longer, shorter, different, otherwise. If, then, we recognize how form can represent thinking—or, more precisely, reasoning—then it's not a problem to describe a poem's form as a contingent whole. Reasoning is also a contingent whole.

What makes it whole, then? Stein suggests that it's a whole if the thinking satisfies us—if it does well enough for us to continue in our own continuous present, in the contingent wholes that are our daily lives. Part Five's XXIX is the one that begins "A stanza should be thought" but continues as an implied conditional statement that if a stanza is thought, it will bring satisfaction:

> A stanza should be thought
> And if which may they do
> Very well for very well
> And very well for you.[109]

This stanza is easily recognizable as a whole; it's a quatrain in (essentially) iambic trimeter and rhymes on the second and fourth lines. It wouldn't be out of place in a Dickinson poem or the octave of a sonnet. This stanza also can be read as about contingency: "And if which may they do" refers to the stanzas, how they are subject to conditions, and also could describe a wish those conditions should be met. And if the stanza should be thought—both connotations of "should," if instructions are followed and also if conditions are met—then the stanzas will "do/Very well." It's worth noting here that the stanza will do well—not be *good*, an adjective, but do *well*, an adverb—because it's describing a verb. Meditation—thought, reasoning, and lyric poetry—is action.

Just a few stanzas earlier, in Part Five's stanza XXII, Stein asks and, in some ways, answers my question: what is a stanza?

> What is a stanza
> When I say that often as a day
> I feel that it is best to know the way
> That if upon the road where if I went
> I meant to feel that is if as if sent
> The if I came and went
> Or well what is it if it makes it do
> Not only which if not only all or not alike[110]

In this section of a stanza, we see some of the aspects of how a stanza is thought that I've been tracing. A stanza characterized by double negatives and qualifications: "Not only which if not only all." It works on patterns: repeated words and sounds, including the rhymes of day/way, went/sent/went, and even slant rhymes such as feel/well/all. A stanza works variously: "not only all or not alike." But really, a stanza is what works: "it makes it do." Like inductive reasoning, it "makes it do" in daily life, constantly: "often as a day."

While composing *Stanzas in Meditation*, Gertrude Stein, in a letter to Louis Bromfield, wrote: "I am working a lot I am trying to write a long dull poem like the long ones of Wordsworth and it is very interesting to do I was always fond of these long dull poems well anyway make the weather better and come to see us."[111] It's easy to read this letter as changing the subject, but there's a way to think about how writing a long dull poem is "full of weather"—indeed, that's exactly how Gordon Teskey described Edmund Spenser's poetry in the quotation I include in the introduction to this book. There, I write that the forecasting of weather is an example of inductive reasoning: we know about past weather, we have developed working theories, and we can make predictions, and they aren't entirely reliable but they still work, more or less, and they are certainly better than nothing. Earlier in this chapter, I also describe the half-had explanation as like a weather forecast, accurate in its predictions until it's not, when a new prediction is offered. Dydo describes the frustration of reading *Stanzas in Meditation* this way: "As long as I look for consistency, each reading seems to cancel the last as a misreading."[112] But what if this inconsistency isn't a problem the way Dydo thinks it is? What if elucidating contingency is itself how the poem coheres as a whole?

DO YOU UNDERSTAND

Weather is one way that we experience the world together—"well anyway make the weather better and come to see us"—and throughout her work, Stein tries to use inclusive experience to mitigate the contingency of inductive reasoning. We see it in her choice to call herself "Everybody" in *Everybody's Autobiography*. We can also see it in her characteristic questions and assertions from lectures, poetry, and narrative prose, as she repeatedly asks, "do you understand."[113] One of the frustrations of reading Stein is that she seems to be inviting us in, and yet it is hard to imagine what it would be like to *be in*. One of my goals has been to reconcile these impressions. Our persistent difficulty in reading Stein's work is caused by the persistent difficulty of knowing what the facts tell. Knowing what the facts tell is a difficult activity; it is explanation based on inductive reasoning. But Stein teaches us that there is no alternative. It may seem easier to refer to laws and theories, rather than having only half of the necessary information, or not being sure if subjective experience is broad enough to justify understanding. But Stein reminds us that even laws and theories that are accepted by a society as true can change with "startling . . . rapidity." Stein is inviting us not into her house, but into an understanding of why it is difficult to make sense of our own experiences, even in our houses.

In this chapter, I have argued that Stein's work is difficult for the same reason that explaining inductively is difficult. Stein demonstrates how explanation works by theorizing explanation and doing philosophy of explanation. If we try simply to solve Stein's difficulty, we will not see what she is trying to show us—that it is difficult to know what the facts tell. It is difficult to assemble parts into wholes, and to have those wholes be always contingent. She is showing us the criteria of explanation, explanation's risks and rewards. It is difficult to make sense of our experiences in the world based on what we know from our experiences in the world. If we are aware of the contingency of inductive explanation, we can, at least, be sure that we are all facing the same difficulty together. Lyric poetry addresses itself to this difficulty; it offers us a way to experience it as pleasure also. Well anyway, or maybe even very well for you.

Chapter Four

CONSISTENCY AND MARIANNE MOORE

"THE PANGOLIN"

At the end of Marianne Moore's 1932 poem "The Pangolin," the titular animal, an armored anteater, greets the sunrise as he does each morning: with relief.

"Again the sun!"
"anew each day; and new and new and new,"
"that comes into and steadies my soul."[1]

It's as if the pangolin doesn't take the dawn for granted; it's as if he can't assume that just because the sun rose the day before, it will rise today.

The pangolin's attitude or stance toward this literally everyday occurrence echoes David Hume's well-known example of inductive reasoning. Hume writes that "past *experience*" cannot "be extended to future times,"[2] and his first and most famous illustration of (what comes to be called) the problem of induction is the daily sunrise: "*That the sun will not rise tomorrow*, is no less intelligible a proposition, and implies no more contradiction than the affirmation, *that it will rise*."[3] Read in this light, the pangolin's fear that the sun won't rise and his happiness when it does isn't ridiculous, or at least not only ridiculous, but also all too *reasonable*. This empiricist pangolin knows that the past is not a reliable guide to the future. He knows that predictions about what *will* happen based only on what *has* happened will always be problematic, unreliable, and contingent.

In the first two chapters of this book, I argued that the poetry of Walt Whitman and Emily Dickinson, despite enormous aesthetic differences, shares a philosophical ambition. Both show the strength of reasoning based not on abstract laws or theories, but on particular facts, details, and observations. Whitman and Dickinson use their formal poetics—the list and the analogy, respectively—as logical forms. And these forms, enumeration and analogical reasoning, are also the fundamental logical forms of induction. But what induction offers—closeness to lived experience, nimble accommodation of novelty—must be balanced with its drawbacks. The greatest of these drawbacks is the contingency that Hume identifies as the problem of induction: the fragility of any generalization, the risk that any prediction may not hold true. In chapter 3, I discussed how Gertrude Stein recognizes that any generalization based on the facts alone may be falsified by the addition of a new fact; as the classic example says, all swans are white until one sees a single black swan. Inductive reasoning can never be complete, and any explanation based on it must be contingent; a black swan might arrive at any moment. But throughout her oeuvre, Stein proffers facts, and claims that facts alone—one white swan after another—and not general laws or theories can explain, and she argues that the contingency of any resulting explanations is not weakness but strength. This chapter turns to the poetry of Marianne Moore, and here I'll describe how Moore turns induction's contingency—and particularly the problem of predicting based on past experiences—into poetry, or rather, into a formal poetics: an overlapping set of techniques and commitments.

Inductive reasoning is problematic in two ways: first, we can't know what will happen in the future based on what has happened in the past; second, we can't justify inductive reasoning except with more induction. These interrelated problems—the epistemological and the justificatory—are often described as the problem of induction's two horns.[4] While Stein is concerned with the second horn, and how to justify generalization, Moore is more concerned with the first horn, the fundamental epistemological problem. Stein develops aesthetic techniques that respond to the impossible necessity of justifying induction; in addition to her accumulation of facts, her writing in a continuous present seeks to outrun justification. And while

CONSISTENCY AND MARIANNE MOORE

Moore's poetry seems like it could not be more different than Stein's—just as Whitman's seems like it could not be more different than Dickinson's—I'll argue in this chapter that Moore's poetics also are shaped by and in response to her concerns about when inductive reasoning works and when it doesn't. Moore recognizes that any predictions about the future based on the past are both necessary and fragile, and this recognition shapes her poetry. At multiple levels, from her topics to her enjambments, Moore explores how things work and what happens when reliable mechanisms fail. And like the other poems featured in this book, Moore's poems suggest that knowledge and art may not be commensurable, but they can share a set of terms. In so doing, she shows how aesthetics can respond to an epistemological problem.

In this chapter, I'll situate Moore's poetry in the philosophical discussions she would have read and those she wouldn't have; these range from Hume's foundational statement of the problem of induction in the eighteenth century to those that, like modernist poetry, surfaced in the early twentieth century and continue in contemporary philosophy today. My goal isn't to make a claim about Moore's historical context but rather to make a claim on behalf of her poetry by clarifying its philosophical ambitions and stakes.

NOVELTY, MODERNISM, PROBLEMS

How to respond to the new is and has always been a concern, arguably the central concern, for modernist literature and for us as scholars of modernism. We continue to read modernist literature in the light of Ezra Pound's dictum about how to connect the past to the future—"make it new"—as well as through conceptualizations of modernity and its literature as the products of shocking trauma.[5] The uncertain, troubled relation of the past to the future continues to be a live topic for scholars of modernism, important both to how we discuss texts and how we theorize the field. For example, two recent books, Paul Saint-Amour's *Tense Future* and Kate Stanley's *Practices of Surprise in American Literature After Emerson*, both reframe how to understand literary texts of expectation and anticipation, and both continue to use *newness* as, if not a lodestar, at least part of the constellation of modernist studies. Moore does not appear in either Saint-Amour's book or Stanley's, but their arguments—though opposed in certain ways—both help to clarify her titular pangolin's anxiety about what surprises or shocks the future might hold. Both Saint-Amour and Stanley situate their arguments in conversation with Walter Benjamin and his "feeling of vertigo characteristic of the nineteenth century's conception of history."[6] Stanley diverges sharply from Benjamin's account by distinguishing between Benjaminian shock and what she calls "Emersonian surprise,"[7] and argues that Emerson's embrace of surprise, carried on by pragmatists William James and John Dewey, is an intellectual tradition that shapes modernist literature by offering strategies that preserve "a renewable receptivity to unexpected encounters."[8] Modernism, Stanley argues, should not be understood as an "epochal break" from the era before.[9] Saint-Amour reflects Benjamin's account of modernism made anxious by the past forward into an argument about futurity, writing that literature from between the world wars not only carries old wounds, but is also wounded by the anticipation of future violence. Interwar modernism, Saint-Amour argues, is "traumatized by both a past conflagration and the prospect of a worse future one."[10] "The Pangolin" was published in 1936, and like the other interwar texts that Saint-Amour discusses, it could be described as displaying "*pre-traumatic syndrome*."[11] Read with *Tense Future*, the modernism of "The Pangolin" is not due to its having been written at a certain time by a poet who has since come to be celebrated as a canonical modernist, nor to its free verse form, but to its description of the wounded way of life between the wars (which is not in fact *between* the wars at all but constantly under their omnipresent shadows). As Moore was writing "The Pangolin," she read *The Illustrated London News*, and the poem's first line—"Another armored animal!"—recalls, as Victoria Bazin writes, "*The News*'s meticulous descriptions of the marvels of new machine technology," particularly the technology of war.[12] We could even describe the pangolin the way that Jürgen Habermas describes Benjamin: as trying to find "a solution to the paradoxical task of obtaining standards of its own for the contingency of a modernity that had become simply transitory."[13]

I, too, understand modernism as keenly aware of the future's dangerous uncertainty, the potential for inconsistency, and I agree that the fearful anticipation of disaster is part of what makes "The Pangolin" modernist. But the sense of the future, of newness, *being a problem* is older: not modernist, but *modern*, characteristic not of the aesthetic movement but of the changing institutions, technologies, and increasing globalization of the emerging modern world several hundred years earlier. The references in "The Pangolin" include the machines of war, travel, and architecture, and while "the sailboat was the first machine," most of the others—Gargallo, da Vinci, the building of cathedrals—are from Europe's early modern period onward. These allusions include, as I'll linger on more in the next section, that reference to Hume, the modern philosopher who first elucidated the future's unpredictability as a *philosophical* problem. "The Pangolin" represents novelty as both a characteristic problem of modernism, as it's long been understood, and also as a problem with a longer history in the modern era.

While the anxiety and awareness about the future being inconsistent, that surprises or shocks may await, do reach a new pitch, even a crisis, at the beginning of the twentieth century, they do so across different intellectual traditions and disciplines. For example, as I wrote about in this book's introduction, at the beginning of the twentieth century, inductive reasoning becomes a topic again for philosophy. The philosopher Bertrand Russell, a nearly exact contemporary of Moore, writes about Hume and the epistemological problem of induction in 1912's *The Problems of Philosophy*: "Have we any reason, assuming that [laws] have always held in the past, to suppose that they will hold in the future?"[14] Russell shows how fundamental inductive reasoning is, and also how its unreliability is devastating: he writes about Hume in 1945's *A History of Western Philosophy* that if there is no empirical answer to the problem of induction, "there is no intellectual difference between sanity and insanity."[15]

And, of course, the problem of induction can't be solved; there is no empirical answer for the uncertainty of the future; there's no way to prevent the shock or surprise of the new. But there *are* useful ways to respond to it, and one can argue that this is exactly how modernist literature can be described. The aesthetics of modernist literature, Saint-Amour and Stanley agree, though they differ on exactly which, are responses to the problem presented by the new. For Saint-Amour, modernism's strategies, such as the encyclopedic novel, can accommodate new entries and still evoke wholeness (even as "they are thoroughgoing vandals of their *own* totality claims"[16]). For Stanley, too, modernism is marked by aesthetic strategies, bequeathed by Ralph Waldo Emerson, to accommodate the new and so "to open themselves to the surprises of modernity."[17]

"The Pangolin" represents the problem of newness—both the longer history of newness being conceptualized as a problem in the modern era, and the increasing attention to it and anxiety about it in the interbellum rise of modernism—and the poem, like other modernist texts, offers strategies that respond to the problem without solving it. One of these strategies can be described, as Stanley does, as influenced by pragmatism, and although Stanley doesn't read Moore's poetry as pragmatist, other literary scholars have. In the next section, I'll argue that Moore was interested in the problem of novelty, and while pragmatism is one way of categorizing her broad and deep philosophical investments, it's not the only one or even the best.

MOORE'S PHILOSOPHICAL INVESTMENTS

Did Marianne Moore know David Hume's work? Is the pangolin's relief that the sun has risen again a *direct* reference to Hume's famous example of the problem of induction? To the first question: yes, with certainty. Moore studied Hume in her final year at Bryn Mawr, in 1908–1909, when she took two philosophy courses from an influential professor, Theodore de Laguna.[18] And so, then, to the second question: yes, but only probably. It's very likely that the end of "The Pangolin" directly refers to Hume's famous example. But regardless of whether or not Moore's reference to Hume is even provable, what is not in doubt is, by her early twenties, Moore thought about and worried over the larger issues exemplified in Hume's account of the problem of induction: how to reason about the new based only on the old, and how fragile our predictions of the future are when we only have the past to guide us. Moore was invested in the stakes of the intertwined questions of, as she put it in her college notes on de Laguna's lecture on Hume, "How get something new, by mere repetition?"[19] and "What is belief."[20] How does the past produce and predict the future? Or do we only believe that it does retrospectively?

The first philosophy course that Moore took from de Laguna was History of Philosophy in the fall semester, and the second, in spring semester, was General Philosophy; this sequence of courses, which ran chronologically from Classical Greek philosophy through to Empiricism, ended with Hume. Moore's lecture notes from this last month of her college career focus on Hume's ideas of causality, which is where his account of the problem of induction and the famous example are found. She filled up thirteen pages with notes about Hume, including:

> Hume says, <u>necessity ... simply a characteristic of our own imagination</u>. ... Uniformity ... a habit of our own minds. ... Causality—inspires us w belief but doesn't give us truth. ... When you come to a conclusion as a result of reasoning. And you believe it, it has just that sort of vividness in your mind. We believe the impression of our own ideas, how do other ideas get vividness. ... Yet you are not going to quit believing in uniformity of value. Belief so important to us that nature hasn't left it off more demonstrable reasoning. ... Belief without rational ground. ... Without causality—there could be no experience. Your life would be one of chaos. Life of an abs. irrational creature.[21]

Moore is circling around a cluster of terms that describe the power and the perils of inductive reasoning: how the necessary connection between the past and the future is a function of our own reasoning (what philosophers call *necessity*), how we assume that the past will be a good guide to the future (what they call *uniformity*), but that the attribution of cause may merely be a matter of habit (what they call *causality*)—and yet we believe in it. She recognizes and reckons with the knowledge that there is no alternative to believing that inductive reasoning works. The alternative, she writes, is to live as an "irrational creature," echoing Russell's description of the insolvability of the problem of induction as erasing the difference "between sanity and insanity."

Discussion of Moore's interest in philosophy has focused on pragmatism, which makes sense, as Moore was very close with William James's daughter Peggy while both were students at Bryn Mawr. Moore first read James's work at Bryn Mawr, and continued to read more afterward, as well as reading John Dewey's. Literary scholars, including Linda Leavell,[22] David Kadlec,[23] Elisa New,[24] Victoria Bazin,[25] Kristen Case,[26] Rachel Buxton,[27] and others, have all written about interpreting Moore's poetry in light of her knowledge and love of pragmatism.

But I'm concerned in this section with making the argument that Moore's interest in the stakes of certain philosophical questions goes beyond—because it precedes and also motivates—her attention to pragmatism. Given Moore's knowledge of Hume's account of causality, she was probably referring to his example of the problem of induction in the last lines of "The Pangolin," but my tracing of this reference through the archive is not an end but a means. What this reference shows is that her interest in philosophy was both historically broad and also deeply attentive to particular philosophical concerns. Instead of simply reading Moore as interested in pragmatism, we can instead recognize that Moore is interested in pragmatism *because* it offers a way to reason about an unreasonable world, and it is this problem that motivates her investment in philosophy in the first place. In her college notebook she writes that the alternative to believing (however contingently) in causality is to live as an "irrational creature." We might say that Moore's interest in philosophy is about how to live as a *rational* creature, or even more specifically, how to live as a rational creature in an irrational world.

Pragmatism offers one response to empiricism's skepticism. While Hume leaves Moore, at the very end of her college career, with the skeptical knowledge that causality rests only on belief, and that belief, while absolutely necessary, is very possibly false, pragmatism offers her a different orientation toward truth. James writes in *Pragmatism*, delivered as lectures the same year that Moore was studying philosophy, "a new opinion counts as 'true' just in proportion as it gratifies the individual's desire to assimilate the novel in his experience to his beliefs in stock. It must both lean on old truth and grasp new fact; and its success (as I said a moment ago) in doing this, is a matter for the individual's appreciation."[28] For the pragmatist, the uncertain relation of the future to the past is not understood to be a problem at all, and so newness doesn't present real difficulty, and the unreliability of induction, like whether the squirrel "goes round" the tree, in James's famous example, is just one more of the "metaphysical disputes that otherwise might be interminable."[29] Pragmatism doesn't *solve* the problem of induction; it *dissolves* it by arguing that it makes "no practical difference" in how we live.[30]

James had already critiqued the problem of induction thirty years earlier in 1875. Reviewing a book by George Lewes, James took aim at "the skeptical philosophers who have of late predominated in England" who argue that "habitual concurrence of the same phenomena is not a case of dynamic connection at all" and write that "the universe may turn inside out tomorrow, for aught we know."[31] Such skepticism is "possible *ad infinitum*. That we do not all do it is because at a certain point most of us get tired of the play, resolve to stop, and assuming something for true, pass on to a life of action based on that."³² And, anticipating his language in *Pragmatism*, he writes that the "practical difference is nil."³³

Returning to Moore's "The Pangolin" as a case study: the titular pangolin may rejoice at each sunrise, but he never calmly or confidently awaits it. He never "resolve[s] to stop," and, in fact, the contingency of inductive reasoning *does* seem to make a practical difference in his life, which is shaped by his extreme caution. If cruel optimism "exists when something you desire is actually an obstacle to your flourishing,"³⁴ then perhaps James's pragmatism can be understood to be an inverse of cruel optimism: it's a humane optimism, a recognition that, yes, "we desire to know what to *expect* . . . as a matter of fact we do live in a world from which as a rule we know what to expect."³⁵ And so, "Even in regard to that mass of accidents which must be expected to occur in some shape but cannot be accurately prophesied in detail, we set our minds at rest, by saying that the world with all its events has a substantial cause; and when we call this cause God, Love, or Perfection, we feel secure that whatever the future may harbor, it cannot at bottom be inconsistent with the character of this term."³⁶ And, still, even when we end up disappointed, it's good for us, as the child's "false expectation which would make him experience the shock of difference between merely imagining a thing and getting it" is what teaches self-consciousness.³⁷

I'm not the first to note that Moore's pangolin echoes Hume; Siobhan Phillips, in *The Poetics of the Everyday*, also discusses how poetry considers the diurnal courses of, in Moore's words, "sun and moon and day and night," and she touches upon how philosophy, such as Hume's and James's, shares some perspectives with poetry about how to live day-to-day. But Phillips doesn't show that Moore actually read Hume, nor does she understand Hume and James as disagreeing sharply with each other. For her, they align in that each is concerned with making sense of the world as one lives in it: James "amplifies" Hume,³⁸ since "in a world lacking timeless verities, only the patterns of previous events allow one to predict which opinion will lead to future verification,"³⁹ and the pangolin accepts his "diurnal assignment," which is "consensual," and his "assenting 'again' exemplifies a common hope as well as a common chore."⁴⁰ The common chore for all of us in "the disenchanted twentieth-century universe" is to accept that the "contingent but empirical patterns of a physical earth might serve to replace the eternal but unbelievable truths of a metaphysical concept."[41] While Phillips illuminatingly traces the way that modern poets find emotional grounding in the literal movements of our earth, this reading—contingency doesn't present any particular problem as empiricism is the new paradigm that successfully replaces metaphysics—is too sanguine.

Contingency *is* a problem for Moore's pangolin; the world's potential inconsistency and so uncertainty means he's "the prey of fear" and must meet each day "armored." The pangolin offers a different inverse of cruel optimism; it's not the humane optimism offered by James and echoed by Phillips, but a cruel pessimism: a determination not to hold out hope for what might turn out to be untrue, the opposite kind of self-protection. In addition to his scales and closing ear ridges, the pangolin protects himself by expecting the worst. The pangolin sees the truth in Hume's skeptical empiricism, which frames the unpredictable future, our inconsistent world, as a philosophical problem with no solution, one that we encounter (even if we ignore it) on a daily basis. What appears to be an oxymoronic statement about the pangolin—"not afraid of anything is he,/and then goes cowering forth"—is not contradictory at all when read as an expression of the cruel pessimism of empiricist skepticism. Precisely because the pangolin is afraid of *everything*, he doesn't need to be afraid of *anything*: all possible terrible outcomes have already been anticipated, and practical preparations as well as emotional bracing are done.

Trying to prepare for the unpredictable might be impossible, but that doesn't mean it's *irrational*. In the next section, I'll show how Moore's investment in how to reason about the new, in how to be a rational creature, reaches into her poetics. To be clear: I'm less interested in tracing the intellectual influences on Moore and more interested in looking for how she responds to these influences in her poetry and through it. Whether she read Hume and James is a matter of fact, but I care much more about its potential significance: it only matters that Moore thought about philosophical problems, including whether they were problems at all, if it matters for how we read her poems. And while it's not wrong to describe her poetry as echoing pragmatism, it's far better to think of it as discussing and addressing the same problems that pragmatism does. Moore's poetry is not imitative of philosophy; it doesn't simply echo the philosophy she has read; it is, itself, philosophical in offering new understandings of one of the oldest problems of the modern world.

RATIONAL CREATURES: MOORE'S CASE STUDIES OF REASONING

In the *Nicomachean Ethics*, Aristotle distinguishes humans from animals; unlike animals, the human being's *ergon*—function or work—depends on being rational.[42] Moore studied Aristotle's ethics as part of that same yearlong philosophy sequence at Bryn Mawr, and we can suppose that Aristotle's distinction between humans and animals on the basis of rationality, at least in part, lies behind her writing in her lecture notebook that while causality is merely a fragile belief, it's a necessary one, since without it, "Your life would be one of chaos. Life of an abs. irrational creature."

But Moore's own animals—the animals in some of Moore's most famous poems, including the pangolin—show that it's not always clear what the criteria for rationality are or even could be. Expecting the future to resemble the past is rational, and yet, at the same time, trusting inductive reasoning may not make a lot of sense. Moore's animals, in their survival strategies, are either—or both, simultaneously—sensibly cautious and unreasonably paranoid as they try to predict the future based on the past. In this section, I'll argue that Moore uses animals to show that what looks irrational may in fact be the best strategy, and that even what appears to be the best strategy may turn out, retrospectively, to have been reasonable after all, to have been true. She's charting the extent of induction's epistemological powers and finding that they are real and even formidable.

Moore's poems about fish, pelicans, ostriches, snails, jerboas, nautiluses, and other animals, are among her greatest, and, additionally, she translated the *Fables* of La Fontaine, which use wolves, frogs, goats, sheep, weasels, and more as their characters. *Pace* Aristotle, Moore's animals can be described as behaving rationally. The animals of the *Fables* speak, plan, deceive, and presumably are meant to be read as allegories of human behavior in part because of their obvious rationality. Moore's own poetry is different; as Robin G. Schulze writes, "Moore's animals remain animals." But the animals in her poems still can be described as behaving logically. For example—reaching again for my touchstone—the pangolin, with his "gritequipped gizzard" is also a "night miniature artist engineer." The characteristics that seem extraneous or excessive—"armor seems extra," writes Moore about the pangolin—are, in fact, crucial to the animal's strategy of self-protection. The pangolin's particular genius has to do with his various ways of protecting himself: "the closing ear-ridge"; his "contracting nose and eye apertures"; how he rolls "into a ball"; his "sting-proof scales."[43] So although he walks "peculiarly," there's a reason: "that the outside/edges of his hands may bear the weight and save the/claws/for digging."

"Man and beast/each with a splendor . . . each with an excellence!" Moore exclaims in "The Pangolin." Each of Moore's animals have their particular, even peculiar, logical strategies for survival that may appear irrational to an observer in how exaggeratedly cautious they are. So we might say that the paper nautilus's "thin glass shell," along with the rest of her dedication to her eggs, the way she "guards it/day and night," barely surviving herself, is her excellence. The jellyfish "floats away/From you" in water that it turns suddenly "cloudy"; this is its excellence. And, too, the ostrich's "great neck revolves with compass-needle nervousness/when he stands guard" over his nest. All of these examples, like that from "The Pangolin," describe how animals protect themselves or their offspring.

I'm emphasizing this point because the logic of survival modeled by Moore's animals displays the strength of inductive reasoning, but it also displays its weakness. My argument, though, isn't about whether or not the animals are logical, but notes that one can't always tell the difference. Based on past experience, *it works* for the pangolin to walk peculiarly on the edges of his hands, for the nautilus to construct a shell to protect her eggs, for the jellyfish to escape from a grasping hand by releasing an ink cloud, and for the ostrich to use its long neck to survey in all directions. But also, of course, *sometimes it doesn't work*. Sometimes all of the animal's careful, even paranoid, preparations don't successfully prepare it for the dangers it encounters. In "He 'Digesteth Harde Yron,'" the poem in praise of the ostrich, Moore writes of how all of the great birds except the ostrich have been hunted to extinction.

>   Although the aepyornis
>   or roc that lived in Madagascar and
>   the moa are extinct,
>   the camel-sparrow, linked
>   with them in size—the large sparrow
>   Xenophon saw walking by a stream—was and is
>   a symbol of justice.

CONSISTENCY AND MARIANNE MOORE

> This bird watches his chicks with
> a maternal concentration-and he's
> been mothering the eggs
> at night six weeks—his legs
> their only weapon of defense.
> He is swifter than a horse; he has a foot hard
> as a hoof; the leopard
>
> is not more suspicious. How
> could he, prized for plumes and eggs and young
> used even as a riding-beast, respect men
> hiding actor-like in ostrich skins, with the right hand
> making the neck move as if alive
> and from a bag the left hand strewing grain, that ostriches
>
> might be decoyed and killed![44]

The ostrich's caution, its vigilance, how it could not be "more suspicious," has kept it alive so far, but not all ostriches have survived, nor is the future survival of the species guaranteed.

> Six hundred ostrich-brains served
> at one banquet, the ostrich-plume-tipped tent
> and desert spear, jewel-
> gorgeous ugly egg-shell
> goblets, eight pairs of ostriches
> in harness, dramatize a meaning
> always missed by the externalist.
>
> The power of the visible
> is the invisible, as even where
> no tree of freedom grows,
> so-called brute courage knows.
> Heroism is exhausting, yet
> it contradicts a greed that did not wisely spare
> the harmless solitaire

> or great auk in its grandeur;
> unsolicitude having swallowed up
> all giant birds but an alert gargantuan
> little-winged, magnificently speedy running-bird.
> This one remaining rebel
> is the sparrow-camel.[45]

Moore describes the ostrich as heroic, but "heroism is exhausting." The ostrich is rightfully suspicious of humans, since in our "greed," humans mock ostriches to trap and kill them. The great auk, the moa, and the aepyornis have all vanished, but describing this as "unsolicitude" is understatement: these birds have all been hunted to extinction. The ostrich might well be next. Its excellence, its suspicion, may save it, but may not.

One could say that the "harde yron" of the poem's title is not just a reference to John Lyly's claim in his 1578 *Euphues* that the "Estrich" eats iron to "preserve his health," but a metaphor: the ostrich continues to swallow the inedible—to do the nearly impossible—to continue its life and that of its children.[46] One could call this a "preservation of its health," but only in the same key of ironic understatement as calling rapacious hunting "unsolicitude." The ostrich can run fast, kick powerfully, and turn its head to look behind it, but none of those will reliably save it from its only predators: humans. Is the ostrich's extreme caution excessive or inadequate? It's impossible to say. Moore's use of the self-protective behavior of animals shows that inductive reasoning is both rational and not. The necessity of its caution is not in doubt, but its sufficiency can only be known retrospectively.

One might object that the rationality here isn't necessarily the animals' own. It could be argued that Moore's animals are displaying the logic of their physiognomy rather than their own ability to reason; one could point to Moore's Christian faith and describe her as interested in divine design, or to her interest in science and describe these behaviors as evolutionary adaptations. If one were interested in Moore's faith, or her relationship to science, this objection would have teeth. Even if one's ultimate aim was to determine Moore's stance on Aristotle's distinction between humans and animals, rather than use that as a lens to examine her account of rationality, there would be significant implications. But for this chapter, it simply doesn't matter very much. My point is that Moore's interest in the epistemology of predictability predates her interest in pragmatism and it continues to be visible in her poetry for decades.[47]

So then, rather than thinking that her philosophical interest is in pragmatism, Moore's interest in pragmatism is one expression of a set of philosophical concerns that lie beneath it: that reasoning about the future based on the past is part of our daily lives and habits of mind, that it's unreliable, and also that it's impossible to forgo or avoid. Whether the design of the pangolin's hand, the nautilus's shell, the jellyfish's ink, or the ostrich's neck are evolutionary or divine in origin may change the ultimate object of these poems' praise—the source of their splendor, their excellence—but it just doesn't change the immediate problems and solutions that these animals literally embody. These animals continue to survive because of their logical behaviors, because what has worked will probably, though never definitely, continue to work. In other words, the response that Moore outlines to the future's inconsistency is that animals themselves can remain consistent in their behaviors.

MOORE'S CONTINUOUS PRESENT

In "Composition As Explanation," Gertrude Stein describes writing in the "continuous present," which involves "beginning again and again and again."[48] In chapter 3, I described "Composition As Explanation" as part of Stein's justification of induction, or anyway, an end-run around critiques of it. Moore also writes in a continuous present tense, though she doesn't identify it as such, and it's not Stein's present, with its embrace of trying different attempts or directions. Moore's present tense is *is*, which has no beginning; it has always been. An ostrich has always run fast and been suspicious: it "was and is," as Moore writes in "He 'Digesteth Harde Yron.'"[49] The jellyfish "opens, and/It closes" and then it continues, just the same: "It opens and it/Closes."[50] A pangolin has always had "scale/lapping scale with spruce-cone regularity."[51] Moore is not interested in evolution. Anything known about the future based on what's known about the past is valid and true, but will only be valid and true if everything continues as it is. If *how it is now* is also *how it has always been*, then also, just maybe, that is *how it will always be*.

In this section, I'll widen my reading of Moore's interest in predictability, the first horn of Hume's problem, the epistemological aspect of induction. Previously, I argued that Moore's animals are occasions for her to think through her philosophical interests in reasoning about the future: what she, in her college notebooks, using the philosophical terms, calls "necessity" as she writes about Hume's account of causal inference, and "uniformity," that the future will resemble the past. But animals aren't the only ways she's thinking through these problems. Moore's continuous present—her description of how something works, how it has always worked, how it continues to work—is also found in her attention to inanimate objects. Indeed, the line between animal and object—whether machine or piece of art—in Moore's poetry isn't always clear. It's blurred by her very tight focus on function, on what animals and objects share because of what both *do and keep doing*. We can describe this as her attention to mechanisms.

In philosophy of science—the contemporary branch of philosophy that grew out of logical empiricism, which was itself the school of thought that took Hume's skeptical empiricism seriously—philosophers working on scientific explanation have turned their attention toward mechanisms. Identifying how mechanisms work, they suggest, allows us to understand how things work, and thereby conceptualize causality and so how explanation should work to make predictions. This philosophical conversation largely stems from Wesley Salmon's 1984 *Scientific Explanation and the Causal Structure of the World*, in which he writes, "I do maintain that scientific explanation is designed to provide understanding, and such understanding results from *knowing how things work*. In this sense, the theory of scientific explanation that I have been attempting to develop is an expression of a *mechanical philosophy*."[52] Salmon is critiquing the then-dominant theory of scientific explanation, Carl G. Hempel's deductive-nomological theory of explanation, which—as I discussed in chapter 3—argues that an explanation works deductively to show that a phenomenon is predictable because it is a logical consequence of a law.[53] Salmon, on the other hand, seeks to theorize how scientific explanation can work nondeductively, eschewing abstract laws and theories, and to do so, he argues, "the correct explanation will involve a different set of causal mechanisms. We should note explicitly that all of these putative causal explanations are probabilistic."[54] Probability is inductive, and attention to causal mechanisms allows one to "provide understanding" about "how things work" while also avoiding deductive laws. And like other nondeductive reasoning, "Mechanisms can be indefinitely local, particular, and contingent."[55]

The pangolin's excellence is due to his mechanisms, both biomechanical, and, in Moore's descriptions, actually mechanical. His movements are described as "the not unchain-like machine-like/form and frictionless creep of a thing/made graceful by adversities, con-//versities."[56] Daniel Tiffany takes this reading further; for him, Moore's animal-machines are allegorical and anamorphic images of the power of imagery as he traces it through both literature and quantum mechanics.[57] In addition to likening animals to machines, she also does the reverse and likens machines to living beings. In Moore's "Four Quartz Crystal Clocks," the clocks are "the world's exactest clocks," and they "work well."[58] But they must be kept at a stable temperature because of their sensory sensitivity, their capacity to feel like that of an organism: "a quartz prism when/the temperature changes, feels/the change."[59] Moore's steamroller is described as a kind of large, stupid animal; she scolds it, in "To a Steam Roller": "You lack half wit. You crush all the particles down/into close conformity, and then walk back and forth/on them."[60] For Barbara Johnson, the steamroller's surprising legs reveal the poem's confusion of objects and humans: "the poem uses an anthropomorphism that refers to human form . . . but it is humanity behaving like a machine. 'You lack half wit,' too, expresses a difference between persons and things that becomes tangled in confusion."[61] She points out, "there is no attempt to hide, in this poem, the human stakes represented by things—the poem is not interested in getting to the thingness of the thing by stripping away the human presence."[62] Johnson is concerned with the distinctions between persons and things, but what persons and things share in Moore's poetry is that they keep on keeping on.

Aesthetic objects are like this too in Moore's poems: for Moore, particular aesthetic objects and also whole species both endure through their ongoing operations, their specific skillful "excellence." The poem "The Fish" presents its titular animals more like sculpture than living creatures: "The Fish//wade through black jade."[63] And, again, the reverse is also true; animals are also compared to aesthetic objects in addition to mechanical objects, as aesthetic objects are described as if alive. In "An Egyptian Pulled Glass Bottle in the Shape of a Fish," the blue, yellow, and white cosmetic vessel from 1350 BC, displayed in the British Museum, where Moore visited in 1911, is described as if it's alive: "that/Spectacular and nimble animal the fish,/Whose scales turn aside the sun's sword by their polish."[64] The Parthenon (or Elgin) marbles are also displayed at the British Museum, and they find their way into "The Paper Nautilus," when the white, ridged paper nautilus's "thin glass shell" is compared to the carved marble "lines in the mane of/a Parthenon horse."[65] Like John Keats's poems similarly set in the British Museum—"On Seeing the Elgin Marbles" and "Ode on a Grecian Urn"—Moore's, though different in tone, also praise endurance and consistency. But while Keats's poems look with painful ambivalence into a future in which a particular speaker has been outlived by the aesthetic objects that remain, and remain the same, Moore praises continued functioning rather than specific identity. It doesn't matter very much in her poems if an individual fish survives as long as fish in general do; but also the specific fish bottle is valuable because it is the only one of its kind and so its continued endurance under the blows of the "sun's sword" is praiseworthy. Both are examples of survival by functioning in the same ongoing and unchanging ways.

Moore's most famous example of mechanisms, of how art and animals both always work as they always have, how they are "machine-like," is in her poem "Poetry." Moore asks for poems with "a place for the genuine," and her first examples of the criteria for the genuine in art are the biomechanics of animals—humans, *us*—in reaction to it: "Hands that can grasp, eyes/that can dilate, hair that can rise/if it must."[66] These—our—actions are "genuine" not only because they are unconscious or unfeigned, but because they are "useful."[67] Our hands that can grasp, the dilation of our eyes, and the piloerection of our hair are useful for us as animals—for dealing with objects, darkness, and temperature—and they are useful as we handle art objects as well. In the next stanza, too, Moore presents "case after case" of the biomechanical movements of animals—"the bat/holding on upside down or in quest of something to//eat, elephants pushing, a wild horse taking a roll, a tireless wolf under/a tree"—as comparable to an encounter with art or even with other phenomena, like those that "the immovable critic twinkling his skin like a horse that feels a flea, /the base-/ball fan, the statistician" may encounter.[68] "All these phenomena are important," she asserts; "are"—this statement is in her continuous present.[69] This is how art has always functioned, and this is why it endures.

How art endures is how everything endures, at least so far. Animals (including humans) and objects (including both mechanical and aesthetic objects) are presented by Moore as having always functioned as they do now. But while Keats is confident that the Parthenon marbles and Grecian urns will last forever, and though he knows and mourns the fact that he himself will not, Moore frequently admits doubt about whether what works now will continue to work, even if it always has. Some objects, and even some animal species, seem indestructible; the fish-shaped Egyptian pulled-glass bottle and the ecosystem of the sea in "The Fish" are presented as if they will simply grow older and older in their respective contexts, absorbing and reflecting the blows of ocean and sunlight without damage. But others don't.

Often, Moore's continuous present is balanced against an uncertain and contingent future. Her animals know that what has worked for them in the past may fail next time. The paper nautilus labors and fights for a safe future, but that poem concludes with the grammar of uncertainty, ending on a preposition and in the subjunctive mood: "as if they knew love/is the only fortress/strong enough to trust to."[70] Moore's objects also may not continue to work. While the "Four Quartz Crystal Clocks" at this present moment "work well," they are very delicate, and that poem ends with an image of the continued inexorable approach of the future, with a depiction of Jupiter enforcing the coming of each day over his own father, Chronos, whose thwarted cannibalism of his children was an attempt to stop time by preventing his children from succeeding him.[71]

And as philosophers of science have continued to write about mechanisms, they have not denied their unreliability. Peter Machamer, Lindley Darden, and Carl F. Craver, in an influential article, write, straightforwardly, "In many fields of science what is taken to be a satisfactory explanation requires providing a description of a mechanism."[72] Expecting explanations to rely on laws is, inverting Hempel's stance, "problematic,"[73] but not because mechanisms are always reliable; they are not: "Mechanisms are regular in that they work always or for the most part in the same way under the same conditions."[74] Nonetheless, "We should not be tempted to follow Hume and later logical empiricists into thinking that the intelligibility of activities (or mechanisms) is reducible to their regularity."[75]

Moore's animals most clearly dramatize the impossibility of preparing for the unknown, but Moore's attention to the problem of prediction extends further. And by recognizing that she's not confined to zoology but is rather paying attention to consistent functioning, to mechanisms, by including the working of mechanical and aesthetic objects, then the epistemological issue at stake in her poetry comes into clearer focus. Moore writes about how animals, machines, and art all work in a continuous present, but this tense does not imply certain knowledge of the future, or even a future. In many poems, Moore carefully stops at the immediate moment and, like the pangolin, doesn't feel completely confident that tomorrow, in all its newness, will resemble today.

HOW MOORE WORKS

Scholars and critics who write about Moore frequently describe a particular set of strategies that comprise what can be called *Moore's* excellence, her splendor: what makes Moore's poems function, what makes them continue to work so that they endure a century later. Roughly, many of these strategies fall into two categories: her descriptive precision and her collage poetics.[76]

Moore is widely understood as describing expertly, exactly, precisely. Her poetry has long been noted for what she calls in "An Octopus," a "capacity for fact."[77] Wallace Stevens wrote in an essay on "He 'Digesteth Harde Yron,'" "this poem has an extraordinarily factual appearance."[78] This description of Moore as an exact collector or describer continues: in the introduction to *Twenty-First Century Marianne Moore*, Elizabeth Gregory and Stacy Carson Hubbard write, "One might say that the title of Moore's first authorized book, *Observations*, aptly names all of her poems, which simultaneously offer commentary and teach us to see anew."[79] The account of Moore as fussily preoccupied with factual details is obviously gendered, as Natalia Cecire discusses in her article "Marianne Moore's Precision" and also in her book *Experimental*. In the earlier article, Cecire writes, "Precision is perhaps the most widely agreed-upon feature of Moore's poetics,"[80] and she quotes Bonnie Costello, Evelyn Feldman, Michael Barsanti, and Robin Schulze characterizing Moore's exact descriptions in almost identical language. In her later book, she develops her reading of Moore's precision as an "epistemic virtue."[81]

The other common account of Moore's method is that her poems collect and juxtapose. Moore's poetics has been described as curatorial and influenced by the Museum of Natural History, and also classificatory, influenced by the Dewey Decimal System. (The Rosenbach Museum and Library, which houses Moore's archives, has permanently installed her Greenwich Village living room on its third floor, including over 2,500 personal objects.) Here, too, there is some sexist grumbling about how Moore's collections are amateurish, as Dan Chiasson has noted;[82] as just one example, Robert Bly writes that her poetry is "knickknacks carefully arranged" in "a treasure-house—a feminine one."[83] But the description still holds. Johnson writes about the incongruity of what Moore chooses to include: "Moore's collection of quotations resembles a magpie's nest more than a traditional list of prior greatest hits ready to be used in allusions."[84] Roger Gilbert reframes her selections and groupings of details and quotations as an "array of techniques" that "confer categorical status on a series of instances that initially appear as pure parataxis."[85]

This second account of Moore's poetry, the account of her form as collecting, sits easily with the first account of her content of precise descriptions. One can move in either direction from form to content or back: Moore's investment in imagery grows until it accumulates into a form akin to a *wunderkammer* that includes imagery quoted from other texts, or Moore's investment in the poetic form of collages requires the acquisition of vivid images for juxtaposition. In chapter 1, while discussing the poetry of Walt Whitman, I noted that there's no opposition between form and content in philosophic logic, and that the binary we've accepted as obvious in literary studies may (or need) not be.

So now, rather than identifying the exactness of Moore's imagery as the content of her collage poetics, or her form as its container, I want to note that if we don't think of one following the other, if we remember that content can be formal, we can recognize that both *factual precision* and *gathering together disparate facts* are aspects of the logical forms of inductive reasoning. This book's chapter on Walt Whitman described his enumeration as the latter, and chapter 2 argued that Emily Dickinson's analogies involved the former. I am not comparing Moore's poetic form to logical form the way that describing her poetics as collage or curatorial implicitly compares them to other media and practices; I am saying that Moore's form *is* logical, and so already involves the content. Inductive reasoning, we might say, *also* has a capacity for fact; it connects empirical facts, and the more, and more precise, the better. Inductive reasoning's logical forms require the empirical observations of particulars, then the development of a working theory that, by looking at those particulars together, offers predictive power.

By describing Moore's precision and her collecting as different facets or moments of the same story of how her poems model inductive reasoning, we can do more than merely link together what's been identified as her poems' frequent form and content—we can also do better at reading other aspects and characteristics of her poetry. For example, her descriptions are known for their precision, and yet her collage poetics veer toward eclectic miscellany. Even if one disregards the blatant sexism of comparing her poems to attics full of forgotten tchotchkes, Johnson's description of her poems as akin to a "magpie's nest" sticks because Moore's selections *are* surprising. While there's no contradiction between precision and eclecticism, there is some contrast in these most common stories about Moore's methods. But inductive logical forms are both precise and inconsistent. The particulars they gather are empirical, the premises may be extremely clear and detailed—but the conclusions, the more abstract working theories, have an inherent capriciousness in their unreliability. Their predictive power can easily go rogue.

By thinking of Moore's poetics as attentive to this uncertain predictability, to how things have always worked and how they might not work in the future, we can connect another characteristic aspects of Moore's poetics: dramatic enjambments. Her lines and line endings are usually understood in the context of her use of syllabic verse, which Moore used in 1924's *Observations* and in the great poems published in the mid-1930s, and which remains "Moore's recognized signature."[86] If a line must end after a certain number of syllables, it is to be expected and yet also often creates surprising, even vertiginous, enjambments. Moore, as she said in her well-known *Paris Review* interview with Donald Hall, would write one stanza and then would "try to have successive stanzas identical with the first."[87] The result is that the poem "maintain[s] the syllabic count of its linescheme through grammatical sequences that are independent of the design, often startlingly so."[88] In other words, her stanzaic forms themselves are "mechanical" in that they work as they always have in the past, even as that specific action veers closer and closer to being puzzling or untenable.

We can see how this works in the "The Fish," which is typical in that Moore's enjambments are expected because of the poem's syllabic meter, and yet also jarring, increasingly so as the poem unrolls and each successive stanza's syllabic pattern must repeat the first. The title itself is enjambed with the first line: "The Fish//wade/through black jade."[89] A little later in the poem, Moore stretches prepositional phrases across first a line break—"the side/of the wave"—and then a stanza break—"the submerged shafts of the//sun."[90] The phrase—"of the"—breaks differently each time, first before, then after, first at the beginning of a line, then at its end:

> The barnacles, which encrust the side
> of the wave, cannot hide
>   there, for the submerged shafts of the sun,
>
> split like spun
>   glass, move themselves with spotlight swiftness
>   into the crevices—[91]

As the poem continues, the enjambments assert increasing dramatic force. Moore splits a line across a hyphen:

> pink
> rice-grains, ink-
>   bespattered jellyfish, crabs like green[92]

And then, turning the dial to eleven, Moore splits a single word across two lines:

> All
> external
>   marks of abuse are present on this
>   defiant edifice—
>   all the physical features of
>
> ac-
> cident—lack
>   of cornice, dynamite grooves, burns, and

> hatchet strokes, these things stand
>> out on it; the chasm-side is
>
> dead.[93]

The bifurcating of "accident" is shocking. Its intensity overshadows even the stanza break "is//dead," which in another poem would have risked hamminess. Hugh Kenner wrote that Moore's line endings—in this poem in particular—display "implacable arbitrariness."[94] This description risks self-contradiction: can something be rigidly haphazard or inflexibly capricious? Yes: this is exactly how the ostrich, the clocks, and Moore's poetic form itself works. They are both implacable in continuing as they always have, consistently. As it sometimes turns out, they may appear arbitrary to onlookers, and their behavior may someday, inconsistently, no longer work in the way it once did.

Moore's formal poetics can be read broadly as explorations of logical predictability. Other scholars have written about Moore's interest in "conscientious inconsistency," as she calls it in "The Mind is an Enchanting Thing."[95] Cliff Mak compares her poetry to slapstick films that offer an "alternative logic of failure."[96] He focuses on syllabic meter, writing that it "provided Moore with a way to re-conceive of language as entirely malleable, fluid, and unpredictable" that "allowed her to dramatize the slapstick physics of her ever-falling, ever-failing social ethics."[97] And Moore's enjambments exceed the accounts that tether them to her use of syllabic verse. While preset numbers of syllables in a line can create abrupt line endings, Moore did not exclusively use syllabics and has cliff's-edge enjambments in many poems. Cecire notes, "many of Moore's most important poems ... are written in free verse, and many others ... were at first written in syllabic stanzas but were soon revised into free verse."[98] Pushing back against the equation of Moore's precision to her use of "the fussy, obsessive counting" associated with syllabic meter,[99] Cecire writes, "Moore's precision has often been located in her form, which is in turn often reduced to her use of 'syllabics,' as if the mere presence of poetic meter were unusual in a poem, and as if syllabic meter were the defining feature of Moore's poetics. Yet as a gloss for 'precision,' formal regularity has little explanatory power."[100]

Indeed, in "The Pangolin," which is written in free verse, Moore has enjambments every bit as dramatic as those in "The Fish." Only one-third of the poem's nearly one hundred lines are end-stopped, and the enjambments immediately pile up, line lapping line, at the poem's beginning:

> Another armored animal–scale
> > lapping scale with spruce-cone regularity until they
> form the uninterrupted central
> > tail-row![101]

The poem splits a hyphenated compound adjective—"the fragile grace of the Thomas-/of-Leighton Buzzard Westminster Abbey wrought-iron/vine"—and, as in "The Fish," a single word is split for an enjambment across a stanza break:

> > Pangolins are not aggressive animals; between
> > dusk and day they have the not unchain-like machine-like
> > > form and frictionless creep of a thing
> > > > made graceful by adversities, con-

versities.[102]

There's a pun here, of course—by splitting off the prefix "con" from "versities," Moore is calling attention to this verse as verse. How the pangolin moves forward—"form and frictionless creep"—is also how the poem moves forward. Both are made graceful, foot by foot, by the difficulties of carrying on.

The pangolin's form is described as "machine-like," and it's striking that multiple scholars—while describing other aspects of Moore's work—describe her poetry as machine-like. Margaret Holley's 1984 essay on Moore's syllabic verse argued that her poems were developed by both "organic and mechanical modes";[103] as Moore claimed never to " 'plan' a stanza" but then would have other stanzas mechanically follow the syllabic line lengths of the first.[104] Mak quotes Kenner on Buster Keaton and applies it to Moore: "Moore, in the repose of her factual precision, is not far from this idiosyncratic comic lineage. As much as Keaton's films, her poetry might be described as 'study after study of moral imperturbability trapped by mechanism.'"[105] And Cecire writes that her precision aesthetics should be understood as "embodying the aesthetics of the machine."[106] Her poems work, and they work as they always have. How do they work? Machine-like. We might say that her mechanisms, the things she always does, the things that have always worked, are having mechanisms. We may never be able to have laws that are dependable, but we still can feel hopeful that what has worked in the past will work in the future.

GRACE NOTES

So far, I've talked about how the future is contingent for animals, machines, and aesthetic objects. The future is also contingent for humans. By this I mean the obvious, at every register from tripping on a shoelace to climate change. Earlier, I argued that when Moore notes that, without inductive reasoning, "Your life would be one of chaos. Life of an abs. irrational creature." We, like the pangolin, are also armored animals; the poem begins by implicitly comparing the pangolin to us. What counts as rational is not so clear, though. It's also not clear for humans how we should prepare for an unpredictable future. What is our excellence?

Earlier I wrote that James does not *solve* the problem of induction, but *dissolves* it. He does not engage with it; he escapes it. Ludwig Wittgenstein takes up that same move in the *Philosophical Investigations*, in which he dissolves one philosophical problem after another. For Wittgenstein, the real aim of philosophy is exactly that kind of escape from the problems that philosophers have constructed by using language badly, and so he tries "to shew the fly the way out of the fly-bottle."[107] But one of Wittgenstein's most famous interpreters, Stanley Cavell, uses this same move again and he does it a bit differently. Cavell takes up the Cartesian problem of other minds—the epistemological uncertainty that we can ever *know* that another person is real—and shows that one can escape from this problem by realizing that the problem is in the wrongheaded use of certain terms. Cavell argues that we should offer, and seek, not *knowledge* of others but *acknowledgment* of them.[108] But—and this is as important for me as his revelatory reframing of our relationships to others as one of ethics rather than one of epistemology—he insists on "the truth of skepticism."[109] Being skeptical of another person is a tragedy but not exactly an intellectual error; it has a logic.[110] Usually Cavell's central argument is presented the other way around—the skeptic who says that she cannot *know* that other people are real is not making a solipsistic mistake; the truth of skepticism is a devastating problem from which, if one accepts its terms, there is no escape; the response is not a *solution* to it, but a *stance*—so the emphasis is on the humane reframing of knowledge into acknowledgment. But part of Cavell's remarkable great-heartedness is in the honoring of skepticism's truth *also*, that skepticism is not merely, as in Wittgenstein's words, an "illusion." Othello is not stupid in being taken in by Iago, as Cavell writes about in the remarkable last pages of *The Claim of Reason*.[111] For contrast, look at Richard Rorty, one of pragmatism's more recent standard-bearers, Cavell's contemporary, and, in many ways, his foil. Rorty writes in a review of *The Claim of Reason* that Cavell exaggerates the importance of skepticism: "He *takes for granted* that the 'philosophical problems' with which we infect freshman by assigning Descartes and Berkeley are something the freshman really needs—not just so that he can understand history, but so that he can be in touch with himself, with his own humanity."[112] For Rorty, "our inability to say what would count as confirming or disconfirming a given solution to a problem is a reason for setting the problem aside."[113]

In Moore's poetry, we see her turn over again and again an epistemological problem that grows out of Enlightenment empiricism—not that of other minds but that first horn of the problem of induction. She does not escape it; she does not set it aside; it never fades to an illusion to her. Nor does she solve it. Like Cavell does, she finds a stance toward the problem, an adequate response to it. We see it most clearly in "The Pangolin," where she names it *grace*. The quality of grace is produced when something or someone continues its work even in the face of contingency, when one knows that the world is inconsistent but acts as if it weren't. It is our human excellence.

In "The Pangolin," Moore uses the word *grace* seven times. Moore describes the pangolin as having the "the fragile grace of the Thomas-/of-Leighton Buzzard Westminster Abbey wrought-iron vine," referring to a thirteenth-century ironworker named Thomas from the town of Leighton Buzzard, known for his work on Queen Eleanor of Castile's tomb in Westminster Abbey. The pangolin's tail is a "graceful tool, as a prop or hand or broom or ax." As Srikanth Reddy notes, "One critical approach to reading this text construes religious grace as the author's true subject."[114] Reddy disagrees on the grounds that "To interpret a poem as employing animals as a pretext for exploring religious matters or human nature is to classify it as an allegory or a fable,"[115] and the poem itself describes those who think a pangolin is "a living fable" as "simpletons."[116] Reddy argues instead that Moore shows how "this concept might continue to signify across a variety of segregated disciplines."[117]

Moore then seems to leave the anteater behind completely as she launches into a very long and complex rhetorical question about grace and its different meanings by imagining the construction of a medieval cathedral:

> To explain grace requires
>   a curious hand. If that which is at all were not forever,
> why would those who graced the spires
>   with animals and gathered there to rest, on cold luxurious
>   low stone seats——a monk and monk and monk——between the thus
>   ingenious roof supports, have slaved to confuse
>   grace with a kindly manner, time in which to pay a debt,
>   the cure for sins, a graceful use
>   of what are yet
>   approved stone mullions branching out across
>   the perpendiculars?[118]

"To explain grace requires/a curious hand": this is the infinitive statement just before the long rhetorical question. It is confusing—in Moore's Presbyterian church, grace is necessarily causeless and therefore resistant to explanation—so how could one, then, explain grace? Reddy calls it "an uncertain proof," because it is "wary of dogma and doctrine," but argues that it works via philology: the monks "confused/grace" by "fusing together various segregated fields of human activity under the rubric of a single term" and so "anatomiz[ing] a concept."[119] In other words, for Reddy, Moore *does* explain grace, but does so inductively, through far-flung examples alone. In chapter 3, I wrote that Stein uses explanation as a case study to insist that we can say why things happen using only the particularity of our own experiences. Moore, like Stein, is not explaining as much as writing about what might count as an explanation, and like Stein, as Reddy writes, she offers not an abstract large-scale law or theory, not a dogma or doctrine, that would underwrite deductive certainty, but only particulars. Unlike Stein, though, Moore does not insist that explanations based on inductive reasoning work as well or better than those based on deduction. Rather, even if explanations based on inductive reasoning are the best option, they're still not an ideal one, and this is a problem, both intellectually and emotionally. One might be able to explain this way and it might work, since it has in the past. But it also might not. If it does, if it succeeds, that's grace—a debt has not been called in, not yet, and also the stone mullions have held so far—but for Moore, the best example of grace is living with the uncertainty. Grace describes movement, even the sense of movement, and specifically the movement of being consistent in an inconsistent world.

Monk and monk and monk: it's an earlier version of the line from the end: "new and new and new." Monks follow monks, generations after generations, for the many centuries that it takes to build a cathedral. And grace is grace is grace, whether it's biomechanical, aesthetic, ethical, religious, or architectural. Just in this passage, grace is decorative art—adorning spires with gargoyles—and it is also generous, "a kindly manner"—and the grace period of repayment. It is the "cure for sins"—the grace of God (Moore was raised in the household of her Presbyterian minister grandfather)—and also the skilled engineering behind the support of window transoms—"stone mullions."

The point of this rhetorical question is *why*—"If that which is at all were not forever,/why"—*why* do the monks purposefully conflate the different meanings of grace? They "slaved to confuse" them. Why? What is an explanation for this behavior? Because, Moore suggests, the understanding of grace as meaning beauty, kindness, mercy, salvation, and design, is at the root of their belief that the things they make and do may last into the future. Grace branches out across the perpendiculars; like a flying buttress, it supports impossible weight: the weight that this belief is not false, though it's impossible to justify, no matter how many examples one assembles.

We can't justify the expectation of the sun's rising every day just because it always has. We can't explain it by describing its past behavior; it rises "new and new and new." Grace, we could say, describes a stance toward demands for justification: not that they're irrelevant, or incorrect, but just unanswerable. They're to be lived with, or maybe within, but not completely without. Often conditions are described as *necessary but not sufficient*, and we might say that grace is *sufficient but never necessary*. The pangolin has the "form and frictionless creep of a thing/made graceful by adversities, con// versities."[120] Grace, Moore tells us, is grace-under-pressure, and the pressure is the feeling of contingency, the awareness of inconsistency, the knowledge that things may not last, the hope they will, the joy when they do, the acceptance when they don't. (Can I call the monks' attitude not a humane pessimism but a superhuman one?)

The unreliability, the unpredictability, the unknowable and inexplicable and unjustifiable causes are real, and they cause real difficulty. But grace, as a term, is how one moves on and forward anyway. It's another way of identifying the same problem that Hume does, but of not being trapped by it while also not fully escaping from it. It denies its devastating power without refusing its grasp. And the "curious hand" that can explain grace is not the monks'—not the human hand—but the unusual hand of the pangolin, who we are told walks "peculiarly, that the outside/edges of his hands may bear the weight."[121] Open to the chance that the sun might not rise, steadied when it does; recognizing the dawn as grace makes the pangolin graceful. There is no solution to the problem of induction, but grace is a term that describes moving through the world peculiarly, and so bearing the weight.

Chapter Five

COHERENCE AND ELIZABETH BISHOP

COMPLETE COMPREHENSION

In Elizabeth Bishop's poem "The Fish," the speaker tells a fish story: one that starts small and spirals out as it grows larger and larger.[1]

> I caught a tremendous fish
> and held him beside the boat
> half out of water, with my hook
> fast in a corner of his mouth.
> He didn't fight.
> He hadn't fought at all.
> He hung a grunting weight,
> battered and venerable
> and homely. Here and there
> his brown skin hung in strips
> like ancient wallpaper,
> and its pattern of darker brown
> was like wallpaper:
> shapes like full-blown roses
> stained and lost through age.
> He was speckled with barnacles,

fine rosettes of lime,
and infested
with tiny white sea-lice,
and underneath two or three
rags of green weed hung down.
While his gills were breathing in
the terrible oxygen
—the frightening gills,
fresh and crisp with blood,
that can cut so badly—
I thought of the coarse white flesh
packed in like feathers,
the big bones and the little bones,
the dramatic reds and blacks
of his shiny entrails,
and the pink swim-bladder
like a big peony.[2]

The speaker assigns the fish a pronoun and proceeds to catalogue his exterior appearance: his "grunting weight," "his brown skin hung in strips," his scales "speckled with barnacles,/fine rosettes of lime,/and infested/with tiny white sea-lice."

And then there is what appears to be a description of the fish's insides:

the coarse white flesh
packed in like feathers,
the big bones and the little bones,
the dramatic reds and blacks
of his shiny entrails,
and the pink swim-bladder
like a big peony.

It's remarkably easy to forget, precisely because of the vividness of this imagery, that this account of the fish's tissues and organs is *not* a description. The speaker cannot describe observing the fish's flesh, bones, or entrails because she never sees inside this fish—she throws it back into the water whole and living at the end of the poem. Rather, the speaker says, "*I thought of* the coarse white flesh." This account of the tremendous fish's insides, then, is not a moment of literally looking at the fish. It's a moment of thinking about, of metaphorically looking into it. It's not a description of what she can see, nor is it imagination, which, as Shakespeare says, "bodies forth the forms of things unknown."[3] It's inference; from what Bishop's speaker can observe of the fish's outward appearance, and what she knows about fish anatomy, she infers about this fish's internal organs and muscles.[4]

Inference is the process by which we reason from what is true to what else is true; it's the foundation of logical reasoning. What does inductive inference about the fish offer Bishop's speaker? Not prediction, nor knowledge, nor mastery, nor security, as for Walt Whitman, Emily Dickinson, Gertrude Stein, and Marianne Moore. Rather, for Bishop, it leads to coherence: a powerful enough inference can make everything fit together. And when everything fits together, everything is comprehensible. The poem ends:

> I stared and stared
> and victory filled up
> the little rented boat,
> from the pool of bilge
> where oil had spread a rainbow
> around the rusted engine
> to the bailer rusted orange,
> the sun-cracked thwarts,
> the oarlocks on their strings,
> the gunnels—until everything
> was rainbow, rainbow, rainbow!
> And I let the fish go.[5]

Bishop's speaker looks, and looks into, until, in a transcendent moment, "Everything/was rainbow, rainbow, rainbow!" That thrice-repeated "rainbow" overwhelms the reader, with its perfect rhyme with "go," making a neat final couplet. But the rainbow saturates the sight because it brings "everything" together: the air and the water, the speaker and the fish. "Everything" rhymes on "strings," and it ties up the poem's conceptual loose strings: the fishing line can be released because the physical possession of the fish is insignificant compared to the way the fish is caught in and by the speaker's sense of how everything coheres.

In this chapter, I'll argue that Elizabeth Bishop's poetics, like the other poets I've discussed in this book, are shaped by her attention to reasoning. But rather than use the forms of induction and face the problem of induction, Bishop uses another form of nondeductive logic—inference to the best explanation, which is also known as abduction. Like those of inductive reasoning, abductive inferences are non-necessary—it is not necessarily the case that if the premises are true, the conclusion is also true—but abduction does not oppose deduction as much as invert it or even co-opt it through its prioritization of explanation. In this chapter, I'll show that Bishop similarly prioritizes inferences that promise large-scale understanding, or what she calls in "Arrival at Santos," "complete comprehension."[6] By recognizing Bishop's use of this philosophic form, by recognizing her adaptation of it into a poetic form, we can see that her poems are not just illustrating philosophy's abstractions with the richness of poetic example, but are themselves doing philosophic work.

INFERENCE

Throughout her career, Bishop offers images of how nondeductive inference works and the powerful understanding it promises. I'll provide a brief, whirlwind survey here, with the promise to return to some of these poems later in this chapter. "The Fish" is just one example of how Bishop repeatedly depicts a speaker inferring about a hidden interior of an object or place based on what she can see of the exterior.[7] Early in Bishop's career, in "The Monument," the speaker wonders what is inside the stacked wooden boxes of the mysterious monument:

> It may be solid, may be hollow.
> The bones of the artist-prince may be inside
> or far away on even drier soil.
> But roughly but adequately it can shelter
> what is within (which after all
> cannot have been intended to be seen).[8]

COHERENCE AND ELIZABETH BISHOP

In the middle of Bishop's career, in the poems written in Brazil while living with her longtime partner Lota de Macedo Soares, her speakers desire to peer into the opaque Amazonian rainforest. In "Arrival at Santos," her speaker looks out at the Brazilian coastline, identifying what she can see—"Here is a coast; here is a harbor," alongside churches and warehouses—and noting what she can't see without "driving to" it—"the interior." She mocks herself:

> Oh, tourist,
> is this how this country is going to answer you
>
> and your immodest demands for a different world,
> and a better life, and complete comprehension
> of both at last, and immediately,
> after eighteen days of suspension?[9]

Another poem about arrival on the Brazilian coast rewinds several centuries and casts the drive to the interior as sexual violence. "Brazil, January 1, 1502" begins by comparing Bishop's contemporary Brazil to the Brazil she imagines Europeans seeing upon their arrival hundreds of years before:

Januaries, Nature greets our eyes
exactly as she must have greeted theirs:
every square inch filling in with foliage—
big leaves, little leaves, and giant leaves,
blue, blue-green, and olive,
with occasional lighter veins and edges,
or a satin under leaf turned over;
monster ferns
in silver-gray relief,
and flowers, too, like giant water lilies
up in the air—up, rather, in the leaves—
purple, yellow, two yellows, pink,
rust red and greenish white;
solid but airy; fresh as if just finished
and taken off the frame.[10]

The poem ends, after this catalogue of leaves and petals, with parallel images of the violation of the forest and assault of its inhabitants:

> they ripped away into the hanging fabric,
> each out to catch an Indian for himself—
> those maddening little women who kept calling,
> calling to each other (or had the birds waked up?)
> and retreating, always retreating, behind it.[11]

The native women are unreachable—at least for a time—behind the abundance of visible foliage that hides them in the invisible interior of the forest. Their presence is inferred, but they cannot be seen any more than the "artist-prince" of "The Monument."[12]

Later in Bishop's life, as an image of what can only be inferred about and not seen firsthand, she substitutes for the Brazilian rainforest the woods of the American Northeast. For example, in "The Moose," the speaker cannot see into "the impenetrable wood" from which the moose appears and into which she disappears.[13] In "Cape Breton," her speaker desires to see into the interior of a landscape, but cannot:

> Whatever the landscape had of meaning appears to have been abandoned,
> unless the road is holding it back, in the interior,
> where we cannot see.[14]

Houses are also impenetrable, or, as she writes in "Sestina," "inscrutable."[15] In the poem "The End of March" the speaker remembers a boarded-up beach shack. She infers based on the exterior about what the interior must be like:

> There must be a stove; there *is* a chimney,
> askew, but braced with wires,
> and electricity, possibly
> —at least, at the back another wire
> limply leashes the whole affair
> to something off behind the dunes.[16]

Due to the stove, she could make "*a grog a l'américaine*," and because there's a wire, there must be "A light to read by—perfect!"[17] In "Filling

Station," the speaker wonders if the filling station is also a house—"Do they live in the station?" she asks about the "Father" and "greasy sons"— and observes the "cement porch" and its furnishings, but no further.[18]

Sometimes Bishop's speakers try to see the physical insides not of animals, objects, forests, or houses, but the nonphysical emotional and psychological interiority of *people*. She desires to see what lies within her beloved's heart in "O Breath" in nearly anatomical terms. In the first ten lines of this near-sonnet, the speaker examines the skin of her lover's chest, unable to see the heart moving within:

> Beneath that loved   and celebrated breast,
> silent, bored really   blindly veined,
> grieves, maybe,   lives and lets
> live, passes   bets,
> something moving   but invisibly,
> and with what clamor   why restrained
> I cannot fathom   even a ripple.[19]

The speaker wants to "fathom" her lover's heart to know if it beats for her, if her love is "equivocal" or "equivalent."[20] And, famously, in "In the Waiting Room," her young speaker tries to look into herself:

> But I felt: you are an *I*,
> you are an *Elizabeth*,
> you are one of *them*.
> *Why* should you be one, too?
> I scarcely dared to look
> to see what it was I was.
> I gave a sidelong glance
> —I couldn't look any higher—"[21]

The speaker is not asking about her "big bones and the little bones" but she is inferring about her own interior, her own identity, based on what she can observe of "boots, hands, the family voice/I felt in my throat."[22]

This first point—that Bishop infers about what can't be seen rather than merely describing what can—cuts against the oldest account of her poetics. Traditionally, Bishop has been described as "all eye," a poet whose work is comprised of meticulous observations, a poet who looks at the world with a keen gaze. David Kalstone titled his 1970 review of her *Complete Poems* "All Eye."[23] Robert Lowell, introducing Bishop at a poetry reading, called her "the famous eye."[24] Randall Jarrell writes, "All her poems have written underneath, *I have seen it*."[25] This outdated and obviously gendered characterization of Bishop as a describer has been pushed against for the last several decades by critics who argue that her gaze is skeptical,[26] ironic,[27] willful and controlling,[28] and more. Nearly as long as this account of Bishop has existed, it has also been resisted. Lee Edelman, in his 1985 essay on "In the Waiting Room," writes about how Bishop "encouraged . . . misreadings by characterizing her poetry as 'just description,'" and that her poetry anticipates those misreadings and even courts them as an evasive strategy.[29] More recently, Gillian White, Claire Seiler, and Zachariah Pickard all recast the long-standing account of Bishop as a describer.[30] But even on a more basic level: while identifying Bishop as the writer of brilliant descriptions does have some truth to it, it's wrong on its face: Randall Jarrell says that Bishop's poems claim the authority of witness—"I have seen it"—*but she hasn't seen it*. Her speakers fail or choose not to see the inside of the fish, the monument, the forest, the beach shack, her beloved's chest, or themselves.

My argument that Bishop uses inference rather than relying on description also cuts against a more recent characterization. In the last several decades as Bishop's poetry has become enshrined in syllabi and anthologies, critics have written about what they describe as her modesty and restraint."[31] In 2006, *The New York Times*'s David Orr described her as "withholding."[32] The Irish novelist Colm Tóibín, in his 2015 book on Bishop's poetry, also uses the word "withholding."[33] These comments are meant as praise, but this characterization of Bishop as restrained, modest, and withholding is frustrating, partly in its contradiction with the earlier characterization of her as "all eye"—if she's an excellent describer, what exactly is being withheld?—and it is also still gendered. (No one praises the William Carlos Williams poem often titled "The Red Wheelbarrow" for being "withholding," though he never tells us what exactly depends upon it.)[34] And yet the characterization of Bishop's poetry as withholding also has some truth. There *is* something held back from readers. But attributing it to Bishop's sense of propriety falls flat. Even though Bishop was not a confessional poet, she was not prim. Her falling out with Marianne Moore was catalyzed by Bishop insisting on using the term "water closet" in the poem "Roosters." Nor is it as simple as identifying her as closeted: her queerness, and her complicated feelings about coming out as gay, may be of a piece with her poetics, but a biographical explanation alone does not suffice.[35] We might imagine that Bishop could tell us what she is withholding, that she could come out with it, come out of it. But what I will argue in this chapter is that she can't—not that she won't, but that she can't—because her poems model the very problem of *not* being able to see inside, and therefore needing to infer rather than being able to know. Bishop isn't the one withholding something from her readers. She is showing us what is withheld from her, and all of us, and how we reason about what we don't know and can't see.

And finally, this argument reframes the existing scholarly conversation about Bishop and philosophy. One group of scholars who read Bishop's poetry alongside philosophy describe her as a pragmatist, and the other group as a skeptic. The description of Bishop as a pragmatist has some obvious force: Bishop was good friends with the pragmatist philosopher John Dewey's daughter, Jane, and met Jane's famous father when all three were living in Key West; they all stayed close for decades.[36] In a letter to Marianne Moore the day after meeting Dewey in 1939, Bishop asked which book of Dewey's she should read.[37] Moore's answer is not preserved, and though there is no record of Bishop having read any of Dewey's philosophy, we know that her Boston apartment in the 1970s included a "six foot section of philosophy,"[38] including four books by Dewey.[39] Bishop writes in a letter to Anne Stevenson, "Another friend who influenced me—*not* with his books but with his character—was John Dewey, whom I knew well and was very fond of."[40] This compliment hints at familiarity with Dewey's work, particularly with his central claim that scientific inquiry is not different in kind than the inquiries we conduct in our daily lives, and that these inquiries are conducted through detailed attention to experience. Dewey writes in *The Structure of Experience*, "Inquiry, in spite of the diverse subjects to which it applies, and the consequent diversity of its special techniques has a common structure or pattern: that this common structure is applied both in common sense and science."[41] For both the expert and the layman, all inquiry starts and ends in empirical experience:

> This experienced material is the same for the scientific man and the man in the street . . . stars, rocks, trees, and creeping things are the same material

of experience for both. These commonplaces . . . indicate that experience, if scientific inquiry is justified, is no infinitesimally thin layer or foreground of nature, but that it penetrates into it, reaching down into its depths, and in such a way that its grasp is capable of expansion; it tunnels in all directions and in so doing brings to the surface things at first hidden—as miners pile high on the surface of the earth treasures brought from below.[42]

Dewey's imagery of vines and pillars and the colloquial but consonance- and assonance-heavy list of "stars, rocks, trees, and creeping things" would not be out of place in a Bishop poem. The inquirer, whether scientist or layman, desires more than to understand only the "infinitesimally thin layer or foreground of nature."[43] Moreover, Dewey argues, the artist does the same type of activity as the scientific or lay inquirer: "The odd notion that an artist does not think and a scientific inquirer does nothing else is the result of converting a difference of tempo and emphasis into a difference in kind."[44]

Victoria Harrison and Frances Dickey both interpret Bishop's poetry in light of her probable reading of Dewey's epistemology. They sharply disagree over Dewey's—and, as a result, Bishop's—realism, the commitment to discovering truth. Harrison argues (through a reading of Richard Rorty's neo-pragmatism) that "Dewey articulated for the modern American period a vision that had its roots in Emersonian thinking and found its way into the poetic practice of such twentieth-century poets as Frost, Stevens, and, I will argue, Elizabeth Bishop."[45] This vision, as Harrison quotes Rorty, includes "a thorough-going abandonment of the notion of discovering the truth which is common to theology and science."[46] Harrison's Dewey and her Bishop resemble Rorty in being anti-realist pragmatists who have "no method for knowing when one has reached the truth, or when one is closer to it than before."[47] Dickey directly opposes this interpretation of Dewey and of Bishop, writing, that "although Dewey may doubt the existence of *unrevisable* truths, his approach by no means denies the possibility of accuracy. . . . Our only access to knowledge about the world must be through our inferences from evidence, and we revise those conclusions as new evidence presents itself. . . . Bishop's interest in Dewey, then, does not make her antirealist."[48] For Dickey, Bishop's process reflects Dewey's realism and commitment to the scientific method: "There are at least two distinct versions of pragmatism. . . . Rorty's *antirealist* pragmatism and a *realist* pragmatist philosophy committed to a model of knowledge based on scientific inquiry. Bishop's poetry, I propose, is more in keeping with this second—but historically first—kind of philosophy."[49] Inferences are, according to Dickey, "the first step toward contact with the world" and one uses "evidence to confirm or correct the truth of one's inferences."[50]

But describing Bishop as a skeptic also makes sense; she often does not seem to have confidence in her inferences. Though Jarrell said Bishop's "poems have written underneath, *I have seen it*,"[51] the poet Gibbons Ruark points out, "If all of her poems have written underneath 'I have seen it,' underneath that is written, 'and I can't be sure what it was.'"[52] V. Joshua Adams calls Bishop's poetry "a literary negotiation with skepticism."[53] Laurel Snow Corelle writes of Bishop, "She was committed to the position that some things are and should remain unknowable. And she abided in that stance."[54] Guy Rotella describes her skepticism as a result of her postmodernism, writing, "Skepticism about givens, about supposedly natural arrangements or authorities whose word is beyond question, is a characteristic feature of Bishop's response to things. It informs her poems, her conversations, her letters, and her childhood memoirs and stories."[55] Susan McCabe argues that Bishop "reminds us at every turn that we cannot know anything fully or absolutely,"[56] and Kirstin Hotelling Zona combines a reading of her restraint and her skepticism under a claim about "skepticism of the essential, coherent subject" and "distrust of the confessional lyric speaker."[57] Edelman writes about how "In the Waiting Room" "effectively positions itself to read its readers," as Bishop shows the "insufficiency of any mode of interpretation that claims to release the meaning it locates 'inside' a text by asserting its own ability to speak from a position of mastery 'outside' of it."[58] Other critics, such as Mutlu Konuk Blasing[59] and Margaret Dickie[60] write that Bishop is not interested in the truth but in how we construct our own perspectives. Thomas Gardner uses Bishop as his "first example of a poetry that is interested in, and increasingly takes place within, spaces where we live out what Stanley Cavell calls 'the truth of skepticism'— the fact that our placement in the world, our condition, is not guaranteed by knowing and is not marked by certainty. Her poems look closely at or acknowledge the limits of our drives to grasp or know or make a home; and they discover that such drives, once forced to operate without guarantees of mastery, are quite powerfully charged and frail and alive."[61] He describes Bishop not only as an outsider, but as a "squatter"—"without a home, without an explanatory sentence to rely on, the speaker discovers the world itself to be 'homely as a house.'"[62]

The significance of the distinction about whether Bishop is a pragmatist or skeptic has to do with whether her inferences lead her to truth. Pragmatists, generally, think that truth is available, if not stable, and skeptics usually disagree on both counts: truth is stable, but not necessarily available. But although Bishop's speakers usually infer what remains unseen, indescribable, and unknown, it does not necessarily follow that they think truth is unavailable. Bishop's speakers have no explanatory sentences to rely on, but they are in the business of making them. Their inferences aim at explanations and tack toward truth.

INFERENCE TO THE BEST EXPLANATION

So far I have described Bishop's inference as interested in trying to answer *what questions*: what is inside the fish, the monument, the forest, the beach shack, and even individual people. Here I'll expand and refine that claim to suggest that Bishop's speakers are interested in *what* as a means to discover *why*. By inferring what lies within or behind, the speakers of Bishop's poems are asking about the cause of the events or phenomena they observe; they are seeking explanations and the comprehension they provide. Why does the speaker of "The Fish" let the fish go? Because she has inferred and made everything cohere in rainbows.[63] In "The Monument," Bishop writes, "'Why did you bring me here to see it?'" and the answer must have to do with whatever is inside the monument.[64] The speaker of "In the Waiting Room" looks into herself because she is trying to answer the unanswerable question, "Why should I be my aunt,/or me, or anyone?"[65] Does any other poet include or allude to so many *why questions* as Bishop in such a comparatively small oeuvre? Even more: "Trouvée" is entirely built around the joke-question "Why did the chicken cross the road?"[66] Crusoe from "Crusoe in England" asks, "Was that why it rained so much?" and "Why didn't I know enough of something?"[67] The newly-formed community of the bus in "The Moose" asks, "Why, why do we feel/(we all feel) this sweet/sensation of joy?"[68] And perhaps most famously, the questions of "Filling Station:" "Why the extraneous plant?/Why the taboret?/Why, oh why, the doily?"[69]

A *why question* asks about causality; we can think about Aristotle's four causes here, but in modern philosophy, we usually think about explanation answering a question that starts *why?* In chapter 3, I argue that Gertrude Stein uses explanation as a case study to defend inductive reasoning. Stein insists, contra to philosophy of science's account of explanation, that, yes, one *can* explain without reference to general laws and based only on the particularity of individual experience. Bishop approaches the relationship of inference to explanation differently. Rather than defending inductive reasoning as the basis of an explanation and saying, like Stein, that laws or theories are unnecessary in order to explain why events and phenomena occur and that one should accept the resulting contingency of prediction as still preferable to deduction, Bishop rejects both laws and also contingency. Like Marianne Moore, as I argue in chapter 4, she is interested in how things work, and how to discover the reliable mechanisms that offer consistency, without relying on deductive reasoning.

Bishop's answer is a method of logical reasoning called inference to the best explanation.

Inference to the best explanation depends on individual experience and perspective, and is particularly relevant in analyzing causality, in reasoning about why events and phenomena occur. The philosopher Peter Lipton writes in his classic book *Inference to the Best Explanation*, "We are forever inferring and explaining, forming new beliefs about the way things are and explaining why things are as we have found them to be."[70] "Other familiar models of induction"[71] move from premises to a conclusion via, for example, enumeration or analogizing, by looking at one's own experience or at mechanisms, and then reasoning.[72] Unlike those traditional forms of induction, inference to the best explanation rotates the means and the ends of logic, and uses reasoning as the compass rather than the destination. Lipton writes: "According to Inference to the Best Explanation, we infer what would, if true, be the best explanation of our evidence. On this view, explanatory considerations are a guide to inference."[73] He elaborates this point: "Far from explanation only coming on the scene after the inferential work is done, the core idea of Inference to the Best Explanation is that explanatory considerations are a guide to inference."[74]

Inference to the best explanation is ampliative; like other forms of induction such as reasoning based on enumeration and analogical reasoning, conclusions contain information that isn't in the premises. I wrote that Bishop's speakers infer about *what* as a means to answer *why* and vice versa; Lipton puts it this way: "The explicit point of explaining is to understand *why* something is the case but, if Inference to the Best Explanation is correct, it is also an important tool for discovering *what* is the case."[75] While Stein was willing to accept contingency as the condition of inductive explanation, Lipton argues that's unnecessary: "the model offers a satisfying explanatory unification of our inductive and explanatory practices."[76]

Inference to the best explanation is the more contemporary term for what pragmatist C. S. Peirce called abduction (in contrast to induction and deduction), and which he described as the "process of forming explanatory hypotheses."[77] This stands in some contrast to how abduction is understood now—as inference to the best explanation, and inductive—and as assessing and justifying hypotheses rather than simply generating more of them.[78] Abduction is on ongoing topic in philosophy; while Bas C. van Fraassen argued in 1989's *Laws and Symmetry* that abductive reasoning is not reliable, a number of philosophers have recently argued that abduction, in Igor Douven's words, is "a cornerstone of scientific methodology."[79] It is of course also a central method in logic, in which it plays "a discreet but fundamental role," in Timothy Williamson's words.[80] Williamson also notes that Bertrand Russell describes abduction as induction when he writes, in 1907, "We tend to believe the premises because we can see that their consequences are true, instead of believing the consequences because we know the premises to be true. But the inferring of premises from consequences is the essence of induction; thus the method in investigating the principles of mathematics is really an inductive method, and is substantially the same as the method of discovering general laws in any other science."[81]

Although readers of this book may not be familiar with the term "inference to the best explanation" and perhaps initially thought "abduction" referred to kidnapping, everyone uses inference to the best explanation and probably just about every day.[82] A classic example of how inference to the best explanation works is the process of medical diagnosis: a patient presents observable symptoms and a doctor infers the invisible cause. The doctor probably does not gather every possible bit of data and generalize, nor invent analogies, nor extrapolate from their own experience, nor begin with biomechanics. Rather, the doctor reasons by selecting the diagnosis that would explain the most.[83] One of Lipton's central case studies is the process by which nineteenth-century Austro-Hungarian physician Ignaz Semmelweis theorized that medical students were infecting obstetric patients via cross-contamination—medical students dissected corpses and then attended women in labor without washing their hands—and the resulting infection was the cause of the high mortality rates from puerperal fever among women delivering in the First Clinic of the Vienna Hospital.

Bishop understood how diagnosis works and how powerful its explanations based on inference can be. She suffered from chronic eczema, asthma, bronchitis, depression, and alcoholism, along with other periodic ailments, and her letters are full of descriptions of coughs, rashes, and fevers.[84] And if an illness was not treatable, then the initial diagnosis became the final word. The most important example is the earliest in Bishop's biography: her mother was diagnosed as permanently insane when Bishop was five, and was confined to a hospital for the remainder of her life.[85] Bishop wrote a short story attributing the death of her childhood friend Gwendolyn to untreated diabetes; David Kalstone describes the story as "insist[ing], perhaps too rigorously, on causation and explanation."[86] When Bishop was six years old, living with her paternal grandparents in Worcester, she was diagnosed with "nervous illnesses," allergies, St. Vitus's Dance, and her first attacks of eczema and asthma.[87] "I felt myself aging, even dying,"[88] she wrote later, and eventually "even the Bishops conceded that Elizabeth was hopelessly unhappy in their house," a diagnosis that allowed her to live with her aunt Maud Boomer Shepherdson in Revere, Massachusetts.[89] In Aunt Maud's care, Bishop read Tennyson, Browning, Emerson, and Carlyle, and within two years of her "rescue," at age eight, began writing her own poetry and stories.[90] Another diagnosis, more than thirty years later, prompted another significant relocation: a few weeks into an around-the-world cruise, during a stop in Rio de Janeiro, Bishop was diagnosed with an allergic reaction to cashew fruit. Her acquaintance Lota de Macedo Soares nursed her over her slow recovery and then became her lover.

The process of diagnosis and the process of writing poetry have a tenuous but continuous biographical connection for Bishop, whose literary talents were crucially supported by the diagnoses that brought her to Aunt Maud and Lota. Her doctor, Anny Baumann, was also her dear friend and the dedicatee of her second book, *A Cold Spring*. Earlier in her life, Bishop herself had considered becoming a doctor rather than a poet, but was encouraged to commit to poetry by Marianne Moore.[91] Bishop repeatedly mentions her medical ambitions in later interviews, even claiming to have enrolled in Cornell's medical school, but given that she had never studied any math or science at Vassar aside from one semester of zoology, it seems unlikely that her interest in medicine was realistic, or even actually medical—she never mentions doctoring when she talks about almost having become a doctor, only that medicine would have been a practical skill and a reliable source of income.[92]

Is it too speculative to offer the idea that Bishop's interest in medicine also has to do with her desire to diagnose, to infer to the best explanation, to look into? Years after deciding against medicine in favor of poetry, Bishop saw an X-ray of Lota's grandchild in utero and could not shake the image from her imagination. As she wrote in a letter, "I have stolen the last x-ray of [the fetus], seated very neatly upside down, with semi-translucent bones, its little spine rather like a pearl necklace—towards the tail, at least,—perfectly beautiful."[93] She wanted to write a poem about it, but never completed it, but it sounds like it could have been not unlike "The Fish," with its "big bones and little bones."[94] Later in her life, after a former lover developed mental illness, Bishop "wrote out in great detail the 'evidence' for her diagnosis of Suzanne... She also used these letters to place this latest episode—her third lover to go mad before her eyes, and the fifth or sixth person if one includes her mother, Robert Lowell, and Margaret Miller—in a context or pattern in her life."[95] By diagnosing Suzanne, Bishop examined her own life, made some inferences, and diagnosed herself.

Bishop also diagnoses herself in her poems. "The Prodigal," written during the same stay at Yaddo as the asthmatically gasping "O Breath," identifies the cause of her alcoholism using "that spiritual exercise of the Jesuits—when they try to think in detail how the thing must have happened"[96] and settles on "one of my aunt's stepsons offered me a drink of rum, in the pigsties, at about nine in the morning."[97] The unpublished poem "A Drunkard," is more straightforward about diagnosing herself as an alcoholic and psychoanalytically inferring the cause of her illness as her mother's neglect; she writes "I was terribly thirsty but mama didn't hear/me calling her" . . .

> But since that night, that day, that reprimand
> that night that day that reprimand—
> I have suffered from abnormal thirst—
> I swear it's true—and by the age
> of twenty or twenty-one I had begun
> to drink, & drink—I can't get enough[98]

COHERENCE AND ELIZABETH BISHOP

And Bishop also diagnoses other people, including Ezra Pound in her poem "Visits to St. Elizabeths." When Bishop was the Poetry Consultant to the Library of Congress from 1949 to 1950, her unofficial duties included visiting Pound, at that time in his fourth year of imprisonment in St. Elizabeths Hospital. Diagnosing Pound had been an activity of both the legal court and the court of public opinion since he pled insanity in 1945 in order to escape a possible death sentence for treason. Seven years later, when Bishop was solicited for a collection of poetry honoring Pound, she contributed this poem, which suggests an invisible cause for Pound's visible condition. While Pound's *Cantos* are populated by heroes, kings, triumphant warriors, and noble sages, the figures populating Bishop's poem are not powerful, triumphant, or noble—they are the collaterally damaged.[99]

> This is the soldier home from the war.
> These are the years and the walls and the door
> that shut on the boy that pats the floor
> to see if the world is round or flat.
> This is a Jew in a newspaper hat
> that dances carefully down the ward,
> walking the plank of a coffin board
> with the crazy sailor
> that shows his watch
> that tells the time
> of the wretched man
> that lies in the house of Bedlam.[100]

Some critics have read this cast of characters as Pound's fellow inmates.[101] But there's a strikingly precise inverted contrast between the figures of "Visits to St. Elizabeths" and the figures of *The Cantos*. There is no heroic Sigismundo Malatesta or Benito Mussolini in Bishop's poem, just "the soldier home from the war"; old, wise Confucius may understand the nature of existence in Pound's *Cantos*, but here at St. Elizabeths there's just a young "boy that pats the floor/to see if the world is there, is flat"; we do not have wily Odysseus, only "the crazy sailor/that shows his watch"; and most tellingly, there aren't evil, conspiring Jewish bankers in St. Elizabeths, just "a Jew in a newspaper hat/that dances carefully down the ward/walking the plank of a coffin board." Even if these are portraits of real inmates, Bishop is having them pull double duty by embodying the negative space of *The Cantos*, representing the powerless people Pound hated or ignored. This is not a world of books come to life, but the opposite: "This is a world of books gone flat."[102] St. Elizabeths, in Bishop's eyes, is a Dantesque hellhole because there, as in the *Inferno*, the punishment echoes the crime, and Pound's crime was not his treason but rather his prejudice and his worship of power that long predated his wartime radio addresses. Robert Dale Parker writes that there is a suggestion that "the house of his decay is of his own building."[103] But it is more than a suggestion; it even goes beyond a diagnosis to a broader indictment of Pound, his work, and his—and our—society. This is an inference to the best explanation, and one that draws together ethics and aesthetics: something close to complete comprehension.

BISHOP'S POETIC AND LOGICAL FORMS

Sometimes forms of reasoning have equivalent poetic forms: listing and enumeration are easily swapped across disciplines, and analogy is recognized by both philosophy and literature. But often, poetic forms aren't recognized also to be logical forms. The argument of this book is that they should be. Bishop uses some traditional poetic forms and some nontraditional poetic forms, which I'll argue below should be understood as part of her attention to causality. She also, like Whitman and Dickinson, uses the catalogue and the analogy, though unlike them, she blends them into embodying the formal qualities of the comparatively formless inference to the best explanation.

Bishop's use of villanelle, sestina, and rhyme can be seen through a historical lens either as an anachronistic oddity, or better as the inverse, as part of a mid-century revival of traditional forms. But her use of poetic forms are also demonstrations of her interest in cause and effect: villanelles, sestinas, and rigorous rhyme schemes all force a poet to follow through on the consequences of initial choices. One striking aspect of Bishop's use of form is that she does not make it look easy; she draws attention to how initial choices lead to difficult consequences.[104] Her rhymes often show the strain, such as when she splits the word "Falls" in "Arrival at Santos," in which "six feet tall" is forced to rhyme with "Glens Fall/s, New York."[105] Similarly, she also splits the word "an" in "Pink Dog," making a feminine rhyme: "Tonight you simply can't afford to be a-/n eyesore. But no one will ever see a."[106] Her villanelle, "One Art," and sestina, "Sestina," are commonly considered to be among the best modern examples of those forms, but not because they show easy, virtuosic command of the language. Rather, they show hard-won and barely-achieved control. In each intricate form, the choice of the initial end words and lines determines much of the rest of the poem, but in Bishop's hands, each prescribed repetition further deforms the initial meanings of the end words or repeating lines, culminating in "Sestina" with the surreal scene of an almanac raining its drawings of moons like tears. In "One Art," the repeating lines, "The art of losing isn't hard to master" and "loss is no disaster" sound confident and cool initially, but by the end of the poem, these lines are revealed to be just sad, self-consoling bravado.[107] Bishop, of course, *means* to show this strain. A notorious perfectionist, she could have found easy rhymes and used end words and lines that do not shift under the pressure of repetition. Bishop means to show the way that one's initial choices result in particular consequences: causes lead, inescapably, to effects.

"Visits to St Elizabeths" is a less traditional but still poetic form, modeled on the ancient nursery rhyme "The House that Jack Built," in which a farmer, cock, priest, man, maiden, cow, dog, cat, malt, and the house that Jack built are all linked through a chain of cause and effect, reinforcing Bishop's poem's claim of the inescapability of appropriate consequences. But here she runs it in the other direction, tracing from effect back to cause as she looks into Pound and explains why he's imprisoned. One of Bishop's biographers, Brett Millier, writes that this nursery rhyme is "a lesson for children on the interrelatedness of events, the inevitable progress of cause to effect. Like this nursery rhyme, Bishop's description opens progressively wider as its causes grow more distant yet more necessary to the final result."[108] More than that, though, each character in the nursery rhyme is introduced in relation to what it is powerful over; the addition of the next line reveals what is powerful over it. It is not only a chain, it is a Darwinian food chain: the malt is eaten by the rat that is killed by the cat that is worried by the dog that is tossed by the cow that is milked by the maiden, etc., until we arrive back at the farmer—Jack?—who grew the malt that lies in his house. Pound may have thought he was Jack, at the top of the food chain, but the rhyme teaches us that Jack is at the mercy of the rat. Bishop's poem, like the nursery rhyme, gathers evidence as it traces back in time to show why things have happened as they did, as it traces up the food chain. Millier writes, " 'The House that Jack Built' . . . posits a series of mutually dependent events that all turn out to promote the marriage of 'the maiden all forlorn' and 'the man all tattered and torn' by 'the priest all shaven and shorn.' "[109] The events are indeed mutually dependent, but I disagree with the optimism of this interpretation; "The House that Jack Built" does not end with the marriage, but rather, with "the farmer sowing his corn." Given that "The House that Jack Built" begins with eating and ends with sowing, it shows not progress but regress. The nursery rhyme emphasizes that even if the links between cause and effect are far-flung and hard to see, this chain is still as inescapable as iron shackles. St. Elizabeths, then, is just the physicalization of Pound's true chains; he is imprisoned by whom he has eaten and by what now eats at him, his actions and their effects. This is as true for the end words of a sestina as it is for Ezra Pound's culpability.

Although Bishop wrote a substantial number of poems in recognizable poetic forms, many are formal in some aspects of their poetics without being villanelles. But in these poems, too, we see forms of reasoning that readers of this book will remember from its earliest chapters. For example, as I began this chapter, I wrote about "The Fish," which is mostly in free verse, and in which the speaker catalogues the fish's exterior appearance: his weight, his skin, his scales. This is not a Whitmanian catalogue; the speaker here lists what she sees not in order to enumerate to a predictive inference, not to generalize about what comes next, but to understand why events have happened as they did. She infers about the fish's interior—"the big bones and the little bones,/the dramatic reds and blacks/of his shiny entrails"—and she uses figurative language: "the coarse white flesh/packed in like feathers" and "the pink swim-bladder/like a big peony." These are similes, and they're very good similes; that comparison of the fish's flesh to feathers is so vivid that it evokes an entire evolutionary history. But unlike a Dickinson poem, Bishop isn't setting up analogies between the fish's organs and flowers that work with multiple terms in order to make sense of something unknown. If there's an analogy here, it's an implicit one between the speaker of the poem in her world of air and the fish in his watery world. And even then, the speaker doesn't reason about the fish's world by means of her own, or the reverse, but, if anything, seeks to infer to the best explanation: how water and air combine in rainbows, and why she released the fish back to its own element.

In multiple poems—including those I surveyed earlier—Bishop uses inference to the best explanation as a poetic form. It's a method of reasoning so commonplace that it goes even more unnoticed than the catalogue or analogy. And inference to the best explanation freely draws on elements of both catalogues and analogies, though with the explicit goal of answering *why* questions. Here—and for much of the rest of this chapter—I'll use as touchstones two of Bishop's most famous poems, "In the Waiting Room" and "Filling Station."

The young speaker of "In the Waiting Room" begins the poem with authority:

In Worcester, Massachusetts
I went with Aunt Consuelo
to keep her dentist's appointment
and sat and waited for her
in the dentist's waiting room.[110]

Our speaker—named Elizabeth—lets us know that she thinks her aunt is a foolish woman, and that even though Elizabeth is not yet seven years old, she can read, and so she reads the *National Geographic* while she waits. A series of images in the magazine frighten this self-possessed little girl: "the inside of a volcano," and nearby, two unprepared-looking explorers, "a dead man slung on a pole," naked breasts. And at the same time, she hears something: "Suddenly, from inside/came an Oh of pain." This is a catalogue—magazine images, and the sound of pain—but it's one that works analogically. What do all these people have in common? Their bodies are all vulnerable, albeit in different situations and for different reasons. The speaker identifies the voice as Aunt Consuelo's voice, but then also immediately says: "it was me: my voice, in my mouth." She was cataloguing a group—vulnerable human bodies—and then found that it went beyond the magazine pages to her aunt, and then beyond her aunt to include herself. The speaker's disorientation is extreme: she describes it as "falling off the round, turning world into cold blue-black space." She says: "nothing stranger has ever happened, nothing stranger could ever happen." She feels like she is "sliding beneath a big black wave, another, and another." And again and again she tries to reason abductively for an explanation of her own existence, the hidden cause of her own identity:[111]

> But I felt: you are an *I*
> you are an *Elizabeth*,
> you are one of *them*.
> *Why* should you be one, too?
> I scarcely dared to look
> to see what it was I was....
> Why should I be my aunt
> or me, or anyone?
> What similarities—
> boots, hands, the family voice
> I felt in my throat, or even
> the *National Geographic*
> and those awful hanging breasts—
> held us all together
> or made us all just one?
> How—I didn't know any
> word for it—how "unlikely"...
> How had I come to be here,
> like them?[112]

Young Elizabeth diagnosing herself, using inference to the best explanation to figure out why she is sitting in the waiting room—a literal waiting room, but also waiting for the inevitable damage to a mortal, female body. She's alone, without parents, in a world where "The War was on." Why is she there, and why is she the person that she is, in her family, and a woman, "one of them?" How can she reason her way into an answer? She's seeking the best explanation that can guide her inference.

"Filling Station" begins much like "In the Waiting Room": a solitary and slightly supercilious speaker catalogues the people and objects around her in a determinedly nonpoetic setting, a gas station this time instead of a dentist's office. She exclaims "oh" and she looks at the people working there:

> Father wears a dirty,
> oil-soaked monkey suit
> that cuts him under the arms,
> and several quick and saucy
> and greasy sons assist him

(it's a family filling station),
all quite thoroughly dirty.[113]

Even within this stanza, one sees inference to the best explanation. Why are these people working at this gas station? Because "it's a family filling station"—the explanation is marked by its placement in parentheses. The speaker asks a series of "why" questions about what she observes. Although the filling station is "quite thoroughly dirty," there's a porch with a wicker sofa, a taboret with a doily on top of it, and a begonia on the doily.

Why the extraneous plant?
Why the taboret?
Why, oh why, the doily?
(Embroidered in daisy stitch
with marguerites, I think,
and heavy with gray crochet.)[114]

Here the catalogue begins expanding to include not just people but objects. Why are these people working at this gas station, and also why are these objects here? How do they fit together?[115] The speaker infers to the best explanation:

Somebody embroidered the doily.
Somebody waters the plant,
or oils it, maybe. Somebody
arranges the rows of cans
so that they softly say:
ESSO—SO—SO—SO
to high-strung automobiles.
Somebody loves us all.[116]

What's the explanation for why the filling station is operated by a family and decorated like a home? Because it *is* a family home. And more: because there's a mother in this family. Her presence is inferred from the effects that her love has caused. Like "The Fish" and so many other poems, "Filling Station" shows a speaker inferring about an interior—a mother, hidden within the home—from the visible exterior—the sons, the plant, the doily, the arrangement of the cans, even, finally, the speaker herself in that final "us all." This is the best explanation.[117]

One should ask, of course, what makes an explanation the best? Lipton distinguishes between "two senses in which something may be the best of competing explanations. We may characterize it as the explanation that it is the most warranted: the 'likeliest' or most probable explanation. On the other hand, we may characterize the best explanation as the one which would, if correct, be the most explanatory or provide the most understanding: the 'loveliest' explanation."[118] Explanations can be likely without being lovely—for example saying that opium puts people to sleep because of its dormitive powers—or explanations can be lovely without being likely—conspiracy theories offer broad understanding but are extremely improbable. He argues that loveliness tracks likeliness: an explanation's power has a rough correlation with its truth.

The speaker of "In the Waiting Room" has a choice between a likely explanation and a lovely one, and they are very far apart. A likely explanation that could answer the question "Why should I be my aunt/or me, or anyone?" is the randomness of physical biology as it happened exactly to produce her. It's very, as the speaker says, "unlikely," that she ended up as herself. A lovely explanation of identity would be on a different plane, metaphysical rather than physical, and would offer a belief in the fates weaving lives, or a theory of embodiment, an idea about what it means to be a woman among other women, a person among other people, and what makes "us all just one." Unfortunately for young Elizabeth, the most likely explanation is that there is no lovely explanation, no great understanding to uncover, no universal order to reveal. But the likely explanation does not satisfy her; a lovely explanation is what the speaker wants, and when she looks into herself—"sidelong. . . . I couldn't look any higher"—she is hoping to see her own loveliness, a reason for her being, a way in which the world fits together and she fits the world. She wants coherence; she does not get it, or not on terms she's willing to accept.

But the speaker of "Filling Station" does. A mother—a parent—is precisely what the young speaker of "In the Waiting Room" lacks. That young speaker tells us in the second line of that poem that she is going to the dentist with her aunt and waiting for her there; we can infer an explanation: that this young Elizabeth has no one else to take care of her, even if we didn't know Bishop's own biography and that she was effectively orphaned as an infant. But in "Filling Station," the softly said so-so-so of the carefully arranged Esso cans becomes the *so* of the "*somebody*" who "loves us all." Maternal love is the gasoline of the world; somebody loving us all is what fuels us all. This is a lovely explanation, and not merely because it's quite lovely, or even because it's about love. It's a lovely explanation because maternal love provides the most understanding of what causes the filling station's decor, it explains this filling station, and also *everything*. It's a conspiracy theory and it tracks with truth.

In "The Fish," the speaker looks at "where oil had spread a rainbow ... until everything/was rainbow, rainbow, rainbow!"[119] Oil coats everything in "Filling Station" as well, and also here is an image of the coherence provided by a lovely explanation. The poem begins:

Oh, but it is dirty!
—this little filling station,
oil-soaked, oil-permeated
to a disturbing, over-all
black translucency.
Be careful with that match![120]

Everything is oily; the speaker makes this point repeatedly: "Father wears a dirty,/oil-soaked monkey suit" and she wonders if someone "waters the plant,/or oils it, maybe." Even the doily has *oily* within it; the very word is filled with oil. The oiliness of the filling station covers everything: an "overall/black translucency." It might appear that in "Filling Station," unlike "The Fish," the oil is "disturbing" and not rainbowed. But here, too, everything coheres: the speaker begins the poem as an outsider, infers to the best explanation about what lies beyond what she can see or imagine, and ends the poem as counted within the first person plural of "us all."

The speaker, as she examines the porch behind the filling station, asks, "Why the extraneous plant?" The power of a lovely explanation is that it, in its fullest extension, claims that *nothing is extraneous*. The decorative objects initially appeared extraneous because the speaker has not yet fully inferred the explanation that this filling station is a "family filling station" and that this is their home, decorated, with love, by the unseen and unnamed mother. The speaker herself begins the poem as an outsider, appearing to be extraneous to this scene, remarking with apparent disgust, "Oh, but it is dirty!"[121] But the plant is not extraneous, neither is the taboret, neither is the doily—and neither is she. By the end of the poem, she has catalogued a group of people she initially thinks are different than her, and then included objects that analogically belong to that category as well, and then finds herself included. This is the same progression that the young speaker of "In the Waiting Room" pursues as she finds that the group she catalogues—first far away in the pages of a magazine, then her aunt, then aspects of the other people in the waiting room—includes herself. But young Elizabeth finds no loveliness, nothing that justifies the first person plural that "held us all together." There is also an "us all" in the last line of "Filling Station" as the speaker states the loveliest explanation, the one that leaves nothing outside of it, that promises total coherence, and that uses coherence as a confirmation of truth: "Somebody loves us all."

COHERENCE

I've been using coherence in its colloquial meaning—how things fit together, and how, by fitting together, make sense. Other scholars have written about Bishop's poems and coherence. Since the early 1980s, Helen Vendler repeatedly discussed Bishop's poetry as committed to coherence (like other lyric poets).[122] She writes "to wring significance out of the random is the chief task of many of Bishop's lyric narrators . . . and the inability to make a connection among random signifiers (neighbors, an aunt's cry of pain, pictures of 'savages,' the name 'Elizabeth') literally makes the six-year-old Bishop ill, faint with nausea. The bizarre commandment to 'make it cohere' under which lyric poets (more than all other writers) serve, makes incoherence an anguish of peculiar magnitude for them."[123] Three years later, in a scholarly journal rather than a magazine, Vendler repeats her sense of Bishop creating coherence, writing, "Abstracting from particulars to make a coherent sketch of social reality seems to Bishop very like what mapmakers do."[124] Skipping forward several decades, Claire Seiler writes about the coherence of Bishop's 1955 book *A Cold Spring* and notes its interest in "the possibility of knowledge";[125] Stephanie Burt calls epiphanic coherence illusory in Bishop's poems, as "Other poets use rainbows as gestures towards exactly the promise of coherence, of continuity . . . which Bishop's own rainbows almost always abjure";[126] Langdon Hammer lectures on how "Sandpiper" is "a meditation on the challenges of locating coherence in a shifting world";[127] and Gillian White describes how Bishop "wrestles with the great weight of modernism's doubt," including its "forms of coherence."[128] The term pops up repeatedly in the recent collection *Elizabeth Bishop in Context* in essays about race,[129] dreams,[130] travel,[131] and religion.[132]

But coherence is also a term in philosophy of explanation, where it refers to how well explanatory theories fit together, how well they fit the world, and the extent to which fitting together guarantees truth. Philosophers Luc Bovens and Stephan Hartmann write, "the story that we gather about some small corner of the world is a coherent story, then this gives us at least some reason to believe it. Some philosophers propose to recruit this item of common sense to combat sceptical worries: it is the very coherence of the story about the world that warrants our confidence."[133] They note that other philosophers—including ones whose work I've drawn on in this book, such as Thomas Kuhn and Wesley Salmon—have written about consistency among theories, or in Salmon's words, "*inductive* relations of fittingness."[134] But as Erik J. Olsson writes in *Against Coherence*, "coherence theorists have been unable to reach anything like a consensus on how to define their central notion ... there is no way to specify an informative notion of coherence that would allow us to draw even the minimal conclusion that more coherence means a higher likelihood of truth."[135]

Lipton's term for explanations with a great deal of power—loveliness—is drawn from aesthetics, and it has been criticized on those grounds.[136] Here though I want to run Lipton's insight the other direction: the way in which a poem hangs together, which is aesthetic, is also a matter of explanatory coherence: it has a relationship to truth. In other words, Lipton describes logic as not just coherent but lovely, and I describe poetics as not just lovely but coherent.

That literary studies has an interest in coherence was argued recently by Elaine Auyoung, who notes "a more profound but largely unacknowledged convention that defines our discipline: an interest in coherence."[137] Auyoung quotes Lipton's work, and also that of Anahid Nersessian and Jonathan Kramnick in which they describe literary interpretation as a variety of explanation, and she argues, "While not every philosopher agrees with Lipton on the relationship between loveliness and likeliness, they all presume that truth is the goal of any explanation. What they seek to determine is how, in the face of competing explanations, we settle on the explanation most likely to be the 'actual' one. This philosophic perspective brings into relief something striking about the explanatory work that literary interpretation performs: assessing the likelihood or probability of the interpretive inferences that other critics make is not our primary interest."[138] Auyoung's claim is not that literary scholars interpret literary texts with an eye toward coherence; a good overview of this long-accepted argument is in Caroline Levine's first chapter of *Forms*, titled "Whole," in which she describes how Cleanth Brooks and other New Critics "sediment the field's sense of form as bounded unity."[139]

Auyoung's argument is not even that critics "identify a subset of the text that coheres in a way we did not expect." Rather, it's that an argument of a literary scholar will "cohere, independent of whether we [other literary scholars] find it convincing." In other words, in literary scholarship, "even when we are skeptical of other critics' inferences," we value loveliness. Auyoung focuses on scholarship about Jane Austen's *Emma*; she writes about how Austen "thematizes the act of reading letters, solving riddles, and unscrambling anagrams alongside the more difficult work of reading other people, or making inferences about them based on their observable behavior" but notes that the "representation of these activities in the narrative is distinct from the processes involved in the literal act of reading the text itself."[140]

One could read Bishop's poems like this, as thematizing inference, and indeed, I do read them that way initially in this chapter's second section. But in representing inference, they are also modeling inference, they are taking the form of inference to the best explanation as a poetic form, and they are showing how abductive reasoning works. Moreover, Bishop's poetry, unlike Auyoung's account of literary scholarship, does link together coherence and truth—the lovelier the explanation, the less is extraneous, the more coherent, and the more comprehension it provides. In philosophy, coherence serves to "combat sceptical worries." So too in Bishop's poems.

In Bishop's poems, loveliness tracks likeliness, and coherence supports truth. We can see this in what she says about truth, such as her assertion about "The Fish": "I always tell the truth in my poems. With 'The Fish,' that's exactly how it happened. It was in Key West, and I did catch it just as the poem says. That was in 1938. Oh, but I did change one thing; the poem says he had five hooks hanging from his mouth, but actually he only had three. Sometimes the poem makes its own demands."[141] This sounds like a contradiction, or at least an exaggeration, as if she's admitting that it's a fish story, but instead she's asserting that the number of fishhooks is irrelevant at worst and useful at best to the coherence of the poem. The poem's inferences are not falsified by additional information; additional information only adds to the poem's coherence, only serves to combat skepticism and not warrant it. Another example: Bishop writes to John Frederick Nims in 1979 about footnoting her poems in the anthology he's editing, "I'm going to take issue with you—rather violently—about the idea of footnotes. With one or two exceptions (I'll mention them later) I don't think there should be ANY footnotes. . . . 'Insinglass' is in the dictionary; so is 'gunnel' (see 'gunwale'); so is 'thwarts' [these words occur in 'The Fish']. One of my few exceptions is the ESSO-Exxon note to 'Filling Station' . . . the cans are arranged to say so-so-so, etc., so I don't think *that* has to be explained. However—most of them might well not know *that* so-so-so was—perhaps still is in some places—the phrase people use to calm and soothe horses."[142] This information is not extraneous—nothing is extraneous, it adds to the poem's coherence—but neither is necessary.

NEWNESS

Inductive reasoning is ampliative: you can learn new things by means of this logic, things that were not part of the premises. Will they necessarily be true? No. Will they likely be? Maybe. Is that enough? Probably. In the introduction to this book, I wrote that modern poetry and inductive reasoning are both about encountering newness, and both offer techniques by which newness is made sense of or just managed. But inductive reasoning also offers new comprehension. To end, here is part of one last poem by Bishop, "Song for the Rainy Season," written while Bishop was living happily in Brazil with her longtime partner, Lota. In other poems, her speakers gaze on houses from the outside, ask about them, and find them "inscrutable." Now, in this "open house" she shares with Lota, they are on the inside: "Hidden, oh hidden/in the high fog/the house we live in."[143]

"Song for the Rainy Season" uses figurative language that echoes "O Breath" but then rewrites it. In the much later "Song for the Rainy Season," the same imagery of rib cage and breath depicts a loving symbiotic ecosystem:

the brook sings loud
from a rib cage
of giant fern; vapor
climbs up the thick growth
effortlessly, turns back,
holding them both,
house and rock,
in a private cloud.[144]

Our speaker is loved in return this time, her beloved's heart beats for her; she begins with the evidence of being loved, and then infers what would be the best explanation of this fact. The cause she identifies is very lovely: her beloved's heart beats for her—she knows it does this time—because a heart full of love beats openly beneath everything. Everything is in love, everything is reciprocal, and everything is legible and reasonable, even the mildew's map, the "ordinary brown/owl gives us proof he can count," and the "fat frogs/shrilling for love."[145] It's both likely and lovely. It's complete comprehension, and even if just for this brief time, coherent and true.

CONCLUSION
The Sonnet's Logic and Gwendolyn Brooks

PIVOTING

This book began with the claim that poetry can be philosophical no matter its topic or references, because poems are philosophical in how they reason. My account of how poetry reasons risks being misunderstood as a claim that poems show thinking. That's not what I am arguing; indeed, that's an assertion too obvious to argue. But one way of describing this book is to say that, by showing how poetic forms are also logical forms, I attempt to take that statement seriously and to make good on the intuition behind it that we accept, and indeed widely and easily share.

Until now, I've followed the forms of reasoning into poetry, identifying how poems are always already logical, and providing vocabulary drawn from philosophy to name and more fully understand aspects of poetics that we've seen but haven't always recognized as epistemological. Chapters 1 and 2 chart the fundamental forms of inductive reasoning—the list and the analogy—and demonstrate that, because these are also the characteristic forms of Walt Whitman and Emily Dickinson, they are also fundamental forms of modern American poetry. Chapters 3 and 4 describe how modernist poets, Gertrude Stein and Marianne Moore in particular, take up inductive reasoning in their poetry and address its problems, both the epistemological and the justificatory. Chapter 5 argues that we see another attempt to reckon with the promise and perils of reasoning nondeductively in Elizabeth Bishop's use of the philosophic form of reasoning called inference to the best explanation.

For all of these poets, inductive reasoning is not adapted into poetic use, but rather, their poems locate the underlying shared structures and powers of logic and lyric—*both logic and lyric work by connecting particulars.* By connecting particulars, both inductive reasoning and modern poetry offer a way to hold and make sense of lived experience in the world. The results might be, by any objective lights, wrong, but also this way of holding details together is worth it anyway, and not just because it allows us to honor subjective perspectives. Ultimately, inductive reasoning, this problematic logic, may end up being more reliable than deduction because of how it can assimilate newness. Modern poetry takes on novelty—it makes it new—as an asset and aptitude. And so: poetry shows how induction's great problem, novelty, which is also one of the defining problems of modern philosophy, can, from another angle, be recognized as a great strength.

In this conclusion, I'll rotate this argument once again by making a claim for what poetics has long known about its own relation to reasoning and also its own resources. I'll discuss the sonnet—often considered the most exemplary form of the lyric—and I'll focus on what I'll argue is the lynchpin of the sonnet's logical form and also its most defining feature: the volta.[1] The website of the Poetry Foundation, in "Learning the Sonnet," notes the sonnet's traditional bipartite form of octave and sestet, which are "often called the proposition and resolution. Dividing them is the *volta*, or turn. Thus, a problem or question is often presented in the first section of a sonnet and then, via the pivot made by the turn, resolved or given new perspective in the second."[2] Paul Fussell calls the two parts of a sonnet not proposition and resolution but "complication followed by resolution—an archetype of the common act of problem-solving, or deciding, or even rationalizing," and he describes the volta as "the turn which will open up for solution the problem advanced by the octave."[3] *The Princeton Encyclopedia of Poetry and Poetics* defines the sonnet by framing it explicitly relative to thinking and centers the volta as thought's pivot or fulcrum: "With respect to the It[alian] pattern (by far the most widely used of the three), it will be observed that a two-part division of thought is invited, and that the octave offers an admirably unified pattern and leads to the volta or 'turn' of thought in the more varied sestet."[4] Later, in defining the volta, this same point is emphasized: the volta is "a decisive 'turn in thought.'"[5]

The sonnet form is commonly described relative not just to thinking but specifically and directly to argument, reasoning, and logic. Stephanie Burt and David Mikics describe the sonnet's "internal logic" in the introduction to their anthology of sonnets and explain that "Rapturous praise, bitter exclamation, and step-by-step reasoning frequently intertwine in its concise shape."[6] In the introductions to their anthology, Edward Hirsch writes that the sonnet "thinks on its feet,"[7] and Eavan Boland describes it as "this highly reasonable, toughly reasoning form."[8] Helen Vendler does not bother making a case for repeatedly describing "the argument of the poem" in her book on Shakespeare's sonnets; that a sonnet makes an argument is presented as self-evident.[9]

A sonnet is distinct from a quatorzain—it's more than just a fourteen-line poem—not just in how it divides into pieces but in how those pieces lean on and build off of each other. That is: the volta, the hinge between parts, is what makes the whole of the sonnet more than the sum of those parts. From the oldest Sicilian sonnets, the two-part structure of octave and sestet has been definitional. Burt and Mikics trace how "The Sicilian school borrowed the octave from the *strambotto*, a peasant song. The sonnet, however, was no song. It was asymmetrical, suited to meditative logic rather than music. . . . The arrival of the sonnet marks an inward turn in Italian poetry: lyric purifies itself, and becomes reflection on reflection."[10] Scholars and poets write repeatedly that sonnets show self-awareness of their status as lyric poems and as sonnets, and even more so as sonnets as exemplary of lyric poetry. Jahan Ramazani writes of the sonnet that "the genre's memory of its history, conventions, structures, and tropes is so rich, its tradition of self-metaphorization so strong, its self-awareness so intensified by its compression, that sonnets often talk about themselves when talking about love, race, nationality, the natural environment, or another subject."[11] In the introduction to this book, I wrote that reasoning in poems should count as what philosophers call *metalogic* because the poems discussed in this book are using logic to make arguments, and also the arguments they are making are about how logic works and what it can do. Similarly, the sonnet is often what Ramazani calls a "metasonnet."[12] Sonnets not only talk about themselves, but also, in the words of Burt and Mikics, "lyric verse has become a way of talking to oneself."[13] The representation of reflection and self-reflection, the analysis and the awareness of that analysis, distinguishes the sonnet. But even if a sonnet doesn't directly refer to itself as a sonnet, it's still recursive on the level of what Marjorie Levinson calls "the poem's self-understanding" and "self-assembly."[14] This sort of recursion is embodied in the sonnet form due to its self-reflexive reassessment of itself in its own second half.

I've been using the vocabulary of philosophy to analyze poetry; could I reverse this route and trace the sonnet form, as a form of logical argument, back into philosophy? While I don't know of philosophic writing that works entirely or neatly in the sonnet form, elements of it—the opening problem, the address to a beloved, the two-part argument, and certainly the volta—are found from Plato through Wittgenstein. But that's not what I need to do here, now at the end of this book. Rather than trace poetics back into philosophy, what this conclusion will show, *without* importing the vocabulary of philosophical reasoning, is how poetry can be—*is*—logical. The sonnet is a form of reasoning; it's one that poets and literary scholars already know. Step by step, meter by meter, iambic or not: sonnets and inductive reasoning both show what it means to think on your feet.

How do sonnets reason? What distinguishes their logic? The sonnet has traditional content—a first-person speaker, a nonnarrative reflection, conventional subjects including passion—and formal poetics—its compact or even restrictive fourteen lines, lines that are pentameter-ish in length, probably one of a few rhyme schemes. A sonnet's relation to reasoning can be seen in its traditional use of the conceit, which could be seen as a variety of analogical reasoning.[15] Burt and Mikics quote the character of Anne Elliot in Jane Austen's *Persuasion* describing sonnets as "fraught with the apt analogy."[16] I discuss analogical reasoning in this book's chapter 2, but that isn't the only or even the primary aspect of a sonnet's logic. The sonnet's relation to thinking, and particularly to logical argument, is most fundamentally not due to the analogies, lists, explanations, or other thought that it might include, nor is it due to the sonnet's frequent reflection on its own status as a sonnet in a long tradition.

Rather, the sonnet is a form of logical argument because of the volta that makes it a sonnet in the first place. The volta, or turn, is an attribute of both a poem's content and its form.[17] Traditionally the volta marks the pivot between the opening proposition of the octave and the resolution of the sestet, but sonnets can turn elsewhere too; a Shakespearean sonnet often turns before the final couplet, between the twelfth and thirteenth lines, even if it also has an earlier volta.[18] *The Princeton Encyclopedia of Poetry and Poetics* defines the volta as "the gap or break" in a sonnet, and notes "the turn is effected in white space, i.e. in the gap between stanzas."[19] Similarly, Fussell writes, "the turn occurs somewhere in the white space that separates line 8 from line 9, and that line 9 simply reflects or records it."[20] Thus, "something very important, something indeed indispensable ... happens at the turn: we are presented there with a logical or emotional shift by which the speaker enables himself to take a new or altered or enlarged view of his subject."[21] In connecting language across a gap, the volta is an epitome of both logic and lyric.

Of course, one could say that the sonnet form only *resembles* logic. For example, Fussell, after writing about the sonnet's "structures of reasoning" and "logical and rhetorical organization," also writes that "the Shakespearean sonneteer 'to solve his problem' tend to make the Shakespearean sonnet a little showplace of rhetoric or advocacy or logic—or mock-logic."[22] David Bromwich writes that the sonnet is both "close to syllogism" and "close to prayer."[23] I understand this as stating the proximity of the sonnet to logical argument, and also the recognition that the sonnet is not, or need not be, deductive in its reasoning. But of course, logic does not need to be syllogistic; logic can be nondeductive. And, as this book argues, logic in poems can be, and often is, nondeductive—without being mock-logic.

As Graham Priest writes, logic can be defined as "what follows from what."[24] The forms of deductive reasoning keep your thinking in a straight line. The forms of inductive reasoning let you think around corners. The forms of inductive reasoning accommodate novelty—*they turn.*

VOLTAS

Voltas characterize sonnets as a form of reasoning because logic is also about the move from proposition to resolution. Reasoning is motivated by having a problem; logic responds to a problem. Logic tells us what follows what, how thought follows thought, and how to represent that movement on the page. What makes a volta count as a volta is that what comes after it is at least a little different from what preceded it—it's an altered angle, an idea reframed—so the volta shows reasoning but a particular variety, a kind of reasoning that's open to newness or even requires it. Lines of poetry follow each other on the page but the logic of the volta can be unpredictable. This is a logic that embraces contingency, the awareness that the argument could have turned down another path, and the willingness to address a problem slantwise. The volta does not claim logical necessity but it does assert that an argument which may not be logically impeccable can nonetheless be perfect on its own terms.[25] Elsewhere in this book I wrote about forms of reasoning that philosophy has names for that poetics does not, though these forms are in practice shared; here, with the sonnet and particularly with the volta, poetics has a name for a form that philosophy doesn't.

In the introduction to this book, I read three poems closely; two are sonnets: "Nomad Exquisite" by Wallace Stevens and "kitchenette building" by Gwendolyn Brooks. Looking to sonnets to demonstrate how poems reason, of course, was not coincidental; sonnets are exactly where one should look to see formal logic in poetry. I didn't discuss voltas then, and I'll take the opportunity now to return to these poems and pay attention to their turns.

"Nomad Exquisite," one long sentence broken into three stanzas, rotates its glance in between the stanzas, each of which has a different subject:

As the immense dew of Florida
Brings forth
The big-finned palm
And green vine angering for life,

As the immense dew of Florida
Brings forth hymn and hymn
From the beholder,
Beholding all these green sides
And gold sides of green sides,

And blessed mornings,
Meet for the eye of the young alligator,
And lightning colors

> So, in me, come flinging
> Forms, flames, and the flakes of flames.[26]

Its sharpest turn, like that of a Shakespearean sonnet, falls between the twelfth and thirteenth lines, with a final couplet turning to the speaker of the poem. Here the poem transforms the literal sunrise into a figurative one as it shifts from the world outside to the world inside. The turn to "So, in me" is the resolution to the logic of "as X, as Y . . . so Z," or as I described it in the introduction, *this, then this, then this*. Each of these points follow, but not directly, not fully predictably, not quite with logical necessity, but they do follow. And so the speaker is motivated into speech, into writing this poem, at its end, as a consequence.

I also discussed "kitchenette building" by Gwendolyn Brooks in the introduction to this book. Despite her well-known ambivalence about the form, Brooks is one of the great American writers of sonnets.[27] Karen Jackson Ford writes of "Brooks's irrepressible interest in the sonnet" and how "the sonnet was the poetic structure in which Brooks was able to explore her ethical and political questions about literary form."[28] She traces Brooks's investment in the sonnet to her reading of "Robert Hillyer's *First Principles of Verse* (1938), a critical volume she was introduced to in 1941 by Inez Cunningham Stark, a wealthy white woman who led a poetry workshop for African Americans at the South Side Community Center."[29] Ford argues that "What reading Hillyer would have shown Brooks, perhaps inadvertently, is that poetic forms can argue with themselves, or, as his term 'thought structure' acknowledges, that sonnets can *think*."[30] Nothing exemplifies this more than the sonnet and its turns.

"kitchenette building" is a sonnet that turns at least twice: once toward the dream between the first and second stanza, and once away from it, between the third and fourth stanzas:

> We are things of dry hours and the involuntary plan,
> Grayed in, and gray. "Dream" makes a giddy sound, not strong
> Like "rent," "feeding a wife," "satisfying a man."
>
> But could a dream send up through onion fumes
> Its white and violet, fight with fried potatoes

And yesterday's garbage ripening in the hall,
Flutter, or sing an aria down these rooms

Even if we were willing to let it in,
Had time to warm it, keep it very clean,
Anticipate a message, let it begin?

We wonder. But not well! not for a minute!
Since Number Five is out of the bathroom now,
We think of lukewarm water, hope to get in it.[31]

A sonnet is distinct from a quatorzain because of its internal logic, and that's why I can call this thirteen-line poem a sonnet in the first place: it has a sonnet's logic.[32] Different sonnet variations have different formulations of sonnet logic, but they all negotiate how the parts are components of a whole, how one part connects to another, and how the parts are connected by turns. Vendler writes about the difference between the earlier Italian sonnets of octave and sestet and the later English ones: "The four units of the Shakespearean sonnet can be set in any number of logical relations to one another: successive and equal; hierarchical; contrastive; analogous; logically contradictory; successively 'louder' or 'softer.'"[33] (Vendler's frequent practice of developing new descriptive terms for poems—often putting them in quotes as with "'louder' or 'softer'"—is obliquely behind this book's sense of additional vocabulary for poetics being useful.)

Brooks's "kitchenette building," like a Shakespearean sonnet, falls into four units with logical relations to one another. Unlike Shakespeare's, Brooks's has a final tercet rather than a couplet, and unlike Shakespeare's couplets, the turn to Brooks's last stanza does not "symbolize," as Vendler writes, "the distance from one's own experience necessitated by an analytic stance," nor does it echo an aphorism that "represents the speaker's despair at solving by himself, in personally formulated language, the conundrum presented by the sonnet."[34] The "further twist," as Burt and Mikics describe the Shakespearean sonnet's final couplet, is that the speakers appear to turn away from an analytic stance, to have no solution, not even a trite one, to their problem. Indeed, their problem appears to be dismissed as an inevitable condition, and therefore not to have the status of problem or even to be available to reasoning, logic, or thought at all.

CONCLUSION

And yet there's one further twist, and it is that *this problem becomes available to reasoning* when we read this poem as a sonnet, with an argument, with logical coherence, with definitional connection between parts and wholes, with voltas. If we do, then we can recognize that there's also something of a turn in the middle of this poem, between the second and third stanzas as the collective speakers imagine the dream entering their homes. There's a pause as the dream is half-visualized, almost faintly heard, coming before the speakers turn, or return, to their consideration of the unremunerated labor that protecting and nurturing a dream would demand. The volta—if we identify it as a volta, and therefore describe the poem as a sonnet—shows the space where the dream could have entered and where it's briefly, if wordlessly, considered. Tess Taylor wonders, "Could a dream live inside this poem? Similarly, could this poem be a sonnet? Maybe. Maybe not," before asserting that it is indeed a sonnet: "In 'kitchenette building,' the sonnet gives breath-space to the half-dream that might be taken away."[35] Or even more than showing the space, the volta in this poem holds open that space. (In Moore's words from "The Pangolin," it makes a window, or "mullion," by "branching out across/the perpendiculars."[36])

In the introduction to this book, I wrote about how "kitchenette building" is almost a sonnet, in that it's thirteen and not fourteen lines, and the dream is almost called into being. If we see that there's a gap in the middle of the poem, if we see that it's a volta, we can understand this poem as a sonnet. And then we can see that the empty space left in the poem—the missing line—is a way to imagine that there's a protected space left for the dream too. The structure of the sonnet, and of the kitchenette, and of racist and misogynistic American society, I wrote, has a lacuna left in it that belongs to something else. In the introduction, I wrote that Brooks shows how powerful deductive laws are, how much of life they determine . . . but also that they don't determine everything. There's a gap between deductive necessity and logical necessity. That fissure, the blank space, the openness, which I described in the introduction in terms of inductive logic—how it can accommodate novelty that deduction can't—can also be described as the sonnet's volta. "The turn is effected in white space," writes the *Princeton Encyclopedia of Poetry and Poetics*, and also, writes Gwendolyn Brooks, it is "white and violet."[37] Even if its speakers can't quite see around a corner, the poem's form shows the corner is truly there. The sonnet holds open that gap; it turns and finds there can be an opening for something new. By reading this sonnet as a sonnet, we can see that it's responding to a problem, and that the poem's negative space is its positive claim.

"A LOVELY LOVE"

Brooks's use of the sonnet form has been widely interpreted in light of her subsequent disuse of it; this reading is demonstrably important and true.[38] Brooks did abandon the sonnet form as part of her emerging anti-racist political commitments.[39] But also, we do her sonnets a disservice if we don't recognize that they are already thinking—or even better, reasoning—about problems and how they can be reframed. In Brooks's sonnets, her speakers encounter racism, misogyny, and capitalism and their resulting exhaustion, fear, and violence. Her sonnets don't offer solutions to these problems but they are reasoning about them and finding ways to respond to them that are epistemological and not just aesthetic.

Many poems, many sonnets, have one big turn, and some have more, like the several swerves in Brooks's "kitchenette building." Next I will discuss another one of Gwendolyn Brooks's sonnets, "A Lovely Love," published fifteen years after "kitchenette building." This sonnet also uses the sonnet form to show how forms of reasoning can be forms of poetry, and what these forms restrict and what they enable. "A Lovely Love" has big twists and turns; we could describe it as high-voltage.

> Let it be alleys. Let it be a hall
> Whose janitor javelins epithet and thought
> To cheapen hyacinth darkness that we sought
> And played we found, rot, make the petals fall.
> Let it be stairways, and a splintery box
> Where you have thrown me, scraped me with your kiss,
> Have honed me, have released me after this
> Cavern kindness, smiled away our shocks.
> That is the birthright of our lovely love
> In swaddling clothes. Not like that Other one.
> Not lit by any fondling star above.
> Not found by any wise men, either. Run.
> People are coming. They must not catch us here
> Definitionless in this strict atmosphere.[40]

CONCLUSION

Like "kitchenette building," this sonnet, in a form, considers forms. In "kitchenette building," the societal forms of racist and capitalist American society oppress the first-person speakers, who can only begin to imagine something, a vague dream, that eludes diminishment. In "A Lovely Love," the speaker is also sometimes plural, not a group of people in a similar class, race, and gender formation—impoverished Black women in Chicago—but a pair of lovers seeking a place to love. In "kitchenette building," the heterosexual partnerships are economic, involving, for each half of the couple, "'feeding a wife,' 'satisfying a man'" but here the couple requires no compensation from each other. Rather, they make a wish that the world fulfills: "Let it be alleys. Let it be a hall." We don't find ourselves in a kitchenette, but at the beginning of this sonnet, the form that Wordsworth famously called a "narrow room," the speakers enter a building.[41] It's not a home but despite or because of that, it might be a refuge for them. "A Lovely Love" poses a similar question about forms as "kitchenette building" does: is there a form that can support rather than restrict a dream? If a dream is something that's unexpected and new and can be hard for people to understand? Yes, this sonnet suggests: the form that can hold a dream is the sonnet form, something that usually comes in two slightly unlike halves—like a couple or couplet—and something full of unexpected turns.

"A Lovely Love" is easily recognizable as a sonnet and one could describe it as a fairly standard one. It takes romantic love as a subject and location as a problem: the lovers seek a place to love. It's intensely libidinal—"your kiss," "our shocks," "our lovely love." It's set in the liminal—alleys, hall, stairways. Both of these—unrestrained passion running up against the restrictions of their society, and also the restrictive architecture of narrow spaces—are characteristic topics of the sonnet and have been for centuries. Formally, "A Lovely Love" is also easily categorizable as a sonnet. It has fourteen lines, but more importantly, it divides neatly into an octave and sestet. The octave has an *abbacddc* rhyme scheme—a looser version of the Petrarchan pattern—and closes with a period. The sestet rhymes *efefgg*, and like a Shakespearean sonnet, it ends on a final couplet.[42] The octave's proposition describes what the couple's passion feels like, then there's a volta, and the sestet's resolution makes a claim for what belongs to their love.

But that's not quite right, because it glosses over how this sonnet keeps throwing curves. It has fairly standard end-rhymes, but in addition, it's dense with surprising internal rhymes and slant rhymes. Nearly every line has a sound that connects unexpectedly; just a few include: alleys/hall/petals/fall, epithet/thought/sought/rot, cheapen/hyacinth, thrown me/honed me, one/fondling/found/men/Run/coming. The octave, with its twisted syntax, is hard to parse. For example, I understand it as expressing a wish for a hidden and protected space where the lovers can meet, then recognizing that nowhere is safe—even the secluded hallway has a janitor who calls them names—and then hyacinth darkness ends and they're on the move again. But . . . what is "hyacinth darkness"? And what's the grammatical subject of the verbs "rot, make the petals fall"? "Rot" at first could be mistaken for a noun or even an exclamation, but is presumably a verb. It could be read as the imperative mood in parallel to "Let it be alleys. Let it be a hall," or, alternatively, with the subjects "epithet and thought" that, in addition to "cheapen," also "rot, make petals fall." The rest of the octave is not much easier. Is the "splintery box" finally a place where the lovers can meet, an unfinished closet, say, or is it a place of danger, even, if a coffin, death? These lines are charged with eroticism and violence; when Brooks writes, with the "me" as the repeated recipient of a beloved's overwhelming power, "Where you have thrown me, scraped me with your kiss,/Have honed me, have released me after this," I hear an echo of John Donne: "Take me to you, imprison me, for I,/Except you enthral me, never shall be free,/Nor ever chaste, except you ravish me."[43] Then there's a turn, and the volta's different, comparing their love to the birth of Christianity: "swaddling clothes," "fondling star," "found by wise men." And, as with "hyacinth darkness," what is a "fondling star"?

Nearly every line turns and turns again. But voltas are what make the sonnet's logic; they don't weaken it but emphasize it. They underline how the sonnet holds its parts together *because* of and not *despite* unexpected swerves. Here, in "A Lovely Love," the sonnet coheres not just due to the constant surprising turns, the new images, but because of the implicit claim that the couple's love is also itself that same kind of extraordinary and unforeseen phenomenon. They are also novel. They themselves are surprised; they "smiled away our shocks." Their love is new, still in "swaddling clothes." The speaker compares their love to Christianity—even in the octave, it rises from "a splintery box" and is "released . . . after this Cavern kindness"—but in the sestet, its imagery is connected not to the resurrection but to the birth of Jesus, whose arrival was "lit" by a "fondling star," and "found by wise men." Like a new religion, their love is precipitated by a miracle, unexplained by previous laws and theories, but bringing with it a new way of making sense of the world. Their love is unlike that "Other one"; its birthright is not divine nor human authority—stars, wise men—but instead the pleasure found at the margins—alleys, halls, stairways.

In "kitchenette building," the speakers appear to despair of the possibility that their lives could admit novelty, something that's not in the "involuntary plan." We could say that their lives are defined in "a strict atmosphere," while the dream, both "white and violet," is "Definitionless." And the hole left in "kitchenette building"—a hole that makes the sonnet a whole—implicitly leaves an opening for the dream to run through these spaces, to "Flutter, or sing an aria down these rooms." Maybe it's still waiting in an alley or hall or stairway.

In "A Lovely Love," the speakers do not have power, but claim it nonetheless: their love has a "birthright." They can find spaces to make their own because, like the sonnet form, they can think on their feet. "Run," the speaker instructs. They are entitled not to embody established power but to elude it. "People are coming"—maybe the janitor javelining? Regardless—"They must not catch us here/Definitionless in this strict atmosphere." Where is that *here*? It's their various passageways where they've found to meet, all of which are dark but can take you somewhere; unlike a room, all have more than one exit for escape. But it's also the room of poetry, the stanza: the strict atmosphere of the sonnet, where you can still run, make love, find surprises, be surprising, go somewhere, and stay definitionless.

In "kitchenette building," deductive necessity is not logical necessity. We know this because "the involuntary plan" isn't quite—the dream has eluded its grasp and thereby strengthened the sonnet's logic as it turns, as it runs. The speakers could also turn and run—it's still possible—the form holds an alley or hallway open for them. And that's what the speakers of "A Lovely Love" do. What they show us, though, is that the sonnet is not scanty imprisonment but a form that can support a dream. It's a logical form that is also lyric.

BRIDGEWORK

The sonnet is often understood to stand at the center of the category of lyric poetry, and the volta is at the center (definitionally as well as literally) of the sonnet. Sonnets synecdochically represent all lyric poems; voltas,

CONCLUSION

similarly, stand for sonnets. Voltas, then, even if they aren't found in most poems, are a useful case study for an important aspect of what makes lyric poetry lyric: its logic. When we describe a poem, any poem, as *lyric*, part of what we mean is *that it turns*. It absorbs novelty into its form. For example, there is one poem in this book's introduction that is not a sonnet—Ezra Pound's "In a Station of the Metro"—and it also turns, dramatically, between its two lines. I wrote in the introduction that although I've read that poem countless times, I can still be surprised by the beginning of the second line, "Petals." Isn't this a volta? After all, as I noted then but am considering anew now, Hugh Kenner calls "petals" not just a significant word but "the pivotal word." It's important, but specifically because of its status as a turning point.

One of the implications of this book is about the modern lyric poem. I began this book by stating that a poem can be philosophical in its logic, regardless of whether or not its topics, perspective, or allusions are drawn from philosophy. Further, both modern philosophy and modern poetry are invested in the uncertain powers of inductive reasoning. But induction is not drawn from philosophy into poetry; inductive reasoning comprises a set of logical forms shared between poetry and philosophy because the challenge of making sense of the world, especially when the world is unpredictable, is also shared. The still more expansive version of this argument is that logic is a constitutive feature of the modern lyric poem. It's not just that some poems are logical; it's not just that this book outlines a category into which some poems can be placed. Rather, we can talk about modern poetry relative to logic because part of what makes the lyric poem lyric *is* its logic: how it connects particulars and parts. How proceeding inductively allows poetry to incorporate, and even benefit, from novelty. How a poem pivots; how a poem connects; how a poem knows what's enough to go on.

Here's one more sonnet by Brooks; "the rites for Cousin Vit" was published in 1949 between the early "kitchenette building" and the later "A Lovely Love."

> Carried her unprotesting out the door.
> Kicked back the casket-stand. But it can't hold her,
> That stuff and satin aiming to enfold her,
> The lid's contrition nor the bolts before.
> Oh oh. Too much. Too much. Even now, surmise,

She rises in the sunshine. There she goes,
Back to the bars she knew and the repose
In love-rooms and the things in people's eyes.
Too vital and too squeaking. Must emerge.
Even now she does the snake-hips with a hiss,
Slops the bad wine across her shantung, talks
Of pregnancy, guitars and bridgework, walks
In parks or alleys, comes haply on the verge
Of happiness, haply hysterics. Is.[44]

Like Brooks's other sonnets, "the rites for Cousin Vit" considers cramped architecture—here the coffin rather than the hallway or home, but still the sonnet form's "narrow room"—and not just what it would take to escape, but what turns can occur within its strictures. In "kitchenette building," the dream almost exists in the almost-apartment, and in "A Lovely Love," the speakers manage, albeit with a series of close calls, to stay "Definitionless in this strict atmosphere." But here, Cousin Vit, named for life itself, cannot be confined even by death. Unnamed pallbearers "Carried her unprotesting out the door./Kicked back the casket-stand" but death "can't hold her."[45] The funeral rites may have happened but those formalities are superseded by another kind of form, that of the sonnet form.[46]

This sonnet is exemplary of the sonnet because it turns and turns and turns. Michael Theune locates the volta very early in the sonnet: "Gwendolyn Brooks's 'the rites for Cousin Vit' contains another of the earliest major voltas in a sonnet: it occurs about halfway through the second line."[47] Ramazani writes that in this sonnet, Brooks "distributes the volta."[48] The poem keeps turning; it is always "Too much" for effective confinement. Even though Vit emerges from the coffin in the second line, later, in the ninth line, the traditional place for a volta, she does so again: "Too vital and too squeaking. Must emerge."

Vit "Must emerge" but arises not speaking but "squeaking"—too much for death and also "Oh oh. Too much. Too much" for language. The exclamation of "Oh oh" is something between the poetic invocative or apostrophic "O" and the near moan of "uh oh." The poem keeps pivoting and, like the speakers of "A Lovely Love," Vit finds her ways to the ungoverned, liminal spaces, including the boundaries of grammar. She "talks/Of pregnancy, guitars and bridgework, walks/In parks or alleys, comes haply on the verge/Of happiness, haply hysterics. Is." Talking and walking are set up in parallel: she takes both to their limits. She comes also "haply on the verge/Of happiness"; arriving at the border of happiness by luck, but also by punning. She "haply hysterics," meaning that she has hysterics by chance and is spinning out of control, or, alternatively, by condensing *happily* into "haply," she is laughing with joy. Vit "Is"—the poem ends with this single word sentence, insisting on her presence. But she achieves that presence by turns on different levels. She "Is" by twisting the largest structures—death and the sonnet—and also the smallest—the individual word, even a single syllable.

Voltas are usually thought of as *between* lines or stanzas, pivoting from one moment to another, and so represented by emptiness, a blank space, the white page. How can we think of a structure made *by* turns? The poem offers an image for a form made entirely of pivoting: Vit "does the snake-hips with a hiss." That "hiss," like the speaker's exclamations and puns and Vit's own "squeaking," shows how Vit twists language; how she spins its sounds away from and back to meaning. But also, the dance called the "snake-hips" is another representation of turning. Popularized by Earl "Snakehips" Tucker in the 1920s, it looks shockingly modern, easily imaginable as a solo performance in Alvin Ailey's groundbreaking 1960 "Revelations" mixed with the twist and moonwalking. In other words: it's all voltas.

Vit "talks/Of pregnancy, guitars and bridgework." We can read all of these as images of this poem that creates structures to hold what can't be held still: birth, music that exceeds the hollow wood form of the instrument, and even—though bridgework here means dentures—the work of connection. The snakehips dance is one more, as is this sonnet. The volta need not be understood as a gap or a silence, nor a lack of order or expectation. But rather, a volta can be understood as a bridge, as infrastructure, as structure itself. The speaker insists that snakehipping her way through this sonnet is not contrary to the sonnet tradition's relation to reasoning, but central to it. She moves directly from the exclamation of "Oh oh. Too much. Too much" to the language of inference: "Even now, surmise,/She rises in the sunshine." A surmise is a conjecture, and it can suggest an ungrounded assumption.

One could, and some philosophers have, described inductive reasoning as only surmise or mere surmise. While induction might have a close relationship to evidence, its inferences are not ever adequately supported by it. However, in the sonnet tradition, there's a slightly different way to read "surmise," which emphasizes how, by incorporating new evidence, by being potentially falsifiable—by working inductively—it brings one closer to truth. John Keats's "On First Looking into Chapman's Homer" ends with the sestet relating how the speaker felt when he "heard Chapman speak out loud and bold":

> Then felt I like some watcher of the skies
> When a new planet swims into his ken;
> Or like stout Cortez when with eagle eyes
> He stared at the Pacific—and all his men
> Looked at each other with a wild surmise–
> Silent, upon a peak in Darien.[49]

Here, a surmise is "Silent" but it depicts a sudden, even "wild" shift. In this image, Cortez "and all his men" suddenly realize that there is another ocean than the one they just traversed; their previous conception of the world's geography is instantly falsified.[50] Keats compares this realization to that of an astronomer identifying a "new planet," as William Herschel did in 1781 when he discovered Uranus, the first such identification since antiquity.[51] The "new planet" doesn't "swim[]" into the sight of the "watcher of the skies"—rather, it "swims into his ken," meaning his understanding. With the recognition that Uranus is not a star but a planet, the whole previous conception of the solar system's geography is also instantly falsified. So too with the speaker himself reading Chapman's new translation of Homer—what came before is now wrong. But with a "wild surmise," Cortez and his men, the astronomer, and the speaker all have a new and better understanding. Their reasoning, by incorporating new evidence, by turning, tacks ever closer to the truth. Surmise, like each day's sunrise, in the words of Marianne Moore's "The Pangolin," is "new and new and new." But pivoting doesn't mean unsteadiness; Moore's poem shows us that this novelty "steadies."[52]

The weakness of inductive reasoning is that any new piece of evidence might falsify, that is, overturn—that is, *turn*—a working theory. The strength of inductive reasoning is that its turns are, therefore, *what it is*. Its turns are what it is, and in this, it's like a sonnet, and also, more generally, like the modern poem, and also like modernity. For Earl "Snakehips" Tucker, Cousin Vit, and all of us: there is no still point of the turning world.

CONCLUSION

RESOLUTION

Modern poetry, like inductive reasoning, is made of turns, of voltas. The occasion of modernism is the surprises and shocks of modernity, the difficulty of living through novelty, the modern world's turns. Modern literature represents those turns formally, and modern poetry's experiments and innovations have been identified as making it new and thereby making it difficult. But while voltas are difficult, and their particular difficulty is that of novelty, this is not how this kind of turn in poetry should be understood. And, therefore—since voltas epitomize the sonnet form, which itself epitomizes the lyric poem—that isn't how poetry should be understood either. Nor, indeed, modernism.

A volta is not an empty space or break; it is not a disjunction but a conjunction. Moreover, a volta pivots in response to a problem. In a sonnet, the volta comes after the end of the octave's proposition, when the proposition has run out of steam or even run aground. The sestet is the resolution to the problem of the octave, but the sestet does not *solve* the octave's problem—it turns instead. It might appear that the poem turns away, but even rotating tangentially still turns the initial problem itself: it looks at it differently, it adjusts its grasp. By turning, the volta reframes the problem. The volta doesn't solve a problem because a *resolution* is not quite the same as a *solution*. A resolution doesn't simply answer a problem because it doesn't accept the problem's initial term; rather, it adjusts its stance relative to the problem. By reframing the octave, by being new, a volta changes the proposition's difficulty, the extent to which it even *is* a problem. And then the sestet can move forward.

A focus of this book has been what philosophers call the problem of induction, but as I'm arguing, modern poems reframe induction's bridgework, the way inductive reasoning connects luminous details, induction's conjunctions. In modern poetry, we see induction's unreliability turned into a strength. Modern poems show how novelty—a pivot, a new perspective—can reframe novelty itself as a problem. Modern poems, full of difficulty, are also made of the constant reframing of that difficulty. Modern poems, full of novelty, also make use of that novelty for epistemological ends and not just aesthetic ones. These turns are what make logic *logic* and also the lyric *lyric*. Modern poems turn so they can go on. This is a kind of resolution. It's also a kind of resolve.

ACKNOWLEDGMENTS

One way of describing this book is that it's about how the unexpected can be difficult, and I wrote it through surprising happinesses and disorienting losses. This book exists only because at crucial moments, as institutions and luck failed, the people close to me helped. It's a privilege to name and thank them.

At the University of Chicago, where I began the first fragments of this book, I thank Suzanne Buffam, Maud Ellmann, and Srikanth (Chicu) Reddy—without their rock-solid support, I would not have finished my PhD; I remain grateful. The members of the Poetics Workshop taught me much of what I learned in graduate school about good poetry and real thinking: V. Joshua Adams, Stephanie Anderson, Joel Calahan, Michael Hansen, Joshua Kotin, Patrick Morrissey, and Chalcedony Wilding. Thank you to Kristian Kerr for the Thomas Street years.

I express my appreciation for the National Endowment for the Humanities and the Bill and Carol Fox Center for Humanistic Inquiry at Emory University, and Keith Anthony. The time granted by a postdoctoral fellowship allowed me to imagine this book. From that year at Emory, I particularly thank John Lysaker and Nathan Suhr-Sytsma, and I remember, here and always, Rebecca Munson.

The tremendous luck of getting an academic job—it could easily have been otherwise—meant that I was able to continue working on this book.

ACKNOWLEDGMENTS

In particular, from my years at West Virginia University, I thank Rose Casey, who I met as a colleague but very quickly became a dear friend, which in this case also meant both a co-conspirator and an inspiration. I am grateful to the West Virginia Humanities Council and the WVU Humanities Center for their financial support.

My thanks to the Notre Dame Institute for Advanced Study for my semester there as a fellow, and to my undergraduate research assistants August Bonacci and Abigail Whalen. I also thank Brad Gregory, Kristian Olsen, Carolyn Sherman, and Don Stelluto. I'm lucky to have found friends during my brief months at Notre Dame: I thank Harvey Brown, Nan Z. Da, Clare Kim, Sara Marcus, Kate Marshall, Joseph Rosenberg, and Yasmin Solomonescu.

And I'm extraordinarily fortunate to have landed, just as this book went to press, among wonderful new colleagues at Reed College. I am already grateful for their welcome.

Thank you to the Rosenbach Library and to Elizabeth Fuller. An earlier version of chapter 1 was published as "Walt Whitman's Formalism," in the "Logic and Literary Form" special issue of *Poetics Today* 41, no. 1 (2020): 59–81, edited by Jeffrey Blevins and Daniel Benjamin Williams, whom I thank for their useful feedback. An earlier version of chapter 3 was published as "Explanation in Composition: Gertrude Stein and the Contingency of Inductive Reasoning," *jml: Journal of Modern Literature* 39, no. 3 (2016): 95–113. I thank Robert Caserio for asking for it, and for his kindness to me at a crucial moment when I was a graduate student.

Thank you to Philip Leventhal at Columbia University Press; I will always be grateful for his patient support. Thank you to Emily Simon. Thank you to Sarah Osment, who built the cogent and elegant index. And my thanks also to Aaron Obedkoff for his help reading the proofs and checking citations.

I'm grateful to the people who read pieces of this book over the years and lent their intelligence to show me how to improve it: V. Joshua Adams, Kasia Bartoszynska, Natalia Cecire, Erica Fretwell, Devin Garofalo, Nick Gaskill, Brian Glavey, Walt Hunter, Oren Izenberg, Joshua Kotin, Emily Ogden, and Dora Zhang. They are also some of the friends that made academia where I wanted to stay, and let me add to that list: Stephanie Anderson, Kristin Grogan, Eric Hayot, David Hobbs, Kamran Javadizadeh, Anna Kornbluh,

ACKNOWLEDGMENTS

Michael LeMahieu, Megan Quigley, Lisi Schoenbach, Dan Sinykin, and Lindsay Turner.

More friends: thank you to Emily Chilko, Kate Chilko and Andrew Sylvester, Kate Ferguson and Adam Atherton, Laura Hyde and Erin Hult, Theresa McCulla and Brian Goldstein, Daisy Pitkin and Scott Buchanan, Jillian Wein Riley and Andy Riley, Alana Sagin, Laura Ward, and Anna Weincrot. Thank you to my reading group and my writing group—the Half-Lung Club and everyone in my group texts—and thank you to Bartlett Street. Thank you to Anne O'Donnell; I would be lost without her wisdom. I thank Joshua Kotin again; he has bolstered me for decades now. My debt to Oren Izenberg is long-lasting and ongoing; I thank him again. And my thanks to Brian Glavey; he always tells me the truth.

Three of my grandparents lived to see me begin this book (and to meet their great-grandchildren), and I think of the fourth every day: Karl and Dé Winant and Melvin and Yvonne Rogow loved music, literature, the world, and me, all unflaggingly, and their memories are blessings. I'm grateful for Steve and Alison Hilsabeck, who always show up for us when we need them. Thank you to my sister and brother, Carmen and Gabriel Winant, whose commitments to their work and to the world continue to inspire me.

This book is for my parents, Howard Winant and Deborah Rogow. They made me feel capable and cherished; they gave me the world and showed me how to work toward its repair. Thank you to Geoff Hilsabeck. Every page of this book could have been a love letter that began "Dear Geoff"—which is what I used to write when I got stuck in my dissertation—and so every page is that love letter, written over so many years in the past and looking to the future. Thank you also to our children, Esther and Zeke Hilsabeck: you are the best new things.

NOTES

Introduction: Philosophical Poetry

1. See, for example, Paul de Man, "Literary History and Literary Modernity," *Daedalus* 99, no. 2 (Spring 1970): 384–404; Michael Levenson, "Novelty, Modernity, Adjacency," *New Literary History* 42, no. 4 (Autumn 2011): 663–80; Michael North, *Novelty: A History of the New* (University of Chicago Press, 2013); and Jed Rasula, "Make It New," *Modernism/Modernity* 17, no. 4 (November 2010): 713–33.
2. North, *Novelty: A History of the New*.
3. David Hume, *An Enquiry Concerning Human Understanding*, ed. Stephen Buckle (Cambridge University Press, 2007), 29.
4. There are compelling accounts of modernism as concerned not with novelty but with daily ordinariness, including books by Liesl Olson, *Modernism and the Ordinary* (Oxford University Press, 2009) and Siobhan Phillips, *The Poetics of the Everyday: Creative Repetition in Modern American Verse* (Columbia University Press, 2009). Inductive reasoning is concerned with novelty, and it's also the philosophic logic that is depended on daily by everyone—and it shows that a confrontation with novelty *is* ordinary. As Ian Hacking writes, at the beginning of *An Introduction to Probability and Inductive Logic*, "Good news; Inductive reasoning is a guide in life. . . . It plays a much larger part in everyday affairs than deductive reasoning." Ian Hacking, *An Introduction to Probability and Inductive Logic* (Cambridge University Press, 2001), xi.
5. The syllogism, for example, can take the form:

> All A are B.
> All B are C.
> Therefore all A are C.

INTRODUCTION

 Inductive reasoning does not have a set of established forms, but in this book's first chapter I identify the list as a common inductive form, and in the second chapter I focus on the analogy. For a longer discussion of logical form, see chapter 1.

6. Ana Schwartz, "Anne Bradstreet, Arsonist?," *New Literary History* 52, no. 1 (2021): 119–43, 137.
7. Graham Priest, *An Introduction to Non-Classical Logic: From If to Is*, 2nd ed. (Cambridge University Press, 2008), xviii.
8. Ezra Pound, *Selected Poems of Ezra Pound* (New Directions, 1957), 35.
9. Hugh Kenner, *The Pound Era* (University of California Press, 1971), 187.
10. Kenner, *The Pound Era*, 185.
11. Sianne Ngai talks about the aesthetic judgment of "interesting" similarly as a kind of working theory: "What is striking is the consistency of the judgment's function: that of ascribing value to that which seems to differ, in a yet-to-be-conceptualized way, from a general expectation or norm whose exact concept may itself be missing at the moment of judgment"; she writes, "The question of how we use nonaesthetic, concept-based judgments to support feeling-based aesthetic judgments, including ones based on complicated mixtures of displeasure with pleasure, is worth examining more closely in light of the fact that we do it all the time, without recourse to general principles"; and she notes, "Frank Sibley puts it in more technical language recalling Hume's problem of induction." Sianne Ngai, *Our Aesthetic Categories: Zany, Cute, Interesting* (Harvard University Press, 2012), 112, 118.
12. I discuss this later in this introduction.
13. In addition to Kenner's reading of this poem, I'm informed by the work of Daniel Tiffany. See Daniel Tiffany, *Radio Corpse: Imagism and the Cryptaesthetic of Ezra Pound* (Harvard University Press, 1998).
14. Scholarship on Ezra Pound has produced dozens if not hundreds of articles and books on the influence of certain schools of philosophy—or single philosophers or theorists—on the *Cantos*. For example, on Neoplatonism in the *Cantos*, see Peter Liebregts, *Ezra Pound and Neoplatonism* (Fairleigh Dickinson University Press, 2004); on Confucianism, see Chungeng Zhu, "Ezra Pound: The One-Principle Text," *Literature and Theology* 20, no. 4 (2006): 394–410; on social credit economic theory, see, among many others, Richard Sieburth, "In Pound We Trust: The Economy of Poetry/The Poetry of Economics," *Critical Inquiry* 14, no. 1 (1987): 142–72.
15. Pound's espousal of successive aesthetic theories merge with one another, and then, by the "Usura" canto, connect with social-credit economics into a theory of value that may or may not cohere; Eliot's aesthetic commitments link up with his Christianity; Stevens forges an aesthetics-in-lieu-of-religion "supreme fiction."
16. Marjorie Perloff, in "Pound/Stevens: Whose Era?" details the assembled literary scholars on each side, arguing, "The split goes deep, and its very existence raises what I take to be central questions about the meaning of Modernism—indeed about the meaning of poetry itself in current literary history and theory." Marjorie Perloff, *The Dance of the Intellect: Studies in the Poetry of the Pound Tradition* (Cambridge University Press, 1985), 2.

INTRODUCTION

17. Susan Stewart, *Poetry and the Fate of the Senses* (University of Chicago Press, 2002), 42.
18. Daniel Albright, *Lyricality in English Literature* (University of Nebraska Press, 1985), vii–viii. In Walt Hunter's essay "Lyric and Its Discontents," he notes that claiming confusion about lyric's definition is itself a convention. He quotes Rene Wellek writing, "One must abandon attempts to define the general nature of the lyric or the lyrical," and identifies it as an "adaptation of Samuel Johnson's remark, in his *Lives of the English Poets*, that 'to circumscribe poetry by a definition will only show the narrowness of the definer.'" Walt Hunter, "Lyric and Its Discontents," *Minnesota Review* 79 (2012): 78–90, 78.
19. Jackson's lyricization thesis—that the lyric was invented through the practice of lyric reading, or as she writes in *Dickinson's Misery*, "from the mid-nineteenth century through the beginning of the twenty-first century, to be lyric is to be read as lyric"—has been widely influential, and also has been sharply disputed. Virginia Jackson, *Dickinson's Misery* (Princeton University Press, 2005), 6. Jonathan Culler, for example, in 2015's *Theory of the Lyric*, argues that Jackson's account of lyricization "conflates two quite different historical operations"; the first is the rise of "lyric as the intense expression of the poet" in the nineteenth century and the second is "the critical operation by which Anglo-American New Criticism, after the 1940s, takes the poem away from the historical author and treats it as the *speech* of a persona." Culler, *Theory of the Lyric*, 84. Jackson then responds to Culler in 2023's *Before Modernism*, arguing that it is Culler who has overlooked history, because "if we place Culler's project against the racialized background of nineteenth-century American poetics, we can see that . . . the history of American poetics has been expertly constructed as a bridge that connects ideas of the expressive lyric to ideas of the fictive lyric speaker, since this forgotten chapter in that history so explicitly racialized the relation between the two. What has been historically irresponsible has been the omission of nineteenth-century American poetics (aside from the usual nods to Whitman and Dickinson) from theories of the lyric." Virginia Jackson, *Before Modernism: Inventing American Lyric* (Princeton University Press, 2023), 52.
20. Virginia Jackson, "Lyric," in *The Princeton Encyclopedia of Poetry and Poetics*, 4th ed., ed. Roland Greene, Stephen Cushman, Claire Cavanagh, Jahan Ramazani, and Paul F. Rouzer (Princeton University Press, 2012), 826.
21. Stephanie Burt, "What Is this Thing Called Lyric?," *Modern Philology* 113, no. 3 (2016): 422–40, 429.
22. I'm referring here to the Wittgensteinian concept of family resemblance, specifically as it governs the rules of a language-game, here the language-game of what we mean by "lyric." To quote from the *Stanford Encyclopedia of Philosophy* about how Wittgenstein advises eschewing definitions of words: "Instead of these symptoms of the philosopher's 'craving for generality,' he points to 'family resemblance' as the more suitable analogy for the means of connecting particular uses of the same word. There is no reason to look, as we have done traditionally—and dogmatically—for one, essential core in which the meaning of a word is located and which is, therefore, common to all uses of that word. We should, instead, travel with the word's uses through 'a complicated network of similarities overlapping and criss-crossing' (*PI* 66)." Anat Biletzki and Anat Matar, "Ludwig Wittgenstein," *The Stanford Encyclopedia of Philosophy* (Fall 2023 Edition), ed.

Edward N. Zalta and Uri Nodelman, https://plato.stanford.edu/archives/fall2023/entries/wittgenstein. Reading the lyric this way is already in practice, i.e., this is how I understand Stephanie Burt's addendum at the end of a long list of prior definitions of the lyric that a lyric poem is "a poem that descends from, or resembles, other poems often called lyric." Burt, "What Is this Thing Called Lyric?," 425.

23. For example, Hunter describes how the unexpected detail may be "either a gap or an excess in a text," and this is a common theme in "attempts to locate the essence of lyric." Hunter, "Lyric and Its Discontents," 78. See also Michael Theune, *Structure and Surprise* (Teachers & Writers Collaborative, 2007).
24. Mark W. Booth, *The Experience of Songs* (Yale University Press, 1981), 4.
25. Booth, *The Experience of Songs*, 23–24.
26. Albright, *Lyricality in English Literature*, ix
27. Albright, *Lyricality in English Literature*, 31. Similarly, Robert von Hallberg also agrees that "Lyric poetry is a genre of song," and describes the musicality of poetic language as an aspect of its novelty: "Musicality is known not by itself, but rather in relation to what it is not, viz. conventional speech between strangers." Robert von Hallberg, *Lyric Powers* (University of Chicago Press, 2008), 144, 146. Von Hallberg's point is the pleasure offered by musicality in contrast to rote small talk, but I note that his definition depends how music feels surprising in its unconventionality, though it is of course also rule-governed.
28. For another account of poetry working "slantwise," see Anahid Nersessian, *The Calamity Form* (University of Chicago Press, 2020), 19.
29. Helen Vendler, *Our Secret Discipline* (Harvard University Press, 2007), 118.
30. Allen Grossman, *True-Love: Essays on Poetry and Valuing* (University of Chicago Press, 2009), 15.
31. Allen Grossman, *The Sighted Singer* with Mark Halliday (Johns Hopkins University Press, 1992), 233.
32. Grossman, *The Sighted Singer*, 239.
33. Grossman, *The Sighted Singer*, 247.
34. These are just a few examples, and here are a few more: Barbara Johnson attends to poetry's surprises so consistently that *The Surprise of Otherness* becomes the subtitle of a posthumous collection of her essays and the throughline of the preface. Melissa Feuerstein et al., "Editors Preface," in *The Barbara Johnson Reader: The Surprise of Otherness*, ed. Melissa Feuerstein et al. (Duke University Press, 2014); Oren Izenberg's description of what comes to be called the avant-garde tradition, with its "repeated promises of originality and continual discoveries of discontinuity,... The privileging of unending novelty." Oren Izenberg, *Being Numerous: Poetry and the Ground of Social Life* (Princeton University Press, 2011), 6; also Nersessian's "Pindaric leap" between particulars in the paratactic poem. Nersessian, *The Calamity Form*, 20.
35. Culler, *Theory of the Lyric*, 38.
36. Jackson's book *Dickinson's Misery* has the subtitle "A Theory of Lyric Reading." Hunter writes, "The work of Virginia Jackson in *Dickinson's Misery* (2005) is a watershed moment in the slow process of decommissioning the lyric. In Jackson's book, the question of 'why' the lyric emerges at various points in history replaces the question of 'what' the lyric is and supplements the question of 'how' the lyric works." Hunter, "Lyric and Its Discontents," 79.

INTRODUCTION

37. Culler, *Theory of the Lyric*, 87.
38. Culler, *Theory of the Lyric*, 90.
39. For example, Jackson writes that "obvious inflection [of the language of slavery] does continue to surprise literary historians, since it has not been understood as the racialization of the structure of American poetics itself." Virginia Jackson, *Before Modernism* (Princeton University Press, 2023), 32.
40. Priest, *An Introduction to Non-Classical Logic*, xviii.
41. I see this account of lyric poetry using novelty to address philosophical problems in Allen Grossman's work as well as that of his erstwhile students and interlocutors Sharon Cameron, Oren Izenberg, and their own erstwhile students, including Joshua Kotin and V. Joshua Adams—including myself—as well as in Stanley Cavell's work on skepticism and the work in literary studies that follows in his tradition.
42. "Skepticism concerning other minds is not skepticism but tragedy." Stanley Cavell, *The Claim of Reason* (Oxford University Press, 1999), xxiii. For other examples of literary scholarship that takes up this question, see, in addition to Allen Grossman's, the work of Oren Izenberg and V. Joshua Adams.
43. As mentioned in footnote 14, Pound's philosophic influences ranged broadly and idiosyncratically and included economic and aesthetic theories of value; literary scholarship on Pound tends to isolate single influences. Scholarship on Stevens and philosophy, on the other hand, synthesizes the influences on Stevens and his portrayal of them; they're more easily synthesizable, and also, Stevens is already acknowledged as "the philosopher's poet," as Bart Eeckhout writes in a recent article of that title. Bart Eeckhout, "The Philosopher's Poet: Twenty-First-Century Perspectives on Wallace Stevens," *Transatlantica*. no. 1 (December 1, 2020). Stevens's use of philosophy is introductory material; Eeckhout previously wrote a chapter called "Stevens and Philosophy" for *The Cambridge Companion to Wallace Stevens*. Bart Eeckhout, "Stevens and Philosophy," in *The Cambridge Companion to Wallace Stevens*, ed. John N. Serio (Cambridge University Press, 2007). In *Wallace Stevens in Context*, there are two chapters on Stevens's philosophic influences, "American Philosophy" and "European Philosophy," as well as one on "Aesthetics" and one on "Abstraction." Glen MacLeod, ed., *Wallace Stevens in Context* (Cambridge University Press, 2017). Literary scholars have traced the philosophic influences on Stevens; see, for example, Charles Altieri, "Poetic Thinking," in *The New Wallace Stevens Studies*, ed. Bart Eeckhout and Gül Bilge Han (Cambridge University Press, 2021); Joshua Kotin, *Utopias of One* (Princeton University Press, 2017); Marjorie Levinson, *Thinking Through Poetry: Field Reports on Romantic Lyric* (Oxford University Press, 2018); and Rachel Malkin, "Public Desires, Private Desires: The Satisfactions of Stevens and Stanley Cavell," *The Wallace Stevens Journal* 36, no. 1 (2012): 105–33. There's also a cluster of writing on Stevens and pragmatism, including Olson, *Modernism and the Ordinary*; Jonathan Levin, *The Poetics of Transition* (Duke University Press, 1999); and Heather Cass White, "Pragmatist Poetics in Wallace Stevens and Marianne Moore," *The Wallace Stevens Journal* 31, no. 2 (Fall 2007): 148–70. And it's also well known that Stevens's poetry is used as an example by philosophers; Alain Badiou, Stanley Cavell, Simon Critchley, and Peter Hare have all written about how Stevens's poetry illustrates and illuminates

INTRODUCTION

philosophic ideas or problems. See Alain Badiou, *The Age of Poets: And Other Writings on Twentieth-Century Poetry and Prose*, trans. Emily Apter and Bruno Bosteels (Verso, 2014); Stanley Cavell, "Reflections on Wallace Stevens at Mount Holyoke," in *Artists, Intellectuals, and World War II: The Pontigny Encounters at Mount Holyoke College, 1942–1944*, ed. Christopher Benfey and Karen Remmler (University of Massachusetts Press, 2006), 61–79; Simon Critchley, *Things Merely Are: Philosophy in the Poetry of Wallace Stevens* (Routledge, 2005); and Peter Hare, *Pragmatism with Purpose*, ed. Joseph Palencik et al. (Fordham University Press, 2015). Hare's essays on Stevens could be grouped with the literary critics writing about pragmatism, of course, and it's also worth noting that he's the late husband of celebrated American poet Susan Howe, who has also written about Stevens. I became aware of Hare's writings from Eeckhout, "The Philosopher's Poet."

44. Wallace Stevens, *Collected Poetry & Prose* (Library of America, 1997), 77.
45. Charles Altieri, "Exemplification and Expression," in *A Companion to the Philosophy of Literature*, ed. Garry L. Hagberg and Walter Jost (Wiley-Blackwell, 2010), 491–507, 499.
46. My thinking here is indebted to Oren Izenberg. See, for example: "Some—or perhaps many—poems may coherently be regarded as investigatory devices rather than as primarily aesthetic or rhetorical performances; or, more precisely—that their aesthetic and rhetorical performances should be regarded as a crucial part of their investigatory means. We don't need to invent new kinds of knowing specific to poems." Oren Izenberg, "How to Know Everything," in *The Poetry of Emily Dickinson: Philosophical Perspectives*, ed. Elisabeth Camp (Oxford University Press, 2021), 95.
47. Gertrude Stein, *The Autobiography of Alice B. Toklas* (Vintage, 1990), 200.
48. I've written elsewhere about Pound's use of the theories of explanation. See Johanna Winant, "Ezra Pound and the Form of Explanation," *Paideuma: Modern and Contemporary Poetry and Poetics* 42 (2015): 171–96.
49. Mueller writes, for example, of Donne's "Take heede of Loving Mee": "The first two stanzas of this poem are cast in the logical form of a 'dilemma,'—a disjunctive syllogism in which two propositions are presented as mutually exclusive alternatives, 'Either X or Y,' from which the inference follows: 'Not X and Y.'" Janel Mueller, ed., *John Donne: Selected Writings*, 21st-Century Oxford Authors (Oxford University Press, 2015), 501. Also see Katrin Ettenhuber, *The Logical Renaissance: Literature, Cognition, and Argument, 1479–1630* (Oxford University Press, 2024).
50. Paul Fussell, *Poetic Meter and Poetic Form* (Random House, 1965), 168.
51. Gordon Teskey, *Spenserian Moments* (Harvard University Press, 2019), 12.
52. Logic, of course, isn't that interesting to what comes to be called the Continental tradition, who are more like James and late Wittgenstein in seeing no problem of induction at all, but spend no time talking about it. But Nietzsche talks about the new in literary history and literary modernity. See Paul de Man, *Blindness and Insight: Essays in the Rhetoric of Contemporary Criticism*, 2nd ed. (University of Minnesota Press, 1983).
53. Alfred North Whitehead, *Science and the Modern World*, Lowell Lectures, 1925 (The Free Press, 1967), 23.

INTRODUCTION

54. Bertrand Russell, "The Regressive Method for Discovering the Premises of Mathematics [1907]," in *Essays in Analysis*, ed. Douglas Lackey (George Braziller, 1945), 273–74.
55. Bertrand Russell, *A History of Western Philosophy* (Simon & Schuster, 1967), 673.
56. Charles S. Peirce, *Writings of Charles S. Peirce: A Chronological Edition, Volume 1: 1857–1866*, ed. Max H. Fitsch et al (Indiana University Press, 1982). For more on Peirce and inductive reasoning, see also Charles Sanders Peirce, *Reasoning and the Logic of Things*, ed. Kenneth Laine Ketner (Harvard University Press, 1993).
57. William James, *Pragmatism and Other Writings*, ed. Giles Gunn (Penguin Classics, 2000), 29.
58. James, *Pragmatism and Other Writings*, 29.
59. James, *Pragmatism and Other Writings*, 30.
60. James, *Pragmatism and Other Writings*, 32.
61. Karl Britton, "Portrait of a Philosopher," in *Ludwig Wittgenstein: The Man and His Philosophy*, ed. K. T. Fang (University of Michigan Press, 1967), 61. Also see Oswald Hanfling, "Hume and Wittgenstein," in *Impressions of Empiricism*, vol. 9, ed. Godfrey Vesey (Royal Institute of Philosophy, 1976).
62. Ludwig Wittgenstein, *Tractatus Logico-Philosophicus*, 2nd ed., Routledge Classics (Routledge, 2001), 47.
63. Ludwig Wittgenstein, *On Certainty*, ed. G. E. M. Anscombe and G. H. von Wright trans. Denis Paul and G. E. M. Anscombe. (Harper & Row, 1972), 37e.
64. From the 1940s, when Carnap was in his early fifties, through the end of his life nearly thirty years later in 1970, Carnap wrote about inductive reasoning. Of a dozen possible citations, here are two examples: Rudolf Carnap, "On Inductive Logic," *Philosophy of Science* 12, no. 2 (1945): 72–97 and Rudolf Carnap, "Inductive Logic and Inductive Intuition," in *The Problem of Inductive Logic*, ed. Imre Lakatos (North-Holland, 1968), 258–314.
65. Carl G. Hempel, *Aspects of Scientific Explanation, and Other Essays in the Philosophy of Science* (The Free Press, 1965).
66. For some critiques of Hempel, see Wesley Salmon and Bas C. van Fraassen. For example, Wesley C. Salmon, *Statistical Explanation and Statistical Relevance* (University of Pittsburgh Press, 1971); Wesley C. Salmon, *Scientific Explanation and the Causal Structure of the World* (Princeton University Press, 1984); and Bas C. van Fraassen, *The Scientific Image* (Oxford University Press, 1980).
67. Carl G. Hempel, "Studies in the Logic of Confirmation," *Mind* 54, no. 213 (1945): 1–26.
68. Karl Popper, *Conjectures and Refutations*, 2nd ed. (Routledge, 2002), 70.
69. Thomas Kuhn, *The Structure of Scientific Revolutions* (University of Chicago Press, 1996). Kuhn's argument has been described as a kind of pragmatism writ large; see, for example, Bojana Mladenović, *Kuhn's Legacy: Epistemology, Metaphilosophy, and Pragmatism* (Columbia University Press, 2017).
70. W. V. O. Quine, *Ontological Relativity & Other Essays* (Columbia University Press, 1969), 72.
71. Ian Hacking, *The Taming of Chance* (Cambridge University Press, 1990), 4.

72. Descriptions of New Criticism as inductive reasoning appear, but in the tone of an afterthought or an obvious statement. Here are two examples: Ian Watt says "Practical Criticism" is "inductive rather than deductive" in his legendary close reading of the first paragraph of *The Ambassadors*. Ian Watt, "The First Paragraph of *The Ambassadors*: An Explication," *Essays in Criticism* 3 (1960): 250. Nearly sixty years later, Gillian White writes that New Criticism uses "close, inductive formalist reading practices." Gillian White, "Poetics of Contingency," *Textual Practice* 32, no. 3 (2018): 532. These quotes are typical in that both Watt and White are building to another point (in both cases about the autonomy of the text) and so the inductive reasoning process behind close reading is tangential and their comments noting it are glancing.

73. T. S. Eliot, *The Sacred Wood and Major Early Essays*, Dover on Literature & Drama (Dover, 1998), 128.

74. George Steiner, "On Difficulty," *The Journal of Aesthetics and Art Criticism* 36, no. 3 (1978): 263–76.

75. Leonard Diepeveen, *The Difficulties of Modernism* (Routledge, 2003), 2.

76. John Guillory, *Cultural Capital: The Problem of Literary Canon Formation* (University of Chicago Press, 1993), 172. Guillory quotes Brooks's writing (drawing on Craig S. Abbott's analysis as well) to make the argument that "the valorization of difficulty as the general quality of poetic language was always an integral part of the New Critical Agenda of canonizing the modernist poets." Guillory, *Cultural Capital*, 169.

77. There are exceptions, of course, especially among recent work in the intersections of literary studies and philosophy. Karen Zumhagen-Yekplé describes a difficulty native to modernist literature (prose, in this case) that also falls between Steiner's tactical and ontological difficulties, a kind of difficulty that resembles that of Wittgenstein's *Tractatus* in that "the real challenge of the book lies in the personally transformative work it demands of readers." This "different order of difficulty" that she identifies in fiction by Joyce, Kafka, Woolf, and Coetzee "poses a deeper and more indefinite sort of difficulty, and with far higher ethical stakes"—not exactly a philosophical problem, but not not one either. Karen Zumhagen-Yekplé, *A Different Order of Difficulty: Literature After Wittgenstein* (University of Chicago Press, 2020), 7. Other scholarship about philosophic problems in literary texts by literary scholars includes (but is not limited to): Robert Chodat, *Worldly Acts and Sentient Things: The Persistence of Agency from Stein to DeLillo* (Cornell University Press, 2008); Izenberg, *Being Numerous*; Kotin, *Utopias of One*; Michael LeMahieu, *Fictions of Fact and Value: The Erasure of Logical Positivism in American Literature, 1945–1975* (Oxford University Press, 2013); Megan Quigley, *Modernist Fiction and Vagueness: Philosophy, Form, and Language* (Oxford University Press, 2015); and V. Joshua Adams's forthcoming book, *Skepticism and Impersonality in Modern Poetry* (Bloomsbury, 2025). See also the work of Cora Diamond, for example, "The Difficulty of Reality and the Difficulty of Philosophy," *Partial Answers: Journal of Literature and the History of Ideas* 1, no. 2 (June 2003): 1–26.

78. Indeterminacy offered Perloff a term to characterize a counter-tradition in modernism—that of Rimbaud, Pound, Stein, Williams, and Ashbery—against what she described as the High Modernist Symbolism of Yeats, Eliot, Auden,

INTRODUCTION

Stevens, and Frost. Marjorie Perloff, *The Poetics of Indeterminacy* (Princeton University Press, 1981), 18.
79. Richard Rorty, *Contingency, Irony, and Solidarity* (Cambridge University Press, 1989); Barbara Herrnstein Smith, *Contingencies of Value* (Cambridge University Press, 1989), 1. Rorty does not cite Herrnstein Smith, but Herrnstein Smith does argue against an earlier essay by Rorty, "Solidarity or Objectivity?" which prefigures the thinking in *Contingency, Irony, and Solidarity*. In her book's final chapter, Herrnstein Smith distinguishes herself from Rorty by embracing radical relativism (which Rorty holds at some distance by holding out "solidarity" as another option) and critiquing Rorty's liberal values, which Rorty himself calls "ethnocentrism." Rorty, *Contingency, Irony, and Solidarity*, 198.
80. Niklas Luhmann, *Social Systems*, trans. John Bednarz, Jr. and Dirk Baecker (Stanford University Press, 1996), 25.
81. David E. Wellbery, "Contingency," in *Neverending Stories: Toward a Critical Narratology* ed. Maria Tatar, Ann Clark Fehn, Ingeborg Hoesterey (Princeton University Press, 1992), 241.
82. Christina Lupton, "Introduction: Literature and Contingency," *Textual Practice* 32, no. 3 (2018): 377.
83. White, "Poetics of Contingency," 529.
84. In her essay, White identifies and discusses the following articles: Charles Altieri, "Contingency as Compositional Principle in Fifties Poetics," in *The Scene of My Selves: New Work on New York School Poets*, ed. Terence Diggory and Stephen Paul Miller (National Poetry Foundation, 2001), 359–84; Michael Palmer, "Poetry and Contingency: Within a Timeless Moment of Barbaric Thought," *Chicago Review* 49, no. 2 (Summer 2003): 65–76; and Marjorie Perloff, "Happy World: What Lyn Hejinian's Poetry Tells Us About Chance, Fortune, and Pleasure," *Boston Review* (February 2001). White also follows Perloff in describing Hejinian's work—especially the essays collected in *The Language of Inquiry*, in which Hejinian uses the adjective "open"—as interested in contingency as well. See Lyn Hejinian, *The Language of Inquiry* (University of California Press, 2000) and Charles Altieri, "Stevens and the Crisis of European Philosophy," *Soundings: An Interdisciplinary Journal* 89, no. 3/4 (Fall/Winter 2006): 255–78.
85. Sianne Ngai, "The Cuteness of the Avant-Garde," *Critical Inquiry* 31 no. 4 (Summer 2005): 811–47, 838.
86. Natalia Cecire writes in her excavation of what is meant by "experimental writing," that the construction of that category by late twentieth-century writers claiming earlier ones as forebears is "a white recovery project." Natalia Cecire, *Experimental: American Literature and the Aesthetics of* (Johns Hopkins University Press, 2019), 29. Cecire was Hejinian's student, and Hejinian's influence, both as a teacher and as the writer of *The Language of Inquiry*, is crucial and visible here. Writing about poetry's underdetermination is one way that these poets and critics were describing the construction of the avant-garde as a category; other versions of this theorization of the avant-garde can be seen in Ngai, "The Cuteness of the Avant-Garde," and another is Cathy Park Hong, "Delusions of Whiteness in the Avant-Garde," *Lana Turner* 7 (November 2014); Bob Perelman, *The Marginalization of Poetry: Language Writing and Literary History* (Princeton University Press, 1996).

87. I thank Natalia Cecire for this point, which I have paraphrased from an exchange we had on Twitter.
88. Charles Bernstein, *Attack of the Difficult Poems: Essays and Inventions* (University of Chicago Press, 2011), 3.
89. Here I am instructed by Sharon Cameron: "All poetry is characterized by problems; put differently, its characteristics, those properties that individuate and distinguish it, also define the specific form of its difficulty." Sharon Cameron, *Lyric Time* (Johns Hopkins University Press, 1979), 18. I am also thinking of Oren Izenberg's discussion of how poetry addresses a philosophical problem: "The poets I am *most* interested to describe throughout this book will thus resist their own will to formal mastery, shy away from the sensory richness of their own strongest work, and undermine the conceptual particularity and moral exemplarity of their poetic vision. At the extremes, they long, threaten, or enjoin themselves to do away with poetry altogether. More precisely, they strive to conceive of or even a produce a 'poetry' without poems; as though the problems with what philosophy calls 'person-concepts'—our definitions of and attempts to give an account of personhood—could be addressed by subverting or destroying the very medium that bears them." Izenberg, *Being Numerous*, 4.
90. See also White's discussion of Brooks's "a song in the front yard," in which ballad rhymes help reveal a child's understanding of systems of injustice. Gillian White, *Lyric Shame: The "Lyric" Subject of Contemporary American Poetry* (Harvard University Press, 2014), 95–96.
91. Gwendolyn Brooks, *The Essential Gwendolyn Brooks*, ed. Elizabeth Alexander (Library of America, 2005), 1.
92. For more on the connections between poetic forms and the structures of capitalism, see Walt Hunter, *Forms of a World: Contemporary Poetry and the Making of Globalization* (Fordham University Press, 2019).
93. Schwartz, "Anne Bradstreet, Arsonist?," 137.
94. Brooks, *The Essential Gwendolyn Brooks*, 1.
95. Brooks, *The Essential Gwendolyn Brooks*, 1.
96. Brooks, *The Essential Gwendolyn Brooks*, 1.
97. Walt Hunter, *The American House Poem, 1945–2021* (Oxford University Press, 2023), 26. Hunter's chapter on Brooks and housing is very useful. For example, in that same chapter, he details the house as a recurrent image from Brooks's juvenilia onward, describes the four kitchenette apartments Brooks lived in with her growing family, and makes the claim for the importance of this poem in Brooks's oeuvre and American poetry: "'Kitchenette building' is a special type of house poem, one in which the temporality of living with a big family in a too-small space transforms the sonnet as a poetic genre. This poem illuminates one of the larger arguments in this book. Housing, as it becomes a preeminent concern both for individual families and for the political and economic identity of the United States, brings old genres to hand while fundamentally altering them." Walt Hunter, *The American House Poem*, 33.
98. Farah Jasmine Griffin, *Who Set You Flowin?: The African-American Migration Narrative* (Oxford University Press, 1995), 108–9.
99. Gwendolyn Brooks, *Selected Poems* (Harper & Row, 1963), 3.
100. Karen Jackson Ford, "The Sonnets of Satin-Legs Brooks," *Contemporary Literature* 48, no. 3 (Fall 2007): 345–73, is a useful survey of Brooks's use of sonnets and

INTRODUCTION

their influence on other poets. Ford argues that the sonnet is central to Brooks's thinking about art: "Brooks may not have written another sonnet after her radicalization in 1967, but she adamantly continued to rely on that form as she pondered aesthetic questions and attempted to formulate a new poetic program that served her political ideals." Ford, "The Sonnets of Satin-Legs Brooks," 346. Although Brooks, after her radicalization in 1967, could neither embrace nor abandon the sonnet, Ford writes, it "was the *question* of the politics of form, so crucial to the new black poetry, that animated Brooks's career, rather than any particular answer she proposed to it. And this questioning always brought her back to the sonnet." Ford, "The Sonnets of Satin-Legs Brooks," 352.

101. My reading of Brooks and "kitchenette building" is influenced by and in conversation with a number of other scholars who theorize the connections between Blackness, literature, and epistemology, and how Brooks's work locates conflict between systemic racism and resistance to it in her use of literary forms. Jacqueline Goldsby writes of Brooks's ballad "Pearl May Lee," which tells the story of a lynching in a "tightly tuned rhyme scheme": "Brooks's clear affinity with ballad aesthetics co-existed with her obvious skepticism toward it, a dissonance which gives rise to the cultural commentary offered through the poem's form." Jacqueline Goldsby, *A Spectacular Secret: Lynching in American Life and Literature* (University of Chicago Press, 2006), 2, 4. Goldsby's book's overall argument is that by "analyzing literary forms as registers or archives of lynching's history," she defines lynching's "cultural logic." Goldsby, *A Spectacular Secret*, 7, 5. Kevin Quashie, writing of Brooks's *Maud Martha*, describes the novel's episodic form as one way Brooks conceptualizes "quiet as a consciousness that gets beyond conflict with the expectations of the outer world." Kevin Quashie, *The Sovereignty of Quiet: Beyond Resistance in Black Culture* (Rutgers University Press, 2012), 47. Instead of "expectations," Michael Clune and Karen Jackson Ford both use the term "pattern." Clune's argument is about how "racial vision proceeds from *example* to *pattern*" in Brooks's poems, but they also "block this desire to see the big picture, and her poems carefully register the frustration this blockage elicits." Michael Clune, *A Defense of Judgment* (University of Chicago Press, 2021), 156, 177. Ford describes Brooks's "keen ambivalence" about formal poetics, especially after her radicalization at the Second Fisk Writers' Conference in 1967. In addition to her essay on Brooks's sonnets, Ford has another about her ballads; about "The Last Quatrain of the Ballad of Emmett Till," she writes, "The last tercet of the poem here figures the insufficiency of the ballad to arrange the wildness of her husband's brutality into stanzas that could keep such a tragedy in check." Karen Jackson Ford, "The Last Quatrain: Gwendolyn Brooks and the Ends of Ballads," *Twentieth Century Literature* 56, no. 3 (2010): 378. She quotes the poem commenting on its own form and the society it depicts: "although the pattern prevailed,/The breaks were everywhere." Brooks, *The Essential Gwendolyn Brooks*, 68." More generally, one could read Brooks's poetry as, in Christina Sharpe's terms, "in the wake" of slavery. Sharpe doesn't discuss Brooks, but her writing is helpful in considering how Brooks's speakers in "kitchenette building" can barely imagine an epistemology beyond capitalism; Sharpe writes, "wake work [is] a mode of inhabiting *and* rupturing this episteme with our known lived and un/imaginable lives." Christina Sharpe, *In the Wake: On Blackness and Being*

INTRODUCTION

(Duke University Press, 2016), 18. Or more generally still, one could read all of these as along the lines of what Fred Moten writes in the first sentence of *In the Break*: "The history of blackness is testament to the fact that objects can and do resist." Fred Moten, *In the Break: The Aesthetics of the Black Radical Tradition* (University of Minnesota Press, 2003).

102. Karen Jackson Ford writes, "In the years following her radicalization, Brooks repeatedly vowed not to write any more sonnets, in 1973, for example, claiming that 'this does not seem to me to be a sonnet time,' and in 1977 reiterating 'that I won't be writing other sonnets.'" Ford, "The Sonnets of Satin-Legs Brooks," 352.

103. I thank the students in my fall 2021 graduate seminar at West Virginia University for talking this reading through with me: Vahid Arefi, Meghan Hutton, Sung Hee Ko, Aerianna McClanahan, and Matthew Powney.

1. WALT WHITMAN'S ENUMERATIONS

1. "Review of Leaves of Grass," *Examiner*, March 22, 1856, 181.
2. Quoted in Edward Waldo Emerson, *Emerson in Concord: A Memoir* (Houghton Mifflin and Company, 1888), 228.
3. Horace Traubel, *With Walt Whitman in Camden*, vol. 4 (Rowman & Littlefield, 1961), 324.
4. Allen Ginsberg, *Howl and Other Poems* (City Lights Books, 1956), 29–30.
5. Harold Bloom, "To the Tally of My Soul: Whitman's Image of Voice," in *The Ordering Mirror: Readers and Contexts* (Fordham University Press, 1993), 53; and Harold Bloom, *The Anatomy of Influence: Literature as a Way of Life* (Yale University Press, 2011), 218.
6. Allen Grossman, "The Poetics of Union in Whitman and Lincoln," in *The American Renaissance Reconsidered* (Johns Hopkins University Press, 1985), 193. Other critics, including Andrew Epstein, Alan Trachtenberg, Matt Cohen, and Aaron Dinen, have taken up the term *tally* in their own critical work on Whitman. See Andrew Epstein, *Attention Equals Life: The Pursuit of the Everyday in Contemporary Poetry and Culture* (Oxford University Press, 2016); Alan Trachtenberg, "The Politics of Labor and the Poet's Work: A Reading of 'A Song for Occupations,'" in *Walt Whitman: The Centennial Essays* ed. Ed Folsom, (University of Iowa Press, 1994): 120–132; and Matt Cohen and Aaron Dinen, "Keeping Tally With Meaning: Reading Numerals in Walt Whitman's Manuscripts," *Walt Whitman Quarterly Review* 34, no. 2 (Fall 2016): 120–45.
7. John B. Mason, "The Poet-Reader Relationship in 'Song of Myself,'" in *Approaches to Teaching Whitman's Leaves of Grass*, ed. Donald D. Kummings (MLA Association of America, 1990), 47. Also see Cristina Beltrán, "Mestiza Poetics: Walt Whitman, Barack Obama, and the Question of Union," in *A Political Companion to Walt Whitman*, ed. John E. Seery (University Press of Kentucky, 2011): 29–95.
8. Matt Sandler, "Kindred Darkness: Whitman in New Orleans," in *Whitman Noir: Black America and the Good Gray Poet* ed. Ivy G. Wilson (University of Iowa Press, 2014), 69.
9. William Pannapacker, "The City," in *A Companion to Walt Whitman* ed. Donald D. Kummings (Wiley-Blackwell, 2006), 45

1. WALT WHITMAN'S ENUMERATIONS

10. I'm grateful to Kamran Javadizadeh for the suggestion of Kelly and to Andrew Epstein for the suggestion of Ammons and Mayer. Epstein describes both Ammons and Mayer as Whitmanian in *Attention Equals Life*, and uses the word *tallying*: "When Ammons calls 'Shit List,' his lengthy exercise in tallying up different types of feces, a poem, it takes its place in a lineage that stems from the catalogs of ancient epic to Whitman's enumerations and beyond." Epstein, *Attention Equals Life*, 20; and, "Mayer deploys ... extravagant documentary lists and Whitman-like catalogs, like the exhaustive tally of the 'titles of all the current books' spotted at the local bookstore." Epstein, *Attention Equals Life*, 172.
11. Caroline Levine, *Forms: Whole, Rhythm, Hierarchy, Network*, (Princeton University Press, 2015), x.
12. Eva von Contzen, "The Limits of Narration: Lists and Literary History," *Style* 50, no. 3 (2016), 256.
13. Paul Jaussen, "Spectral Affordances of the Catalogue," *Comparative Literature* 70, no. 2 (2018): 160.
14. Paul Tankard, "Reading Lists," *Prose Studies* 28, no. 3 (2006): 344.
15. Umberto Eco, *The Infinity of Lists* (Rizzoli, 2009), 327, 131.
16. Robert Belknap, "The Literary List: A Survey of Its Uses and Deployments," *Literary Imagination* 2, no. 1 (2001): 35.
17. Jaussen, "Spectral Affordances of the Catalogue," 171.
18. Jaussen, "Spectral Affordances of the Catalogue," 161; Eva von Contzen, "Die Affordanzen Der Liste" ['The Affordances of the List']," *Zeitschrift für Literaturwissenschaft und Linguistik* 47, no. 3 (2017): 320–21.
19. Martha Nussbaum takes up some of the same questions at the beginning of *Love's Knowledge*, writing, "Literary form is not separable from philosophical content, but is, itself, a part of content—an integral part, then, of the search for and the statement of truth. Martha Nussbaum, *Love's Knowledge: Essays on Philosophy and Literature* (Oxford University Press, 1990), 3. Andrea Gadberry also discusses how philosophy can use literary form, writing that "prose forms can borrow from the techniques of poetry, and literary-critical reading can illuminate instances of poetic force in philosophy." Andrea Gadberry, *Cartesian Poetics: The Art of Thinking* (University of Chicago Press, 2020), 7.
20. I've also written about the congruences between literary form and logical form in "Logical and Literary Form," in *The Cambridge Companion to Philosophy and Literature*, ed. R. Lanier Anderson and Karen Zumhagen-Yekplé (Cambridge University Press, forthcoming).
21. I'm not talking about enumeration as Andrew Piper describes it in his 2018 book, *Enumerations: Data and Literary Study*, where he discusses the computation study of literature and its ability to make meaning by tracking repetitions across large numbers of texts. Andrew Piper, *Enumerations: Data and Literary Study* (University of Chicago Press, 2018). Nor am I discussing induction as a "problem of excess" as Dahlia Porter writes in her 2018 book, *Science, Form, and the Problem of Induction in British Romanticism* (Cambridge University Press, 2018), 3. Porter cites Andrew Piper, *Dreaming in Books: The Making of the Bibliographic Imagination in the Romantic Age* (University of Chicago Press, 2009) as a point of departure. Rather than using "induction" to mean any empirically-derived generalization, as Porter does, drawing on seventeenth-century

science and particularly the Baconian method, I'm using it in the stricter sense of logical inferential reasoning from particulars as it's discussed in philosophy from Hume through the present day.

22. "What we might call the 'formal turn' has been one of the most marked trends in twenty-first-century literary studies." Rachael Scarborough King, "The Scale of Genre," *New Literary History* 52, no. 2 (Spring 2021): 265.
23. Susan J. Wolfson, "Introduction: Reading for Form," in *Reading for Form*, ed. Susan J. Wolfson and Marshall Brown (University of Washington Press, 2006), 3, 14.
24. Marjorie Levinson, "What Is New Formalism?," *PMLA* 122, no. 2 (2007): 558–69, 561.
25. Levine, *Forms*, 2.
26. Cara Lewis describes how "form is so slippery a concept, so multifaceted a word" as she calls for "a responsible, flexible formalism" that can handle "the wide range of formal experiments in modernism" that occur across different media. Cara L. Lewis, *Dynamic Form: How Intermediality Made Modernism* (Cornell University Press, 2020), 9, 11. Her account of form is usefully set alongside that by Levine and Levinson, whose work she discusses, along with Angela Leighton, *On Form* (Oxford University Press, 2007).
27. Sandra Macpherson, "A Little Formalism," *ELH* 82, no. 2 (2015): 386.
28. Jonathan Kramnick and Anahid Nersessian, "Form and Explanation," *Critical Inquiry* 43, no. 3 (2017): 651.
29. Marjorie Levinson, "Response to Jonathan Kramnick and Anahid Nersessian, 'Form and Explanation,'" *Critical Inquiry* 44, no. 1 (2017): 148.
30. My description of our good-faith radical assumption about form here is informed by Donald Davidson's articulation of what he calls "radical interpretation" in the essay "Radical Interpretation" collected in *Inquiries into Truth and Interpretation* (Oxford University Press, 2001). I've written about Davidsonian radical interpretation as it applies to the interpretation of poetry in my essay "Philosophy, Poetry, and the Principle of Charity," in *A Companion to American Poetry*, ed. Mary McAleer Balkun et al. (Wiley-Blackwell, 2022), 120–33.
31. Here I'm disagreeing with King, who writes in "The Scale of Genre," "naming a form is like knowing the answer on a quiz, while naming a genre is like making an argument in an essay." King, "The Scale of Genre," 264. This describes a scholar or critic's activity. One way of describing this chapter—and book's—stance is that forms may be more easily identifiable and identifying them may involve less controversy than identifying genres, but also forms are not just identification; forms may be making arguments of their own.
32. Work such as Naomi Levine's *The Burden of Rhyme* argues that rhyme itself is a literary form—rather than aspect or feature of form—but on the specific grounds that rhyme is "more than a prosodic device in the nineteenth century" because it theorizes "what forms could say and do and mean." Naomi Levine, *The Burden of Rhyme: Victorian Poetry, Formalism, and the Feeling of Literary History* (University of Chicago Press, 2024), 8. See also the work of Meredith Martin and Ben Glaser on meter. Meredith Martin, *The Rise and Fall of Meter* (Princeton University Press, 2012); and Ben Glaser, *Modernism's Metronome: Meter and Twentieth-Century Poetics* (Johns Hopkins University Press, 2020).
33. Robert Hass, *A Little Book on Form: An Exploration into the Formal Imagination of Poetry* (Ecco, 2018), 3.

1. WALT WHITMAN'S ENUMERATIONS

34. Frances Ferguson similarly suggests that what has often been described as *stylistic*—free indirect discourse—should be understood as *formal*, writing "free indirect style is just as formal as any formal feature of poetry." For Ferguson, plot may also be formal: "the marriage plot in Austen. . . . [is] formal to an extraordinary new degree." Frances Feguson, "Jane Austen, *Emma*, and the Impact of Form," in *Reading for Form*, ed. Susan J. Wolfson and Marshall Brown (University of Washington Press, 2006), 234, 239.
35. Indeed, in many ways, we already do recognize content as formal; the conclusion to this book discusses the sonnet form and particularly the volta, which is a formal characteristic of a sonnet (the rhyme scheme usually shifts) that marks a pivot in its content (the argument traditionally shifts too).
36. Ezra Pound, *Personae* (New Directions, 1990), 90; and Ezra Pound, *The Cantos of Ezra Pound* (New Directions, 1996), 538.
37. John Milton, "Note on 'The Verse' Preceding Paradise Lost," in *Complete Poems and Major Prose*, ed. Merritt Y. Hughes (Hackett, 2003), 210.
38. William Wordsworth, *The Major Works*, ed. Stephen Gill (Oxford University Press, 2000), 286.
39. Levine, *Forms*, 8.
40. Martha Nussbaum, "Democratic Desire: Walt Whitman," in *A Political Companion to Walt Whitman*, ed. John E. Seery (University Press of Kentucky, 2011), 107.
41. Betsy Erkkila, *Whitman the Political Poet* (Oxford University Press, 1989), 5.
42. For more on Whitman's formal techniques, see Stephen Cushman, *Fictions of Form in American Poetry* (Princeton University Press, 2014).
43. For a useful discussion of the poems of *Edgar Allan Poe and the Juke Box*, see Oren Izenberg's in the endnotes to his book *Being Numerous: Poetry and the Ground of Social Life* (Princeton University Press, 2011), 211–13.
44. Wordsworth, *The Major Works*, 286.
45. Walt Whitman, *Poetry and Prose*, ed. Justin Kaplan (Library of America, 1982), 6.
46. Alexis de Tocqueville, *Democracy in America*, ed. Richard D. Heffner (Signet Classics, 2001), 183.
47. Patrick Redding, "Whitman Unbound: Democracy and Poetic Form, 1912–1931," *New Literary History* 41, no. 3 (2010): 671.
48. This mood of syllogism is sometimes referred to by its medieval mnemonic BARBARA, since all of its propositions are universal and affirmative.
49. Thomas Pavel, would, I think, disagree with this description of a sonnet; he argues that what makes a sonnet is that it has fourteen lines, and that convention is akin to "social conventions, conventions of polite behavior . . . What is required in these cases is the appreciation and application of the appropriate rule." Thomas Pavel, "Literary Genres as Norms and Good Habits," *New Literary History* 34, no. 2 (2003): 203.
50. Kramnick and Nersessian, "Form and Explanation," 650.
51. Levinson, "Response to Jonathan Kramnick and Anahid Nersessian," 151.
52. Carl G. Hempel, *Aspects of Scientific Explanation, and Other Essays in the Philosophy of Science* (Free Press, 1965), 335.
53. Wesley C. Salmon, *Scientific Explanation and the Causal Structure of the World* (Princeton University Press, 1984), 9. Salmon's answer emphasizes causality, but mostly follows Hempel's D-N model of explanation.

1. WALT WHITMAN'S ENUMERATIONS

54. This is the position held by Bas C. van Fraassen, as Marjorie Levinson points out in her response to "Form and Explanation." See Bas C. van Fraassen, "The Pragmatic Theory of Explanation," in *Theories of Explanation*, ed. Joseph C. Pitt (Oxford University Press, 1988). My favorite version of this argument, though, is found in Mary Hesse, *Models and Analogies in Science* (University of Notre Dame Press, 1965).
55. David Hume, *An Enquiry Concerning Human Understanding*, ed. Stephen Buckle, Cambridge Texts in the History of Philosophy (Cambridge University Press, 2007), 29.
56. Hume recognized that enumeration is the basis of inductive reasoning: "All we can do . . . is to run over several instances and, and examine carefully the principle which binds the different thoughts to each other, never stopping till we render the principle as general as possible. The more instances we examine, and the more care we employ, the more assurance shall we acquire, that the enumeration, which we form from the whole, is complete and entire." Hume, *An Enquiry Concerning Human Understanding*, 20.
57. Whitman, *Poetry and Prose*, 202–203.
58. David S. Reynolds, *Walt Whitman's America: A Cultural Biography* (Vintage Books, 1996), 338.
59. Grossman, "The Poetics of Union in Whitman and Lincoln," 193.
60. Grossman, "The Poetics of Union in Whitman and Lincoln," 188.
61. Whitman, *Poetry and Prose*, 203.
62. Lisi Schoenbach, *Pragmatic Modernism* (Oxford University Press, 2012), 84.
63. On this point, I have depended on Schoenbach's excellent research and follow her in pointing to Ulrich Beck, *Risk Society: Towards a New Modernity* trans. Mark Ritter (Sage, 1992); Anthony Giddens, *The Consequences of Modernity* (Stanford University Press, 1990); Ian Hacking, *The Emergence of Probability: A Philosophical Study of Early Ideas About Probability, Induction, and Statistical Inference*, 2nd ed. (Cambridge University Press, 2006), as well as to Ian Hacking, *The Taming of Chance* (Cambridge University Press, 1990).
64. For how literature engaged with the emergence of insurance, see Jason Puskar, *Accident Society: Fiction, Collectivity, and the Production of Chance* (Stanford University Press, 2012).
65. Schoenbach, *Pragmatic Modernism*, 86. Schoenbach also writes that prediction is "key to understanding modernity as a process and as an intellectual methodology." Schoenbach, *Pragmatic Modernism*, 87.
66. Nelson Goodman, *Fact, Fiction, and Forecast*, 4th ed. (Harvard University Press, 1983), 65.
67. Hilary Putnam agrees, writing, "What we have in Goodman's view, as, perhaps, in Wittgenstein's, are practices, which are right or wrong depending on how they square with our standards." Hilary Putnam, "Foreword to the Fourth Edition," in Goodman, *Fact, Fiction, and Forecast*, ix.
68. Whitman, *Poetry and Prose*, 88.
69. This anticipation is not unique to "Song of Myself"; in "Crossing Brooklyn Ferry," Whitman addresses "You men and women of a generation, or ever so many generations hence."
70. Goodman, *Fact, Fiction, and Forecast*, 73.

2. EMILY DICKINSON'S ANALOGIES

71. Siobhan Phillips, *The Poetics of the Everyday: Creative Repetition in Modern American Verse* (Columbia University Press, 2010), 16.
72. As in the title of Salmon's 1984 book *Scientific Explanation and the Causal Structure of the World*.
73. Ed Folsom and Kenneth M. Price, *Re-Scripting Walt Whitman: An Introduction to His Life and Work*, (Blackwell, 2005), 95.
74. Anne Carson writes of Simonides of Keos that, "Simonides's inscriptional verse [on gravestones] is the first poetry in the ancient Greek tradition about which we can certainly say, these are texts written to be read: literature." That these poems are epitaphs is not accidental, as "memorable naming is the function of poetry." Anne Carson, *Economy of the Unlost* (Princeton University Press, 1999), 78, 41.

2. EMILY DICKINSON'S ANALOGIES

1. Emily Dickinson, *The Poems of Emily Dickinson: Reading Edition*, ed. R. W. Franklin (Belknap Press, 2005), 90.
2. It isn't controversial to argue that, in Elisabeth Camp's words in her introduction to a collection of essays about Dickinson and philosophy, that "Dickinson in particular is an epistemically ambitious poet." Elisabeth Camp, "Introduction: Emily Dickinson's Epistemic Ambitions for Poetry," in *The Poetry of Emily Dickinson: Philosophical Perspectives*, ed. Elisabeth Camp (Oxford University Press, 2021), 1. Later, she asks, "What other motivations are there for poetic form, and what implications might this have for how we might integrate Dickinson's insights into our own philosophizing?" Camp, "Introduction," 16. This chapter addresses, if slantwise, that question. My reading of Dickinson chimes with Joshua Kotin's discussion of Dickinson's poetry as "a limit case of difficulty," and also Oren Izenberg's account of an "analytical Dickinson." Joshua Kotin, *Utopias of One* (Princeton University Press, 2017), 137; Oren Izenberg, "Poems Out of Our Heads," *PMLA* 123, no. 1 (2008): 220.
3. Arguments are valid if they are based on valid logical forms. A logical form is valid if the conclusions necessarily follow from the premises. Deductive logical forms are valid. (Nelson Goodman and Mary Hesse argue for the criteria of validity for nondeductive logical forms, but that remains a controversial idea; most logicians say that the terms valid and invalid simply don't apply to nondeductive reasoning.) An argument is sound if the logical form is valid and the premises are true, making the conclusion also necessarily true.
4. See, for example, the influential structure-mapping theory of Dedre Gentner, "Structure-Mapping: A Theoretical Framework for Analogy," *Cognitive Science* 7, no. 1 (1983): 155–70, as well as work by Mary L. Gick and Keith J. Holyoak, such as "Schema Induction and Analogical Transfer," *Cognitive Psychology* 15 no. 1 (1983): 1–38.
5. Douglas Hofstadter and Emmanuel Sander, *Surfaces and Essences: Analogy as the Fuel and Fire of Thinking* (Basic Books, 2013), 3.
6. Michael Scriven, *Reasoning* (McGraw Hill, 1976), 210.
7. Cass Sunstein, "On Analogical Reasoning," *Harvard Law Review* 106, no. 3 (1993): 741.
8. Lloyd L. Weinreb, *Legal Reason: The Use of Analogy in Legal Argument* (Cambridge University Press, 2005), vii.

9. Joseph Priestley, *The History and Present State of Electricity* (Johnson, 1769), 419.
10. For an analysis of the connections between logical positivism and twentieth-century literature, see Michael LeMahieu, *Fictions of Fact and Value: The Erasure of Logical Positivism in American Literature, 1945–1975* (Oxford University Press, 2013).
11. Mary Hesse, *Models and Analogies in Science* (University of Notre Dame Press, 1965), 7. See also Michael Weisberg, *Simulation and Similarity: Using Models to Understand the World* (Oxford University Press, 2013).
12. Mary S. Morgan, *The World in the Model: How Economists Work and Think* (Cambridge University Press, 2012), 2. See also Mary S. Morgan and Margaret Morrison, eds., *Models as Mediators: Perspectives on Natural and Social Science* (Cambridge University Press, 1999).
13. Morgan, *The World in the Model*, 21.
14. Thomas Kuhn, *The Essential Tension: Selected Studies in Scientific Tradition and Change* (University of Chicago Press, 1977), 246.
15. Tamar Szabó Gendler, *Thought Experiment: On the Powers and Limits of Imaginary Cases* (Garland Publishing, 2000), 1.
16. Roy A. Sorensen, *Thought Experiments* (Oxford University Press, 1992), 227.
17. Nancy Nersessian, "Cognitive Science, Mental Modeling, and Thought Experiments," in *The Routledge Companion to Thought Experiments*, ed. Michael Stuart et al. (Routledge, 2018), 311.
18. John D. Norton, "Thought Experiments in Einstein's Work," in *Thought Experiments in Science and Philosophy*, ed. Tamara Horowitz and Gerald J. Massey (Rowman & Littlefield, 1991), 129.
19. Oren Izenberg has written usefully about the connection between poetry and thought experiments; see Oren Izenberg, "How to Know Everything," in *The Poetry of Emily Dickinson: Philosophical Perspectives*, ed. Elisabeth Camp (Oxford, 2021). See also Geordie McComb, "Thought Experiment, Definition, and Literary Fiction," in *Thought Experiments in Philosophy, Science, and the Arts*, ed. Melanie Frappier et al. (Routledge, 2013).
20. Kuhn, *The Essential Tension*, 263.
21. Scriven, *Reasoning*, 210.
22. Ronald Munson and Andrew Black, *The Elements of Reasoning*, 6th ed. (Wadsworth Cengage Learning, 2012), 113.
23. Hilary Putnam, *The Many Faces of Realism* (Open Court, 1987), 73.
24. Scriven, *Reasoning*, 210.
25. Scriven, *Reasoning*, 211.
26. Hesse, *Models and Analogies in Science*, 74.
27. Hesse, *Models and Analogies in Science*, 57.
28. Scriven, *Reasoning*, 210.
29. Kuhn, *The Essential Tension*, 263–64.
30. Kuhn, *The Essential Tension*, 263.
31. A good roundup of this conversation can be found in David Davies, "Art and Thought Experiments," in *The Routledge Companion to Thought Experiments*, ed. Michael Stuart et al. (Routledge, 2018).
32. Some of the most prominent work on this subject is by Max Black, Stanley Cavell, and Donald Davidson: Max Black, "Metaphor," *Proceedings of the Aristotelian Society* 55 (1954): 273–94; Stanley Cavell, "Aesthetic Problems of Modern Philosophy," in

2. EMILY DICKINSON'S ANALOGIES

Must We Mean What We Say? (Charles Scribner's Sons, 1969), 73–96; and Donald Davidson, "What Metaphors Mean," in *Inquiries into Truth and Interpretation* (Oxford University Press, 1978), 245–64.

33. Devin Griffiths, *The Age of Analogy: Science and Literature Between the Darwins* (Johns Hopkins University Press, 2016), 28.
34. Griffiths, *The Age of Analogy*, 2–3.
35. Dahlia Porter, *Science, Form, and the Problem of Induction in British Romanticism* (Cambridge University Press, 2018), 136.
36. Porter, *Science, Form, and the Problem of Induction in British Romanticism*, 115.
37. Porter, *Science, Form, and the Problem of Induction in British Romanticism*, 136.
38. Griffiths, *The Age of Analogy*, 14.
39. Porter, *Science, Form, and the Problem of Induction in British Romanticism*, 136.
40. Griffiths, *The Age of Analogy*, 18.
41. Porter, *Science, Form, and the Problem of Induction in British Romanticism*, 113.
42. Caroline Levine, *Forms: Whole, Rhythm, Hierarchy, Network.* (Princeton University Press, 2015), 3.
43. Daniel Tiffany, *Toy Medium: Materialism and Modern Lyric* (University of California Press, 2000), 2–3.
44. Tiffany, *Toy Medium*, 5.
45. Another scholar in literary studies who makes an argument along these lines is Dora Zhang in her chapter on analogies in Proust in *Strange Likeness*. Zhang unpacks the significance of how analogical resemblance "concerns relations rather than things," and she describes the "correlational structure of the Proustian universe" as "idiosyncratic, drawing on the accidental connections." Dora Zhang, *Strange Likeness: Description and the Modernist Novel* (University of Chicago Press, 2020): 95, 114. As a result, the descriptions in the *Recherche* "weave a dense net of contingent associations." Zhang, *Strange Likeness*, 115.
46. Porter, *Science, Form, and the Problem of Induction*, 142.
47. Griffiths, *The Age of Analogy*, 29–30.
48. Griffiths, *The Age of Analogy*, 29.
49. Kuhn, *The Essential Tension*, 241.
50. Robert Weisbuch, *Emily Dickinson's Poetry* (University of Chicago Press, 1975), 12. Weisbuch's second chapter focuses on Dickinson's "analogical poetics." Weisbuch, *Emily Dickinson's Poetry*, 11–39. Virginia Jackson has also noted the analogies between body and page in Dickinson's work; see Jackson, *Dickinson's Misery: A Theory of Lyric Reading* (Princeton University Press, 2005), 183, 223. Michael Clune has also written about Dickinson's use of analogies as related to knowledge-making; he writes, "if we restrict our attention to literature's aesthetic qualities, can we abandon philosophical and scientific problems of knowledge? In some cases, the judgment of a works' aesthetic qualities is inextricable from the evaluation of its ideas. In judging that poems by Emily Dickinson and John Keats create compelling depictions of what it is like to die, I will show how they have taught us something new about life and death. The poets' strategy is to present an experience of listening as an analogue to the experience of dying." Michael Clune, *A Defense of Judgment* (University of Chicago Press, 2021), 111.
51. Suzanne Juhasz, "The Irresistible Lure of Repetition and Dickinson's Poetics of Analogy," *The Emily Dickinson Journal* 9, no. 2 (2000): 23–31.

2. EMILY DICKINSON'S ANALOGIES

52. Sharon Cameron, *Lyric Time: Dickinson and the Limits of Genre* (Johns Hopkins University Press, 1979), 35.
53. Cameron, *Lyric Time*, 29.
54. Cameron, *Lyric Time*, 45.
55. Oren Izenberg does not write about analogies in Dickinson, but he does write about how her poetry works—and works well—philosophically, and also based on particular examples. For example, he writes, "for Dickinson the absence of a concept for an experience is not necessarily a crisis.... If Dickinson's poetic mode of bearing out this insight improves on the philosophical mode, it is by means of exemplification—by addressing experience with an argument that is not just a discursive occasion but also an occasion for having an experience in its own right." Izenberg, "Poems Out of Our Heads," 221. And elsewhere he writes about another poem by Dickinson, "the way that the poem, in providing us first with the elemental units of perception, allows space for the drawing of inferences from data. So that even if, as in this poem, it is difficult for us to say *what* proposition is being reached or affirmed, we may still observe the imagistic translation of the note of birdsong into a 'term' of logic." Izenberg, "How to Know Everything," 97. For Izenberg, Dickinson's poetry "conveys experience not discursively, but by exemplification ... in responding to poetry, we take our own experiences as real knowledge about the world." Izenberg, "How to Know Everything," 103. Izenberg's argument is on a similar topic but in tension with V. Joshua Adams's account of Dickinson's "bad logic," and his reading of Dickinson's poetry as first "seek[ing] to resolve the problem of philosophical privacy in formal terms by way of inverted syllogisms that draw third-person conclusions from first-person premises," and thus the poems "deemphasize logic and reemphasize perception.... What we are getting is not inference but testimony disguised as inference." V. Joshua Adams, *Skepticism and Impersonality in Modern Poetry: Literary Experiments with Philosophical Problems* (Bloomsbury, 2025), 21, 44–45.
56. Northrop Frye, *Fables of Identity: Studies in Poetic Mythology* (Harcourt Brace, 1963), 202.
57. Cameron, *Lyric Time*, 35.
58. Jed Deppman, *Trying to Think with Emily Dickinson* (University of Massachusetts Press, 2008), 125.
59. Deppman, *Trying to Think with Emily Dickinson*, 122.
60. Jill Kaufman, "Filmmakers Rewrite the Emily Dickinson Story, Not for the First Time," April 11, 2019, https://www.nepm.org/regional-news/2019-04-11/filmmakers-rewrite-the-emily-dickinson-story-not-for-the-first-time. Christopher Benfey has written about Dickinson's riddles for over thirty years, from a 1986 article in *The New York Times* to this 2019 interview. Christopher Benfey, "The Riddles of Emily Dickinson," *New York Times*, May 18, 1986, https://www.nytimes.com/1986/05/18/books/the-riddles-of-emily-dickinson.html.
61. Christopher Benfey, *A Summer of Hummingbirds: Love, Art, and Scandal in the Intersecting Worlds of Emily Dickinson, Mark Twain, Harriet Beecher Stowe, and Martin Johnson Heade* (Penguin Books, 2009), 210.
62. Dickinson, *The Poems of Emily Dickinson*, 501.
63. I recognize that I could be misunderstood and sound as though I am personifying poems here, and I don't mean to be granting agency to poems in that way.

2. EMILY DICKINSON'S ANALOGIES

However, I am not happy saying that poems "contain," "structure," or even "exemplify" reasoning. We don't have good language to talk about the work that form does if it's not containing.

64. Sharon Cameron, *Choosing Not Choosing: Dickinson's Fascicles* (University of Chicago Press, 1992).
65. Some of these poems include the following, referred to by their first lines: "The rainbow never tell me/That gust and storm are by—," "Flowers—Well—if anybody/Can the extasy define," "'Arcturus' is his other name—/I'd rather call him 'Star!,'" "A science—so the Savans say,/'Comparative Anatomy'—," "Will there really be a 'morning?'/Is there such a thing as 'Day?,'" "If the foolish, call them 'flowers'—/Need the wiser, tell?," "'A transport' one cannot contain/May yet, a transport be—," and "The Skies cant keep their secret!/They tell it to the Hills—."
66. Dickinson, *The Poems of Emily Dickinson*, 61.
67. Dickinson, *The Poems of Emily Dickinson*, 86 (in "If the foolish, call them '*flowers*'—").
68. Cameron, *Lyric Time*, 29.
69. Adrienne Rich, "Vesuvius at Home," *Parnassus Review* 5, no. 1 (1976); Adrienne Rich, *Poetry and Prose: Poetry, Prose, Reviews and Criticism*, 2nd ed. Albert Gelpi et al. (W. W. Norton, 2018), 193.
70. Eve Kosofsky Sedgwick, *Tendencies* (Duke University Press, 1993).
71. Much has been written about pragmatism and American literature, including this short list of relevant scholarship: Kristen Case, *American Pragmatism and Poetic Practice: Crosscurrents from Emerson to Susan Howe* (Camden House, 2011); Paul Grimstad, *Experience and Experimental Writing: Literary Pragmatism from Emerson to the Jameses* (Oxford University Press, 2013); Richard Poirier, *Poetry and Pragmatism* (Harvard University Press, 1992); Lisi Schoenbach, *Pragmatic Modernism* (Oxford University Press, 2011); Kate Stanley, *Practices of Surprise in American Literature After Emerson* (Cambridge University Press, 2018); and Renee Tursi, "Emily Dickinson, Pragmatism, and the Conquests of Mind," in *Emily Dickinson and Philosophy*, ed. Jed Deppman et al. (Cambridge University Press, 2013).
72. William James, *Pragmatism and Other Writings*, ed. Giles Gunn (Penguin Classics, 2000), 34.
73. James, *Pragmatism and Other Writings*, 30.
74. C. S. Peirce, "How to Make Our Ideas Clear," *Popular Science Monthly* 12 (1878): 286–302.
75. For example, John Dewey writes that the truth lies in "its functional or instrumental use." John Dewey, *Studies in Logical Theory* (University of Chicago Press, 1903), 75.
76. Dickinson, *The Poems of Emily Dickinson*, 341–42.
77. Dickinson, *The Poems of Emily Dickinson*, 342.
78. Theo Davis, *Ornamental Aesthetics* (Oxford University Press, 2016).
79. Aristotle, *Poetics*, trans. Anthony Kenny (Oxford World's Classics, 2013), 47.
80. Cameron, *Lyric Time*, 66.
81. Susan Stewart, "On ED's 754/764," *New Literary History* 45, no. 2 (2014): 253–70.
82. Cameron, *Lyric Time*, 67.
83. See also Oren Izenberg's writing about poetry and thought experiments, for example, in Izenberg, "How to Know Everything."

84. See, for example, Susan Howe's description of Dickinson's fascicles: "By continually interweaving expectation and categories they checkmate inscription to become what the reader offers them." Susan Howe, *The Birth-Mark: Unsettling the Wilderness in American Literary History* (Wesleyan University Press, 1993), 136.
85. Davis, *Ornamental Aesthetics*, 94. For more on how analogy in literary texts have a contingent relationship to truth, see Dora Zhang on the contingency of analogy in Proust's *Recherche*. She writes, "The work of art, according to the *Recherche* itself, is a place that harbors the possibility of contingency and surprise, one that, to a reader willing to internalize and interpret its impressions, may yield truths of her own." Zhang, *Strange Likeness*, 115. In Zhang's reading of Proust, analogy's contingency leads to personal truths, but not necessarily truths about the world.
86. Davis, *Ornamental Aesthetics*, 12.
87. Davis, *Ornamental Aesthetics*, 11.
88. Michael Clune reads this poem as a successful analogy, "a convincing experiential analogue to death." Clune, *A Defense of Judgment*, 115.
89. Dickinson, *The Poems of Emily Dickinson*, 265–66.
90. Richard Jean So, "All Models Are Wrong," *PMLA* 132, no. 3 (2017): 668–73, 668.
91. So, "All Models Are Wrong," 670.
92. So, "All Models Are Wrong," 672.
93. Social scientists may not describe modeling as nondeductive because they use models *as deductive laws*, drawing conclusions from the abstractions that they represent. But the creation of these models is the process of nondeductive reasoning, as Mary Hesse argues.
94. So, "All Models Are Wrong," 669. In her introduction to her essays collected in *Thinking Through Poetry*, Marjorie Levinson characterizes one of her goals as "to set aside both classical and intuitive pictures of subjects and objects, entities and environments, in favor of models of recursively self-organizing fields of spatial, temporal, and logical kinds." Marjorie Levinson, *Thinking Through Poetry: Field Reports on Romantic Lyric* (Oxford University Press, 2018), 19.
95. Levinson, *Thinking Through Poetry*, 294.
96. Levinson, *Thinking Through Poetry*, 295.
97. Levinson, *Thinking Through Poetry*, 293.
98. Levinson, *Thinking Through Poetry*, 294n113.
99. Kuhn, *The Essential Tension*, 241, 264.

3. CONTINGENCY AND GERTRUDE STEIN

1. Gertrude Stein, *Writings, 1903–1932*, vol. 1. (Library of America, 1998), 62.
2. Stein, *Writings, 1903–1932*, 62.
3. In *The Autobiography of Alice B. Toklas*, Stein famously called Ezra Pound "a village explainer, excellent if you were a village, but if you were not, not." Gertrude Stein, *The Autobiography of Alice B. Toklas* (Vintage, 1990), 200. Evan Kindley describes a tension between how "modernist difficulty by nature resists understanding and explanation; it prefers simple aesthetic facticity," and yet the modernists "were passionate explainers." Evan Kindley, *Poet-Critics and the Administration of Culture* (Harvard University Press, 2017), 1–2. I half-agree with Kindley and

3. CONTINGENCY AND GERTRUDE STEIN

half-disagree with his characterization—this present chapter argues that modernist facticity and explanation aren't at odds.
4. Friedrich Nietzsche, *Beyond Good and Evil*, trans. Helen Zimmern (Tribeca Books, 2013), 118.
5. Carl G. Hempel, *Aspects of Scientific Explanation, and Other Essays in the Philosophy of Science* (Free Press, 1965), 334.
6. By "empirical" Hempel does not mean "scientific," but rather, "conforming to certain basic levels of objectivity," including the use of "publicly ascertainable evidence" and abandonment if better theories come along. He makes a point of including the social sciences as well as the natural sciences. Hempel, *Aspects of Scientific Explanation*, 334.
7. Hempel, *Aspects of Scientific Explanation*, 337. D-N explanations often, but not always, depend on laws that establish cause, see Hempel, *Aspects of Scientific Explanation*, 352.
8. Mary Hesse, *Models and Analogies in Science* (University of Notre Dame Press, 1965).
9. Bas C. van Fraassen, "From a View of Science to a New Empiricism," in *Images of Empiricism: Essays on Science and Stances, with a Reply from Bas C. van Fraassen*, ed. Bradley Monton and Bas C. van Fraassen (Oxford University Press, 2007), 343; and Bas C. van Fraassen, *The Scientific Image* (Oxford University Press, 1980).
10. Peter Lipton, *Inference to the Best Explanation* (Routledge, 2004), 1.
11. Hempel, *Aspects of Scientific Explanation*, 380.
12. Hempel, *Aspects of Scientific Explanation*, 400.
13. Hempel, *Aspects of Scientific Explanation*, 403.
14. Hempel, *Aspects of Scientific Explanation*, 410.
15. Wesley C. Salmon, *Scientific Explanation and the Causal Structure of the World* (Princeton University Press, 1984), 9.
16. Stein, *Writings, 1903–1932*, 8.
17. Stein, *Writings, 1903–1932*, 9, 62.
18. Stein, *Writings, 1903–1932*, 739.
19. See Liesl Olson, *Modernism and the Ordinary* (Oxford University Press, 2009); Lisi Schoenbach, *Pragmatic Modernism* (Oxford University Press, 2012); Lisa Ruddick, *Reading Gertrude Stein: Body, Text, Gnosis* (Cornell University Press, 1990); Wendy Steiner, *Exact Resemblance to Exact Resemblance: The Literary Portraiture of Gertrude Stein* (Yale University Press, 1978); Steven Meyer, *Irresistible Dictation: Gertrude Stein and the Correlations of Writing and Science* (Stanford University Press, 2002); Jennifer Ashton, *From Modernism to Postmodernism: American Poetry and Theory in the Twentieth Century* (Cambridge University Press, 2005); Robert Chodat, *Worldly Acts and Sentient Things: The Persistence of Agency from Stein to DeLillo* (Cornell University Press, 2008); Jonathan Levin, *The Poetics of Transition: Emerson, Pragmatism, and American Literary Modernism* (Duke University Press, 1999); Joan Richardson, *A Natural History of Pragmatism: The Fact of Feeling from Jonathan Edwards to Gertrude Stein* (Cambridge University Press, 2007); and Natalia Cecire, *Experimental: American Literature and the Aesthetics of Knowledge* (Johns Hopkins University Press, 2019).
20. Louis Menand, *The Metaphysicals Club* (Farrar, Straus and Giroux, 2001), xii.

3. CONTINGENCY AND GERTRUDE STEIN

21. William James, *Pragmatism and Other Writings*, ed. Giles Gunn (Penguin Classics, 2000), 115.
22. William James, *Essays in Radical Empiricism* (Harvard University Press, 1976), 22.
23. Steven Meyer, *Irresistible Dictation: Gertrude Stein and the Correlations of Writing and Science* (Stanford University Press, 2002), 21.
24. Meyer, *Irresistible Dictation*, 4. See also William James, *The Principles of Psychology*, vol. 2. (Henry Holt and Company, 1890), 221.
25. Chodat, *Worldly Acts and Sentient Things*, 34.
26. Chodat, *Worldly Acts and Sentient Things*, 38–39.
27. Chodat, *Worldly Acts and Sentient Things*, 39.
28. Chodat, *Worldly Acts and Sentient Things*, 41.
29. Chodat, *Worldly Acts and Sentient Things*, 42.
30. Natalia Cecire's account of reading Stein relative to ideas about objectivity is useful here as well; she writes, "I wish to hold off the slippage ... in which objectivity becomes equated with scientificity and various other values." Cecire, *Experimental*, 101–2.
31. Stein, *Writings, 1903–1932*, 345.
32. Stein, *Writings, 1903–1932*, 433.
33. Gertrude Stein, *Lectures in America* (Beacon Press, 1985), 40.
34. Gertrude Stein, *Everybody's Autobiography* (Exact Change, 2004), 177.
35. Stein, *Writings, 1903–1932*, 345.
36. Stein, *Writings, 1903–1932*, 444.
37. Gertrude Stein, *Writings, 1932–1946*, vol. 2, 2 vols. (Library of America, 1998), 418.
38. Gertrude Stein, *Blood on the Dining-Room Floor* (Dover, 2008), 6.
39. Gertrude Stein, *The Making of Americans* (Dalkey Archive Press, 1995), 595.
40. See Carl Van Vechten, "How to Read Gertrude Stein," in *Critical Essays on Gertrude Stein*, ed. Michael J. Hoffman (G. K. Hall & Co, 1986); Bruce Kellner, "How to Read Gertrude Stein," in *A Gertrude Stein Companion*, ed. Bruce Kellner (Greenwood Press, 1988); "Reading Gertrude Stein," in Randa Dubnick, *The Structure of Obscurity: Gertrude Stein, Language, and Cubism* (University of Illinois Press, 1984); "Reading Gertrude Stein," in Elizabeth Fifer, *Rescued Readings: A Reconstruction of Gertrude Stein's Difficult Texts* (Wayne State University Press, 1992); and "On Reading Gertrude Stein," in Ellen E. Berry, *Curved Thought and Textual Wandering: Gertrude Stein's Postmodernism* (The University Michigan Press, 1992).
41. Marjorie Perloff, *The Poetics of Indeterminacy* (Princeton University Press, 1981), 107, 98.
42. Marjorie Perloff, *Wittgenstein's Ladder: Poetic Language and the Strangeness of the Ordinary* (University of Chicago Press, 1996).
43. Steiner, *Exact Resemblance*, x.
44. Marianne DeKoven, *A Different Language: Gertrude Stein's Experimental Writing* (University of Wisconsin Press, 1983), xiv.
45. Catharine R. Stimpson, "The Somagrams of Gertrude Stein," in *Critical Essays on Gertrude Stein*, ed. Michael J. Hoffman (G. K. Hall & Co, 1986), 191.
46. Richard Poirier, *Trying It Out in America: Literary and Other Performances* (Farrar, Straus and Giroux, 1999), 190.
47. Poirier, *Trying It Out in America*, 184.

3. CONTINGENCY AND GERTRUDE STEIN

48. Marjorie Perloff, "Abstraction & Unreadability: Gertrude Stein's Portraits: The Case of Christian Berard," *Vlak* 2 (2011): 156.
49. Natalia Cecire, "Ways of Not Reading Gertrude Stein." *ELH* 82, no. 1 (Spring 2015): 304. This argument is further developed in her book, as when she writes, "The complex relationship between gender and objectivity—not only a philosophical relationship but also a very practical historical one bearing on what scientific activities counted as *work* (and should be published and paid for accordingly)." Cecire, *Experimental*, 94.
50. Deborah M. Mix, *A Vocabulary for Thinking: Gertrude Stein and Contemporary North American Women's Innovative Writing* (University of Iowa Press, 2007), 3.
51. Ulla E. Dydo, *Gertrude Stein: The Language That Rises: 1923-1934* (Northwestern University Press, 2008), 28.
52. Poirier, *Trying It Out in America*, 198.
53. Poirier, *Trying It Out in America*, 189.
54. Perloff, *Wittgenstein's Ladder*, 84-85.
55. Chodat, *Worldly Acts and Sentient Things*, 41.
56. Chodat, *Worldly Acts and Sentient Things*, 51.
57. Cecire reads Stein, especially early in her career, as attempting "antivisuality objectivity," which even early in her career can be seen in her medical work as "an intensified objectivity, one that no longer attempts to represent specimens as such but rather turns to abstract mental structures, burning away contingency." Cecire, *Experimental*, 180, 104.
58. "Since, unfortunately, the version of Miss Gertrude Stein's 'An elucidation' printed in the April number of Transition, while containing the correct words, presented them in the wrong order (through an inadvertence in the printing establishment), the text has been rearranged and is offered as a supplement." Elliot Paul, "Supplement," *transition* (1927); Karen Leick, *Gertrude Stein and the Making of an American Celebrity* (Routledge, 2009), 97.
59. Gertrude Stein, *A Stein Reader*, ed. Ulla E. Dydo (Northwestern University Press, 1993), 429.
60. Dydo, *Gertrude Stein*, 46.
61. Dydo, *Gertrude Stein*, 59, 69.
62. Lucy Daniel, *Gertrude Stein* (Reaktion Books, 2009), 142.
63. Dydo, *Gertrude Stein*, 47.
64. Stein, *A Stein Reader*, 430.
65. Stein, *A Stein Reader*, 431-36.
66. Dydo, *Gertrude Stein*, 57
67. Dydo, *Gertrude Stein*, 57.
68. Dydo, *Gertrude Stein*, 59.
69. Donald Davidson, *Essays on Actions and Events* (Oxford University Press, 2001), 3.
70. Stein, *Writings, 1903-1932*, 522.
71. Stein, *Writings, 1903-1932*, 523.
72. Stein, *Writings, 1903-1932*, 520.
73. Stein, *Writings, 1903-1932*, 520.
74. Steiner, *Exact Resemblance*, 168.
75. Bruce Bassoff, "Gertrude Stein's 'Composition As Explanation,'" *Twentieth Century Literature* 24, no. 1 (1978): 76.

76. Michael J. Hoffman, *Gertrude Stein* (Twayne Publishers, 1976), 105.
77. Bob Perelman, *The Trouble with Genius: Reading Pound, Stein, Joyce, and Zukofsky* (University of California Press, 1994), 152.
78. Ashton, *From Modernism to Postmodernism*, 31.
79. Ashton, *From Modernism to Postmodernism*, 32.
80. Ashton, *From Modernism to Postmodernism*, 51–52.
81. Ashton, *From Modernism to Postmodernism*, 60–61.
82. Stein, *Writings, 1903–1932*, 521.
83. Stein, *Writings, 1903–1932*, 521–22.
84. Thomas Kuhn, *The Structure of Scientific Revolutions* (University of Chicago Press, 1996), 7.
85. Gertrude Stein, *Stanzas in Meditation: The Corrected Edition*, ed. Susannah Hollister and Emily Setina (Yale University Press, 2012), 59.
86. Stein, *Stanzas in Meditation*, 204.
87. See Susannah Hollister and Emily Setina, "Preface," in *Stanzas in Meditation: The Corrected Edition*, ed. Susannah Hollister and Emily Setina (Yale University Press, 2012), viii; and Dydo, *Gertrude Stein*, 489–502.
88. Here I'll note Cecire's essay about Stein's unreadability titled "Ways of Not Reading Gertrude Stein," and also her argument in her book about Stein's double negatives: "The multiple negations in this passage . . . strikingly suggest the complex position of the subject who must constantly self-regulate." Cecire, *Experimental*, 87–88.
89. Stein, *Stanzas in Meditation*, 57.
90. Stein, *Stanzas in Meditation*, 72.
91. Stein, *Stanzas in Meditation*, 123.
92. Stein, *Stanzas in Meditation*, 124.
93. Stein, *Stanzas in Meditation*, 168.
94. Chad Bennett, *Word of Mouth: Gossip and American Poetry* (Johns Hopkins University Press, 2018), 75.
95. I talk about Luhmann and contingency at greater length in the introduction to this book.
96. Dydo, *Gertrude Stein*, 502–3.
97. Dydo reads Stein's entire oeuvre this way, writing, "Often her whole opus now seems a single extended work. True, each piece is self-contained, with a center and boundaries, but each also leads to or echoes others in mirrorings that move and shimmer across boundaries. Such bleedings or spills suggest links and changes from piece to piece." Dydo, *Gertrude Stein*, 472.
98. Ashton, *From Modernism to Postmodernism*, 31.
99. Caroline Levine, *Forms: Whole, Rhythm, Hierarchy, Network* (Princeton University Press, 2015), 24.
100. Virginia Jackson, *Dickinson's Misery: A Theory of Lyric Reading* (Princeton University Press, 2013), 8.
101. Bennett, *Word of Mouth*, 54.
102. Bennett, *Word of Mouth*, 54.
103. Donald Sutherland, "The Turning Point: Preface to the 1956 *Stanzas in Meditation*," in *Stanzas in Meditation: The Corrected Edition*, ed. Susannah Hollister and Emily Setina (Yale University Press, 2012), 38.

104. Sutherland, "The Turning Point," 34.
105. Susannah Hollister and Emily Setina, "Appendix B," in *Stanzas in Meditation: The Corrected Edition*, ed. Susannah Hollister and Emily Setina (Yale University Press, 2012), 262.
106. Hollister and Setina, "Appendix B," 262–63.
107. Stein, *Stanzas in Meditation*, 100, 128, 145, 184, 215.
108. Stein, *Stanzas in Meditation*, 181.
109. Stein, *Stanzas in Meditation*, 204.
110. Stein, *Stanzas in Meditation*, 197.
111. Quoted in Dydo, *Gertrude Stein*, 507.
112. Dydo, *Gertrude Stein*, 503.
113. Stein, *Blood on the Dining-Room Floor*, 6.

4. CONSISTENCY AND MARIANNE MOORE

1. Marianne Moore, *The Poems of Marianne Moore*, ed. Grace Schulman (Viking, 2003), 226.
2. David Hume, *An Enquiry Concerning Human Understanding*, ed. Stephen Buckle, Cambridge Texts in the History of Philosophy (Cambridge University Press, 2007), 35.
3. Hume, *An Enquiry Concerning Human Understanding*, 29.
4. I'm grateful to Abigail Whalen, at the time an undergraduate philosophy major at Notre Dame University and my research assistant while I was a fellow at the Notre Dame Institute for Advanced Study, for helping me understand the details of the formal philosophical proof.
5. See, for example, "Some Motifs in Baudelaire," in Walter Benjamin, *Illuminations* (Mariner Books, 2019); Paul Fussell, *The Great War and Modern Memory*, New Edition (Oxford University Press, 2013).
6. Walter Benjamin, *The Arcades Project*, ed. Rolf Tiedemann, trans. Howard Eiland and Kevin McLaughlin (Harvard University Press, 1999), 14.
7. Kate Stanley, *Practices of Surprise in American Literature After Emerson* (Cambridge University Press, 2018), 11.
8. Stanley, *Practices of Surprise in American Literature After Emerson*, 8.
9. Stanley, *Practices of Surprise in American Literature After Emerson*, 12.
10. Paul Saint-Amour, *Tense Future: Modernism, Total War, Encyclopedic Form* (Oxford University Press, 2015), 10.
11. Saint-Amour, *Tense Future*, 14.
12. Victoria Bazin, *Marianne Moore and the Cultures of Modernity* (Ashgate, 2010), 159; See also Rachel Galvin, *News of War: Civilian Poetry 1936–1945* (Oxford University Press, 2017); and Emily Setina, "Marianne Moore's Postwar Fables and the Politics of Indirection," *PMLA* 131, no. 5 (October 2016): 1256–73.
13. Jürgen Habermas, *The Philosophical Discourse of Modernity*, trans. Frederick G. Lawrence (MIT Press, 1987), 10.
14. Bertrand Russell, *The Problems of Philosophy* (Oxford University Press, 1997), 64.
15. Bertrand Russell, *A History of Western Philosophy* (Simon & Schuster, 1967), 673.
16. Saint-Amour, *Tense Future*, 10.

17. Stanley, *Practices of Surprise in American Literature After Emerson*, 4.
18. Moore writes about him frequently in letters to her family, including describing him as a "wonder." Quoted in Bazin, *Marianne Moore and the Cultures of Modernity*, 30.
19. Marianne Moore, "Lecture Notebook," 1906, VII:11:06, Rosenbach Library.
20. Moore, "Lecture Notebook."
21. Moore, "Lecture Notebook."
22. Linda Leavell, "Marianne Moore, the James Family, and the Politics of Celibacy," *Twentieth Century Literature* 49, no. 2 (Summer 2003): 219–45.
23. David Kadlec, *Mosaic Modernism: Anarchism, Pragmatism, Culture* (Johns Hopkins University Press, 2000).
24. Elisa New, *The Line's Eye: Poetic Experience and American Sight* (Harvard University Press, 1999).
25. Bazin, *Marianne Moore and the Cultures of Modernity*.
26. Kristen Case, *American Pragmatism and Poetic Practice: Crosscurrents from Emerson to Susan Howe* (Camden House, 2011).
27. Rachel Buxton, "Marianne Moore and the Poetics of Pragmatism," *The Review of English Studies* 58, no. 236 (2007): 531–51.
28. William James, *Pragmatism and Other Writings*, ed. Giles Gunn (Penguin Classics, 2000), 32.
29. James, *Pragmatism and Other Writings*, 24–25.
30. James, *Pragmatism and Other Writings*, 146.
31. William James, *Essays, Comments, and Reviews* (Harvard University Press, 1987), 305.
32. James, *Essays, Comments, and Reviews*, 307.
33. James, *Pragmatism and Other Writings*, 303. Here, readers of Ludwig Wittgenstein will see one way that James influenced Wittgenstein's work; Wittgenstein writes, "Philosophy is a struggle against the bewitchment of our understanding by the resources of our language." and philosophical problems are "illusions," and when they are handled correctly, "philosophical problems should *completely* disappear." Ludwig Wittgenstein, *Philosophical Investigations*, rev. 4th ed. (Wiley-Blackwell, 2009), §109, §110, §133.
34. Lauren Berlant, *Cruel Optimism* (Duke University Press, 2011), 1.
35. James, *Essays, Comments, and Reviews*, 304.
36. James, *Essays, Comments, and Reviews*, 305.
37. William James, *The Principles of Psychology*, Vol. 2. (Henry Holt and Company, 1890), 359.
38. Siobhan Phillips, *The Poetics of the Everyday: Creative Repetition in Modern American Verse* (Columbia University Press, 2010), 42.
39. Phillips, *The Poetics of the Everyday*, 41.
40. Phillips, *The Poetics of the Everyday*, 28.
41. Phillips, *The Poetics of the Everyday*, 16.
42. Aristotle, *The Nicomachean Ethics*, ed. Lesley Brown, trans. David Ross, New Edition, Oxford World's Classics (Oxford University Press, 2009), 11–12.
43. Moore gives the animal gendered pronouns throughout the poem; I follow her.
44. Moore, *The Poems of Marianne Moore*, 243.
45. Moore, *The Poems of Marianne Moore*, 244.

4. CONSISTENCY AND MARIANNE MOORE

46. John Lyly, *Euphues: The Anatomy of Wit and Euphues and His England*, ed. Leah Scragg (Manchester University Press, 2003), 100.
47. It's also visible in her prose; see Helen Thaventhiran, *Radical Empiricists: Five Modernist Close Readers* (Oxford University Press, 2015). Thaventhiran, however, interprets Moore as "embarrassed about explanation." Thaventhiran, *Radical Empiricists*, 27.
48. Gertrude Stein, *Writings, 1903–1932*, Vol. 1. (Library of America, 1998), 522.
49. Moore, *The Poems of Marianne Moore*, 243.
50. Moore, *The Poems of Marianne Moore*, 14.
51. Moore, *The Poems of Marianne Moore*, 224.
52. Wesley C. Salmon, *Scientific Explanation and the Causal Structure of the World* (Princeton University Press, 1984), 240–41.
53. Carl G. Hempel, *Aspects of Scientific Explanation, and Other Essays in the Philosophy of Science* (Free Press, 1965), 337. D-N explanations often, but not always, depend on laws that establish cause. See Hempel, *Aspects of Scientific Explanation*, 352. Holly Andersen puts it this way: "Mechanisms as a characteristic form of explanation were originally developed as an alternative to a then-dominant way of understanding explanation as necessarily involving laws." Holly Andersen, "What Would Hume Say? Regularities, Laws, and Mechanisms," in *The Routledge Handbook of Mechanisms and Mechanical Philosophy*, ed. Stuart Glennan and Phyllis Illari (Routledge, 2017), 157. For more on mechanisms, see Stuart Glennan and Phyllis Illari, eds., *The Routledge Handbook of the Philosophy of Mechanisms* (Routledge, 2017), and also, published the same year by one of the editors, Stuart Glennan, *The New Mechanical Philosophy* (Oxford University Press, 2017).
54. Salmon, *Scientific Explanation and the Causal Structure of the World*, 268.
55. Andersen, "What Would Hume Say? Regularities, Laws, and Mechanisms," 158.
56. Moore, *The Poems of Marianne Moore*, 225.
57. Daniel Tiffany, *Toy Medium: Materialism and Modern Lyric* (University of California Press, 2000), 277.
58. Moore, *The Poems of Marianne Moore*, 235.
59. Moore, *The Poems of Marianne Moore*, 235.
60. Moore, *The Poems of Marianne Moore*, 92.
61. Barbara Johnson, *Persons and Things* (Harvard University Press, 2010), 29.
62. Johnson, *Persons and Things*, 30.
63. Moore, *The Poems of Marianne Moore*, 127.
64. Moore, *The Poems of Marianne Moore*, 173.
65. Moore, *The Poems of Marianne Moore*, 239.
66. Moore, *The Poems of Marianne Moore*, 135.
67. Moore, *The Poems of Marianne Moore*, 135.
68. Moore, *The Poems of Marianne Moore*, 135.
69. Moore, *The Poems of Marianne Moore*, 135.
70. Moore, *The Poems of Marianne Moore*, 239.
71. Moore, *The Poems of Marianne Moore*, 236.
72. Many philosophers of science tend to use physics for their case studies, but Peter Machamer, Lindley Darden, and Carl F. Craver note that the importance of mechanisms in biology have been argued for by a number of philosophers including

4. CONSISTENCY AND MARIANNE MOORE

William Bechtel and Robert C. Richardson, Stuart Kauffman, William Wimsatt, Richard M. Burian, and others. Machamer et al., "Thinking About Mechanisms," *Philosophy of Science* 67, no. 1 (2000): 3–4.

73. "We find Glennan's reliance on the concept of a 'law' problematic because, in our examples, there are rarely 'direct causal laws' to characterize how activities operate." Machamer et al., "Thinking About Mechanisms," 4.
74. Machamer et al., "Thinking About Mechanisms," 3.
75. Machamer et al., "Thinking About Mechanisms," 21. "When a prediction made on the basis of a hypothesized mechanism fails, then one has an anomaly and a number of responses are possible. If the experiment was conducted properly and the anomaly is reproducible, then perhaps something other than the hypothesized mechanism schema is at fault, such as hypotheses about the set-up conditions. If the anomaly cannot be resolved otherwise, then the hypothesized schema may need to be revised. One might abandon the entire mechanism schema and propose a new one. Alternatively, one can revise a portion of the failed schema." Machamer et al., "Thinking About Mechanisms," 17.
76. See, for example, the section titled "Moore's Methods," in Elizabeth Gregory and Stacy Carson Hubbard, ed., *Twenty-First Century Marianne Moore: Essays from a Critical Renaissance* (Palgrave Macmillan, 2018); and also Bartholomew Brinkman, "Scrapping Modernism: Marianne Moore and the Making of the Modern Collage Poem," *Modernism/Modernity* 18, no. 1 (2011): 43–66. More generally, see Marjorie Perloff, "Collage and Poetry," in *Encyclopedia of Aesthetics*, ed. Michael Kelly (Oxford University Press, 1998), 1:384–87.
77. Moore, *The Poems of Marianne Moore*, 171.
78. Wallace Stevens, *The Necessary Angel: Essays on Reality and the Imagination* (Vintage Books, 1942), 95.
79. Gregory and Hubbard, *Twenty-First Century Marianne Moore*, 4.
80. Natalia Cecire, "Marianne Moore's Precision," *Arizona Quarterly: A Journal of American Literature, Culture, and Theory* 67, no. 4 (Winter 2011): 83.
81. Natalia Cecire, *Experimental: American Literature and the Aesthetics of Knowledge* (Johns Hopkins University Press, 2019), 144.
82. Dan Chiasson, "All About My Mother: Marianne Moore's Family Romance," *New Yorker*, November 11, 2013.
83. Robert Bly, *American Poetry: Wildness and Domesticity* (Harper & Row, 1990), 11.
84. Johnson, *Persons and Things*, 29.
85. Roger Gilbert, "'These Things:' Moore's Habits of Adduction," in *Twenty-First Century Marianne Moore: Essays from a Critical Renaissance* (Palgrave Macmillan, 2018), 35–36. Gilbert also writes that "Moore's imagination obeys a logic" that's neither inductive nor deductive: "While she is certainly capable of reasoning from general precepts to particular cases and vice versa, Moore's most distinctive habit of mind may be to form unlikely groupings of items and let larger principles emerge from their interstices." Gilbert, *Twenty-First Century Marianne Moore*, 33. I admit that I'm confused by this; letting "larger principles emerge" from "groupings of items" *is* inductive reasoning. But Gilbert uses the verb "to

4. CONSISTENCY AND MARIANNE MOORE

adduce," which implies that he sees Moore's "items" as serving as evidence, which is to say that he doesn't see her poetics as reasoning but doing something more like citational rhetoric.
86. Fiona Green, "Moore's Numbers," in *Twenty-First Century Marianne Moore: Essays from a Critical Renaissance*, ed. Elizabeth Gregory and Stacy Carson Hubbard (Palgrave Macmillan, 2018), 51.
87. Donald Hall, "Marianne Moore, The Art of Poetry No. 4," *The Paris Review* 26 (Summer–Fall 1961).
88. Margaret Holley, "The Model Stanza: The Organic Origin of Moore's Syllabic Verse," *Twentieth Century Literature* 30, no. 2/3 (1984): 182.
89. Moore, *The Poems of Marianne Moore*, 127.
90. Moore, *The Poems of Marianne Moore*, 127.
91. Moore, *The Poems of Marianne Moore*, 127.
92. Moore, *The Poems of Marianne Moore*, 127.
93. Moore, *The Poems of Marianne Moore*, 127–128.
94. Hugh Kenner, *A Homemade World: The American Modernist Writers* (Johns Hopkins University Press, 1989), 99.
95. Moore, *The Poems of Marianne Moore*, 258.
96. Cliff Mak, "On Falling Fastidiously: Marianne Moore's Slapstick Animals," *ELH* 83, no. 3 (Fall 2016): 879.
97. Mak, "On Falling Fastidiously," 884.
98. Cecire, *Experimental*, 127.
99. Cecire, *Experimental*, 128.
100. Cecire, "Marianne Moore's Precision," 86.
101. Moore, *The Poems of Marianne Moore*, 224.
102. Moore, *The Poems of Marianne Moore*, 225.
103. Holley, "The Model Stanza," 187.
104. Hall, "Marianne Moore, The Art of Poetry No. 4."
105. Mak, "On Falling Fastidiously," 883.
106. Cecire, *Experimental*, 118.
107. Wittgenstein, *Philosophical Investigations*, §309.
108. "We think skepticism must mean that we cannot know the world exists, and hence that perhaps there isn't one (a conclusion some profess to admire and others to fear). Whereas what skepticism suggests is that since we cannot know the world exists, its presentness to us cannot be a function of knowing. The world is to be accepted; as the presentness of other minds is not to be known, but acknowledged." Stanley Cavell, *Must We Mean What We Say?*, Updated ed. (Cambridge University Press, 2002), 298.
109. Stanley Cavell, *The Claim of Reason* (Oxford University Press, 1999), 496.
110. In Cavell's account, "the cause of skepticism" is "the attempt to convert the human condition, the condition of humanity, into an intellectual difficulty, a riddle." Cavell, *The Claim of Reason*, 493.
111. Cavell, *The Claim of Reason*, 490–91.
112. Richard Rorty, *Consequences of Pragmatism* (University of Minnesota Press, 1982), 181.
113. Rorty, *Consequences of Pragmatism*, xxiii.

4. CONSISTENCY AND MARIANNE MOORE

114. As an example, Reddy cites Linda Leavall, *Marianne Moore and the Visual Arts: Prismatic Color* (Louisiana State University Press, 1995); Srikanth Reddy, *Changing Subjects: Digressions in Modern American Poetry* (Oxford University Press, 2012), 37–38.
115. Reddy, *Changing Subjects*, 38.
116. Moore, *The Poems of Marianne Moore*, 225.
117. Reddy, *Changing Subjects*, 45.
118. Moore, *The Poems of Marianne Moore*, 225.
119. Reddy, *Changing Subjects*, 47–48.
120. Moore, *The Poems of Marianne Moore*, 225.
121. Moore, *The Poems of Marianne Moore*, 224.

5. COHERENCE AND ELIZABETH BISHOP

1. Multiple scholars have described "The Fish" as a "fish story," including but not limited to Anne Colwell, "The One That Got Away: Elizabeth Bishop's 'Damned "Fish,"'" *Journal X* 3, no. 2 (2020): 172–81; Stephen Cushman, *Fictions of Form in American Poetry* (Princeton University Press, 1993); and Jeredith Merrin, *An Enabling Humility: Marianne Moore, Elizabeth Bishop, and the Uses of Tradition* (Rutgers University Press, 1990).
2. Elizabeth Bishop, *Poems*, ed. Saskia Hamilton (Farrar, Straus and Giroux, 2011), 43.
3. William Shakespeare, *A Midsummer Night's Dream*, ed. Barbara A. Mowat and Paul Werstine, Folger Shakespeare Library (Simon & Schuster, 2016), 143. This reading runs against those by James Longenbach and James McCorkle, both of whom write about imagination enabling the speaker's description of the fish's interior, and somewhat contra to Lucy Alford's account of the speaker's "imagined gutting" of the fish. See James Longenbach, *Modern Poetry After Modernism* (Oxford University Press, 1997); James McCorkle, *The Still Performance: Writing, Self, and Interconnection in Five Postmodern American Poets* (University of Virginia Press, 1989); and Lucy Alford, *Forms of Poetic Attention* (Columbia University Press, 2020).
4. Alford writes about this moment: "The speaker's contemplation begins to move past surface and into the imagined fleshy interior. The speaker knows fish, knows fishing and gutting and scaling, and the textures of flayed interior of a fish's body." Alford, *Forms of Poetic Attention*, 68.
5. Bishop, *Poems*, 44.
6. Bishop, *Poems*, 87.
7. In Stephen Cushman's words about this poem, it's a "journey to the interior." Cushman, *Fictions of Form in American Poetry*, 131.
8. Bishop, *Poems*, 26.
9. Bishop, *Poems*, 87.
10. Bishop, *Poems*, 89.
11. Bishop, *Poems*, 90.
12. Bishop, *Poems*, 26.

5. COHERENCE AND ELIZABETH BISHOP

13. Bishop, *Poems*, 192.
14. Bishop, *Poems*, 65.
15. Bishop, *Poems*, 121.
16. Bishop, *Poems*, 200.
17. Bishop, *Poems*, 200.
18. Bishop, *Poems*, 125.
19. Bishop, *Poems*, 77.
20. Bishop, *Poems*, 77. This poem has been read by Adrienne Rich and others as a poem about Bishop's homosexuality; see Adrienne Rich, "The Eye of the Outsider: On the Poetry of Elizabeth Bishop," *Boston Review*, June 1, 1984, https://www.bostonreview.net/articles/rich-the-eye-of-the-outsider/. While Bishop's poem is calculatedly gender-neutral, its drama is entirely concerned with the information that is being withheld from the speaker, not by the speaker from the reader. Victoria Harrison, following Rich, writes of it, "Bishop's privacy about her intimate relationships is respected by the surreal imagery, the rejection of narrative and grammatical cohesion, and the white spaces, which can only suggest what must be left unsaid." Victoria Harrison, *Elizabeth Bishop's Poetics of Intimacy* (Cambridge University Press, 1993), 64. Robert Dale Parker notes Bishop's interest in interiors and ties it to her examination of her own creativity: "What in her, then, whether under her power or not, will produce it? What in her femininity, in her own filling station of body and mind, will shape her art?" He later traces it to her homosexuality and her interest in women's bodies. "Bishop repeatedly wants to explore interiors, whether of dolls or people, filling stations or geography. As far back as an editorial for her high school magazine, she insists on the primacy of what lies inside, using metaphors that would erupt again when she wrote 'In the Waiting Room' so many years later.... That same curiosity about the interior and its link to her imagination continues throughout her publishing career, from, at the beginning, 'The Weed' and 'The Fish,'... through 'Gwendolyn' and 'Filling Station' and 'In the Waiting Room.' While—as she says in 'Gwendolyn'—she always handles things ever so carefully, Bishop wants to know just what hides inside and underneath, especially inside and underneath women's bodies." Robert Dale Parker, *The Unbeliever: The Poetry of Elizabeth Bishop* (University of Illinois Press, 1988), 28, 141. Betsy Erkkila also reads her interest in the interior as self-interest, that "driving to the interior" means her return to her memories, her past. Betsy Erkkila, *The Wicked Sisters: Women Poets, Literary History, and Discord* (Oxford University Press, 1992), 139.
21. Bishop, *Poems*, 180.
22. Lee Edelman writes about this poem that "There is no inside in this poem that can be distinguished from its outside: the cry emanates from inside the dentist's office, and from inside the waiting room, and from inside the *National Geographic*, and from inside 'The Waiting Room.'" Lee Edelman, "The Geography of Gender: Elizabeth Bishop's 'In the Waiting Room,'" *Contemporary Literature* 26, no. 2 (1985): 196.
23. David Kalstone, "All Eye," *The Partisan Review* 37, no. 2 (1970), 310.
24. Angus Cleghorn and Jonathan Ellis, "Chronology," in *The Cambridge Companion to Elizabeth Bishop*, ed. Angus Cleghorn and Jonathan Ellis, 24.

25. Randall Jarrell, *Poetry and the Age* (University of Florida Press, 2001), 181.
26. Guy Rotella, *Castings: Monuments and Monumentality in Poems by Elizabeth Bishop, Robert Lowell, James Merrill, Derek Walcott, and Seamus Heaney* (Vanderbilt University Press, 2004).
27. Lloyd Schwartz writes, "Elizabeth Bishop is one of our great ironists. Irony is a question of tone of voice. The awareness of tone evolves from the perception of juxtaposition." Lloyd Schwartz, *That Sense of Constant Readjustment: Elizabeth Bishop's North & South* (Garland Publishing, 1987), 3.
28. Bonnie Costello writes, "Bishop is a profoundly visual poet with an eye for the particular and mutable. Thus these questions of mastery promote new ways of seeing in time.... She sets her eye not on the transcendental fade-out or on the modernist fixed object, but on the panorama and minutiae of a changing world which she tentatively orders and interprets." Bonnie Costello, *Elizabeth Bishop: Questions of Mastery* (Harvard University Press, 1993), 2.
29. Edelman, "The Geography of Gender," 181.
30. Gillian White, *Lyric Shame: The "Lyric" Subject of Contemporary American Poetry* (Harvard University Press, 2014); Claire Seiler, *Midcentury Suspension: Literature and Feeling in the Wake of World War II* (Columbia University Press, 2020); and Zachariah Pickard, *Elizabeth Bishop's Poetics of Description* (McGill-Queen's University Press, 2009).
31. See Parker, *The Unbeliever*; and Kirstin Hotelling Zona, *Marianne Moore, Elizabeth Bishop, and May Swenson: The Feminist Poetics of Self-Restraint* (University of Michigan Press, 2002).
32. David Orr, "Rough Gems: Edgar Allan Poe & the Juke Box," *New York Times*, April 2, 2006, sec. Books, https://www.nytimes.com/2006/04/02/books/review/rough-gems.html.
33. Colm Tóibín, *On Elizabeth Bishop*, Writers on Writing 7 (Princeton University Press, 2015), 166.
34. There's a discussion of Williams and Bishop in Gillian White's *Lyric Shame*, especially regarding "a tradition of likenesses." White, *Lyric Shame*, 56–57.
35. Although Brian Glavey doesn't discuss Bishop at any length in *The Wallflower Avant-Garde*, I am informed by his writing, "Aesthetic form thus functions both as a means to shore up provisional identities and to help us escape from them entirely. Both are queer not only in the sense that their ways of binding and unbinding us to the world are analogous to the operations of sexuality itself but also because, for non-normative subjects whose attachments cannot be taken for granted, the projects of sustaining and suspending identity can become equally urgent." Brian Glavey, *The Wallflower Avant-Garde: Modernism, Sexuality, and Queer Ekphrasis* (Oxford University Press, 2015), 3; See also White, *Lyric Shame*, 44.
36. Bishop had John and Jane Dewey over for dinner on February 18, 1939. Brett C. Millier, *Elizabeth Bishop: Life and the Memory of It* (University of California Press, 1992), 146. John Dewey knew Bishop well enough to write letters of recommendation in support of her successful applications to the Houghton Mifflin Poetry Prize and to the Guggenheim Foundation. Millier, *Elizabeth Bishop*, 187. In 1947, Bishop visited Dewey without Jane's company at his house in Hubbards,

5. COHERENCE AND ELIZABETH BISHOP

Nova Scotia during a trip to see her Canadian relatives. And, during one of her long stays in New York, Dewey lent Bishop his apartment from November through May. Millier, *Elizabeth Bishop*, 180.

37. Elizabeth Bishop, *One Art: Letters*, ed. Robert Giroux (Farrar, Straus and Giroux, 1994), 80.
38. George Monteiro, ed., *Conversations with Elizabeth Bishop* (University Press of Mississippi, 1996), 134.
39. Elizabeth Bishop, "Index Cards of Bishop's Library at Lewis Wharf" (Vassar College Library, n.d.), Elizabeth Bishop Archive, Box 111. The books are: *Human Nature and Conduct, Individualism Old and New, Jefferson*, and *Intelligence in the Modern World*.
40. Elizabeth Bishop, *Elizabeth Bishop: Poems, Prose, and Letters*, ed. Robert Giroux and Lloyd Schwartz (Library of America, 2008), 846.
41. John Dewey, *The Philosophy of John Dewey*, ed. John J. McDermott (University of Chicago Press, 1973), 224.
42. Dewey, *The Philosophy of John Dewey*, 250.
43. It is tempting to imagine Bishop recalling this passage of Dewey's when she writes to Robert Lowell, "Have you ever gone through caves?" (She is also remembering a specific long ago experience in Mexico and using it to describe her current state of depression.) Elizabeth Bishop, *One Art: Letters*, ed. Robert Giroux (Farrar, Straus and Giroux, 1994), 517. It might be even more tempting to read this passage with "Squatter's Children," when Bishop writes, "The children play at digging holes./The ground is hard; they try to use/one of their father's tools.... Their laughter spreads/effulgence in the thunderheads,/weak flashes of inquiry/ direct as is the puppy's bark." Bishop, *Poems*, 93.
44. John Dewey, *Art as Experience* (Perigree, 1934), 15.
45. Harrison, *Elizabeth Bishop's Poetics of Intimacy*, 4.
46. Richard Rorty, *Consequences of Pragmatism: Essays 1972-1980* (University of Minnesota Press, 1982), 151.
47. Rorty, *Consequences of Pragmatism*, 165-66, quoted in Harrison, *Elizabeth Bishop's Poetics of Intimacy*, 6.
48. Frances Dickey, "Bishop, Dewey, Darwin: What Other People Know," *Contemporary Literature* 44, no. 2 (2003): 309.
49. Dickey, "Bishop, Dewey, Darwin," 302-3.
50. Dickey, "Bishop, Dewey, Darwin," 304.
51. Jarrell, *Poetry and the Age (1953)*, 181.
52. Quoted in Anne Colwell, *Inscrutable Houses: Metaphors of the Body in the Poems of Elizabeth Bishop* (University of Alabama Press, 1997), 6, from Gibbons Ruark's unpublished lecture notes.
53. V. Joshua Adams, *Skepticism and Impersonality in Modern Poetry: Literary Experiments with Philosophical Problems* (Bloomsbury, 2025), 23.
54. Laurel Snow Corelle, *A Poet's High Argument: Elizabeth Bishop and Christianity* (University of South Carolina Press, 2008), 10.
55. Rotella, *Castings*, 18-19.
56. Susan McCabe, *Elizabeth Bishop: Her Poetics of Loss* (Penn State University Press, 1994), xiv.

5. COHERENCE AND ELIZABETH BISHOP

57. Zona, *Marianne Moore, Elizabeth Bishop, and May Swenson*, 3, 7.
58. Edelman, "The Geography of Gender," 188.
59. Mutlu Konuk Blasing, *Politics and Form in Postmodern Poetry: O'Hara, Bishop, Ashbery, and Merrill* (Cambridge University Press, 1995).
60. Margaret Dickie, *Stein, Bishop, & Rich: Lyrics of Love, War, & Place* (University of North Carolina Press, 1997).
61. Thomas Gardner, *Regions of Unlikeness: Explaining Contemporary Poetry* (University of Nebraska Press, 1999), 33.
62. Gardner, *Regions of Unlikeness*, 63, 69.
63. Alford frames this question as "why didn't the fish fight this time, after so many victories?" and notes "contemplation reveals not only the object's present but its history." Alford, *Forms of Poetic Attention*, 68.
64. Bishop, *Poems*, 26.
65. Bishop, *Poems*, 181.
66. Bishop, *Poems*, 172.
67. Bishop, *Poems*, 184.
68. Bishop, *Poems*, 193.
69. Bishop, *Poems*, 125.
70. Peter Lipton, *Inference to the Best Explanation* (Routledge, 2004), 1.
71. Lipton, *Inference to the Best Explanation*, 208.
72. These are, of course, the subjects of the previous four chapters.
73. Lipton, *Inference to the Best Explanation*, 19.
74. Lipton, *Inference to the Best Explanation*, 56.
75. Lipton, *Inference to the Best Explanation*, 66.
76. Lipton, *Inference to the Best Explanation*, 209.
77. C. S. Peirce, *Collected Papers of Charles Sanders Peirce*, ed. Charles Hartshorne and Paul Weiss (Harvard University Press, 1931), 5:172, quoted in Igor Douven, "Abduction," in *The Stanford Encyclopedia of Philosophy*, ed. Edward N. Zalta, Summer 2021, https://plato.stanford.edu/archives/sum2021/entries/abduction/.
78. Igor Douven, *The Art of Abduction* (MIT Press, 2022), 42.
79. Bas C. van Fraassen, *Laws and Symmetry* (Oxford University Press, 1989), 131–50; Douven, *The Art of Abduction*, 7; see also Rom Harré, *Varieties of Realism: A Rationale for the Natural Sciences* (Blackwell, 1986); Lipton, *Inference to the Best Explanation*. Douven quotes Timothy Williamson: "The abductive methodology is the best science provides." Timothy Williamson, Timothy Williamson, "Semantic Paradoxes and Abductive Methodology," in *Reflections on the Liar*, ed. Bradley Armour-Garb (Oxford University Press, 2017), 335. 334–35. He also quotes Ernan McMullin who writes abduction is "the inference that makes science." Ernan McMullin, *The Inference That Makes Science* (Marquette University Press, 1992). For more on abduction, the entry on it in the *Stanford Encyclopedia of Philosophy* is a good place to start, with a useful bibliography. I'll note here that I draw largely on Lipton because I find his account of abduction the clearest and most useful for literary studies, and indeed, it has already been cited by at least one other—Elaine Auyoung, "What We Mean by Reading," *New Literary History* 51, no. 1 (2020): 93–114—which I note later in this chapter. Because I am writing here for scholars of poetics and philosophers interested in literature, I do not wrestle with some of the most contentious aspects of abduction, such as its

relationship to Bayesian confirmation theory—for that, see Lipton, Douven, and many others.
80. Williamson, *Doing Philosophy*, 91.
81. Bertrand Russell, "The Regressive Method for Discovering the Premises of Mathematics [1907]," in *Essays in Analysis*, ed. Douglas Lackey (George Braziller, 1945), 273–274.
82. See Kevin McCain and Ted Poston, "Best Explanations: An Introduction," in *Best Explanations: New Essays on Inference to the Best Explanation* (Oxford University Press, 2017).
83. Douven concurs, writing, "abduction is the predominant mode of reasoning in medical diagnosis," and devotes two chapters to it in Douven, *The Art of Abduction*, See also John R. Josephson and Susan G. Josephson, *Abduction Inference: Computation, Philosophy, Technology* (Cambridge University Press, 1994); and Stefan Dragulinescu, "Inference to the Best Explanation and Mechanisms in Medicine," *Theoretical Medicine and Bioethics* 37, no. 3 (2016): 211–32.
84. For example, Millier writes of Bishop's asthma, "The condition dominated her life between 1934 and 1951." Millier, *Elizabeth Bishop*, 75.
85. Millier, *Elizabeth Bishop*, 11.
86. David Kalstone, *Becoming a Poet* (University of Michigan Press, 1989), 158.
87. Millier, *Elizabeth Bishop*, 27.
88. Bishop, *Elizabeth Bishop: Poems, Prose, and Letters*, 425.
89. Millier, *Elizabeth Bishop*, 28.
90. Millier, *Elizabeth Bishop*, 28.
91. She says this repeatedly in letters and interviews, but to offer one source: "I wanted to be a doctor, too, and I got myself enrolled at Cornell Medical School. I think Marianne Moore discouraged me from going on with that." Monteiro, *Conversations with Elizabeth Bishop*, 24.
92. Monteiro, *Conversations with Elizabeth Bishop*, 24, 57, 93, 112; Millier, *Elizabeth Bishop*, 44.
93. Elizabeth Bishop, "Letters to Lloyd Frankenburg and Loren Maciver" (Vassar College Library, 1959), 30.4. Also see Bishop, *One Art: Letters*, 373.
94. Millier, *Elizabeth Bishop*, 266.
95. Millier, *Elizabeth Bishop*, 429–30.
96. Elizabeth Bishop and Robert Lowell, *Words in Air: The Complete Correspondence Between Elizabeth Bishop and Robert Lowell*, ed. Thomas Travisano and Saskia Hamilton (Farrar, Straus and Giroux, 2008), 171.
97. Bishop, *One Art: Letters*, 479.
98. Bishop, *Poems*, 319.
99. I am building upon the work of Bishop's biographer Brett Millier, who writes, "When after seven years Elizabeth finally distilled her visits to Pound into a poem, she placed him at the center of a vortex of madness on the hospital ward, surrounded by, defined by, the characters he had attempted to screen out of his literary conversations." Millier, *Elizabeth Bishop*, 281. See also Colwell, *Inscrutable Houses*, 165. She notes that Pound "is grouped with those he once despised."
100. Bishop, *Poems*, 133.
101. For example, Lloyd Schwartz and Sybil P. Estess write, "As Ezra Pound is revealed through the expanding stanzas (modeled on 'This is the house that Jack built') of

5. COHERENCE AND ELIZABETH BISHOP

'Visits to St. Elizabeths,' his simple nobility is smothered by the weakness, fragility, and insipidity of the other inmates." Lloyd Schwartz and Sybil P. Estess, *Elizabeth Bishop and Her Art* (University of Michigan Press, 1983), 155.
102. Bishop, *Poems*, 132.
103. Parker, *The Unbeliever*, 116.
104. White writes, "Called by early modernist ethical poetics to epistemic maturity, and all the while doubting its premises, Bishop turns to dramatize the problem of trying, and failing, to shirt the shame of forms of poetic meaning making." White, *Lyric Shame*, 71.
105. Bishop, *Poems*, 87–88.
106. Bishop, *Poems*, 213.
107. Bishop, *Poems*, 198.
108. Millier, *Elizabeth Bishop*, 281.
109. Millier, *Elizabeth Bishop*, 280.
110. Bishop, *Poems*, 179.
111. Bishop, *Poems*, 180.
112. Bishop, *Poems*, 181.
113. Bishop, *Poems*, 125.
114. Bishop, *Poems*, 125.
115. In her reading of Bishop as a metadiscursive poet, White writes of this poem that it "tak[es] pains to confuse what is inside the frame of the poem and what is outside it. Are we the ones who are making these connections? Who has arranged things this way?" White, *Lyric Shame*, 82–83.
116. Bishop, *Poems*, 126.
117. Izenberg writes of this poem, "Bishop turns the word 'so' itself into a thing to be seen, and makes seeing the thing make all the difference. Conflating the object that the word is with the causality that the word denotes, the poet of 'Filling Station' insists that the act of perception itself can serve of evidence that we too are seen, and known.... To see 'so'—not once, but many times, metered, arranged and arrayed, is to feel the force of the word as an argument. The materialization of the word, its transformation into soothing whisper or deliberate pattern, offers concrete *evidence* for the conclusion of universal love." Oren Izenberg, *Being Numerous: Poetry and the Ground of Social Life* (Princeton University Press, 2011), 104.
118. Lipton, *Inference to the Best Explanation*, 59.
119. Alford describes the oil in "The Fish" "blurring the boundaries between things" and not as coherence but "a miracle of convergence." Alford, *Forms of Poetic Attention*, 69.
120. Bishop, *Poems*, 125.
121. "Filling Station" appears in *Questions of Travel*, which Bishop wrote in Brazil, and it's reasonable to wonder if there's racial and national differences between speaker and the family working. Certainly, this would be another way the poem chimes with "In the Waiting Room," in which the young speaker racializes the images of women in the *National Geographic*. But *Questions of Travel* is divided into two halves—"Brazil" and "Elsewhere"—and "Filling Station" appears in "Elsewhere," alongside poems depicting Bishop's childhood in Nova Scotia, though it is not clear that this speaker is a child, like that of other poems in this half of the book.

5. COHERENCE AND ELIZABETH BISHOP

122. For a discussion of the stakes of describing Bishop as a lyric poet, see White, *Lyric Shame*. There's also a useful account of the lyric as an interpretive frame in reading Bishop's poetry in Claire Seiler, *Midcentury Suspension: Literature and Feeling in the Wake of World War II* (Columbia University Press, 2020).
123. Helen Vendler, "Life Studies," *New York Review of Books*, February 16, 1984, https://www.nybooks.com/articles/1984/02/16/life-studies/.
124. Helen Vendler, "The Poems of Elizabeth Bishop," *Critical Inquiry* 13, no. 4 (1987): 836.
125. Seiler, *Midcentury Suspension*, 42.
126. Stephanie Burt, "Elizabeth Bishop at the End of the Rainbow," in *Reading Elizabeth Bishop*, ed. Jonathan Ellis (Edinburgh University Press, 2019), 325.
127. Langdon Hammer, "ENGL 310: Modern Poetry," Open Yale Courses, Lecture 24—Elizabeth Bishop, https://oyc.yale.edu/english/engl-310/lecture-24.
128. White, *Lyric Shame*, 56.
129. "The inferiority within is the traveller's ambivalence towards coherence, symbolized through the other." Sandeep Parmar, "Race," in *Elizabeth Bishop in Context*, ed. Angus Cleghorn and Jonathan Ellis (Cambridge University Press, 2021), 337.
130. "Bishop is interested in the risk involved in dreams, as in works of art; they allow us to explore uncharted territory, but they also undermine the coherent structures that make conscious life possible." Bonnie Costello, "Dreams," in *Elizabeth Bishop in Context*, ed. Angus Cleghorn and Jonathan Ellis (Cambridge University Press, 2021), 295.
131. "Bishop was concerned about coherence and continuity." Jeffrey Gray, "Travel," in *Elizabeth Bishop in Context*, ed. Angus Cleghorn and Jonathan Ellis (Cambridge University Press, 2021), 282.
132. "For Elizabeth, life was given the semblance of coherence and meaning through words that had special value because they were validated by adults whom she trusted and whose faith was never in doubt." Cheryl Walker, "Religion," in *Elizabeth Bishop in Context*, ed. Angus Cleghorn and Jonathan Ellis (Cambridge University Press, 2021), 259. And while Brian Glavey does not focus on Elizabeth Bishop's poetry in *The Wallflower Avant-Garde*, it's useful to read her poetry, and not just her ekphrastic poems, alongside his book's theorization of queer ekphrasis as "a particularly useful mode for thinking about this sort of relational formalism." Glavey, *The Wallflower Avant-Garde*, 4. Glavey describes form in terms of coherence: "a vision of impossible coherence produced via iterations of imitation and failure." Glavey, *The Wallflower Avant-Garde*, 7.
133. Luc Bovens and Stephan Hartmann, "Solving the Riddle of Coherence," *Mind*, New Series 112, no. 448 (2003): 601.
134. Wesley C. Salmon, "Rationality and Objectivity in Science or Tom Kuhn Meets Tom Bayes," in *Scientific Theories*, ed. C. Wade Savage (University of Minnesota Press, 1990), 198.
135. Erik J. Olsson, *Against Coherence: Truth, Probability, and Justification* (Oxford University Press, 2005), viii.
136. See Alexander Bird's critique of IBE as "Panglossian": " For IBE to lead frequently to the truth, it has to be that the actual world is the loveliest of possible worlds, or at least among the most lovely worlds." Alexander Bird, *Knowing Science* (Oxford University Press, 2023), 196.

137. Auyoung, "What We Mean by Reading," 105.
138. Auyoung, "What We Mean by Reading," 105.
139. Caroline Levine, *Forms: Whole, Rhythm, Hierarchy, Network* (Princeton University Press, 2015), 29. Levine also notes Mary Poovey's earlier statement that "Almost all of the literary criticism published in the US since the 1940s is organized, either explicitly or implicitly, by the trope of the organic whole." Mary Poovey, "The Model System of Contemporary Literary Criticism," *Critical Inquiry* 27, no. 3 (2001): 435. This chimes with Helen Vendler's statement of "the first obligation of a writer, which is to bend the world of matter until it assumes, of its own will (or so it seems), a formal outline, distinctive and coherent." Helen Vendler, "The Creeping Griffon," *New York Review of Books*, September 23, 1982, https://www.nybooks.com/articles/1982/09/23/the-creeping-griffon/.
140. Auyoung, "What We Mean by Reading," 108, 109, 110, 96.
141. Millier, *Elizabeth Bishop*, 196. Edelman uses a shorter version of this quote as an epigraph to his article, and begins his essay with another similar quote: " 'It was all true,' she affirms of 'The Moose,' 'it was all exactly the way I described it except that I said 'seven relatives.' Well, they weren't really relatives, they were various stepsons and so on, but that's the only thing that isn't quite true.' " Edelman, "The Geography of Gender," 179.
142. Bishop, *One Art: Letters*, 638.
143. Bishop, *Poems*, 99.
144. Bishop, *Poems*, 99.
145. Bishop, *Poems*, 99.

CONCLUSION: THE SONNET'S LOGIC AND GWENDOLYN BROOKS

1. For example, Northrop Frye writes about Shakespeare's sonnets that their author is not exactly Shakespeare himself: "the true father or shaping spirit of the poems is the form of the poem itself, and this form is a manifestation of the universal spirit of poetry." Northrop Frye, *Anatomy of Criticism: Four Essays* (Princeton University Press, 2020), 98.
2. Rachel Richardson, "Learning the Sonnet," in *Poetry Foundation*, Article for Students, August 29, 2013, https://www.poetryfoundation.org/articles/70051/learning-the-sonnet.
3. Paul Fussell, *Poetic Meter and Poetic Form* (Random House, 1965), 125, 116.
4. T. V. F. Brogan et al., "Sonnet," in *The New Princeton Encyclopedia of Poetry and Poetics* ed. Alex Preminger, Terry V. F. Brogan, and Frank Warnke (Princeton University Press, 1993), 1167–1170.
5. T. V. F. Brogan, "Volta," in *The New Princeton Encyclopedia of Poetry and Poetics* ed. Alex Preminger, Terry V. F. Brogan, and Frank Warnke (Princeton University Press, 1993), 1367.
6. Stephanie Burt and David Mikics, "Introduction," in *The Art of the Sonnet* (Harvard University Press, 2010), 3, 6.
7. Edward Hirsch, "My Own Acquaintance," in *The Making of a Sonnet*, ed. Eavan Boland and Edward Hirsch (W. W. Norton, 2008), 39.

CONCLUSION

8. Eavan Boland, "Discovering the Sonnet," in *The Making of a Sonnet*, ed. Eavan Boland and Edward Hirsch (W. W. Norton, 2008), 53.
9. Helen Vendler, *The Art of Shakespeare's Sonnets* (Harvard University Press, 1997), 24.
10. Burt and Mikics, "Introduction," 7.
11. Jahan Ramazani, "Self-Metaphorizing 'American' Sonnets," in *The American Sonnet: An Anthology of Poems and Essays*, ed. Dora Malech and Laura T. Smith (University of Iowa Press, 2022), 134. See also Jennifer Wagner-Lawlor, *A Moment's Monument: Revisionary Poetics and the Nineteenth-Century English Sonnet* (Fairleigh Dickinson University Press, 1998).
12. Ramazani, "Self-Metaphorizing 'American' Sonnets," 138.
13. Burt and Mikics, "Introduction," 8.
14. Marjorie Levinson, *Thinking Through Poetry: Field Reports on Romantic Lyric* (Oxford University Press, 2018), 85, 263.
15. Burt and Mikics write, "The poet's work took expression as a series of striking, governing images (called conceits). The poet was a soldier in love's wars; his passion a ship lost in a storm; an icy fire burned within him. His beloved's face was a garden or a set of assembled metaphors (known as a blazon): her teeth like pearls, her lips like cherries, her eyes like bright suns." Burt and Mikics, "Introduction," 12.
16. Jane Austen, *Persuasion*, ed. Gillian Beer (Penguin Books, 2003), 79.
17. I've written about the overlap of logical form and poetic form both in chapter 1 of this book and in an essay in the *Cambridge Companion to Literature and Philosophy*, ed. Lanier Anderson and Karen Zumhagen-Yekplé (Cambridge University Press, forthcoming).
18. "The clearest modern definition of 'sonnet' specifies a poem of fourteen lines in iambic pentameter ... divided by its rhymes, and by its internal logic, in one of two ways [Italian or Shakespearean] ... The volta (or turn) in the sonnet ... normally comes at the end of the octave, and the further twist that the Shakespearean form often puts in the last two lines." Burt and Mikics, "Introduction," 3.
19. Brogan, "Volta," 1367.
20. Paul Fussell, *Poetic Meter and Poetic Form*, rev. ed. (McGraw Hill, 1979), 115–16.
21. Fussell, *Poetic Meter and Poetic Form*, 116.
22. Fussell, *Poetic Meter and Poetic Form*, 120, 122.
23. David Bromwich, "Introduction," in *American Sonnets: An Anthology*, ed. David Bromwich (Library of America, 2007), xxxviii.
24. Graham Priest, *An Introduction to Non-Classical Logic: From If to Is*, 2nd ed. (Cambridge University Press, 2008), xviii.
25. "Normally, too, a definite pause is made in thought development at the end of the eighth line, serving to increase the independent unity of an octave that has already progressed with the greatest economy in rhyme sounds. . . The sestet, on the other hand, with its element of unpredictability, its usually more intense rhyme activity (three rhymes in six lines coming after two in eight) and the structural interdependence of the tercets, implies an acceleration in thought and feeling." Brogan et al., "Sonnet," 1168.
26. Wallace Stevens, *Collected Poetry & Prose* (Library of America, 1997), 77.
27. I cite a number of essays from *The American Sonnet* in this conclusion, in part because Brooks's sonnets are the focus of five different essays, more than any other writer's. *The American Sonnet: An Anthology of Poems and Essays*, ed. Dora

Malech and Laura T. Smith (University of Iowa Press, 2022). For Brooks's ambivalence about the sonnet, see Karen Jackson Ford, "The Sonnets of Satin-Legs Brooks," *Contemporary Literature* 48, no. 3 (Fall 2007): 345–73.
28. Ford, "The Sonnets of Satin-Legs Brooks," 358.
29. Ford, "The Sonnets of Satin-Legs Brooks," 356.
30. Ford, "The Sonnets of Satin-Legs Brooks," 357.
31. Gwendolyn Brooks, *The Essential Gwendolyn Brooks*, ed. Elizabeth Alexander (Library of America, 2005), 1.
32. In an essay from which I also cite in this book's introduction, Tess Taylor writes: "What do we make of this sonnet—or almost sonnet—that *almost* lets a dream sing inside rooms that are *almost* apartments? What do we make of this domestic interior, in which we overhear voices of speakers, who are not even sure they can call themselves speakers, open by calling themselves 'things'? Who speak in a chorus of voices, as if distinction itself were too much luxury? These are not quite sonnet's subjects: A building, its inhabitants, and the strange, possible, uncertain space by which dream allows us to feel human at all. On the level of form, we're in uncertain space as well: Although this thirteen-line poem is a not-quite sonnet, it gains its energy from its nearness to sonnet, from its proximity and also abnegation of the fourteenth line woven through. We hear the aural possibility of the sonnet set in long syllabic lines that easily could be but have not been relineated. The poem's opening tercet has thirty-eight syllables, two short of the forty that would lend themselves to iambic quatrains. Those leggy lines have fourteen and twelve syllables, while in the rest of the quatrains, the lines have ten or eleven syllables. The poem's second stanza is not a tercet but a quatrain, again hoveringly suggesting sonnet space. Could a dream live inside this poem? Similarly, could this poem be a sonnet? Maybe. Maybe not." Tess Taylor, "But Could a Dream: Form and Freedom in Gwendolyn Brooks's Domestic Sonnets," in *The American Sonnet: An Anthology of Poems and Essays*, ed. Dora Malech and Laura T. Smith (University of Iowa Press, 2022), 328.
33. Vendler, *The Art of Shakespeare's Sonnets*, 22.
34. Vendler, *The Art of Shakespeare's Sonnets*, 25, 26.
35. Taylor, "But Could a Dream," 329.
36. Marianne Moore, *The Poems of Marianne Moore*, ed. Grace Schulman (Viking, 2003), 225.
37. Brogan, "Volta," 1367; Brooks, *The Essential Gwendolyn Brooks*, 1.
38. Karen Jackson Ford writes, "The legend of Gwendolyn Brooks's stylistic shift from traditional Anglo-American prosody to free verse and the ideals of the black aesthetic is well known by her readers and abundantly chronicled by her critics. Of the many forms the poet employed in her long writing career, the sonnet in particular has come to represent the very question of poetic form for Brooks." Ford, "The Sonnets of Satin-Legs Brooks," 345.
39. Lisa L. Moore writes, "Brooks famously gave up received verse forms after being challenged to do so by students at historically Black Fisk University when she visited there in 1967, but for the rest of her career, the sonnet continued to be Brooks's touchstone." Lisa L. Moore, "The Sonnet Is Not a Luxury," in *The American Sonnet: An Anthology of Poems and Essays*, ed. Dora Malech and Lisa T. Smith (University of Iowa Press, 2022), 224.

40. Brooks, *The Essential Gwendolyn Brooks*, 75.
41. William Wordsworth, *The Major Works*, ed. Stephen Gill (Oxford University Press, 2000), 286. Jon Woodson writes of this poem that it "signifies on Shakespeare's 'lovely boy' sonnets," and that "nearly every word in Brooks's sonnet is severally cross-referential" with Shakespeare; additionally, "nearly every word is an index leading to an element associated with alchemy." Jon Woodson, "Gwendolyn Brooks's Esoteric Sonnet 'A Lovely Love' as an Alchemical Metatext," in *The American Sonnet: An Anthology of Poems and Essays*, ed. Dora Malech and Laura T. Smith (University of Iowa Press, 2022), 334, 336, 337.
42. Fussell writes, of the distinction between Petrarchan and Shakespearean sonnets, "To turn at line 9 and to resolve in six lines is a very different emotional operation than to turn at line 13 and resolve in two." Brooks is doing both. Fussell, *Poetic Meter and Poetic Form*, Revised Edition, 124.
43. John Donne, *The Complete English Poems*, ed. A. J. Smith (Penguin Books, 1977), 314.
44. Brooks, *The Essential Gwendolyn Brooks*, 52.
45. Ramazani describes how in this sonnet, "at the diegetic level, the casket, perhaps recalling Shakespeare's sonnet tombs, is meant to ritually contain the 'unprotesting' corpse of Cousin Vit, 'But it can't hold her'—a woman who seems to defy casket and 'contrition,' sexual and social propriety and gender norms. . . . Brooks's sonnet flaunts its ordering but also its variance and rule twisting: its first two iambic lines open with trochees consistent with African American syncopation." Ramazani, "Self-Metaphorizing 'American' Sonnets," 141–42.
46. Ramazani writes of this sonnet that it could be read as something between "Culler's ritual model and Theodor Adorno's notion of the idiosyncratic individuality of lyric," asking "Is this elegiac sonnet 'the rites' for the deceased, as the title and ritual model might suggest, or is it about or perhaps even in tension with such rites?" Ramazani, "Self-Metaphorizing 'American' Sonnets," 143, 141.
47. Michael Theune, "Strange Voltas," in *The American Sonnet: An Anthology of Poems and Essays*, ed. Dora Malech and Laura T. Smith (University of Iowa Press, 2022), 269.
48. Ramazani, "Self-Metaphorizing 'American' Sonnets," 141.
49. John Keats, *The Complete Poems*, ed. John Barnard, 3rd ed. (Penguin Books, 1988), 72.
50. Keats has substituted Cortez for Balboa; for more on this ostensible error, see Erica McAlpine, *The Poet's Mistake* (Princeton University Press, 2020).
51. Colin Stuart, "The Discovery of Uranus," *Royal Museums Greenwich* (blog), March 13, 2020, https://www.rmg.co.uk/stories/blog/astronomy/discovery-uranus?_gl=1*12lijjt*_up*MQ..*_ga*MTczNjM4MTgzMC4xNzMyNzkoMzM4*_ga_4MH5VEZTEK*MTczMjc5NDMzOC4xLjAuMTczMjc5NDMzOC4wLjAuMA..*_ga_7JJ3J5DBF6*MTczMjc5NDMzOC4xLjAuMTczMjc5NDMzOC4wLjAuMA.
52. Moore, *The Poems of Marianne Moore*, 226.

BIBLIOGRAPHY

Adams, V. Joshua. *Skepticism and Impersonality in Modern Poetry: Literary Experiments with Philosophical Problems*. Bloomsbury, 2025.
Albright, Daniel. *Lyricality in English Literature*. University of Nebraska Press, 1985.
Alford, Lucy. *Forms of Poetic Attention*. Columbia University Press, 2020.
Altieri, Charles. "Contingency as Compositional Principle in Fifties Poetics." In *The Scene of My Selves: New Work on New York School Poets*, ed. Terence Diggory and Stephen Paul Miller, 359–84. National Poetry Foundation, 2001.
Altieri, Charles. "Poetic Thinking." In *The New Wallace Stevens Studies*, ed. Bart Eeckhout and Gül Bilge Han. Cambridge University Press, 2021.
Altieri, Charles. "Stevens and the Crisis of European Philosophy." *Soundings: An Interdisciplinary Journal* 89, no. 3/4 (Fall/Winter 2006): 255–78.
Altieri, Charles. "Exemplification and Expression." In *A Companion to the Philosophy of Literature*, ed. Garry L. Hagberg and Walter Jost, 491–507. Wiley-Blackwell, 2010.
Andersen, Holly. "What Would Hume Say? Regularities, Laws, and Mechanisms." In *The Routledge Handbook of Mechanisms and Mechanical Philosophy*, ed. Stuart Glennan and Phyllis Illari. Routledge, 2017.
Aristotle. *Poetics*. Trans. Anthony Kenny. Oxford World's Classics, 2013.
Aristotle. *The Nicomachean Ethics*. Ed. Lesley Brown. Trans. David Ross. Oxford World's Classics, 2009.
Ashton, Jennifer. *From Modernism to Postmodernism: American Poetry and Theory in the Twentieth Century*. Cambridge University Press, 2005.
Austen, Jane. *Persuasion*. Ed. Gillian Beer. Penguin Classics, 2003.
Auyoung, Elaine. "What We Mean by Reading." *New Literary History* 51, no. 1 (2020): 93–114.
Badiou, Alain. *The Age of Poets: And Other Writings on Twentieth-Century Poetry and Prose*. Trans. Emily Apter and Bruno Bosteels. Verso, 2014.

BIBLIOGRAPHY

Bassoff, Bruce. "Gertrude Stein's 'Composition As Explanation.'" *Twentieth Century Literature* 24, no. 1 (1978): 76–80.

Bazin, Victoria. *Marianne Moore and the Cultures of Modernity*. Ashgate, 2010.

Beck, Ulrich. *Risk Society: Towards a New Modernity*. Trans. Mark Ritter. Sage, 1992.

Belknap, Robert. "The Literary List: A Survey of Its Uses and Deployments." *Literary Imagination* 2, no. 1 (2001): 35–54.

Beltrán, Cristina. "Mestiza Poetics: Walt Whitman, Barack Obama, and the Question of Union." In *A Political Companion to Walt Whitman*, ed. John E. Seery, 59–95. University Press of Kentucky, 2011.

Benfey, Christopher. *A Summer of Hummingbirds: Love, Art, and Scandal in the Intersecting Worlds of Emily Dickinson, Mark Twain, Harriet Beecher Stowe, and Martin Johnson Heade*. Penguin Books, 2009.

Benfey, Christopher. "The Riddles of Emily Dickinson." *New York Times*, May 18, 1986. https://www.nytimes.com/1986/05/18/books/the-riddles-of-emily-dickinson.html.

Benjamin, Walter. *The Arcades Project*. Ed. Rolf Tiedmann. Trans. Howard Eiland and Kevin McLaughlin. Harvard University Press, 1999.

Benjamin, Walter. *Illuminations*. Mariner Books, 2019.

Bennett, Chad. *Word of Mouth: Gossip and American Poetry*. Johns Hopkins University Press, 2018.

Berlant, Lauren. *Cruel Optimism*. Duke University Press, 2011.

Bernstein, Charles. *Attack of the Difficult Poems: Essays and Inventions*. University of Chicago Press, 2011.

Berry, Ellen. *Curved Thought and Textual Wandering: Gertrude Stein's Postmodernism*. University of Michigan Press, 1992.

Biletzki, Anat, and Anat Matar, "Ludwig Wittgenstein." *The Stanford Encyclopedia of Philosophy* (Fall 2023). Ed. Edward N. Zalta and Uri Nodelman. https://plato.stanford.edu/archives/fall2023/entries/wittgenstein/.

Bird, Alexander. *Knowing Science*. Oxford University Press, 2023.

Bishop, Elizabeth. *Elizabeth Bishop: Poems, Prose, and Letters*. Ed. Robert Giroux and Lloyd Schwartz. Library of America, 2008.

Bishop, Elizabeth. "Index Cards of Bishop's Library at Lewis Wharf." Vassar College Library. Elizabeth Bishop Archive, n.d.

Bishop, Elizabeth. "Letters to Lloyd Frankenburg and Loren Maciver." Vassar College Library, 1959.

Bishop, Elizabeth. *One Art: Letters*. Edited by Robert Giroux. Farrar, Straus and Giroux, 1994.

Bishop, Elizabeth. *Poems*. Ed. Saskia Hamilton. Farrar, Straus and Giroux, 2011.

Bishop, Elizabeth, and Robert Lowell. *Words in Air: The Complete Correspondence Between Elizabeth Bishop and Robert Lowell*. Ed. Thomas Travisano and Saskia Hamilton. Farrar, Straus and Giroux, 2008.

Black, Max. "Metaphor." *Proceedings of the Aristotelian Society* 55 (1954): 273–94.

Blasing, Mutlu Konuk. *Politics and Form in Postmodern Poetry: O'Hara, Bishop, Ashbery, and Merrill*. Cambridge University Press, 1995.

Bloom, Harold. *The Anatomy of Influence: Literature as a Way of Life*. Yale University Press, 2011.

Bloom, Harold. "To the Tally of My Soul: Whitman's Image of Voice." In *The Ordering Mirror: Readers and Contexts*. Fordham University Press, 1993.

BIBLIOGRAPHY

Bly, Robert. *American Poetry: Wildness and Domesticity.* Harper & Row, 1990.
Boland, Eavan. "Discovering the Sonnet." In *The Making of a Sonnet.* Ed. Eavan Boland and Edward Hirsch. W. W. Norton, 2008.
Boland, Eavan, and Mark Strand, eds. *The Making of a Poem: A Norton Anthology of Poetic Forms.* Reprint Edition. W. W. Norton, 2001.
Booth, Mark W. *The Experience of Songs.* Yale University Press, 1981.
Bovens, Luc, and Stephan Hartmann. "Solving the Riddle of Coherence." *Mind,* New Series 112, no. 448 (2003): 601–33.
Brinkman, Bartholomew. "Scrapping Modernism: Marianne Moore and the Making of the Modern Collage Poem." *Modernism/Modernity* 18, no. 1 (2011): 43–66.
Britton, Karl. "Portrait of a Philosopher." In *Ludwig Wittgenstein: The Man and His Philosophy.* Ed. K. T. Fang. University of Michigan Press, 1967.
Brogan, T. V. F. "Volta," In *The New Princeton Encyclopedia of Poetry and Poetics* Ed. Alex Preminger, Terry V. F. Brogan, and Frank Warnke. Princeton University Press, 1993.
Brogan, T. V. F., L. J. Sillman, C. S. Scott, and J. Lewin. "Sonnet." In *The New Princeton Encyclopedia of Poetry and Poetics* Ed. Alex Preminger, Terry V. F. Brogan, and Frank Warnke. Princeton University Press, 1993.
Bromwich, David. "Introduction." In *American Sonnets: An Anthology*, ed. David Bromwich. Library of America, 2007.
Brooks, Cleanth. *The Well Wrought Urn: Studies in the Structure of Poetry (1947).* Harcourt Brace, 1970.
Brooks, Gwendolyn. *Selected Poems.* Harper & Row, 1963.
Brooks, Gwendolyn. *The Essential Gwendolyn Brooks.* Ed. Elizabeth Alexander. Library of America, 2005.
Burt, Stephanie. "Elizabeth Bishop at the End of the Rainbow." In *Reading Elizabeth Bishop*, ed. Jonathan Ellis, 321–36. Edinburgh University Press, 2019.
Burt, Stephanie. "What Is This Thing Called Lyric?" *Modern Philology* 113, no. 3 (February 2016): 422–40.
Burt, Stephanie, and David Mikics. "Introduction." In *The Art of the Sonnet*, ed. Stephanie Burt and David Mikics. Harvard University Press, 2010.
Buxton, Rachel. "Marianne Moore and the Poetics of Pragmatism." *The Review of English Studies* 58, no. 236 (2007): 531–51.
Cameron, Sharon. *Choosing Not Choosing: Dickinson's Fascicles.* University of Chicago Press, 1992.
Cameron, Sharon. *Lyric Time: Dickinson and the Limits of Genre.* Johns Hopkins University Press, 1979.
Camp, Elisabeth. "Introduction: Emily Dickinson's Epistemic Ambitions for Poetry." In *The Poetry of Emily Dickinson: Philosophical Perspectives*, ed. Elisabeth Camp. Oxford University Press, 2021.
Carnap, Rudolf. "Inductive Logic and Inductive Intuition." In *The Problem of Inductive Logic*, ed. Imre Lakatos, 258–314. North-Holland, 1968.
Carnap, Rudolf. "On Inductive Logic." *Philosophy of Science* 12, no. 2 (1945): 72–97.
Carnap, Rudolf. *The Continuum of Inductive Methods.* University of Chicago Press, 1952.
Carson, Anne. *Economy of the Unlost.* Princeton University Press, 1999.

Case, Kristen. *American Pragmatism and Poetic Practice: Crosscurrents from Emerson to Susan Howe.* Camden House, 2011.
Cavell, Stanley. *The Claim of Reason.* Oxford University Press, 1999.
Cavell, Stanley. *Must We Mean What We Say?* Updated ed. Cambridge University Press, 2002.
Cavell, Stanley. "Reflections on Wallace Stevens at Mount Holyoke." In *Artists, Intellectuals, and World War II: The Pontigny Encounters at Mount Holyoke College, 1942-1944,* ed. Christopher Benfey and Karen Remmler, 61-79. University of Massachusetts Press, 2006.
Cecire, Natalia. *Experimental: American Literature and the Aesthetics of Knowledge.* Johns Hopkins University Press, 2019.
Cecire, Natalia. "Marianne Moore's Precision." *Arizona Quarterly: A Journal of American Literature, Culture, and Theory* 67, no. 4 (Winter 2011): 83-110.
Cecire, Natalia. "Ways of Not Reading Gertrude Stein." *ELH* 82, no. 1 (Spring 2015): 281-312.
Chiasson, Dan. "All About My Mother: Marianne Moore's Family Romance." *New Yorker,* November 11, 2013.
Chodat, Robert. *Worldly Acts and Sentient Things: The Persistence of Agency from Stein to DeLillo.* Cornell University Press, 2008.
Clune, Michael. *A Defense of Judgment.* University of Chicago Press, 2021.
Cohen, Matt, and Aaron Dinen. "Keeping Tally With Meaning: Reading Numerals in Walt Whitman's Manuscripts." *Walt Whitman Quarterly Review* 34, no. 2 (Fall 2016): 120-45.
Colwell, Anne. *Inscrutable Houses: Metaphors of the Body in the Poems of Elizabeth Bishop.* University of Alabama Press, 1997.
Colwell, Anne. "The One That Got Away: Elizabeth Bishop's 'Damned "Fish."'" *Journal X* 3, no. 2 (2020): 172-81.
Corelle, Laurel Snow. *A Poet's High Argument: Elizabeth Bishop and Christianity.* University of South Carolina Press, 2008.
Costello, Bonnie. "Dreams." In *Elizabeth Bishop in Context,* ed. Angus Cleghorn and Jonathan Ellis, 291-301. Cambridge University Press, 2021.
Costello, Bonnie. *Elizabeth Bishop: Questions of Mastery.* Harvard University Press, 1993.
Critchley, Simon. *Things Merely Are: Philosophy in the Poetry of Wallace Stevens.* Routledge, 2005.
Culler, Jonathan D. *Theory of the Lyric.* Harvard University Press, 2015.
Cushman, Stephen. *Fictions of Form in American Poetry.* Princeton University Press, 1993.
Daniel, Lucy. *Gertrude Stein.* Reaktion Books, 2005.
Davidson, Donald. *Essays on Actions and Events.* Oxford University Press, 2001.
Davidson, Donald. *Inquiries into Truth and Interpretation.* Oxford University Press, 2001.
Davidson, Donald. "What Metaphors Mean." In *Inquiries into Truth and Interpretation,* 245-64. Oxford University Press, 1978.
Davies, David. "Art and Thought Experiments." In *The Routledge Companion to Thought Experiments,* ed. Michael Stuart, Yiftach Fehige, and James Robert Brown. Routledge, 2018.

BIBLIOGRAPHY

Davis, Theo. *Formalism, Experience, and the Making of American Literature in the Nineteenth Century*. Cambridge University Press, 2007.
Davis, Theo. *Ornamental Aesthetics*. Oxford University Press, 2016.
de Man, Paul. "Literary History and Literary Modernity." *Daedalus* 99, no. 2 (Spring 1970): 384–404.
de Man, Paul. *Blindness and Insight, Essays in the Rhetoric of Contemporary Criticism*. 2nd ed. University of Minnesota Press, 1983.
de Toqueville, Alexis. *Democracy in America (1835)*. Ed. Richard D. Heffner. Signet Classics, 2001.
DeKoven, Marianne. *A Different Language: Gertrude Stein's Experimental Writing*. University of Wisconsin Press, 1983.
Deppman, Jed. *Trying to Think with Emily Dickinson*. University of Massachusetts Press, 2008.
Dewey, John. *Art as Experience*. Perigree, 1934.
Dewey, John. *The Philosophy of John Dewey*. Ed. John J. McDermott. University of Chicago Press, 1973.
Dewey, John. *Studies in Logical Theory*. University of Chicago Press, 1903.
Diamond, Cora. "The Difficulty of Reality and the Difficulty of Philosophy." *Partial Answers: Journal of Literature and the History of Ideas* 1, no. 2 (June 2003): 1–26.
Dickey, Frances. "Bishop, Dewey, Darwin: What Other People Know." *Contemporary Literature* 44, no. 2 (2003): 301–31.
Dickie, Margaret. *Stein, Bishop, & Rich: Lyrics of Love, War, & Place*. University of North Carolina Press, 1997.
Dickinson, Emily. *The Poems of Emily Dickinson: Reading Edition*. Ed. R. W. Franklin. Belknap Press, 2005.
Diepeveen, Leonard. *The Difficulties of Modernism*. Routledge, 2003.
Donne, John. *The Complete English Poems*. Ed. A. J. Smith. Penguin Classics. Penguin Books, 1977.
Douven, Igor. "Abduction." In *The Stanford Encyclopedia of Philosophy*. Ed. Edward N. Zalta. https://plato.stanford.edu/archives/sum2021/entries/abduction/.
Douven, Igor. *The Art of Abduction*. MIT Press, 2022.
Dragulinescu, Stefan. "Inference to the Best Explanation and Mechanisms in Medicine." *Theoretical Medicine and Bioethics* 37, no. 3 (2016): 211–32.
Dubnick, Randa. *The Structure of Obscurity: Gertrude Stein, Language, and Cubism*. University of Illinois Press, 1984.
Dydo, Ulla E. *Gertrude Stein: The Language That Rises: 1923–1934*. Northwestern University Press, 2008.
Eco, Umberto. *The Infinity of Lists*. Rizzoli, 2009.
Edelman, Lee. "The Geography of Gender: Elizabeth Bishop's 'In the Waiting Room.'" *Contemporary Literature* 26, no. 2 (1985): 179–96.
Eeckhout, Bart. "The Philosopher's Poet: Twenty-First-Century Perspectives on Wallace Stevens." *Transatlantica. Revue d'études Américaines. American Studies Journal*, no. 1 (December 1, 2020). https://journals.openedition.org/transatlantica/15268.
Eeckhout, Bart. "Stevens and Philosophy." In *The Cambridge Companion to Wallace Stevens*, ed. John N. Serio. Cambridge University Press, 2007.

Eliot, T. S. *The Sacred Wood and Major Early Essays*. Dover, 1998.
Emerson, Edward Waldo. *Emerson in Concord: A Memoir*. Houghton Mifflin and Company, 1889.
Epstein, Andrew. *Attention Equals Life: The Pursuit of the Everyday in Contemporary Poetry and Culture*. Oxford University Press, 2016.
Erkkila, Betsy. *The Wicked Sisters: Women Poets, Literary History, and Discord*. Oxford University Press, 1992.
Erkkila, Betsy. *Whitman the Political Poet*. Oxford University Press, 1989.
Ettenhuber, Katrin. *The Logical Renaissance: Literature, Cognition, and Argument, 1479–1630*. Oxford University Press, 2024.
Examiner. "Review of Leaves of Grass." March 22, 1856.
Feguson, Frances. "Jane Austen, *Emma*, and the Impact of Form." In *Reading for Form*, edited by Susan J. Wolfson and Marshall Brown, 234, 239. University of Washington Press, 2006.
Feuerstein, Melissa, Bill Johnson González, Lili Porten, and Keja Valens. "Editors Preface." In *The Barbara Johnson Reader: The Surprise of Otherness*, ed. Melissa Feuerstein, Bill Johnson González, Lili Porten, and Keja Valens. Duke University Press, 2014.
Fifer, Elizabeth. *Rescued Readings: A Reconstruction of Gertrude Stein's Difficult Texts*. Wayne State University Press, 1992.
Folsom, Ed, and Kenneth M. Price. *Re-Scripting Walt Whitman: An Introduction to His Life and Work*. Wiley-Blackwell, 2005.
Ford, Karen Jackson. "The Sonnets of Satin-Legs Brooks." *Contemporary Literature* 48, no. 3 (Fall 2007): 345–73.
Ford, Karen Jackson. "The Last Quatrain: Gwendolyn Brooks and the Ends of Ballads." *Twentieth Century Literature* 56, no. 3 (2010): 371–95.
Friedrich, Nietzsche. *Beyond Good and Evil*. Trans. Helen Zimmern. Tribeca Books, 2013.
Frye, Northrop. *Anatomy of Criticism: Four Essays*. Princeton University Press, 2020.
Frye, Northrop. *Fables of Identity: Studies in Poetic Mythology*. Harcourt Brace, 1963.
Fussell, Paul. *The Great War and Modern Memory*. New ed. Oxford University Press, 2013.
Fussell, Paul. *Poetic Meter and Poetic Form*. Random House, 1965.
Fussell, Paul. *Poetic Meter and Poetic Form*, Rev. ed. McGraw Hill, 1979.
Gadberry, Andrea. *Cartesian Poetics: The Art of Thinking*. University of Chicago Press, 2020.
Galvin, Rachel. *News of War: Civilian Poetry 1936–1945*. Oxford University Press, 2017.
Gardner, Thomas. *Regions of Unlikeness: Explaining Contemporary Poetry*. University of Nebraska Press, 1999.
Gendler, Tamar Szabó. *Thought Experiment: On the Powers and Limits of Imaginary Cases*. Garland Publishing, 2000.
Gentner, Dedre. "Structure-Mapping: A Theoretical Framework for Analogy." *Cognitive Science* 7, no. 1 (1983): 155–70.

BIBLIOGRAPHY

Gick, Mary L., and Keith J. Holyoak. "Schema Induction and Analogical Transfer." *Cognitive Psychology* 15, no. 1 (1983): 1–38.
Giddens, Anthony. *The Consequences of Modernity*. Stanford University Press, 1990.
Gilbert, Roger. "'These Things': Moore's Habits of Adduction." In *Twenty-First Century Marianne Moore: Essays from a Critical Renaissance*, ed. Elizabeth Gregory and Stacy Carson Hubbard, 33–48. Palgrave Macmillan, 2018.
Ginsberg, Allen. *Howl and Other Poems*. City Lights Books, 1956.
Glaser, Ben. *Modernism's Metronome: Meter and Twentieth-Century Poetics*. Johns Hopkins University Press, 2020.
Glavey, Brian. *The Wallflower Avant-Garde: Modernism, Sexuality, and Queer Ekphrasis*. Oxford University Press, 2015.
Glennan, Stuart. *The New Mechanical Philosophy*. Oxford University Press, 2017.
Glennan, Stuart, and Phyllis Illari, eds. *The Routledge Handbook of the Philosophy of Mechanisms*. Routledge, 2017.
Goldsby, Jacqueline. *A Spectacular Secret: Lynching in American Life and Literature*. University of Chicago Press, 2006.
Goodman, Nelson. *Fact, Fiction, and Forecast*. 4th ed. Harvard University Press, 1983.
Gray, Jeffrey. "Travel." In *Elizabeth Bishop in Context*, ed. Angus Cleghorn and Jonathan Ellis, 277–90. Cambridge University Press, 2021.
Green, Fiona. "Moore's Numbers." In *Twenty-First Century Marianne Moore: Essays from a Critical Renaissance*, ed. Elizabeth Gregory and Stacy Carson Hubbard, 49–66. Palgrave Macmillan, 2018.
Gregory, Elizabeth, and Stacy Carson Hubbard, eds. *Twenty-First Century Marianne Moore: Essays from a Critical Renaissance*. Palgrave Macmillan, 2018.
Griffin, Farah Jasmine. *Who Set You Flowin?: The African-American Migration Narrative*. Oxford University Press, 1995.
Griffiths, Devin. *The Age of Analogy: Science and Literature Between the Darwins*. Johns Hopkins University Press, 2016.
Grimstad, Paul. *Experience and Experimental Writing*. Oxford University Press, 2013.
Grossman, Allen. *The Long Schoolroom: Lessons in the Bitter Logic of the Poetic Principle*. University of Michigan Press, 1997.
Grossman, Allen. "The Poetics of Union in Whitman and Lincoln." In *The American Renaissance Reconsidered*. ed. Walter Benn Michaels and Donald E. Pease, 183–208. Johns Hopkins University Press, 1985.
Grossman, Allen. *The Sighted Singer* with Mark Halliday. Johns Hopkins University Press, 1991.
Grossman, Allen. *True-Love: Essays on Poetry and Valuing*. University of Chicago Press, 2009.
Guillory, John. *Cultural Capital: The Problem of Literary Canon Formation*. University of Chicago Press, 1993.
Habermas, Jürgen. *The Philosophical Discourse of Modernity*. Trans. Frederick G. Lawrence. MIT Press, 1987.
Hacking, Ian. *An Introduction to Probability and Inductive Logic*. Cambridge University Press, 2001.

BIBLIOGRAPHY

Hacking, Ian. *The Emergence of Probability: A Philosophical Study of Early Ideas About Probability, Induction, and Statistical Inference.* 2nd ed. Cambridge University Press, 2006.
Hacking, Ian. *The Taming of Chance.* Cambridge University Press, 1990.
Hall, Donald. "Marianne Moore, The Art of Poetry No. 4." *The Paris Review* 26. (Summer-Fall 1961.) (Summer-Fall 1961).
Hammer, Langdon. "ENGL 310: Modern Poetry." Open Yale Courses, Lecture 24—Elizabeth Bishop. https://oyc.yale.edu/english/engl-310/lecture-24.
Hanfling, Oswald. "Hume and Wittgenstein." In *Impressions of Empiricism.* vol. 9. Ed. Godfrey Vesey. Royal Institute of Philosophy, 1976.
Hare, Peter. *Pragmatism with Purpose.* Ed. Joseph Palencik, Douglas R. Anderson, and Steven A. Miller. Fordham University Press, 2015.
Harré, Rom. *Varieties of Realism: A Rationale for the Natural Sciences.* Blackwell, 1986.
Harrison, Victoria. *Elizabeth Bishop's Poetics of Intimacy.* Cambridge University Press, 1993.
Hass, Robert. *A Little Book on Form: An Exploration into the Formal Imagination of Poetry.* Ecco, 2018.
Hejinian, Lyn. *The Language of Inquiry.* University of California Press, 2000.
Hempel, Carl G. *Aspects of Scientific Explanation, and Other Essays in the Philosophy of Science.* Free Press, 1965.
Hempel, Carl G. "Studies in the Logic of Confirmation." *Mind* 54, no. 213 (1945): 1–26.
Hesse, Mary. *Models and Analogies in Science.* University of Notre Dame Press, 1965.
Hesse, Mary, and L. Jonathan Cohen, eds. *Applications of Inductive Logic.* Clarendon Press, 1980.
Hirsch, Edward. "My Own Acquaintance." In *The Making of a Sonnet.* Ed. Eavan Boland and Edward Hirsch. W. W. Norton, 2008.
Hoffman, Michael J. *Gertrude Stein.* Twayne Publishers, 1976.
Hofstadter, Douglas, and Emmanuel Sander. *Surfaces and Essences: Analogy as the Fuel and Fire of Thinking.* Basic Books, 2013.
Holley, Margaret. "The Model Stanza: The Organic Origin of Moore's Syllabic Verse." *Twentieth Century Literature* 30, no. 2/3 (1984): 181–91.
Hollister, Susannah, and Emily Setina. "Appendix B." In *Stanzas in Meditation: The Corrected Edition.* Ed. Susannah Hollister and Emily Setina. Yale University Press, 2012.
Hollister, Susannah, and Emily Setina. "Preface." In *Stanzas in Meditation: The Corrected Edition.* Ed. Susannah Hollister and Emily Setina. Yale University Press, 2012.
Hong, Cathy Park. "Delusions of Whiteness in the Avant-Garde." *Lana Turner* 7, November 2014.
Howe, Susan. *The Birth-Mark: Unsettling the Wilderness in American Literary History.* Wesleyan University Press, 1993.
Hume, David. *An Enquiry Concerning Human Understanding.* Ed. Stephen Buckle. Cambridge University Press, 2007.
Hunter, Walt. *The American House Poem, 1945–2021.* Oxford University Press, 2023.
Hunter, Walt. *Forms of a World: Contemporary Poetry and the Making of Globalization.* Fordham University Press, 2019.
Hunter, Walt. "Lyric and Its Discontents." *Minnesota Review* 79 (2012): 78–90.

Izenberg, Oren. *Being Numerous: Poetry and the Ground of Social Life*. Princeton University Press, 2011.
Izenberg, Oren. "How to Know Everything." In *The Poetry of Emily Dickinson: Philosophical Perspectives*. Ed. Elisabeth Camp. Oxford University Press, 2021.
Izenberg, Oren. "Poems Out of Our Heads." *PMLA* 123, no. 1 (2008): 216–22.
Jackson, Virginia. *Before Modernism*. Princeton University Press, 2023.
Jackson, Virginia. *Dickinson's Misery: A Theory of Lyric Reading*. Princeton University Press, 2013.
Jackson, Virginia. "Lyric." In *The Princeton Encyclopedia of Poetry and Poetics*, 4th ed., ed. Roland Greene, Stephen Cushman, Claire Cavanagh, Jahan Ramazani, and Paul F. Rouzer, 826–34. Princeton University Press, 2012.
James, William. *Essays, Comments, and Reviews*. Harvard University Press, 1987.
James, William. *Essays in Radical Empiricism*. Harvard University Press, 1976.
James, William. *Pragmatism and Other Writings*. Ed. Giles Gunn. Penguin Classics, 2000.
James, William. *The Principles of Psychology*, vol. 2. Henry Holt and Company, 1890.
Jarrell, Randall. *Poetry and the Age (1953)*. University of Florida Press, 2001.
Jaussen, Paul. "Spectral Affordances of the Catalogue." *Comparative Literature* 70, no. 2 (2018): 160–75.
Johnson, Barbara. *Persons and Things*. Harvard University Press, 2010.
Josephson, John R., and Susan G. Josephson. *Abduction Inference: Computation, Philosophy, Technology*. Cambridge University Press, 1994.
Juhasz, Suzanne. "The Irresistible Lure of Repetition and Dickinson's Poetics of Analogy." *The Emily Dickinson Journal* 9, no. 2 (2000): 23–31.
Kadlec, David. *Mosaic Modernism: Anarchism, Pragmatism, Culture*. Johns Hopkins University Press, 2000.
Kalstone, David. "All Eye." *The Partisan Review* 37, no. 2. 1970.
Kalstone, David. *Becoming a Poet*. University of Michigan Press, 1989.
Keats, John. *The Complete Poems*. 3rd ed. Edited by John Barnard. Penguin Classics. Penguin Books, 1988.
Kellner, Bruce. "How to Read Gertrude Stein." In *A Gertrude Stein Companion*. Edited by Bruce Kellner. Greenwood Press, 1988.
Kenner, Hugh. *A Homemade World: The American Modernist Writers*. Johns Hopkins University Press, 1989.
Kenner, Hugh. *The Pound Era*. University of California Press, 1971.
Kermode, Frank. *The Sense of an Ending: Studies in the Theory of Fiction*. Oxford University Press, 1966.
Killingsworth, M. Jimmie. *Cambridge Introduction to Walt Whitman*. Cambridge University Press, 2007.
Kindley, Evan. *Poet-Critics and the Administration of Culture*. Harvard University Press, 2017.
King, Rachael Scarborough. "The Scale of Genre." *New Literary History* 52, no. 2 (Spring 2021): 261–84.
Kotin, Joshua. *Utopias of One*. Princeton University Press, 2017.
Kramnick, Jonathan, and Anahid Nersessian. "Form and Explanation." *Critical Inquiry* 43, no. 3 (2017): 650–69.

Kuhn, Thomas. *The Essential Tension: Selected Studies in Scientific Tradition and Change*. University of Chicago Press, 1977.
Kuhn, Thomas. *The Structure of Scientific Revolutions*. 3rd ed. University of Chicago Press, 1996.
Leavall, Linda. *Marianne Moore and the Visual Arts: Prismatic Color*. Louisiana State University Press, 1995.
Leavall, Linda. "Marianne Moore, the James Family, and the Politics of Celibacy." *Twentieth Century Literature* 49, no. 2 (Summer 2003): 219–45.
Leick, Karen. *Gertrude Stein and the Making of an American Celebrity*. Routledge, 2009.
Leighton, Angela. *On Form*. Oxford University Press, 2007.
LeMahieu, Michael. *Fictions of Fact and Value: The Erasure of Logical Positivism in American Literature, 1945–1975*. Oxford University Press, 2013.
Levenson, Michael. "Novelty, Modernity, Adjacency." *New Literary History* 42, no. 4 (Autumn 2011): 663–80.
Levin, Jonathan. *The Poetics of Transition: Emerson, Pragmatism, and American Literary Modernism*. Duke University Press, 1999.
Levine, Caroline. *Forms: Whole, Rhythm, Hierarchy, Network*. Princeton University Press, 2015.
Levine, Naomi. *The Burden of Rhyme: Victorian Poetry, Formalism, and the Feeling of Literary History*. University of Chicago Press, 2024.
Levinson, Marjorie. "Response to Jonathan Kramnick and Anahid Nersessian, 'Form and Explanation.'" *Critical Inquiry* 44, no. 1 (2017): 144–55.
Levinson, Marjorie. *Thinking Through Poetry: Field Reports on Romantic Lyric*. Oxford University Press, 2018.
Levinson, Marjorie. "What Is New Formalism?" *PMLA* 122, no. 2 (2007): 558–69.
Lewis, Cara L. *Dynamic Form: How Intermediality Made Modernism*. Cornell University Press, 2020.
Liebregts, Peter. *Ezra Pound and Neoplatonism*. Fairleigh Dickinson University Press, 2004.
Lipton, Peter. *Inference to the Best Explanation*. Routledge, 2004.
Longenbach, James. *Modern Poetry After Modernism*. Oxford University Press, 1997.
Luhmann, Niklas. *Social Systems*. trans. John Bednarz, Jr. and Dirk Baecker. Stanford University Press, 1996.
Lupton, Christina. "Introduction: Literature and Contingency." *Textual Practice* 32, no. 3 (2018): 375–79.
Lyly, John. *Euphues: The Anatomy of Wit and Euphues and His England*. Ed. Leah Scragg. Manchester University Press, 2003.
Machamer, Peter, Lindley Darden, and Carl F. Craver. "Thinking about Mechanisms." *Philosophy of Science* 67, no. 1 (2000): 1–25.
MacLeod, Glen, ed. *Wallace Stevens in Context*. Cambridge University Press, 2017.
Macpherson, Sandra. "A Little Formalism." *ELH* 82, no. 2 (2015): 385–405.
Mak, Cliff. "On Falling Fastidiously: Marianne Moore's Slapstick Animals." *ELH* 83, no. 3 (Fall 2016): 873–98.
Malech, Dora, and Laura T. Smith, eds. *The American Sonnet: An Anthology of Poems and Essays*. University of Iowa Press, 2022.
Malkin, Rachel. "Public Desires, Private Desires: The Satisfactions of Stevens and Stanley Cavell." *The Wallace Stevens Journal* 36, no. 1 (2012): 105–33.

BIBLIOGRAPHY

Marx, Karl, and Friedrich Engels. *The Communist Manifesto [Trans. Samuel Moore, First Published 1888]*. Penguin Classics, 1967.
Mason, John B. "The Poet-Reader Relationship in 'Song of Myself.'" In *Approaches to Teaching Whitman's Leaves of Grass*. Ed. Donald D. Kummings. MLA Association of America, 1990.
McAlpine, Erica. *The Poet's Mistake*. Princeton University Press, 2020.
McCabe, Susan. *Elizabeth Bishop: Her Poetics of Loss*. Penn State University Press, 1994.
McComb, Geordie. "Thought Experiment, Definition, and Literary Fiction." In *Thought Experiments in Philosophy, Science, and the Arts*, ed. Mélanie Frappier, Letitia Meynell, and James Robert Brown. Routledge, 2013.
McCorkle, James. *The Still Performance: Writing, Self, and Interconnection in Five Postmodern American Poets*. University of Virginia Press, 1989.
McCain, Kevin, and Ted Poston. "Best Explanations: An Introduction." In *Best Explanations: New Essays on Inference to the Best Explanation* ed. Kevin McCain and Ted Poston. Oxford University Press, 2017.
McMullin, Ernan. *The Inference That Makes Science*. Marquette University Press, 1992.
Martin, Meredith. *The Rise and Fall of Meter*. Princeton University Press, 2012.
Menand, Louis. *The Metaphysicals Club*. Farrar, Straus and Giroux, 2001.
Merrin, Jeredith. *An Enabling Humility: Marianne Moore, Elizabeth Bishop, and the Uses of Tradition*. Rutgers University Press, 1990.
Meyer, Steven. *Irresistible Dictation: Gertrude Stein and the Correlations of Writing and Science*. Stanford University Press, 2002.
Michaels, Walter Benn, and Donald E. Pease. *The American Renaissance Reconsidered*. Johns Hopkins University Press, 1985.
Millier, Brett C. *Elizabeth Bishop: Life and the Memory of It*. University of California Press, 1992.
Milton, John. "Note on 'The Verse' Preceding Paradise Lost." In *Complete Poems and Major Prose*. Ed. Merritt Y. Hughes. Hackett, 2003.
Mix, Deborah M. *A Vocabulary for Thinking: Gertrude Stein and Contemporary North American Women's Innovative Writing*. University of Iowa Press, 2007.
Mladenović, Bojana. *Kuhn's Legacy: Epistemology, Metaphilosophy, and Pragmatism*. Columbia University Press, 2017.
Monteiro, George, ed. *Conversations with Elizabeth Bishop*. University Press of Mississippi, 1996.
Moore, Lisa L. "The Sonnet Is Not a Luxury." In *The American Sonnet: An Anthology of Poems and Essays*. Ed. Dora Malech and Lisa T. Smith. University of Iowa Press, 2022.
Moore, Marianne. "Lecture Notebook," 1906. VII:11:06. Rosenbach Library.
Moore, Marianne. *The Poems of Marianne Moore*. Ed. Grace Schulman. Viking, 2003.
Morgan, Mary S. *The World in the Model: How Economists Work and Think*. Cambridge University Press, 2012.
Morgan, Mary S., and Margaret Morrison, eds. *Models as Mediators: Perspectives on Natural and Social Science*. Cambridge University Press, 1999.
Moten, Fred. *In the Break: The Aesthetics of the Black Radical Tradition*. University of Minnesota Press, 2003.
Mueller, Janel. *John Donne*. Twenty-first-Century Oxford Authors. Oxford University Press, 2015.

Munson, Ronald, and Andrew Black. *The Elements of Reasoning*. 6th ed. Wadsworth Cengage Learning, 2012.

Nersessian, Anahid. *The Calamity Form*. University of Chicago Press, 2020.

Nersessian, Nancy. "Cognitive Science, Mental Modeling, and Thought Experiments." In *The Routledge Companion to Thought Experiments*, ed. Michael Stuart, Yiftach Fehige, and James Robert Brown. Routledge, 2018.

New, Elisa. *The Line's Eye: Poetic Experience and American Sight*. Harvard University Press, 1999.

Ngai, Sianne. *Our Aesthetic Categories: Zany, Cute, Interesting*. Harvard University Press, 2012.

Ngai, Sianne. "The Cuteness of the Avant-Garde." *Critical Inquiry* 31 no. 4 (Summer 2005): 811–47.

Nietzsche, Friedrich. *Beyond Good and Evil*. trans. Helen Zimmern. Tribeca Books, 2013.

North, Michael. *Novelty: A History of the New*. University of Chicago Press, 2013.

Norton, John D. "Thought Experiments in Einstein's Work." In *Thought Experiments in Science and Philosophy*. Ed. Tamara Horowitz and Gerald J. Massey. Rowman & Littlefield, 1991.

Nussbaum, Martha. "Democratic Desire: Walt Whitman." In *A Political Companion to Walt Whitman*. Ed. John E. Seery. University Press of Kentucky, 2011.

Nussbaum, Martha. *Love's Knowledge: Essays on Philosophy and Literature*. Oxford University Press, 1990.

Olson, Liesl. *Modernism and the Ordinary*. Oxford University Press, 2009.

Olsson, Erik J. *Against Coherence: Truth, Probability, and Justification*. Clarendon Press, 2005.

Orr, David. "Rough Gems: Edgar Allan Poe & the Juke Box." *New York Times*, April 2, 2006. sec. Books. https://www.nytimes.com/2006/04/02/books/review/rough-gems.html.

Palmer, Michael. "Poetry and Contingency: Within a Timeless Moment of Barbaric Thought." *Chicago Review* 49, no. 2 (Summer 2003): 65–76.

Pannapacker, William. "The City." In *A Companion to Walt Whitman* ed. Donald D. Kummings. Blackwell, 2006.

Parker, Robert Dale. *The Unbeliever: The Poetry of Elizabeth Bishop*. University of Illinois Press, 1988.

Parmar, Sandeep. "Race." In *Elizabeth Bishop in Context*, ed. Angus Cleghorn and Jonathan Ellis, 337–46. Cambridge University Press, 2021.

Paul, Elliot. "Supplement." *Transition*, 1927.

Pavel, Thomas. "Literary Genres as Norms and Good Habits." *New Literary History* 34, no. 2 (2003): 201–10.

Peirce, C. S. "How to Make Our Ideas Clear." *Popular Science Monthly* 12, no. Jan. (1878): 286–302.

Peirce, Charles Sanders. *Collected Papers of Charles Sanders Peirce*. Ed. Charles Hartshorne and Paul Weiss. Harvard University Press, 1931.

Peirce, Charles Sanders. *Reasoning and the Logic of Things*. Ed. Kenneth Laine Ketner. Harvard University Press, 1993.

Peirce, Charles Sanders. *Writings of Charles S. Peirce: A Chronological Edition, Volume 1: 1857–1866*. Ed. Max H. Fitsch et al. Indiana University Press, 1982.

BIBLIOGRAPHY

Perelman, Bob. *The Marginalization of Poetry: Language Writing and Literary History.* Princeton University Press, 1996.
Perelman, Bob. *The Trouble with Genius: Reading Pound, Stein, Joyce, and Zukofsky.* University of California Press, 1994.
Perloff, Marjorie. "Abstraction & Unreadability: Gertrude Stein's Portraits: The Case of Christian Berard." *Vlak* 2 (2011): 156–61.
Perloff, Marjorie. "Collage and Poetry." In *Encyclopedia of Aesthetics*, 1st ed., ed. Michael Kelly, 1:384–87. Oxford University Press, 1998.
Perloff, Marjorie. *The Dance of the Intellect: Studies in the Poetry of the Pound Tradition.* Cambridge University Press, 1985.
Perloff, Marjorie. "Happy World: What Lyn Hejinian's Poetry Tells Us About Chance, Fortune, and Pleasure." *Boston Review*, February 2001.
Perloff, Marjorie. *The Poetics of Indeterminacy.* Princeton University Press, 1981.
Perloff, Marjorie. *Wittgenstein's Ladder: Poetic Language and the Strangeness of the Ordinary.* University of Chicago Press, 1996.
Phillips, Siobhan. *The Poetics of the Everyday: Creative Repetition in Modern American Verse.* Columbia University Press, 2009.
Pickard, Zachariah. *Elizabeth Bishop's Poetics of Description.* McGill-Queen's University Press, 2009.
Piper, Andrew. *Dreaming in Books: The Making of the Bibliographic Imagination in the Romantic Age.* University of Chicago Press, 2009.
Piper, Andrew. *Enumerations: Data and Literary Study.* University of Chicago Press, 2018.
Poirier, Richard. *Poetry and Pragmatism.* Harvard University Press, 1992.
Poirier, Richard. *Trying It Out in America: Literary and Other Performances.* Farrar, Straus and Giroux, 1999.
Poovey, Mary. "The Model System of Contemporary Literary Criticism." *Critical Inquiry* 27, no. 3 (2001): 408–38.
Popper, Karl. *Conjectures and Refutations.* 2nd ed. Routledge, 2002.
Porter, Dahlia. *Science, Form, and the Problem of Induction in British Romanticism.* Cambridge University Press, 2018.
Pound, Ezra. *The Cantos of Ezra Pound.* New Directions, 1996.
Pound, Ezra. *Personae.* Rev. ed. New Directions, 1990.
Pound, Ezra. *Selected Poems of Ezra Pound.* New Directions, 1957.
Priest, Graham. *An Introduction to Non-Classical Logic: From If to Is.* 2nd ed. Cambridge University Press, 2008.
Priestley, Joseph. *The History and Present State of Electricity.* Johnson, 1769.
Puskar, Jason. *Accident Society: Fiction, Collectivity, and the Production of Chance.* Stanford University Press, 2012.
Putnam, Hilary. "Foreword to the Fourth Edition." In *Fact, Fiction, and Forecast* by Nelson Goodman. 4th ed. Harvard University Press, 1983.
Quashie, Kevin. *The Sovereignty of Quiet: Beyond Resistance in Black Culture.* Rutgers University Press, 2012.
Quigley, Megan. *Modernist Fiction and Vagueness: Philosophy, Form, and Language.* Oxford University Press, 2015.
Quine, W. V. O. *Ontological Relativity & Other Essays.* Columbia University Press, 1969.

Ramazani, Jahan. "Self-Metaphorizing 'American' Sonnets.' " In *The American Sonnet: An Anthology of Poems and Essays*, ed. Dora Malech and Laura T. Smith. University of Iowa Press, 2022.
Rasula, Jed. "Make It New." *Modernism/Modernity* 17, no. 4 (November 2010): 713–33.
Redding, Patrick, "Whitman Unbound: Democracy and Poetic Form, 1912–1931." *New Literary History* 41, no. 3 (2010): 669–90.
Reddy, Srikanth. *Changing Subjects: Digressions in Modern American Poetry*. Oxford University Press, 2012.
Reynolds, David S. *Walt Whitman's America: A Cultural Biography*. Vintage Books, 1996.
Rich, Adrienne. "The Eye of the Outsider: On the Poetry of Elizabeth Bishop." *Boston Review*, June 1, 1984. https://www.bostonreview.net/articles/rich-the-eye-of-the-outsider/.
Rich, Adrienne. "Vesuvius at Home." *Parnassus Review* 5, no. 1 (1976).
Richardson, Joan. *A Natural History of Pragmatism: The Fact of Feeling from Jonathan Edwards to Gertrude Stein*. Cambridge University Press, 2007.
Richardson, Rachel. "Learning the Sonnet." In *Poetry Foundation*, Article for Students, August 29, 2013. https://www.poetryfoundation.org/articles/70051/learning-the-sonnet.
Rorty, Richard. *Consequences of Pragmatism: Essays 1972–1980*. University of Minnesota Press, 1982.
Rorty, Richard. *Contingency, Irony, and Solidarity*. Cambridge University Press, 1989.
Rotella, Guy. *Castings: Monuments and Monumentality in Poems by Elizabeth Bishop, Robert Lowell, James Merrill, Derek Walcott, and Seamus Heaney*. Vanderbilt University Press, 2004.
Ruddick, Lisa. *Reading Gertrude Stein: Body, Text, Gnosis*. Cornell University Press, 1990.
Russell, Bertrand. *A History of Western Philosophy*. Simon & Schuster, 1967.
Russell, Bertrand. *Essays in Analysis*, ed. Douglas Lackey. George Braziller, 1945.
Russell, Bertrand. *The Problems of Philosophy*. Oxford University Press, 1997.
Saint-Amour, Paul. *Tense Future: Modernism, Total War, Encyclopedic Form*. Oxford University Press, 2015.
Salmon, Wesley C. "Rationality and Objectivity in Science or Tom Kuhn Meets Tom Bayes." In *Scientific Theories*, ed. C. Wade Savage, 175–204. University of Minnesota Press, 1990.
Salmon, Wesley C. *Scientific Explanation and the Causal Structure of the World*. Princeton University Press, 1984.
Salmon, Wesley C. *Statistical Explanation and Statistical Relevance*. University of Pittsburgh Press, 1971.
Sandler, Matt. "Kindred Darkness: Whitman in New Orleans." In *Whitman Noir: Black America and the Good Gray Poet* ed. Ivy G. Wilson. University of Iowa Press, 2014.
Schoenbach, Lisi. *Pragmatic Modernism*. Oxford University Press, 2011.
Schwartz, Ana. "Anne Bradstreet, Arsonist?" *New Literary History* 52, no. 1 (2021): 119–43.
Schwartz, Lloyd. *That Sense of Constant Readjustment: Elizabeth Bishop's North & South*. Garland Publishing, 1987.

BIBLIOGRAPHY

Schwartz, Lloyd, and Sybil P. Estess. *Elizabeth Bishop and Her Art*. University of Michigan Press, 1983.
Scriven, Michael. *Reasoning*. McGraw Hill, 1976.
Sedgwick, Eve Kosofsky. *Tendencies*. Duke University Press, 1993.
Seery, John E. *A Political Companion to Walt Whitman*. University Press of Kentucky, 2011.
Seiler, Claire. *Midcentury Suspension: Literature and Feeling in the Wake of World War II*. Columbia University Press, 2020.
Setina, Emily. "Marianne Moore's Postwar Fables and the Politics of Indirection." *PMLA* 131, no. 5 (October 2016): 1256–73.
Shakespeare, William. *A Midsummer Night's Dream*. Ed. Barbara A. Mowat and Paul Werstine. Folger Shakespeare Library. Simon & Schuster, 2016.
Sharpe, Christina. *In the Wake: On Blackness and Being*. Duke University Press, 2016.
Sieburth, Richard. "In Pound We Trust: The Economy of Poetry/The Poetry of Economics." *Critical Inquiry* 14, no. 1 (1987): 142–72.
Smith, Barbara Herrnstein. *Contingencies of Value*. Cambridge University Press, 1989.
So, Richard Jean. "All Models Are Wrong." *PMLA* 132, no. 3 (2017): 668–73.
Sorensen, Roy A. *Thought Experiments*. Oxford University Press, 1992.
Spiers, Elizabeth. "The Art of Poetry XXVII: Elizabeth Bishop." *Paris Review*, 1981.
Stanley, Kate. *Practices of Surprise in American Literature After Emerson*. Cambridge University Press, 2018.
Stein, Gertrude. *A Stein Reader*. Ed. Ulla E. Dydo. Northwestern University Press, 1993.
Stein, Gertrude. *The Autobiography of Alice B. Toklas*. Vintage, 1990.
Stein, Gertrude. *Blood on the Dining-Room Floor*. Dover, 2008.
Stein, Gertrude. *Everybody's Autobiography*. Exact Change, 2004.
Stein, Gertrude. *Lectures in America*. Beacon Press, 1985.
Stein, Gertrude. *The Making of Americans*. Dalkey Archive Press, 1995.
Stein, Gertrude. *Stanzas in Meditation: The Corrected Edition*. Ed. Susannah Hollister and Emily Setina. Yale University Press, 2012.
Stein, Gertrude. *Writings, 1903–1932*. Vol. 1. Library of America, 1998.
Stein, Gertrude. *Writings, 1932–1946*. Vol. 2. Library of America, 1998.
Steiner, George. "On Difficulty." *The Journal of Aesthetics and Art Criticism* 36, no. 3 (1978): 263–76.
Steiner, Wendy. *Exact Resemblance to Exact Resemblance: The Literary Portraiture of Gertrude Stein*. Yale University Press, 1978.
Steinlight, Emily. *Populating the Novel: Literary Form and the Politics of Surplus Life*. Cornell University Press, 2018.
Stevens, Wallace. *Collected Poetry & Prose*. Library of America, 1997.
Stewart, Susan. "On ED's 754/764." *New Literary History* 45, no. 2 (2014): 253–70.
Stewart, Susan. *Poetry and the Fate of the Senses*. University of Chicago Press, 2002.
Stimpson, Catherine R. "The Somagrams of Gertrude Stein." In *Critical Essays on Gertrude Stein*, ed. Michael J. Hoffman. G. K. Hall & Co., 1986.
Stuart, Colin. "The Discovery of Uranus." *Royal Museums Greenwich* (blog), March 13, 2020. https://www.rmg.co.uk/stories/blog/astronomy/discovery-uranus.
Sunstein, Cass. "On Analogical Reasoning." *Harvard Law Review* 106, no. 3 (1993).

Sutherland, Donald. "The Turning Point: Preface to the 1956 *Stanzas in Meditation*." In *Stanzas in Meditation: The Corrected Edition*, ed. Susannah Hollister and Emily Setina. Yale University Press, 2012.

Tankard, Paul. "Reading Lists." *Prose Studies* 28, no. 3 (2006): 337–60.

Taylor, Tess. "But Could a Dream: Form and Freedom in Gwendolyn Brooks's Domestic Sonnets." In *The American Sonnet: An Anthology of Poems and Essays*, ed. Dora Malech and Laura T. Smith. University of Iowa Press, 2022.

Teskey, Gordon. *Spenserian Moments*. Harvard University Press, 2019.

Thaventhiran, Helen. *Radical Empiricists: Five Modernist Close Readers*. Oxford University Press, 2015.

Theune, Michael. "Strange Voltas." In *The American Sonnet: An Anthology of Poems and Essays*, ed. Dora Malech and Laura T. Smith. University of Iowa Press, 2022.

Theune, Michael. *Structure and Surprise*. Teachers & Writers Collaborative, 2007.

Tiffany, Daniel. *Radio Corpse: Imagism and the Cryptaesthetic of Ezra Pound*. Harvard University Press, 1998.

Tiffany, Daniel. *Toy Medium: Materialism and Modern Lyric*. University of California Press, 2000.

Tocqueville, Alexis de. *Democracy in America*. Reissue. ed. Richard D. Heffner. Signet Classics, 2001.

Tóibín, Colm. *On Elizabeth BIshop*. Princeton University Press, 2015.

Trachtenberg, Alan. "The Politics of Labor and the Poet's Work: A Reading of 'A Song for Occupations.'" In *Walt Whitman: The Centennial Essays*, ed. Ed Folsom University of Iowa Press, 1994.

Traubel, Horace. *With Walt Whitman in Camden*. Vol. 4. Rowman & Littlefield, 1961.

Tursi, Renee. "Emily Dickinson, Pragmatism, and the Conquests of Mind." In *Emily Dickinson and Philosophy*, ed. Jed Deppman, Marianne Noble, and Gary Lee Stonum. Cambridge University Press, 2013.

van Fraassen, Bas C. *The Scientific Image*. Oxford University Press, 1980.

van Fraassen, Bas C. *Laws and Symmetry*. Oxford University Press, 1989.

van Fraassen, Bas C. "The Pragmatic Theory of Explanation." In *Theories of Explanation*. Ed. Joseph C. Pitt. Oxford University Press, 1988.

van Fraassen, Bas C. *Science and Stances, with a Reply from Bas C. van Fraassen*. Ed. Bradley Monton and Bas C. van Fraassen. Oxford University Press, 2007.

Van Vechten, Carl. "How to Read Gertrude Stein." In *Critical Essays on Gertrude Stein*. ed. Michael J. Hoffman. G. K. Hall & Co., 1986.

Vendler, Helen. *The Art of Shakespeare's Sonnets*. Harvard University Press, 1997.

Vendler, Helen. "The Creeping Griffon." *New York Review of Books*, September 23, 1982. https://www.nybooks.com/articles/1982/09/23/the-creeping-griffon/.

Vendler, Helen. "Life Studies." *New York Review of Books*, February 16, 1984. https://www.nybooks.com/articles/1984/02/16/life-studies/.

Vendler, Helen. *Our Secret Discipline*. Harvard University Press, 2007.

Vendler, Helen. "The Poems of Elizabeth Bishop." *Critical Inquiry* 13, no. 4 (1987): 825–38.

von Contzen, Eva. "Die Affordanzen Der Liste" [The affordances of the list]. *Zeitschrift Für Literaturwissenschaft Und Linguistik* 47, no. 3 (2017): 317–26.

von Contzen, Eva. "The Limits of Narration: Lists and Literary History." *Style* 50, no. 3 (2016): 241–60.

von Hallberg, Robert. *Lyric Powers*. University of Chicago Press, 2008.
Wagner-Lawlor, Jennifer. *A Moment's Monument: Revisionary Poetics and the Nineteenth-Century English Sonnet*. Fairleigh Dickinson University Press, 1998.
Walker, Cheryl. "Religion." In *Elizabeth Bishop in Context*, ed. Angus Cleghorn and Jonathan Ellis, 256–65. Cambridge University Press, 2021.
Watson, Jamie Carlin, and Robert Arp. *Critical Thinking: An Introduction to Reasoning Well*. Bloomsbury Academic, 2015.
Watt, Ian. "The First Paragraph of The Ambassadors: An Explication." *Essays in Criticism* 3 (1960): 250–74.
Weinreb, Lloyd L. *Legal Reason: The Use of Analogy in Legal Argument*. Cambridge University Press, 2005.
Weisberg, Michael. *Simulation and Similarity: Using Models to Understand the World*. Oxford University Press, 2013.
Weisbuch, Robert. *Emily Dickinson's Poetry*. University of Chicago Press, 1975.
Wellbery, David E. "Contingency." In *Neverending Stories: Toward a Critical Narratology* ed. Maria Tatar, Ann Clark Fehn, Ingeborg Hoesterey. Princeton University Press, 1992.
White, Gillian. *Lyric Shame: The "Lyric" Subject of Contemporary American Poetry*. Harvard University Press, 2014.
White, Gillian. "Poetics of Contingency." *Textual Practice* 32, no. 3 (2018): 529–50.
White, Heather Cass. "Pragmatist Poetics in Wallace Stevens and Marianne Moore." *The Wallace Stevens Journal* 31, no. 2 (Fall 2007): 148–70.
Whitehead, Alfred North. *Science and the Modern World*. Lowell Lectures, 1925. The Free Press, 1967.
Whitman, Walt. *Poetry and Prose*. ed. Justin Kaplan. Library of America, 1982.
Williamson, Timothy. "Semantic Paradoxes and Abductive Methodology," in *Reflections on the Liar*, ed. Bradley Armour-Garb. Oxford University Press, 2017.
Williamson, Timothy. *Doing Philosophy: From Common Curiosity to Logical Reasoning*. Oxford University Press, 2018.
Winant, Johanna. "Ezra Pound and the Form of Explanation." *Paideuma: Modern and Contemporary Poetry and Poetics* 42 (2015): 171–96.
Winant, Johanna. "Logical and Literary Form." In *Cambridge Companion to Philosophy and Literature*, ed. R. Lanier Anderson and Karen Zumhagen-Yekplé. Cambridge University Press, forthcoming.
Winant, Johanna. "Philosophy, Poetry, and the Principle of Charity." In *A Companion to American Poetry*, ed. Mary McAleer Balkun, Jeffrey Gray, and Paul Jaussen, 120–132. Wiley-Blackwell, 2022.
Wittgenstein, Ludwig. *On Certainty*, ed. G. E. M. Anscombe and G. H. von Wright. trans. Denis Paul and G. E. M. Anscombe. Harper & Row, 1972.
Wittgenstein, Ludwig. *Philosophical Investigations*. Rev. 4th ed. Wiley-Blackwell, 2009.
Wittgenstein, Ludwig. *Tractatus Logico-Philosophicus*. 2nd ed. Routledge Classics. Routledge, 2001.
Wolfson, Susan J., and Marshall Brown, eds. *Reading for Form*. University of Washington Press, 2006.
Woodson, Jon. "Gwendolyn Brooks's Esoteric Sonnet 'A Lovely Love' as an Alchemical Metatext." In *The American Sonnet: An Anthology of Poems and Essays*. ed. Dora Malech and Laura T. Smith. University of Iowa Press, 2022.

Wordsworth, William. *The Major Works*. ed. Stephen Gill. Oxford University Press, 2000.
Zhang, Dora. *Strange Likeness: Description and the Modernist Novel*. University of Chicago Press, 2020.
Zhu, Chungeng. "Ezra Pound: The One-Principle Text." *Literature and Theology* 20, no. 4 (2006): 394–410.
Zona, Kirstin Hotelling. *Marianne Moore, Elizabeth Bishop, and May Swenson: The Feminist Poetics of Self-Restraint*. University of Michigan Press, 2002.
Zumhagen-Yekplé, Karen. *A Different Order of Difficulty: Literature After Wittgenstein*. University of Chicago Press, 2020.

INDEX

abduction, 27, 28, 81, 142, 152, 226n79, 227n83; in Bishop, 27, 142, 152. *See also* inference: to the best explanation

Adams, V. Joshua, 195n41; on Bishop's skepticism, 149; on Dickinson's "bad logic," 210n55

aesthetics, 1, 6, 7, 77, 111, 113, 133, 156, 165

Albright, Daniel: on defining lyric poetry, 7, 8, 10

Alford, Lucy, 222n3; on Bishop's "The Fish," 222n4, 226n63, 228n119

Alighieri, Dante, 39

Altieri, Charles, 21, 199n83; on "Nomad Exquisite," 13

Ammons, A. R., 31, 203n10

analogy, 3, 6, 26, 51, 53, 110, 156, 169, 172; in Bishop, 158; contingency of, 74, 77; in Dickinson, 6, 51–52, 59–74, 77, 129, 212n88; and ethics, 55; failures of, 58, 71; and feminist epistemology, 67; in law, 53; literary form of, 59, 65; in literary studies, 56–59, 212n85; and reasoning, 27, 51–56, 58–59, 61, 64, 68, 74, 77, 80, 159; in philosophy of science, 53–55, 57; powers of, 58–59, 72, 77; and pragmatism, 67, 68, 77

Andersen, Holly: on mechanisms, 219n53

Aristotle, 56, 77, 79, 103, 119; on metaphor, 70; *Nicomachean Ethics*, 119; on syllogism, 38

Ashton, Jennifer: on Stein's "problematic of wholeness," 97–98, 102

aubade, 11

Austen, Jane: *Persuasion*, 172

Auyoung, Elaine, 226n79; on literary criticism's coherence, 165–66

Badiou, Alain, 195n43

Bassoff, Bruce: on "Composition as Explanation," 96–97

Bazin, Victoria, 112, 115

Benfey, Christopher: on Dickinson's riddles, 61, 62, 210n60

Benjamin, Walter, 112

Bennett, Chad: on "paraliptic" gossip in Stein, 102; on *Stanzas in Meditation*, 103, 104

Bernstein, Charles: "The Difficult Poem," 21

Bird, Alexander, 229n136

Bishop, Elizabeth, 17, 27, 28, 139–67; abduction in, 27, 28, 142, 152; "Arrival at Santos," 142–43, 156; "Brazil, January 1, 1502," 143; "Cape Breton," 144; *A Cold Spring*, 153, 164; "Crusoe in England," 150; and diagnosis, 153–54, 156; "A Drunkard," 154; "The End of March," 144; "Filling Station," 144–45, 150, 159–64, 167, 223n20, 228n117, 228n121; "The Fish," 139–42, 146, 150, 154, 158, 161, 163, 166, 167, 222n1, 222n3, 222n4, 223n20, 228n119; inference in, 27, 28, 141–42, 146, 151–53, 156, 158–61, 166, 170; "The Monument," 142, 144, 150; "The Moose," 144, 150, 230n141; "O Breath," 145, 154, 167; "One Art," 157; "Pink Dog," 156; "The Prodigal," 154; questions in, 150, 159, 161; *Questions of Travel*, 228n121; "Roosters," 147; "Sestina," 144, 157; "Song for the Rainy Season," 167; "Squatter's Children," 225n43; "Trouvée," 150; "Visits to St. Elizabeths," 155–57, 227n101; "In the Waiting Room," 159–64, 223n20, 228n121
Black, Max, 208n32
Blasing, Mutlu Konuk, 149
Bloom, Harold: on Whitman's lists, 30
Boland, Eavan: on the sonnet's reason, 171
Booth, Mark: on the unexpected in lyric poetry, 8
Box, George E. P., 74
Bradstreet, Anne, 3, 23
Bromwich, David: on sonnets and syllogism, 173
Brooks, Cleanth, 35, 103, 166
Brooks, Gwendolyn, 22–26, 29, 37, 174–84, 200n96, 201n99, 201n100, 202n101, 232n38, 232n39, 233n42; "kitchenette building," 22–26, 174–79, 181, 182, 183, 200n96, 201n100; "A Lovely Love," 178–83; "the rites for Cousin Vit," 182–85, 233n45
Burt, Stephanie: on coherence in Bishop, 164; on defining lyric poetry, 7, 194n22; on sonnets, 231n18; on the sonnet's "internal logic," 171–72, 176, 231n15
Buxton, Rachel, 115

Cameron, Sharon, 70, 195n41; on Dickinson's use of analogy, 66–67, 68, 70; on Dickinson and definition, 61, 62; on Dickinson's imagery, 60; on poetry's problems, 200n88
Camp, Elisabeth: on Dickinson, 207n2
Carnap, Rudolf, 19, 45, 55, 197n63
Carson, Anne: on Simonides of Keos, 207n74
Case, Kristen, 115
causality, 5, 45, 79, 114–16, 119, 124, 150–51, 153, 205n53; in Bishop, 156, 228n117
Cavell, Stanley, 11, 195n43, 208n32; on the problem of other minds, 10, 134; on skepticism, 11, 68, 134, 135, 195n41, 195n42, 221n108, 221n110; on "the truth of skepticism," 67, 134, 149
Cecire, Natalia: on "experimental writing," 199n85; on gender and objectivity, 128, 215n49; on Moore's precision, 132, 134; on reading Stein, 214n30; on Stein's "anti-visual objectivity," 215n57; on Stein's unreadability, 89, 216n88
Chaucer, Geoffrey: *The Parliament of Fowls*, 31
Chiasson, Dan, 129
Chodat, Robert: on Stein, 84, 91, 96, 198n76
Clune, Michael: on Brooks, 201n100; on Dickinson's analogies, 209n50, 212n88
coherence, 10, 35, 177; in Bishop, 28, 141, 162–67, 229n129, 229n131, 229n132
consistency, 165, 192n11; in Moore, 28, 126, 151; in Stein, 87, 107
contingency, 12, 17, 20–21, 48, 68, 76, 99, 110, 112, 117, 174, 199n83, 212n85, 216n95; in Bishop, 151, 152; in Dickinson, 71–72, 74; in Moore, 117, 118, 135, 137; in Stein, 27–28, 78, 82, 97, 99–102, 104, 106–108, 215n57

INDEX

Corelle, Laurel Snow: on Bishop, 149
Costello, Bonnie: on Bishop's eye, 224n28; on Bishop's dreams, 229n130
Craver, Carl F., 127, 220n72
Critchley, Simon, 196n43
Culler, Jonathan: on how lyric works, 9, 10; on Jackson's lyricization thesis, 193n19
Cushman, Stephen, 222n6

Darden, Lindley, 127, 220n72
Davidson, Donald, 208n32; on causal explanation, 95–96; on "radical interpretation," 204n30
Davis, Theo: on contingency in Dickinson, 72; on Dickinson's "ornamental" poetry, 69
deduction, 2, 3, 10, 14–16, 22, 26, 28, 38, 40, 45–46, 48, 79, 82, 152, 173, 207n3; and abduction, 28, 142; and analogy, 51–55, 60, 74; in Dickinson, 67; and explanation, 19, 40, 44, 54, 79–81, 124; in "kitchenette building," 22–26, 177, 181; limits of, 22, 48, 66, 81, 170; and Moore, 136, 151, 220n85; and novelty, 26; and philosophy of science, 67–68; and prediction, 151; rejection of, 6; in social sciences, 212n93; and the sonnet, 173; Stein's refusal of, 28, 84, 90, 91, 94, 99; in Whitman, 43, 47
DeKoven, Marianne: on Stein and *écriture feminine*, 89
de Laguna, Theodore, 114
Deppman, Jed: on Dickinson's definitional impulse, 61, 62
Dewey, John, 45, 68, 112, 147–48, 211n13, 224n36; *The Structure of Experience*, 147–48; on truth, 211n75
Dickie, Margaret, 149
Dickey, Frances: on Dewey and Bishop, 148
Dickinson, Emily, 6, 16, 26, 27, 50–77, 106, 156, 158, 193n19, 207n2, 209n50, 210n55, 210n60, 212n84; analogies in, 50–77, 110, 129, 169, 209n50; "'Arcturus' is his other name—," 66, 211n65; "The Juggler's Hat," 50–52, 61–62, 65, 69, 70; "I heard a Fly buzz—when I died—," 72–74; "My Life had stood—a Loaded Gun—," 69–72; "There is no Frigate like a Book," 62–65, 69, 70
Diepeveen, Leonard: on difficulty, 20
difficulty, 20–21, 82; aesthetic, 21–22, 27; in Dickinson, 27, 51, 52, 71–72, 74, 77, 207n2; epistemological, 17, 27, 221n110; and form, 79; of induction, 27, 51, 52, 55, 82, 99–101; literary, 20; modernist, 2, 198n75, 198n76, 213n3; ontological, 20; and novelty, 186; poetic, 200n88; of prediction, 28, 45; in Stein, 79, 82, 85, 88–93, 95, 99, 100, 101, 102, 108; and unreliability, 138; in Whitman, 27
Donne, John: "Holy Sonnet XIV," 180
Douven, Igor, 226n79; on abduction, 152, 227n83
Dydo, Ulla: on Stein, 88, 90, 92–95, 102, 107, 216n97

Eco, Umberto, 31
Edelman, Lee, 230n141; on Bishop's "description," 146; on "In the Waiting Room," 149, 223n22
Eeckhout, Bart, 195n43
Eliot, T. S., 6, 88, 198n77; on difficulty, 20; *The Sacred Wood*, 103; *The Waste Land*, 89
Emerson, Ralph Waldo, 113, 153
empiricism, 19, 53, 66, 110, 114, 118, 124, 127, 135; radical, 83; skeptical, 116, 118, 124. *See also* philosophy of science
Epstein, Andrew, 202n6, 203n10
Erkkila, Betsy, 36; on Bishop's interiors, 223n20
Estess, Sybil P., on "Visits to St. Elizabeths," 227n101
ethics: and analogy, 53–55; in Aristotle, 119; in Cavell, 134; and Pound, 156
experiments: aesthetic, 2, 7, 17, 22 199n85; Black, 33; modernist, 7, 186, 204n26; thought, 54, 56, 57, 66, 77, 208n20, 212n83; Stein's, 85, 89, 92, 128

INDEX

explanation, 39–41, 79–82, 150–51, 219n53; in Bishop, 15, 153–66, 170; and deduction, 44, 79, 80; and induction, 87; limits of, 88, 136, 213n3; and lyric poetry, 100–104; in Moore, 136–37, 219n47; and Pound, 196n47; predictive, 87; scientific, 19, 40, 54, 124; in Stein, 28, 78–79, 81–88, 91–103, 107–108, 110, 123, 136. *See also* inference: to the best explanation

fact, 10, 27–28, 68, 129; in Dickinson, 73; and induction, 19; in Moore, 128, 129; in Stein, 78–95, 97–103, 108, 110

Ferguson, Frances: on free indirect discourse, 205n34

Foot, Philippa, 54

Ford, Karen Jackson: on Brooks's interest in the sonnet, 232n38

form, 3, 11, 31–40, 49, 57, 59, 64–65, 204n30; and coherence, 124n229; and content, 26, 31–32, 34–36, 38–39, 64–65, 129, 203n19; and free verse, 26, 36–38; literary and logical, 3, 22, 26–27, 38, 39, 52–53, 58–59, 64–65, 77, 101, 156–64, 172, 181–82, 203n19, 203n20; and logic, 26, 38–42, 44, 105; poetic, 6, 11, 15, 22, 24, 26, 27, 29, 37, 49, 64–65, 71, 76–77, 174, 207n2. *See also* analogy; inference; list; lyric poetry; sestina; sonnet; syllogism; villanelle

free verse: in Bishop, 158; in Brooks, 232n38; as form, 26, 36–38; in Moore, 132; in Whitman, 36–38, 44, 65

Frege, Gottlob, 16

Frye, Northrop, 9; on Dickinson's definitional impulse, 60–61; on Shakespeare's sonnets, 230n1

Fussell, Paul: on sonnets, 170, 173, 233n42; on syllogism in Marvell, 15

Gadberry, Andrea: on philosophy and literary form, 203n19

Gardner, Thomas: on Bishop's skepticism, 149

generalization, 2, 3, 5, 12, 27, 41, 100, 152, 203n21; in Stein, 27, 28, 87, 110; in Whitman, 41, 42. *See also* Hume, David; induction

Gilbert, Roger: on Moore's adduction, 220n85; on Moore's categorical poetics, 129

Ginsberg, Allen, 31; "A Supermarket in California," 30

Glavey, Brian: on aesthetic form, 224n35; on queer ekphrasis, 229n132

Goldsby, Jacqueline: on Brooks's "Pearl May Lee," 201n100

Goodman, Nelson, 19, 45, 46, 47, 207n3; on prediction, 45–46

Gregory, Elizabeth, 128

Griffin, Farah Jasmine: on "kitchenette building," 24

Griffiths, Devin: on analogy, 56–59

Grossman, Allen: on lyric poetry, 9; on poetic novelty, 8–9; on the problem of other minds, 10, 11; on Whitman, 30, 42

Guillory, John: on literary difficulty, 20, 198n75

Hacking, Ian: on induction, 191n4; on probability, 19

Hare, Peter, 196n43

Harrison, Victoria: on Bishop's pragmatism, 148; Bishop's privacy, 223n20

Hass, Robert: on poetic form, 35

Hayes, Terrence, 37

Heidegger, Martin, 72

Hejinian, Lyn, 199n83

Hempel, Carl G., 19, 39, 40–41, 45, 53, 80, 81, 84, 95; on "empirical," 213n6; on explanation, 40–41, 80, 81, 84

Herschel, William, 185

Hesse, Mary, 54, 206n54, 207n3, 212n93; on analogical reasoning, 53, 55, 80

Hillyer, Robert: *First Principles of Verse*, 175

Hirsch, Edward: on the sonnet, 171

Hoffman, Michael J., 97

INDEX

Hofstadter, Douglas: on analogy and cognition, 53
Holley, Margaret, 133
Hollister, Susannah, 101
Homer: *The Iliad*, 31
Howe, Susan, 196n43; on Dickinson's fascicles, 212n84
Hubbard, Stacy Carson, 128
Hume, David, 19, 41, 47, 51, 79, 82, 109, 110, 113–18, 127, 138; on enumeration, 206n56; on the problem of induction, 41, 109
Hunter, Walt: on "kitchenette building," 24, 200n96; on lyric poetry, 194n23

indeterminacy, 17, 20–21, 71, 72, 74, 77, 89, 198n77. *See also* contingency
induction, 2–4, 16, 17–19, 28, 40, 152, 167, 173, 184, 203n21; and close reading, 20; contingency of, 98, 110; enumerative, 26, 32, 41, 44, 47–48, 110, 192n5; and epistemology, 110; and justification, 55, 110; in modern American poetry, 3, 5, 7, 13, 14, 16, 21, 22, 29, 100, 170, 172, 182, 186; in Moore, 109–11, 113, 115, 117, 119–20, 122, 129–30, 134, 136, 169; and prediction, 45, 46, 47; problems of, 10, 11, 14, 17–19, 41, 45, 47, 48, 51, 55, 78, 80–82, 91, 93, 98, 109–11, 113–16, 120, 122, 134–35, 138, 142, 185–86, 192n11; power of, 28, 48, 77, 98, 100, 107, 182, 185–86; temporality of, 4; in Stein, 78–79, 82, 85, 87, 92–95, 97–101, 104, 107–108, 151, 169; in Whitman, 32, 40–41, 44, 47–49. *See also* analogy; inference: to the best explanation
inference, 3, 5, 6, 18, 19, 28, 55; to the best explanation, 27, 28, 81, 142, 150–52, 156, 159–61, 166, 170; in Bishop, 141, 146, 150–53, 156, 159–61, 166, 170; in Brooks, 184; causal, 124; predictive, 44; scientific, 19, 226n79. *See also* abduction
Izenberg, Oren, 194n34, 195, 196n46, 208n20; on "Filling Station," 228n117; on how poetry works philosophically, 210n55

Jackson, Virginia: on "Filling Station," 228n117; on reading lyric poetry, 9; on lyricization, 103
James, William, 19, 28, 83, 84, 85, 89, 112, 115, 116, 117, 118, 134, 196n51; on facts as explanation, 83, 87; on induction, 18; on pragmatic reasoning, 68, 116; and Wittgenstein, 218n33
Jameson, Fredric, 33
Jarrell, Randall: on Moore as witness, 146, 149
Jaussen, Paul: on the catalogue form, 31
Javadizadeh, Kamran, 203n10
Johnson, Barbara: on Moore's anthropomorphism, 125; on poetry's surprises, 125

Kadlec, David, 115
Kalstone, David, 146
Keats, John, 127, 209n50, 233n50; "Ode on a Grecian Urn," 126, 127; "On First Looking into Chapman's Homer," 185; "On Seeing the Elgin Marbles," 126, 127
Kelly, Donika, 31
Kenner, Hugh, 132, 133, 182
Kindley, Evan: on modernist difficulty, 212n4
King, Rachael Scarborough, 204n22
Kramnick, Jonathan, 165; on explanation, 39–40; on form's ambiguity, 34
Kuhn, Thomas: 48, on induction, 19; on revolutionary science, 54–55; on scientific explanation, 99; on thought experiments, 77

Leavell, Linda, 115
Levine, Caroline, 31, 33, 36, 57, 64, 204n26; on the expansion of form, 33; on wholeness, 103, 166, 230n139
Levine, Naomi: on rhyme, 204n32
Levinson, Marjorie, 40, 76, 77, 204n26, 206n54, 212n94; on form's "conceptual clarity," 34; on new formalism, 33; on poetic "self-understanding," 172; on poetic recursion, 75, 76

INDEX

Lewis, Cara L.: on "flexible formalism," 204n26
Lipton, Peter, 226n79; on abduction, 81; on likely and lovely explanations, 162, 165; on inference, 151–52
list, 26, 40, 192n5; in Bishop, 140, 144, 156, 158, 159, 161; and induction, 26, 41, 44, 192n5; as logical form, 40, 42; as poetic form; and prediction, 44–48; in Stein, 102; in Whitman, 26, 27, 30–33, 39, 41–44, 46–49, 76, 110, 169, 202n6, 203n10; in Wordsworth, 39
literary studies, 2, 14, 17, 19–20, 32–33, 38, 41, 51, 56, 58, 129, 165, 195n41, 198n76, 204n22, 226n79; and formalism, 76; and pedagogy, 103; quantitative, 74, 75
logic, 4–5, 39, 59, 173; of capitalism, 22, 24; and form, 39, 40, 49, 65, 129; lovely, 165; and lyric poetry, 3, 4, 10, 12–14, 16, 22, 29, 32, 58, 100, 104, 170, 172–74, 176, 180–82, 186; modern debates on, 16, 80, 196n51. *See also* abduction; deduction; induction; inference; metalogic
Longenbach, James, 222n3
Lowell, Robert, 146, 154, 225n43
Luhmann, Niklas: on contingency, 20, 102
Lupton, Christina: on contingency, 21
Lyly, John, 122
lyric poetry, 3, 7–11, 76, 101–103, 108, 170–71, 173, 181–82, 186, 194n23, 194n36; ambiguity of, 7, 193n18, 193n22; in Brooks, 233n46; Bishop's skepticism of, 149; and coherence, 164; and Dickinson, 50, 103; and first-person utterance, 8 and lyric poetry, 3, 4, 10, 12–14, 16, 22, 29, 32, 58, 100, 104, 170, 172–74, 176, 180–82, 186; and music, 7, 194n27; and novelty, 7–11, 182, 195n41; and reading, 103, 193n19; as recursive, 75; and Stein, 103–104, 106. *See also* sonnet; volta

Machamer, Peter: on mechanisms, 127, 220n75
Macpherson, Sandra: on formalism, 34

Mak, Cliff: on slapstick in Moore, 132–33
Marx, Karl, 33, 45
Mayer, Bernadette, 31, 203n10
McCabe, Susan, 149
McCorkle, James, 222n3
Menand, Louis, 83
metalogic, 13, 171
Meyer, Steven, 83–84
Mikics, David: on sonnets, 231n15, 231n18; on the sonnet's "internal logic," 171, 172, 176
Millier, Brett: on Bishop, 157–58, 227n84, 227n99
Milton, John, 15; on rhyme, 36
Mix, Deborah, 90
modernism, 2, 6, 7, 17, 36, 45, 111–14, 165, 186, 191n4, 192n16, 198n75, 198n76, 198n77, 204n26, 213n3, 224n28, 228n104; American, 2; interwar, 112; and newness, 111, 113–14, 191n4
Moore, Lisa L.: on Brooks's interest in sonnets, 232n39
Moore, Marianne, 17, 27, 28, 88, 109–38, 141, 146, 147, 151, 153, 169, 218n18, 219n47, 227n91; animal poems of, 119–23; collage poetics of, 128–30; consistency in, 28, 126, 151; continuous present in, 123–24; "An Egyptian Pulled Glass Bottle in the Shape of a Fish," 125–27; "The Fish," 125–27, 131–33; "Four Quartz Crystal Clocks," 127; grace in, 28, 133–38; "A Jelly-fish," 123; "He 'Digesteth Harde Yron,'" 120–22, 123, 128; induction in, 109–11, 113, 115, 117, 119–20, 122, 129–30, 134, 136, 169; mechanisms of, 124–28, 133, 151; "The Mind is an Enchanting Thing," 132; "The Octopus," 128; "The Pangolin," 109–10, 112–15, 117–20, 123, 128, 132–35, 137–38, 177, 185; "The Paper Nautilus," 126, 127; philosophical investments of, 114–18; "Poetry," 126; precision in, 128–30, 132–33; predictability in, 123, 127, 130, 132; "To a Steam Roller," 125
Moretti, Franco, 74–75
Morgan, Mary S., 54

INDEX

Moten, Fred, 202n100
Mueller, Janel, 15, 196n48

Nersessian, Anahid, 165; on explanation, 39–40; on form's ambiguity, 34
New, Elisa, 115
New Criticism, 5, 20, 64, 103–104, 166, 193n19, 198n71
newness, 2, 17, 22, 25, 26, 112, 167–68, 186; in Bishop, 167; in Brooks, 181–82; and induction, 2, 110, 173, 170, 177, 191n4; and lyric poetry, 2, 7–12, 170, 173–74, 177, 181–82, 194n27, 195n41; and modernism, 2, 111, 113, 170, 186; in Moore, 113, 114, 116, 128, 185
Ngai, Sianne: on avant-garde poetry, 199n85; on "interesting" as aesthetic judgement, 192n11
Nietzsche, Friedrich, 80, 196n50
Nussbaum, Martha, 36; on philosophy and literary form, 203n19

O'Hara, Frank, 37
Olson, Liesl, 89, 191n4
Oppenheim, Paul, 40, 80
Orr, David, 146

Palmer, Michael, 21
Parker, Robert Dale: on Bishop's interiors, 223n20
Pavel, Thomas: on sonnets, 205n49
Peirce, Charles Sanders, on abduction, 152; on induction, 18; on truth, 68
Perelman, Bob, 97
Perloff, Marjorie, 198n83; on indeterminacy, 20–21, 88–89, 198n77; on the interpretive difficulty of Stein, 88, 90, 91; on modernism, 192n16
Phillips, Siobhan: on Moore, 117–18; on the probability of sunrises, 48
philosophy: and poetry, 1–4, 142. *See also* logic; philosophy of science; pragmatism
philosophy of science, 16, 19, 54, 57, 67, 76, 124, 151
Pickard, Zachariah, 146
Piper, Andrew, 203n21

Plato, 54, 79, 172; *Ion*, 13, 59
poetics: American, 193n19, 195n39; Bishop's, 142, 145, 147, 158, 228n104; Brooks's, 201n100; Dickinson's, 110, 209n50; and the lyric, 7, 10; modernist, 2, 20; Moore's, 27, 28, 110, 118, 128–30, 132, 221n85; and pedagogy, 35; and philosophy, 29, 169, 174; and reason, 4, 26, 170; Stein's, 27, 79, 102; Whitman's, 26, 30, 36, 37, 42, 44, 110
poetry. *See* aubade; free verse; lyric poetry; sestina; sonnet; villanelle; volta
Poirier, Richard, 89
Poovey, Mary: on literary criticism and wholeness, 230n139
Pope, Alexander: *The Rape of the Lock*, 31
Popper, Karl, 53; on induction, 19
Porter, Dahlia, 203n21; on analogy, 57, 58
Pound, Ezra, 12, 14, 36, 88, 155–56, 192n14, 195n43, 198n77, 212n4, 227n99, 227n101; "In a Station of the Metro," 4–6; *The Cantos*, 14, 155–56, 192n14; imprisonment of, 155–57
pragmatism, 16, 18, 19, 27, 28, 67–68, 74, 83, 114–18, 123, 148, 195n43, 197n68, 211n71
prediction, 16, 41, 44–46, 84, 99, 107, 206n65, 220n75; contingency of, 28, 41, 110, 114, 151; and explanation, 19, 44, 81, 88, 95, 107, 124; and generalization, 3, 27; in Moore, 111, 123, 127, 130, 132; in Pound, 6; in Stein, 84, 87, 103; and the weather, 16, 95, 99, 107; in Whitman, 47–48, 48; in Wittgenstein, 18. *See also* induction
Priest, Graham, 73
Priestley, Joseph: on analogy, 53
Putnam, Hilary, 45, 55, 206n67; on inductive logic, 55

Quashie, Kevin: on Brooks's *Maud Martha*, 201n100
Quine, W. V. O.: on induction, 19

Ramazani, Jahan: on "the rites for Cousin Vit," 183, 233n45, 233n46; on sonnets, 171, 183, 233n45, 233n46
Rankine, Claudia, 31
reasoning. *See* abduction; deduction; induction; metalogic
Redding, Patrick, 37
Reddy, Srikanth, 135–36
Retallack, Joan, 101
rhyme: ballad, 200n89; in Bishop, 141, 156–58; in Brooks, 201n11; in Dickinson, 51, 71, as literary form, 204n32; and logic, 39; nursery, 37; slant, 51, 179; in sonnets, 32, 35, 172, 179, 205n35, 231n25; in Stein, 105–107; and Whitman, 36–37, 43
Rich, Adrienne, 223n20
Rorty, Richard, 20, 45, 67, 135, 148, 199n78
Rotella, Guy: on Bishop's skepticism, 149
Ruark, Gibbons, 149
Ruddick, Lisa, 89
Russell, Bertrand, 16, 18, 19, 115, 152; on induction, 18; on induction's epistemological problem, 113

Saint-Amour, Paul, 111–13
Salmon, Wesley, 45, 165; on scientific explanation, 40, 81, 124
Sander, Emmanuel: on analogy and cognition, 53
Schoenbach, Lisi, 89, 206n63; on prediction, 45, 206n65
Schulze, Robin G.: on Moore, 119, 128
Schwartz, Ana: on Anne Bradstreet, 3
Schwartz, Lloyd: on Bishop's irony, 224n27; on "Visits to St. Elizabeths," 227n101
Sedgwick, Eve Kosofsky, 67
Seiler, Claire, 164; on Bishop's *A Cold Spring*, 164
Semmelweis, Ignaz, 152
sestina, 34, 35, 144, 156, 157, 158
Setina, Emily, 101
Shakespeare, William, 141; sonnets of, 171, 176, 230n1, 232n41; *Twelfth Night*, 8
Sharpe, Christina, 201n100

Shelley, Percy Bysshe, 39
Smith, Barbara Herrnstein, 20
sonnet, 34, 35, 36, 37, 38, 106, 170, 200n96, 201n99, 205n49; and Bishop, 145; and Brooks, 22, 24–25, 29, 182–83, 201n99, 201n100, 202n101, 231n27, 232n32, 232n38, 232n39, 233n41, 233n45, 233n46; form of, 170–86, 205n35; logic of, 29, 39, 170–86, 231n18; Petrarchan, 233n42; Shakespearean, 62, 230n1, 233n42; and Stein, 105. *See also* lyric poetry; volta
So, Richard Jean: on modeling and error in quantitative literary studies, 74–75
Stanley, Kate, 111–14
stanza, 101, 104–107, 181; in Stein, 101–102, 104–107
Stein, Gertrude, 17, 27–28, 78–108, 110, 123, 136, 141, 151–52, 169, 198n77, 212n4, 214n30, 215n57, 216n88, 218n97; *The Autobiography of Alice B. Toklas*, 83, 212n4; *Blood on the Dining-Room Floor*, 88; "Composition as Explanation," 79, 96–100, 123; contingency in, 27–28, 78, 82, 97, 99–102, 104, 106–108, 215n57; difficulty of, 79, 82, 85, 88–93, 95, 99, 100, 101, 102, 108; double negatives in, 101–102, 106, 216n88; "An Elucidation," 79, 92–96, 98, 100, 102, 215n58; *Everybody's Autobiography*, 86, 88, 107; explanation in, 28, 78–79, 81–88, 91–103, 107–108, 110, 123, 136; facts in, 78–95, 97–103, 108, 110; generalization in, 27, 28, 87, 110; *Geographical History of America*, 88; induction in, 78–79, 82, 85, 87, 92–95, 97–101, 104, 107–108, 151, 169; "Lifting Belly," 86–88; *The Making of Americans*, 88, 98; philosophical context of, 82–86; *Q.E.D.*, 78, 83, 94, 101; repetition in, 189, 102–103, 105; "Sacred Emily," 102; stanzas in, 104–107; *Stanzas in Meditation*, 85, 90, 100–105, 107; *Tender Buttons*, 86–87, 91, 94; "What is English Literature," 86, 88

INDEX

Steiner, George, 20, 198n76
Steiner, Wendy: on Stein, 89, 96
Stevens, Wallace, 6, 11–14, 128, 148, 174, 192n15, 195n43; "Nomad Exquisite," 11–14, 174
Stewart, Susan, 7, 70
Stimpson, Catharine R.: on Stein's sexual codes, 89, 90
Strand, Mark, 35
Sunstein, Cass: on analogy, 53
Sutherland, Donald, 104
syllogism, 3, 15, 38–40, 55, 173, 191n5, 196n48, 205n48

Tankard, Paul: on lists, 31
Taylor, Tess: on "kitchenette building," 177, 232n32
Teskey, Gordon: "architectonic structure," 24; on Milton and Spenser, 15, 107
Theune, Michael: on "the rites for Cousin Vit," 183
Thomson, Judith Jarvis, 54
Tiffany, Daniel, 57–58, 125, 192n13
Toíbín, Colm, 146

van Fraassen, Bas C., 81, 152, 206n54
Vendler, Helen, 8, 9; on Bishop, 164; on lyric poetry; on sonnets, 171, 176
Victorianism, 38
villanelle, 35, 37, 38, 156, 157, 158
volta, 29, 32, 39, 170–74, 177, 179, 181–84, 186, 205n35, 231n18. *See also* sonnet
von Contzen, Eva, 31
von Hallberg, Robert: on lyric poetry, 194n27

Walker, Cheryl, 229n124
Watt, Ian: on induction in criticism, 198n71
Weisbuch, Robert: on analogy, 59
Wienreb, Lloyd L.: on analogy, 53
Wellbery, David, 20, 21

Wellek, Rene: on lyric poetry, 193n18
White, Gillian, 146, 199n83, 200n89, 224n34; on Bishop and lyric shame, 165, 224n34, 228n104, 228n115; on Bishop as metadiscursive poet, 228n115; on contingency, 21; on New Criticism, 198n71
Whitehead, Alfred North: on induction, 17–18
Whitman, Walt, 16, 26, 27, 30–49, 64, 76, 77, 79, 110, 111, 129, 151, 156, 169, 193n19, 202n6, 203n10, 206n69; and Americanness, 42–44; "Crossing Brooklyn Ferry," 206n69; induction in, 32, 40–41, 44, 47–49; *Leaves of Grass*, 30, 37, 46; lists in, 26, 27, 31–33, 39, 41–44, 46–49, 76, 110, 169, 202n6, 203n10; "Song of Myself," 36, 42–44, 46–47, 206n69; prediction in, 44–48
Williams, William Carlos, 88, 198n77, 224n34; "The Red Wheelbarrow," 146
Williamson, Timothy: on abduction in Russell, 152, 226n79
Wittgenstein, Ludwig, 18, 19, 45, 54, 89, 134, 135, 172, 193n22, 196n51; on "family resemblance," 193n22; on induction, 18; on nonsense, 91; *Philosophical Investigations*, 134; on philosophy, 218n33; *Tractatus Logico-Philosophicus*, 198n76
Wolfson, Susan: on formalism, 33
Woodson, Jon: on "A Lovely Love," 232n41
Wordsworth, William, 107; "Nuns Fret Not at Their Convent's Narrow Room," 36, 37, 39, 179; "She Dwelt Among th' Untrodden Ways," 70

Zhang, Dora: on analogical resemblance, 209n45; on contingency in analogy, 212n85
Zona, Kristin Hotelling, 149
Zumhagen-Yekplé, Karen, 198n76

GPSR Authorized Representative: Easy Access System Europe, Mustamäe tee
50, 10621 Tallinn, Estonia, gpsr.requests@easproject.com

www.ingramcontent.com/pod-product-compliance
Lightning Source LLC
Chambersburg PA
CBHW022044290426
44109CB00014B/981